FREE Test Taking Tips DVD Offer

To help us better serve you, we have developed a Test Taking Tips DVD that we would like to give you for FREE. **This DVD covers world-class test taking tips that you can use to be even more successful when you are taking your test.**

All that we ask is that you email us your feedback about your study guide. Please let us know what you thought about it – whether that is good, bad or indifferent.

To get your **FREE Test Taking Tips DVD**, email freedvd@studyguideteam.com with "FREE DVD" in the subject line and the following information in the body of the email:

a. The title of your study guide.

b. Your product rating on a scale of 1-5, with 5 being the highest rating.

c. Your feedback about the study guide. What did you think of it?

d. Your full name and shipping address to send your free DVD.

If you have any questions or concerns, please don't hesitate to contact us at freedvd@studyguideteam.com.

Thanks again!

CSET Multiple Subject Test Prep Book & Practice Test Questions for the CSET Exam

CSET Multiple Subjects Prep Book Team

Table of Contents

Quick Overview

As you draw closer to taking your exam, effective preparation becomes more and more important. Thankfully, you have this study guide to help you get ready. Use this guide to help keep your studying on track and refer to it often.

This study guide contains several key sections that will help you be successful on your exam. The guide contains tips for what you should do the night before and the day of the test. Also included are test-taking tips. Knowing the right information is not always enough. Many well-prepared test takers struggle with exams. These tips will help equip you to accurately read, assess, and answer test questions.

A large part of the guide is devoted to showing you what content to expect on the exam and to helping you better understand that content. Near the end of this guide is a practice test so that you can see how well you have grasped the content. Then, answer explanations are provided so that you can understand why you missed certain questions.

Don't try to cram the night before you take your exam. This is not a wise strategy for a few reasons. First, your retention of the information will be low. Your time would be better used by reviewing information you already know rather than trying to learn a lot of new information. Second, you will likely become stressed as you try to gain a large amount of knowledge in a short amount of time. Third, you will be depriving yourself of sleep. So be sure to go to bed at a reasonable time the night before. Being well-rested helps you focus and remain calm.

Be sure to eat a substantial breakfast the morning of the exam. If you are taking the exam in the afternoon, be sure to have a good lunch as well. Being hungry is distracting and can make it difficult to focus. You have hopefully spent lots of time preparing for the exam. Don't let an empty stomach get in the way of success!

When travelling to the testing center, leave earlier than needed. That way, you have a buffer in case you experience any delays. This will help you remain calm and will keep you from missing your appointment time at the testing center.

Be sure to pace yourself during the exam. Don't try to rush through the exam. There is no need to risk performing poorly on the exam just so you can leave the testing center early. Allow yourself to use all of the allotted time if needed.

Remain positive while taking the exam even if you feel like you are performing poorly. Thinking about the content you should have mastered will not help you perform better on the exam.

Once the exam is complete, take some time to relax. Even if you feel that you need to take the exam again, you will be well served by some down time before you begin studying again. It's often easier to convince yourself to study if you know that it will come with a reward!

Test-Taking Strategies

1. Predicting the Answer

When you feel confident in your preparation for a multiple-choice test, try predicting the answer before reading the answer choices. This is especially useful on questions that test objective factual knowledge or that ask you to fill in a blank. By predicting the answer before reading the available choices, you eliminate the possibility that you will be distracted or led astray by an incorrect answer choice. You will feel more confident in your selection if you read the question, predict the answer, and then find your prediction among the answer choices. After using this strategy, be sure to still read all of the answer choices carefully and completely. If you feel unprepared, you should not attempt to predict the answers. This would be a waste of time and an opportunity for your mind to wander in the wrong direction.

2. Reading the Whole Question

Too often, test takers scan a multiple-choice question, recognize a few familiar words, and immediately jump to the answer choices. Test authors are aware of this common impatience, and they will sometimes prey upon it. For instance, a test author might subtly turn the question into a negative, or he or she might redirect the focus of the question right at the end. The only way to avoid falling into these traps is to read the entirety of the question carefully before reading the answer choices.

3. Looking for Wrong Answers

Long and complicated multiple-choice questions can be intimidating. One way to simplify a difficult multiple-choice question is to eliminate all of the answer choices that are clearly wrong. In most sets of answers, there will be at least one selection that can be dismissed right away. If the test is administered on paper, the test taker could draw a line through it to indicate that it may be ignored; otherwise, the test taker will have to perform this operation mentally or on scratch paper. In either case, once the obviously incorrect answers have been eliminated, the remaining choices may be considered. Sometimes identifying the clearly wrong answers will give the test taker some information about the correct answer. For instance, if one of the remaining answer choices is a direct opposite of one of the eliminated answer choices, it may well be the correct answer. The opposite of obviously wrong is obviously right! Of course, this is not always the case. Some answers are obviously incorrect simply because they are irrelevant to the question being asked. Still, identifying and eliminating some incorrect answer choices is a good way to simplify a multiple-choice question.

4. Don't Overanalyze

Anxious test takers often overanalyze questions. When you are nervous, your brain will often run wild, causing you to make associations and discover clues that don't actually exist. If you feel that this may be a problem for you, do whatever you can to slow down during the test. Try taking a deep breath or counting to ten. As you read and consider the question, restrict yourself to the particular words used by the author. Avoid thought tangents about what the author *really* meant, or what he or she was *trying* to say. The only things that matter on a multiple-choice test are the words that are actually in the question. You must avoid reading too much into a multiple-choice question, or supposing that the writer meant something other than what he or she wrote.

5. No Need for Panic

It is wise to learn as many strategies as possible before taking a multiple-choice test, but it is likely that you will come across a few questions for which you simply don't know the answer. In this situation, avoid panicking. Because most multiple-choice tests include dozens of questions, the relative value of a single wrong answer is small. Moreover, your failure on one question has no effect on your success elsewhere on the test. As much as possible, you should compartmentalize each question on a multiple-choice test. In other words, you should not allow your feelings about one question to affect your success on the others. When you find a question that you either don't understand or don't know how to answer, just take a deep breath and do your best. Read the entire question slowly and carefully. Try rephrasing the question a couple of different ways. Then, read all of the answer choices carefully. After eliminating obviously wrong answers, make a selection and move on to the next question.

6. Confusing Answer Choices

When working on a difficult multiple-choice question, there may be a tendency to focus on the answer choices that are the easiest to understand. Many people, whether consciously or not, gravitate to the answer choices that require the least concentration, knowledge, and memory. This is a mistake. When you come across an answer choice that is confusing, you should give it extra attention. A question might be confusing because you do not know the subject matter to which it refers. If this is the case, don't eliminate the answer before you have affirmatively settled on another. When you come across an answer choice of this type, set it aside as you look at the remaining choices. If you can confidently assert that one of the other choices is correct, you can leave the confusing answer aside. Otherwise, you will need to take a moment to try to better understand the confusing answer choice. Rephrasing is one way to tease out the sense of a confusing answer choice.

7. Your First Instinct

Many people struggle with multiple-choice tests because they overthink the questions. If you have studied sufficiently for the test, you should be prepared to trust your first instinct once you have carefully and completely read the question and all of the answer choices. There is a great deal of research suggesting that the mind can come to the correct conclusion very quickly once it has obtained all of the relevant information. At times, it may seem to you as if your intuition is working faster even than your reasoning mind. This may in fact be true. The knowledge you obtain while studying may be retrieved from your subconscious before you have a chance to work out the associations that support it. Verify your instinct by working out the reasons that it should be trusted.

8. Key Words

Many test takers struggle with multiple-choice questions because they have poor reading comprehension skills. Quickly reading and understanding a multiple-choice question requires a mixture of skill and experience. To help with this, try jotting down a few key words and phrases on a piece of scrap paper. Doing this concentrates the process of reading and forces the mind to weigh the relative importance of the question's parts. In selecting words and phrases to write down, the test taker thinks about the question more deeply and carefully. This is especially true for multiple-choice questions that are preceded by a long prompt.

9. Subtle Negatives

One of the oldest tricks in the multiple-choice test writer's book is to subtly reverse the meaning of a question with a word like *not* or *except*. If you are not paying attention to each word in the question, you can easily be led astray by this trick. For instance, a common question format is, "Which of the following is…?" Obviously, if the question instead is, "Which of the following is not…?," then the answer will be quite different. Even worse, the test makers are aware of the potential for this mistake and will include one answer choice that would be correct if the question were not negated or reversed. A test taker who misses the reversal will find what he or she believes to be a correct answer and will be so confident that he or she will fail to reread the question and discover the original error. The only way to avoid this is to practice a wide variety of multiple-choice questions and to pay close attention to each and every word.

10. Reading Every Answer Choice

It may seem obvious, but you should always read every one of the answer choices! Too many test takers fall into the habit of scanning the question and assuming that they understand the question because they recognize a few key words. From there, they pick the first answer choice that answers the question they believe they have read. Test takers who read all of the answer choices might discover that one of the latter answer choices is actually *more* correct. Moreover, reading all of the answer choices can remind you of facts related to the question that can help you arrive at the correct answer. Sometimes, a misstatement or incorrect detail in one of the latter answer choices will trigger your memory of the subject and will enable you to find the right answer. Failing to read all of the answer choices is like not reading all of the items on a restaurant menu: you might miss out on the perfect choice.

11. Spot the Hedges

One of the keys to success on multiple-choice tests is paying close attention to every word. This is never more true than with words like *almost*, *most*, *some*, and *sometimes*. These words are called "hedges" because they indicate that a statement is not totally true or not true in every place and time. An absolute statement will contain no hedges, but in many subjects, like literature and history, the answers are not always straightforward or absolute. There are always exceptions to the rules in these subjects. For this reason, you should favor those multiple-choice questions that contain hedging language. The presence of qualifying words indicates that the author is taking special care with his or her words, which is certainly important when composing the right answer. After all, there are many ways to be wrong, but there is only one way to be right! For this reason, it is wise to avoid answers that are absolute when taking a multiple-choice test. An absolute answer is one that says things are either all one way or all another. They often include words like *every*, *always*, *best*, and *never*. If you are taking a multiple-choice test in a subject that doesn't lend itself to absolute answers, be on your guard if you see any of these words.

12. Long Answers

In many subject areas, the answers are not simple. As already mentioned, the right answer often requires hedges. Another common feature of the answers to a complex or subjective question are qualifying clauses, which are groups of words that subtly modify the meaning of the sentence. If the question or answer choice describes a rule to which there are exceptions or the subject matter is complicated, ambiguous, or confusing, the correct answer will require many words in order to be expressed clearly and accurately. In essence, you should not be deterred by answer choices that seem excessively long. Oftentimes, the author of the text will not be able to write the correct answer without offering some qualifications and modifications. Your job is to read the answer choices thoroughly and completely and to select the one that most accurately and precisely answers the question.

13. Restating to Understand

Sometimes, a question on a multiple-choice test is difficult not because of what it asks but because of how it is written. If this is the case, restate the question or answer choice in different words. This process serves a couple of important purposes. First, it forces you to concentrate on the core of the question. In order to rephrase the question accurately, you have to understand it well. Rephrasing the question will concentrate your mind on the key words and ideas. Second, it will present the information to your mind in a fresh way. This process may trigger your memory and render some useful scrap of information picked up while studying.

14. True Statements

Sometimes an answer choice will be true in itself, but it does not answer the question. This is one of the main reasons why it is essential to read the question carefully and completely before proceeding to the answer choices. Too often, test takers skip ahead to the answer choices and look for true statements. Having found one of these, they are content to select it without reference to the question above. Obviously, this provides an easy way for test makers to play tricks. The savvy test taker will always read the entire question before turning to the answer choices. Then, having settled on a correct answer choice, he or she will refer to the original question and ensure that the selected answer is relevant. The mistake of choosing a correct-but-irrelevant answer choice is especially common on questions related to specific pieces of objective knowledge, like historical or scientific facts. A prepared test taker will have a wealth of factual knowledge at his or her disposal, and should not be careless in its application.

15. No Patterns

One of the more dangerous ideas that circulates about multiple-choice tests is that the correct answers tend to fall into patterns. These erroneous ideas range from a belief that B and C are the most common right answers, to the idea that an unprepared test-taker should answer "A-B-A-C-A-D-A-B-A." It cannot be emphasized enough that pattern-seeking of this type is exactly the WRONG way to approach a multiple-choice test. To begin with, it is highly unlikely that the test maker will plot the correct answers according to some predetermined pattern. The questions are scrambled and delivered in a random order. Furthermore, even if the test maker was following a pattern in the assignation of correct answers, there is no reason why the test taker would know which pattern he or she was using. Any attempt to discern a pattern in the answer choices is a waste of time and a distraction from the real work of taking the test. A test taker would be much better served by extra preparation before the test than by reliance on a pattern in the answers.

FREE DVD OFFER

Don't forget that doing well on your exam includes both understanding the test content and understanding how to use what you know to do well on the test. We offer a completely FREE Test Taking Tips DVD that covers world class test taking tips that you can use to be even more successful when you are taking your test.

All that we ask is that you email us your feedback about your study guide. To get your **FREE Test Taking Tips DVD**, email freedvd@studyguideteam.com with "FREE DVD" in the subject line and the following information in the body of the email:

- The title of your study guide.
- Your product rating on a scale of 1-5, with 5 being the highest rating.
- Your feedback about the study guide. What did you think of it?
- Your full name and shipping address to send your free DVD.

Introduction

Function of the Test

The California Subject Examinations for Teachers (CSET) Multiple Subjects Exam is for educators in California who wish to receive credentialing to teach elementary or special education. Required by the state of California, the exam is broken up into three subtests and tests applicants on their knowledge of (1) Reading, Language, Literature, History, and Social Science; (2) Science and Mathematics; and (3) Physical Education, Human Development, and Visual and Performing Arts. In the year 2014, 7,168 applicants attempted to pass the test. Out of this number, 5,223 passed, a rate of 73 percent.

Test Administration

The exam is offered in testing centers across California. Those interested in the test should go to the CSET website www.ctcexams.nesinc.com/about_CSET.asp and search for a testing center near their area. The CSET Multiple Subjects Exam is available year-round by appointment, Monday through Saturday, but excludes some holidays. The three subtests can be taken altogether or separately. Be sure to register at the program website before scheduling your appointment to take the Multiple Subjects Exam I, II, and III.

If you fail one of the subtests, you can take that subtest again until you pass. There is no limit on retesting. However, you must redo the registration on the exam's website. The validity of score for the subtests is good for five years, which means you must earn certification within five years of passing the exam(s).

Test Format

The CSET Multiple Subjects subtests are computer-based exams broken into three separate parts. Subtest I and II allow three hours per subtest, while Subtest III lasts two hours and fifteen minutes. Taking all three subtests in a single session would take five hours, although you would be given the freedom to work on the subtests in any order you decide. Any break taken for any subtest remains part of the allotted testing time.

All three subtests consist of multiple-choice questions as well as constructed-response questions. A summary of the sections of the CSET Multiple Subjects Exam is as follows:

Section	Subjects	Multiple-Choice	Constructed Response	Time
Subtest I	Reading, Language, and Literature	26	2	180 minutes
	History and Social Science	26	2	
Subtest Total:		**52**	**4**	
Subtest II	Science	26	2	180 minutes
	Mathematics	26	2	
Subtest Total:		**52**	**4**	
Subtest III	Physical Education	13	1	135 minutes
	Human Development	13	1	
	Visual and Performing Arts	13	1	
Subtest Total:		**39**	**3**	

Scoring

Scores on the CSET Multiple Subjects Exam are converted to a scale of 100 to 300. The passing score for each subtest is a score of 220. If you choose to take the computer-based test, your score should show immediately after the test. Official scores are sent out from twenty to forty-five days after the test. You can choose who receives the scores.

Recent/Future Developments

Per their website, the CSET Multiple Subjects Subtest II is being redesigned to match the Next Generation Science Standards (NGSS). The first test administration for this development is August 7, 2017, and registration is currently open.

Language and Linguistics

Language Structure and Linguistics

Origins of the English Language

The English language has had many influences over time. It was brought to Britain by Germanic invaders between the fifth and seventh century; however, the language has adopted many dialects, inflections, and elements as time passed. In this section, three major linguistic origin influences will be explored. These include Anglo-Saxon roots, Celtic influences, and Greek and Roman elements.

Anglo-Saxon Roots

In the *Anglo-Saxon* period, also known as the Old English era, a new culture was formed when three Germanic tribes (the Angles, the Saxons, and the Jutes) merged. Anglo-Saxon was first written using the Runic alphabet but was later replaced with the Latin alphabet. For over seven hundred years, Anglo-Saxon roots influenced many dialects throughout kingdoms and regions. There are four main dialects of Old English:

- Northumbrian
- Mercia
- Kentish
- West-Saxon

Changes in dialect during this time period occurred for two main reasons. When Britain converted to Christianity, new words and connotations were borrowed from Old French or Latin languages, which in turn increased Anglo-Saxon's vocabulary. Another event that influenced Old English dialect was when the Viking invaders and Norse settlers merged. In the late 700s, England and Denmark united after the Norse invasions. Instead of being enemies, the two cultures merged and produced a mixture of Anglo-Saxon and Norse languages. The integration of languages produced synonyms and simplified ending sounds of words and inflections.

Celtic Influences

When the Anglo-Saxons arrived in Britain, the Celtic population spoke Latin and Celtic languages. Once the Anglo-Saxons integrated with the Celts, Old English became the primary language. The Celtic language was viewed as mediocre, and therefore many words did not endure the transition. The Celtic language survived in a few regions and split into two main groups, Goidelic (Gaelic) and Brythonic (British). Despite the fact that the Celtic language did not have a drastic influence on many English language words, the Celtic language is apparent in location names. Names of rivers (such as the Yare and Thames) and towns (such as York and London) are just a couple of the lasting language from the Celtic period.

Greek and Roman Influences

When the Romans invaded Britain, Latin became the dominant language of the region and was commonly used for religious purposes. Latin was thought to have been a language of upper class and educated citizens, as opposed to the Celtic language that was disregarded as "ordinary." Much of the Latin language stems from Greek origins.

Many of the Greek morphemes and word patterns that were modified into the Latin language over fifteen hundred years have carried over into the English language today. Words using the *ph* pattern, such as *photograph, philosophy, physical,* and *physician,* derive from the Greek origin. Other word patterns such as *th* (words such as *path, clothe,* and *theory*), *ch* (words such as *churn* and *chart*), *y* (words such as *myth, sky,* and *my*), and *z* (words such as *zebra* and *zeta*) also originate from the Greek origin.

Derivatives and Borrowings

Derivatives are words that are formed from other words, otherwise known as *root words.* Word derivatives add morphemes, or affixes, to the beginning or ending of root words to create new words with new meanings. Below are some of the commonly used derivatives in the English language:

English Language Derivatives:

Root Word	Affix	Derivative
favor	-able	favorable
bare	-ness	bareness
child	-like	childlike
boast	-ful	boastful
whole	-some	wholesome
seven	-th	seventh
west	-ward	westward
north	-ern	northern
health	-y	healthy

Remember, sometimes the spelling of the root word changes once the affix is added to form the derivative. For example, by adding the affix *-iation* to the root word *affiliate,* first drop the *e,* and then add the *-iation,* to form *affiliation.*

Borrowings, otherwise referred to as *loanwords,* are words that are borrowed and incorporated into one's own language originating from a different language. It is not as though the borrowed words are returned like a library book; however, these words tend to relate strongly to the language loaning the words as opposed to the language borrowing the words. For example, the English word *music* is a borrowed word from the French word *musique.* The Spanish word *chofer* is borrowed from the French word *chauffeur.* On the following page, review some of the borrowed words from the Germanic Period, Old English Period, Middle English Period, Early Modern English Period, and the Modern English Period.

English Language Borrowings

Germanic Period

Language	Borrowed Word Examples
Latin	butere (butter), sacc (sack), win (wine)

Old English Period

Language	Borrowed Word Examples
Latin	cest (chest), maegester (master), tigle (tile), circul (circle)
Celtic	brocc (badger), cumb (combe, valley)

Middle English Period

Language	Borrowed Word Examples
French	attorney, baron, boil, crime, question, special
Scandinavian	cake, lump, skirt, ugly, want

Early Modern English Period

Language	Borrowed Word Examples
Arabic	alcove, algebra, orange, sugar, zero
Greek	critic, data, pneumonia, tragedy
Latin	area, compensate, dexterity, vindicate

Modern English Period

Language	Borrowed Word Examples
Dutch	booze, bow, scum, uproar
French	ballet, cabernet, brigade, battalion
German	dunk, hamburger, pretzel, strudel
Italian	balcony, grotto, regatta, zucchini
Russian	icon, vodka
Scandinavian	ski, slalom, smorgasbord
Spanish	alligator, coyote, ranch, tornado
Yiddish	bagel, kosher, oy vey

Word borrowing occurred frequently throughout history. Historical events and trends influence which languages influence one another.

Fundamental Language Structures

Among all languages, it is important to have fundamental structure to clearly communicate. There needs to be a logical way to organize words within a sentence so that people can read, speak, and listen in a meaningful way. There are four components of language structure:

- Morphology
- Semantics
- Syntax
- Phonology

Let's review each independently.

Morphology

Morphology is the study of words. It explores how words are formed using morphemes (words or parts of words that contain their own meanings), as well as their relationship with other words within a language. For example, look at the word *cupcake*. The beginning and ending sounds *c* and *silent e* do not have meaning on their own. However, when combined with other morphemes, this compound word takes on a whole new meaning. Each word, *cup* and *cake,* has independent meanings. When you combine them, a new word, *cupcake,* takes on a completely independent definition.

Morphology examines root words, affixes (prefixes and suffixes), and stems. Not only does it analyze each part of words, morphology also looks at how words are used. Morphology can often answer how words are pronounced or the context in which words are used.

Semantics

Semantics studies the meanings of words, phrases, sentences, and texts. Semantics can be divided into two major categories: lexical semantics and phrasal semantics.

Lexical semantics not only studies individual words, but it also analyzes affixes, compound words, and phrases, whereas phrasal semantics studies the meaning of phrases and words. It looks at word meanings as opposed to how words are used. Lexical semantics compares and contrasts linguistic semantics structures across languages.

Syntax

Generally, sentences are formed using a very simple pattern: Subject + Verb + Object. For example, in "The boy ran down the street," the subject is "The boy," the verb is "ran," and the object is "the street." Syntax provides a set structure to sentences in a language. It provides an order to this sentence to make its meaning clear to the reader. Syntax can create a mood for a reader or express an author's purpose.

Phonology

Phonology is the study of how speech sounds in a language are organized to make words. These patterns of sounds also include the study of phonemes (single units of sounds), syllables (vowel sounds heard within a word), stress or accent (emphasis on a sound or syllable within a word), and intonation (variation of tone or pitch in words). Despite their differences, phonology and phonetics (the study of isolated sounds in words) are often confused. Remember, phonology studies how sounds change in syllables, words, and sentences, as opposed to phonetics, where the focus is on a single speech sound.

Phonemes, Syllables, Onsets, and Rimes

A *phoneme* is commonly referred to as a sound or a group of sounds that differentiate one word from another in a spoken language. Phonemes are language-specific sound units that do not carry inherent meanings, but are simply known as the smallest unit in a language. For example, there are phonemes unique to the English language that do not necessarily exist in other spoken languages. In English, although there are only twenty-six letters, there are forty-four phonemes:

Forty-Four Phonemes in English			
Consonant Sounds		**Vowel Sounds**	
/b/	boy	/a/	bat
/d/	desk	/e/	head
/f/	fall	/i/	dish
/g/	game	/o/	rock
/h/	hand	/u/	muck
/j/	joy	/a/	bake
/k/	king	/e/	meet
/l/	life	/i/	like
/m/	map	/o/	moat
/n/	nail	/yoo/	cube
/p/	park	/e/	alarm
/r/	run	/oo/	doom
/s/	sock	/oo/	nook
/t/	tail	/ou/	mouse
/v/	veil	/oi/	toy
/w/	water	/o/	call
/y/	yawn	/u/	herd
/z/	zebra	/a/	hair
/ch/	chalk	/a/	star
/sh/	shallow		
/th/	thorn		
/hw/	whale		
/zh/	leisure		
/ng/	sing		

Mastery of all forty-four phonemes in oral and written communication is a strong predictor of future reading readiness.

Syllables are defined as one complete unit of pronunciation. Every syllable contains only one vowel sound that can be created by one or more than one vowel. Syllables can consist of vowels that stand alone or combine with consonants. The study of syllables and how they operate help children to become stronger readers and will aid in spelling proficiency. Educators will often introduce new words that contain more than one syllable by teaching children to say and write the syllable. Segmenting a word into its individual syllables, as well as blending syllables into whole words, allows children to see the key parts of a word and provides opportunities for them to strengthen their reading skills.

In the English language, there are six different types of syllables, four of which are syllable combinations:

- Closed syllables: syllables that end in a consonant, as in *bat*, or *it*
- Open syllables: syllables that end with a vowel, as in *he*, *she*, or *we*
- Vowel-consonant-e syllables: syllables that end with a silent *e*, as in *ate*, *wife*, or *mile*
- Vowel team syllables: syllables that work in combination to create a new sound, as in *mouth* or *join*

- Consonant + le syllables: syllables that contain a consonant and end with an *le*, as in *turtle*
- R-Controlled syllables: syllables that contain a vowel followed by the letter *r*, where the *r* controls how the vowel is pronounced, as in *bird* or *word*

A word is broken up into two pieces: onset and rime. The *onset* is the initial phonological unit of any word, whether it is a consonant or a consonant cluster. The *rime* is the string of letters that follows the onset, usually consisting of a vowel or variant vowels along with one or more consonants. Many words in the English language share common features or patterns. These *word families* often share the same letter combinations that form the same or similar sounds. When introducing word families, educators will often initiate activities involving onsets and rimes to help children accurately recognize, read, and spell simple words. The study of onsets and rimes has shown to improve a child's overall literacy skills, increase reading fluency, and strengthen spelling skills. The following word family list illustrates words separated into onset and rime:

Word	Onset	Rime
sun	s	Un
sunny	s	unny
sunshine	s	unshine

Letter-Sound Correspondences

When children begin to learn the various letter-sound correspondences, their phonemic awareness begins to overlap with their awareness of orthography and reading. One of the widely accepted strategies to employ when introducing children to letter-sound correspondences is to begin with those correspondences that occur the most frequently in simple English words. In an effort to help build confidence in young learners, educators are encouraged to introduce only a few letter-sound combinations at a time and provide ample opportunities for practice and review before introducing new combinations. Although there is no formally established order for the introduction of letter-sound correspondences, educators are encouraged to consider the following general guidelines, but they should also keep in mind the needs, experiences, and current literacy levels of the students.

The following is intended as a general guide only:

a
m
t
p
o
n
c
d
u
s
g
h
i
f
b
l
e
r
w
k
x
v
y
z
j
q

As a generally accepted rule, short vowels should be introduced ahead of long vowels, and lowercase letters should be mastered before the introduction of their upper case counterparts.

Spelling conventions in the English language are primarily concerned with three areas: mechanics, usage, and sentence formation.

Mechanics

For primary students who are just beginning to master the alphabetic principle, educators should first concentrate on proper letter formation, the spelling of high-frequency words and sight words, and offer classroom discussions to promote the sharing of ideas. When children begin to write in sentences to share their thoughts and feelings in print, educators may consider the introduction of an author's chair, in which students read their writing out loud to their classmates.

Although the phonetic spelling or invented spelling that primary students employ in these early stages may not be the conventional spelling of certain words, it allows primary students to practice the art and flow of writing. It works to build their confidence in the writing process. This is not the time for educators to correct spelling, punctuation, or capitalization errors as young learners may quickly lose interest in writing and may lose self-confidence.

One strategy to employ early on to help students with proper spelling is to ensure there is an easily accessible and updated word wall that employs high-frequency words and sight words. Students should be encouraged to refer to the word wall while they write.

Usage

Usage concerns itself with word order, verb tense, and subject-verb agreement among other areas. As primary children often have a basic knowledge of how to use oral language effectively in order to communicate, this area of spelling conventions may require less initial attention than the mechanics of spelling. During read-aloud and shared reading activities, educators may wish to point out punctuation marks found in print, model how to read these punctuation marks, and periodically discuss their importance in the reading and writing process.

When children begin to engage in writing exercises, educators may wish to prompt self-editing skills by asking if each sentence begins with a capital and ends with a period, question mark, or exclamation point.

Sentence Formation

Verbs, nouns, adverbs, and adjectives all play significant roles in the writing process. However, for primary students, these concepts are fairly complex to understand. One instruction approach that may prove effective is to categorize a number of simple verbs, nouns, adverbs, and adjectives on index cards by color coordination. Educators can then ask one child to choose a noun card and another student to choose a verb card. The children can then face the class and read their words starting with the noun and then the verb. The students can even try reading the verb first followed by the noun. A class discussion can follow, analyzing whether or not the sentences made sense and what words might need to be added to give the sentence more meaning.

Language Development and Acquisition

Research-Based Approaches for Supporting Language Acquisition and Vocabulary Development for Diverse Learners

<u>Examples of Commonly Used Research-Based Strategies</u>
For the vast majority of people, native language acquisition comes about naturally in childhood. From the time they are born, babies are usually surrounded by the language use of their parents or caregivers. The human brain is hardwired to learn language, meaning that babies do not have to put conscious effort into unraveling the intricacies of grammar or pronunciation; it is something that happens automatically as they are exposed to language. Furthermore, caregivers do not have to formally teach first language skills to babies.

First language acquisition in infancy and early childhood passes through several predictable stages. Babies begin by crying to express a range of emotions like hunger or discomfort. By the time they are two months old, they then begin cooing to convey other emotions, such as happiness and satisfaction. In later months, infants start to experiment with different sounds like babbling and gurgling by repeating simple syllables like "goo goo goo" and "ma ma ma" and show signs of comprehending certain full words. A baby's first word often occurs around one year of age, and for the next six months, the baby can conduct simple communication through one-word expressions like "Daddy," "milk," and "cat."

After they reach eighteen months, young children begin to use two- and three-word utterances to express more complex meaning, such as "Mommy go?" "Don't want to!" and "Where juice?" By the time they are two and a half years old, toddlers enter the telegraphic stage of language where they begin using the grammatical structure of their native language, although not without some problems. A common error is "I goed to school," instead of "I went to school." However, even though young children do make mistakes in their language usage, it is nevertheless remarkable that they achieve functional mastery of a language in such a short amount of time, generally without any formal instruction.

Although acquisition of a first language is largely a natural process of childhood development, *second language acquisition* in older children or adults is quite different. This is partially linked to the critical period hypothesis, which states that language acquisition only occurs readily and naturally during the first few years of life; language acquisition that happens later, perhaps after puberty, is much more difficult and less successful. Children who are not exposed to any language before the age of five or so will have extreme difficulty learning a language later. This seems to indicate that the brain is primed to learn language from birth, but this readiness quickly diminishes after the critical period has been passed.

Although scientists continue to debate the exact significance of a critical period on second language development, learning a second language later in life clearly presents different challenges than learning a first language. In linguistics, *L1* refers to a speaker's native language and *L2* refers to a second language.

L2 acquisition follows different stages from that of L1. L2 acquisition begins with *preproduction*, also known as the *silent stage*, during which the learner is exposed to the new language, but lacks the skills to communicate and may only use body language or other non-verbal expressions. During the early production stage, the L2 learner begins using simple expressions and has limited comprehension ability.

Next is *speech emergence*—the low-intermediate stage. At this point, the language learner can form simple sentences although he or she makes frequent errors in grammar and usage. L2 learners then pass to *intermediate fluency*, where they begin to gain skills in academic or idiomatic language, demonstrate a much higher level of comprehension, and make fewer mistakes in their expressions.

Finally, the learner reaches *advanced fluency*, exhibiting near-native expressive and comprehensive skills. It is worth noting that even with near-native skills, after many years of advanced fluency, L2 learners may continue to speak with a different accent or use certain idiosyncratic expressions that are markedly different from native speakers. Nevertheless, they are certainly fluent.

In 2013, the Census Bureau reported that one in five Americans are speaking a language other than English at home, so language arts instructors will encounter a mixture of native speakers and second language learners in the classroom. In both cases, though, certain goals and strategies remain the same. The purpose of a language arts class is not to teach students language from scratch, but rather to further develop their preexisting knowledge and increase their awareness of how to use language for more effective and meaningful communication.

For both native and non-native English speakers, the exposure to written and spoken language that they receive outside of school impacts their future performance in school. In a notable 1995 study, researchers observed children in low- and high-income families and found that those in high-income households were exposed to 30 million more words during their childhood than those from families on welfare. When researchers followed up on these children in third grade, those who had been exposed to more words early on showed greater success in measures of reading comprehension and vocabulary.

As the early stages of both L1 and L2 acquisition show, learners need language input before they can achieve language output. Providing students with a variety of language resources, both formally and informally, can give them valuable exposure to new means of expression. In class, this exposure can include daily assignments, a classroom library, or a bulletin board with news for students. Educators can also get students in the habit of accessing resources outside of the classroom such as visiting the school or public library, watching, reading, or listening to the news, or reading informally from magazines, blogs, or other sources of interest.

This exposure also relates to two different forms of vocabulary acquisition—through incidental learning or direct instruction. *Incidental learning* occurs when students naturally encounter new vocabulary in context during daily life whereas *direct instruction* occurs through structured lessons and assignments in an academic setting.

In vocabulary development in particular, when it comes to direct instruction, there are several approaches to teaching new words to students. One is the *three-tier approach*, which states that vocabulary can be classified into three levels:

- Tier one—the most basic means of expression, e.g., *eat, school*, and *happy*
- Tier two—general academic words, e.g., *interpret, analyze, develop*
- Tier three—highly-specific words, e.g., *electromagnetic, genocide, sociolinguistic*

Tier three words should be taught within the subjects that they are directly related to rather than in a language arts class. Instead, language arts instruction should focus on tier two words that are broadly applicable to a range of subjects and, therefore, more practical for students.

Another theory of vocabulary development is learning language through chunks or groups of related words. By learning words in context along with other connected words, students are better able to connect vocabulary to areas of prior knowledge and more effectively store new words in their long-term memory. Students also gain a more complete set of tools with which to form new expressions, rather than simply learning new words in isolation. Learning in *semantic chunks*—clusters of five to ten words forming a connected phrase or sentence—is particularly useful for L2 learners in gaining familiarity with how to manipulate vocabulary and combine words to build meaning.

Vocabulary learning can also be conducted through a variety of media, combining visual, auditory, and active cues. One strategy is known as the *total physical response*, where students learn to associate a word with a certain physical reaction. For example, in response to the word *circumference*, students might use their finger to draw a circle in the air. Students can also watch videos related to the vocabulary topic they are learning about or look at visual representations of new words through a picture dictionary. By activating different styles of learning, instructors can provide students with more opportunities to acquire new language skills.

Evaluating the Effectiveness of Specific Strategies

New research on teaching strategies is emerging all the time, and it is important for instructors to stay abreast of new developments while evaluating when and how to implement any changes in their classroom. Instructors should also consider the pros and cons of different approaches to teaching.

In terms of encouraging students to seek outside language resources (noted the section above), the effectiveness differs greatly depending on students' background and home life. Students who must work after school to support themselves or their families may not have much time to stop by the public library or to read for leisure; in this case, instructors need to maximize in-class instruction time. According to another strategy, the three tier approach, tier two words are most important in a language arts classroom. However, some L2 students in the early production or intermediate fluency stages may lack basic tier one skills and struggle with understanding more advanced academic vocabulary.

Also, the integrated approach to learning vocabulary in a group of related words calls on instructors to present words as they are actually used in context, which might involve using some tier three words related to specific fields of study. Is it more effective to focus only on having a broad base of general vocabulary or to spend some time building skills in different specialized areas? This question might be answered differently depending on the needs of students in class.

As they experiment with the effectiveness of new methods of instruction, educators can also move beyond outdated learning practices. Assignments such as getting a list of words to look up in the dictionary are not generally considered effective methods. As discussed earlier, words contain a multitude of meanings that take on importance dependent on context; simply memorizing words outside of context, then, does not provide long-term benefits to students' productive language skills.

Instructor-centered models of learning have also been overturned by more recent pedagogical research. While instructors are a valuable resource of providing information and modeling language use for students, educators simply supply the input while students still need a chance to produce output. This means giving students ample opportunity to practice and apply new vocabulary, calling on students' prior knowledge when introducing new vocabulary, and demonstrating how students can use language skills outside of the classroom.

Interpreting Research and Applying it to Particular Instructional Challenges Related to Language

For instructors, pedagogical research is only as valuable as its real-life application in the classroom. Educators need to be able to use research-based strategies to tackle issues that arise while teaching.

One challenge may be the gap that exists between students who come to class with a high degree of literacy and language skills and students who have had fewer opportunities to develop those skills before entering the classroom. For example, some students have no access to a computer or the Internet at home or have a limited/nonexistent home library. Closing the gap through basic media literacy—perhaps in collaboration with a school media specialist—can empower students to know how to access language resources through the library, Internet, or other sources and how to utilize these resources for both learning and leisure. The concept of vocabulary development through incidental learning holds that students will benefit from any reading material, so instructors can encourage students to pursue their own interests through reading if they seem disinterested in textbook offerings. Asking students to keep a personal reading log or daily journal can encourage them to make reading and writing part of their everyday lives.

Another common problem in language instruction is students forgetting new vocabulary as soon as they learn it. Repetition and reinforcement is key to creating lasting knowledge. Also, as many studies point to the importance of learning vocabulary in context, utilizing contextual learning strategies can help students build onto prior knowledge rather than treat every new word as something strange and unfamiliar. This can be done by prompting students for what they already know when a new concept is introduced in class, introduce possible unfamiliar words that they might encounter in a text, and encourage them to use context clues as they read to make logical guesses about how unknown words are connected to known ones. These strategies further empower learners to utilize the knowledge that they already possess.

Incorporating multimedia resources can also be a powerful tool for providing meaningful instruction for students with a variety of learning styles. If students struggle to remember new vocabulary words, strategies such as total physical response or recognizing a picture associated with the word can provide students with different tools to secure information in their long-term memory.

In terms of research specific to L2 learning, knowledge of the stages of development can help instructors handle frustrations that may arise during second language learning. For example, teachers may worry that students understand nothing during the silent period, but students are absorbing the basic linguistic information that they will need to start forming utterances. Rather than giving up and getting discouraged from the start, instructors can continue providing basic communication information that students will be ready to use within the first few weeks or months of being exposed to a new language.

Literacy

Foundations of Literacy and Reading Development and the Stages of Early Orthographic Development

Developing Language Literacy Skills
It is believed that literacy development is the most rapid between birth and 5 years of age. From birth until around 3 months, babies start to recognize the sounds of familiar voices. Between 3 months and 6 months, babies begin to study a speaker's mouth and listen much more closely to speech sounds. Between 9 months and 12 months, babies can generally recognize a growing number of commonly repeated words, can utter simple words, respond appropriately to simple requests, and begin to attempt to group sounds.

In the toddler years, children begin to rapidly strengthen their communication skills, connecting sounds to meanings and combining sounds to create coherent sentences. The opportunities for rich social interactions play a key role in this early literacy development and help children to understand cultural nuances, expected behavior, and effective communication skills. By age 3, most toddlers can understand many sentences and can begin to generalize by placing specific words into categories. In the preschool years, children begin to develop and strengthen their emergent literacy skills. It is at this stage that children will begin to sound out words, learn basic spelling patterns, especially with rhyming words, and start to develop their fine motor skills. Awareness of basic grammar also begins to emerge with oral attempts at past, present, and future verb tenses.

<u>English Literacy Development</u>
English language literacy can be categorized into four basic stages:

- Beginning
- Early Intermediate
- Intermediate
- Early Advanced

Beginning Literacy
This stage is commonly referred to as *receptive language development*. Educators can encourage this stage in literacy development by providing the student with many opportunities to interact on a social level with peers. Educators should also consider starting a personal dictionary, introducing word flashcards, and providing the student with opportunities to listen to a story read by another peer, or as a computer-based activity.

Early Intermediate Literacy
When a child begins to communicate to express a need or attempt to ask or respond to a question, the child is said to be at the early intermediate literacy stage. Educators should continue to build vocabulary knowledge and introduce activities that require the student to complete the endings of sentences, fill in the blanks, and describe the beginning or ending of familiar stories.

Intermediate Literacy
When a child begins to demonstrate comprehension of more complex vocabulary and abstract ideas, the child is advancing into the intermediate literacy stage. It is at this stage that children are able to challenge themselves to meet the classroom learning expectations and start to use their newly acquired literacy skills to read, write, listen, and speak. Educators may consider providing students with more advanced reading opportunities, such as partner-shared reading, silent reading, and choral reading.

Early Advanced Literacy
When a child is able to apply literacy skills to learn new information across many subjects, the child is progressing toward the early advanced literacy stage. The child can now tackle complex literacy tasks and confidently handle much more cognitively demanding material. To strengthen reading comprehension, educators should consider the introduction to word webs and semantic organizers. Book reports and class presentations, as well as continued opportunities to access a variety of reading material, will help to strengthen the child's newly acquired literacy skills.

<u>Stages of Early Orthographic Development: Learning to Spell</u>
Orthography is the representation of the sounds of a language by written or printed symbols. Learning to spell is a highly complex and cumulative process with each skill building on the previously mastered skill. This is considered *orthographic development*. It is imperative for educators to ensure that each skill is taught in sequential steps in order for children to develop spelling capabilities.

Emergent Spelling: Pre-Communicative Writing Stage
Children may be able to accurately identify various letters of the alphabet but will likely not be able to associate them to their corresponding sounds. Children may be able to string together letter-like forms or letters without a connection to specific phonemes (the smallest units of sound in a given language). Nearing the end of this phase, children progress from writing in all directions to writing in standard convention from left to right.

Letter Name-Alphabetic Stage
At this stage, children begin to understand unique letter-sound correspondence and can begin to differentiate between various consonant sounds. Children may even be able to connect two and three letters together in an attempt to spell a word, but the letters they use will generally only consist of consonants. Most show a clear preference for capital letters.

Within-Word Pattern Stage
With a strengthening ability to recognize and apply letter-sound correspondence, children in this spelling stage can use their understanding of phonics to attempt full words that incorporate vowels. With repeated and consistent exposure and practice, children start to focus on letter combinations, spelling patterns, consonant blends, and digraphs. In this stage, students are becoming aware of homophones and experiment with vowel sound combinations.

Syllables and Affixes Stage
Just as the name suggests, children at this stage are focused on syllables and combining them to form words. Children begin to develop a deeper understanding of the need for vowels to appear in each syllable, and words begin to readily resemble the proper conventions of English spelling to them.

Derivational Relations Stage
In this stage, students learn how spelling relates to meaning. Generalizations about spelling patterns and rules of spelling start to be more readily applied, which allows the child to attempt the spelling of unfamiliar words. Children begin learning about root words and consonant and vowel alterations. It is during this stage that children begin to accumulate a much greater vocabulary base.

Effective Teaching Strategies for Spelling
There are several effective strategies that educators can introduce to facilitate each developmental spelling stage. Strategies focused on alphabetic knowledge, including letter-sound games, are of primary importance in the beginning stages. As spelling skills strengthen, educators may choose to introduce word families, spelling patterns, and word structures. There is some controversy surrounding allowing children to use invented spelling in their writing. Research indicates that, provided there is spelling instruction taking place, allowing invented spelling supports growth in the areas of phonemic awareness, phonics, and general spelling skills.

Roles of Phonological Awareness, Phonics, and Word Recognition Skills in Literacy Development

It is imperative that educators understand the five basic components of reading education. If there is any deficit in any one of these following components, a child is likely to experience reading difficulty:

- Phonemic Awareness
- Phonics
- Fluency
- Vocabulary
- Comprehension

Phonemic Awareness

A phoneme is the smallest unit of sound in a given language and is one aspect under the umbrella of skills associated with phonological awareness. A child demonstrates phonemic awareness when identifying rhymes, recognizing alliterations, and isolating specific sounds inside a word or a set of words. Children who demonstrate basic phonemic awareness will eventually also be able to independently and appropriately blend together a variety of phonemes.

Some classroom strategies to strengthen phonemic awareness may include:

- Introduction to nursery rhymes and word play
- Speech discrimination techniques to train the ear to hear more accurately
- Repeated instruction connecting sounds to letters and blending sounds
- Use of visual images coupled with corresponding sounds and words
- Teaching speech sounds through direct instruction
- Comparing known to unfamiliar words
- Practicing pronunciation of newly introduced letters, letter combinations, and words
- Practicing word decoding
- Differentiating similar sounding words

Phonological and Phonemic Awareness Instruction

Age-appropriate and developmentally appropriate instruction for phonological and phonemic awareness is key to helping children strengthen their reading and writing skills. Phonological and phonemic awareness, or PPA, instruction works to enhance correct speech, improve understanding and application of accurate letter-to-sound correspondence, and strengthen spelling skills. Since skill-building involving phonemes is not a natural process but needs to be taught, PPA instruction is especially important for children who have limited access and exposure to reading materials and who lack familial encouragement to read. Strategies that educators can implement include leading word and sound games, focusing on phoneme skill-building activities, and ensuring all activities focus on the fun, playful nature of words and sounds instead of rote memorization and drilling techniques.

Phonics

Phonics is the ability to apply letter-sound relationships and letter patterns in order to accurately pronounce written words. Children with strong phonics skills are able to recognize familiar written words with relative ease and quickly decipher or "decode" unfamiliar words. As one of the foundational skills for reading readiness, phonics essentially enables young readers to translate printed words into recognizable speech. If children lack proficiency in phonics, their ability to read fluently and to increase vocabulary will be limited, which consequently leads to reading comprehension difficulties.

Emergent readers benefit from explicit word decoding instruction that focuses on letter-sound relationships. This includes practicing sounding out words and identifying exceptions to the letter-sound relationships. A multi-sensory approach to word decoding instruction has also been found to be beneficial. By addressing a wide variety of learning styles and providing visual and hands-on instruction, educators help to bridge the gap between guided word decoding and it as an automatic process.

Role of Fluency in Supporting Comprehension

Fluency

When children are able to read fluently, they read with accuracy, a steady and consistent speed, and an appropriate expression. A fluent reader can seamlessly connect word recognition to comprehension, whether reading silently or aloud. In other words, reading fluency is an automatic recognition and accurate interpretation of text. Without the ability to read fluently, a child's reading comprehension will be limited. Each time a child has to interrupt his or her reading to decode an unfamiliar word, comprehension is impaired.

There are a number of factors that contribute to the success of reading fluency. It is important that students have many opportunities to read. Access to a variety of reading genres at appropriate reading levels and effective reading fluency instruction also play important roles in how successful children will become as fluent readers. The key is to have children repeat the same passage several times in order to become familiar with the words in the text and increase their overall speed and accuracy. Poems are an effective choice when teaching fluency, since they are usually concise and offer rhyming words in an entertaining, rhythmic pattern. Some other instructional strategies to consider include:

- Modeling reading fluency with expression
- Tape-assisted reading
- Echo reading
- Partner reading
- Small group and choral reading

Comprehension
Comprehension is defined as the level of understanding of content that a child demonstrates during and after the reading of a given text. Comprehension begins well before a child is able to read. Adults and educators can foster comprehension by reading aloud to children and helping them respond to the content and relate it to their prior knowledge. Throughout the reading process, the child asks and answers relevant questions confirming her or his comprehension and is able to successfully summarize the text upon completion.

Since reading comprehension encompasses several cognitive processes, including the awareness and understanding of phonemes, phonics, and the ability to construct meaning from text, educators should employ reading comprehension strategies prior to, during, and after reading. Reading comprehension is a lifelong process. As the genres of written text change and written language becomes more complex, it is essential that educators continually reinforce reading comprehension strategies throughout a student's educational career.

Some instructional strategies to consider are:

- Pre-teaching new vocabulary
- Monitoring for understanding
- Answering and generating questions
- Summarizing

Assessment

Decoding, Encoding, and the Stages of Spelling Development

Decoding and encoding are reciprocal phonological skills, meaning that the steps to each are opposite of one another.

Decoding is the application of letter-sound correspondences, letter patterns, and other phonics relationships that help students read and correctly pronounce words. Decoding helps students to recognize and read words quickly, increasing reading fluency and comprehension. The order of the steps that occur during the decoding process are as follows:

- The student identifies a written letter or letter combination.
- The student makes correlations between the sound of the letter or sounds of the letter combination.
- The student understands how the letters or letter combinations fit together.
- The student verbally blends the letter and letter combinations together to form a word.

Encoding is the spelling of words. In order to properly spell words, students must be familiar with letter/sound correspondences. Students must be able to put together phonemes, digraphs or blends, morphological units, consonant/vowel patterns, etc. The steps of encoding are identified below.

- The student understands that letters and sounds make up words.
- The student segments the sound parts of a word.
- The student identifies the letter or letter combinations that correspond to each sound part.
- The student then writes the letters and letter combinations in order to create the word.

Because the stages of decoding and spelling are essentially opposite of one another, they are reciprocal skills. Thus, phonics knowledge supports the development of reading and spelling. Likewise, the development of spelling knowledge reinforces phonics and decoding knowledge. In fact, the foundation of all good spelling programs is their alignment to reading instruction and a student's reading level.

Because of the reciprocal relationship between decoding and encoding, the development of phonics, vocabulary, and spelling are interrelated. The instruction of phonics begins with simple syllable patterns. Phonics instruction then progresses toward more difficult syllable patterns, more complex phonics patterns, the sounds of morphemes, and strategies for decoding multisyllabic words. Through this process, new vocabulary is developed. Sight word instruction should not begin until students are able to decode target words with automaticity and accuracy. Spelling is the last instructional component to be introduced.

Spelling development occurs in stages. In order, these stages are the pre-phonetic stage, the semiphonetic stage, the phonetic stage, the transitional stage, and the conventional stage. Each stage is explained below. Ways in which phonics and vocabulary development fit into the spelling stages are discussed. Instructional strategies for each phase of spelling are suggested.

Spelling development begins with the pre-phonetic stage. This stage is marked by an incomplete understanding of the alphabetic principle. Student understanding of letter-sound correspondences is limited. During the pre-phonetic stage, students participate in precommunicative writing. Precommunicative writing appears to be a jumble of letter-like forms rather than a series of discrete letters. Students' precommunicative writing samples can be used as informal assessments of their understanding of the alphabetic principle and knowledge of letter-sound correspondences.

Pre-phonetic stage of spelling development

The pre-phonetic stage is followed by the semiphonetic stage. In this stage, a student understands that letters represent sounds. The alphabetic principle may be understood, but letter recognition may not yet be fully developed. In this stage, single letters may be used to represent entire words (e.g., *U* for *you*). Other times, multiple syllables within words may be omitted. Writing produced by students in this stage is still virtually unreadable. Teachers may ask students to provide drawings to supplement their writing to better determine what a student intended to write.

Semiphonetc stage of writing

The third stage in spelling development is the phonetic stage. In this stage, students have mastered letter-sound correspondences. Although letters may be written backward or upside down, phonetic spellers are able to write all of the letters in the alphabet. Because phonetic spellers have limited sight vocabulary, irregular words are often spelled incorrectly. However, words that are written may phonetically sound like the spoken word. Additionally, student writing becomes systematic. For example, students are likely to use one letter to represent a digraph or letter blend (e.g., *f* for /ph/).

Phonetic stage of writing

Spelling instruction of common consonant patterns, short vowel sounds, and common affixes or rimes can begin during the phonetic stage. Thus, spelling instruction during the phonetic stage coincides with the instruction of phonics and phonemic awareness that also occurs during this stage of development.

The creation of word walls is advantageous during the phonetic stage of spelling development. On a word wall, words that share common consonant-vowel patterns or letter clusters are written in groups. Students are encouraged to add words to the group. As a result, word walls promote strategic spelling, vocabulary development, common letter combinations, and common morphological units.

The transitional stage of spelling occurs when a student has developed a small sight vocabulary and a solid understanding of letter-sound correspondences. Thus, spelling dependence on phonology decreases. Instead, dependence on visual representation and word structure increases. As sight word vocabulary increases during the transition stage, the correct spelling of irregular words will also increase. However, students may still struggle to spell words with long vowel sounds.

Transitional stage of spelling

Differentiation of spelling instruction often begins during the transitional stage. Instruction ought to be guided by data collected through informal observations and informal assessments. Depending on individual needs, lessons may include sight word recognition, morphology, etymology, reading, and writing. It is during the transitional stage that the instruction of homophones can begin. Homophones are words that sound the same but have different spellings and meanings (e.g., *their* and *there*). Additionally, students should be expected to begin writing full sentences at the transitional stage. Writing will not only reinforce correct spelling of words but also phonics and vocabulary development.

Conventional spelling is the last and final stage of spelling development. This stage occurs after a student's sight word vocabulary recognition is well developed and the student is able to read fluently and with comprehension. By this stage, students know the basic rules of phonics. They are able to deal with consonants, multiple vowel-consonant blends, homophones, digraphs, and irregular spellings. Due to an increase in sight word recognition at this stage, a conventional speller is able to recognize when a word is spelled incorrectly.

Conventional stage

It is at the conventional spelling stage that spelling instruction can begin to focus on content-specific vocabulary words and words with unusual spellings. In order to further reinforce vocabulary development of such content-specific words and apply phonic skills, students should be encouraged to use the correct spelling of such words within various writing activities.

For even the best conventional spellers, some words will still cause consistent trouble. Students can keep track of words that they consistently spell incorrectly or find confusing in word banks so they can isolate and eventually eliminate their individualized errors. Students can use their word banks as references when they come across a word with which they struggle. Students may also spend time consciously committing the words in their banks to memory through verbal or written practice.

Non-Written and Written Communication

Conventions of Language

Identifying Parts of Speech

Nouns

A noun is a person, place, thing, or idea. All nouns fit into one of two types, common or proper.

A *common noun* is a word that identifies any of a class of people, places, or things. Examples include numbers, objects, animals, feelings, concepts, qualities, and actions. *A, an,* or *the* usually precedes the common noun. These parts of speech are called *articles*. Here are some examples of sentences using nouns preceded by articles.

> *A* building is under construction.
> *The* girl would like to move to *the* city.

A *proper noun* (also called a *proper name*) is used for the specific name of an individual person, place, or organization. The first letter in a proper noun is capitalized. "My name is *Mary*." "I work for *Walmart*."

Nouns sometimes serve as adjectives (which themselves describe nouns), such as "hockey player" and "state government."

An abstract noun is an idea, state, or quality. It is something that can't be touched, such as happiness, courage, evil, or humor.

A concrete noun is something that can be experienced through the senses (touch, taste, hear, smell, see). Examples of concrete nouns are birds, skateboard, pie, and car.

A collective noun refers to a collection of people, places, or things that act as one. Examples of collective nouns are as follows: team, class, jury, family, audience, and flock.

Pronouns

A word used in place of a noun is known as a *pronoun*. Pronouns are words like *I, mine, hers,* and *us*.

Pronouns can be split into different classifications (seen below) which make them easier to learn; however, it's not important to memorize the classifications.

- Personal pronouns: refer to people
- First person: we, I, our, mine
- Second person: you, yours
- Third person: he, them
- Possessive pronouns: demonstrate ownership (mine, my, his, yours)
- Interrogative pronouns: ask questions (what, which, who, whom, whose)
- Relative pronouns: include the five interrogative pronouns and others that are relative (whoever, whomever, that, when, where)
- Demonstrative pronouns: replace something specific (this, that, those, these)

- Reciprocal pronouns: indicate something was done or given in return (each other, one another)
- Indefinite pronouns: have a nonspecific status (anybody, whoever, someone, everybody, somebody)

Indefinite pronouns such as *anybody, whoever, someone, everybody*, and *somebody* command a singular verb form, but others such as *all, none,* and *some* could require a singular or plural verb form.

Antecedents

An *antecedent* is the noun to which a pronoun refers; it needs to be written or spoken before the pronoun is used. For many pronouns, antecedents are imperative for clarity. In particular, many of the personal, possessive, and demonstrative pronouns need antecedents. Otherwise, it would be unclear who or what someone is referring to when they use a pronoun like *he* or *this*.

Pronoun reference means that the pronoun should refer clearly to one, clear, unmistakable noun (the antecedent).

Pronoun-antecedent agreement refers to the need for the antecedent and the corresponding pronoun to agree in gender, person, and number. Here are some examples:

The *kidneys* (plural antecedent) are part of the urinary system. *They* (plural pronoun) serve several roles."

The kidneys are part of the *urinary system* (singular antecedent). *It* (singular pronoun) is also known as the renal system.

Pronoun Cases

The subjective pronouns —*I, you, he/she/it, we, they,* and *who*—are the subjects of the sentence.

Example: *They* have a new house.

The objective pronouns—*me, you (singular), him/her, us, them,* and *whom*—are used when something is being done for or given to someone; they are objects of the action.

Example: The teacher has an apple for *us*.

The possessive pronouns—*mine, my, your, yours, his, hers, its, their, theirs, our,* and *ours*—are used to denote that something (or someone) belongs to someone (or something).

Example: It's *their* chocolate cake.
Even Better Example: It's *my* chocolate cake!

One of the greatest challenges and worst abuses of pronouns concerns *who* and *whom*. Just knowing the following rule can eliminate confusion. *Who* is a subjective-case pronoun used only as a subject or subject complement. *Whom* is only objective-case and, therefore, the object of the verb or preposition.

Hint: When using *who* or *whom*, think of whether someone would say *he* or *him*. If the answer is *he*, use *who*. If the answer is *him*, use *whom*. This trick is easy to remember because *he* and *who* both end in vowels, and *him* and *whom* both end in the letter *M*.

Verbs

The *verb* is the part of speech that describes an action, state of being, or occurrence.

A *verb* forms the main part of a predicate of a sentence. This means that the verb explains what the noun (which will be discussed shortly) is doing. A simple example is *time flies*. The verb *flies* explains what the action of the noun, *time*, is doing. This example is a *main* verb.

Helping (auxiliary) verbs are words like *have, do, be, can, may, should, must,* and *will.* "I *should* go to the store." Helping verbs assist main verbs in expressing tense, ability, possibility, permission, or obligation.

Particles are minor function words like *not, in, out, up,* or *down* that become part of the verb itself. "I might *not*."

Participles are words formed from verbs that are often used to modify a noun, noun phrase, verb, or verb phrase.

> The *running* teenager collided with the cyclist.

Participles can also create compound verb forms.

> He is *speaking*.

Verbs have five basic forms: the *base* form, the *-s* form, the *-ing* form, the *past* form, and the *past participle* form.

The *past* forms are either *regular* (*love/loved; hate/hated*) or *irregular* because they don't end by adding the common past tense suffix "-ed" (*go/went; fall/fell; set/set*).

Verb Forms

Shifting verb forms entails *conjugation*, which is used to indicate *tense, voice,* or *mood*.

Verb tense is used to show when the action in the sentence took place. There are several different verb tenses, and it is important to know how and when to use them. Some verb tenses can be achieved by changing the form of the verb, while others require the use of helping verbs (e.g., *is, was,* or *has*).

Present tense shows the action is happening currently or is ongoing:

> I walk to work every morning.

> She is stressed about the deadline.

Past tense shows that the action happened in the past or that the state of being is in the past:

> I walked to work yesterday morning.

> She was stressed about the deadline.

Future tense shows that the action will happen in the future or is a future state of being:

> I will walk to work tomorrow morning.

> She will be stressed about the deadline.

Present perfect tense shows action that began in the past, but continues into the present:

> I have walked to work all week.

> She has been stressed about the deadline.

Past perfect tense shows an action was finished before another took place:

> I had walked all week until I sprained my ankle.

> She had been stressed about the deadline until we talked about it.

Future perfect tense shows an action that will be completed at some point in the future:

> By the time the bus arrives, I will have walked to work already.

Voice

Verbs can be in the active or passive voice. When the subject completes the action, the verb is in *active voice*. When the subject receives the action of the sentence, the verb is in *passive voice*.

> Active: Jamie ate the ice cream.

> Passive: The ice cream was eaten by Jamie.

In active voice, the subject (*Jamie*) is the "do-er" of the action (*ate*). In passive voice, the subject *ice cream* receives the action of being eaten.

While passive voice can add variety to writing, active voice is the generally preferred sentence structure.

Mood

Mood is used to show the speaker's feelings about the subject matter. In English, there is *indicative mood, imperative mood,* and *subjective mood.*

Indicative mood is used to state facts, ask questions, or state opinions:

> Bob will make the trip next week.

> When can Bob make the trip?

Imperative mood is used to state a command or make a request:

> Wait in the lobby.

> Please call me next week.

Subjunctive mood is used to express a wish, an opinion, or a hope that is contrary to fact:

> If I were in charge, none of this would have happened.

> Allison wished she could take the exam over again when she saw her score.

Adjectives

Adjectives are words used to modify nouns and pronouns. They can be used alone or in a series and are used to further define or describe the nouns they modify.

> Mark made us a delicious, four-course meal.

The words *delicious* and *four-course* are adjectives that describe the kind of meal Mark made.

Articles are also considered adjectives because they help to describe nouns. Articles can be general or specific. The three articles in English are: a, an, and the.

Indefinite articles (a, an) are used to refer to nonspecific nouns. The article *a* proceeds words beginning with consonant sounds, and the article *an* proceeds words beginning with vowel sounds.

> A car drove by our house.

> An alligator was loose at the zoo.

> He has always wanted a ukulele. (The first *u* makes a *y* sound.)

Note that *a* and *an* should only proceed nonspecific nouns that are also singular. If a nonspecific noun is plural, it does not need a preceding article.

> Alligators were loose at the zoo.

The *definite article (the)* is used to refer to specific nouns:

> The car pulled into our driveway.

Note that *the* should proceed all specific nouns regardless of whether they are singular or plural.

> The cars pulled into our driveway.

Comparative adjectives are used to compare nouns. When they are used in this way, they take on positive, comparative, or superlative form.

> The *positive* form is the normal form of the adjective:

> > Alicia is tall.

> The *comparative* form shows a comparison between two things:

> > Alicia is taller than Maria.

> *Superlative* form shows comparison between more than two things:

> > Alicia is the tallest girl in her class.

Usually, the comparative and superlative can be made by adding *–er* and *–est* to the positive form, but some verbs call for the helping verbs *more* or *most*. Other exceptions to the rule include adjectives like *bad*, which uses the comparative *worse* and the superlative *worst*.

An adjective phrase is not a bunch of adjectives strung together, but a group of words that describes a noun or pronoun and, thus, functions as an adjective. *Very ugly* is an adjective phrase; so are *way too fat* and *faster than a speeding bullet.*

Adverbs

Adverbs have more functions than adjectives because they modify or qualify verbs, adjectives, or other adverbs as well as word groups that express a relation of place, time, circumstance, or cause. Therefore, adverbs answer any of the following questions: *How, when, where, why, in what way, how often, how much, in what condition,* and/or *to what degree. How good looking is he? He is* <u>very</u> *handsome.*

Here are some examples of adverbs for different situations:

- how: quickly
- when: daily
- where: there
- in what way: easily
- how often: often
- how much: much
- in what condition: badly
- what degree: hardly

As one can see, for some reason, many adverbs end in *-ly.*

Adverbs do things like emphasize (*really, simply,* and *so*), amplify (*heartily, completely,* and *positively*), and tone down (*almost, somewhat,* and *mildly*).

Adverbs also come in phrases.

> The dog ran as <u>though his life depended on it.</u>

Prepositions

Prepositions are connecting words and, while there are only about 150 of them, they are used more often than any other individual groups of words. They describe relationships between other words. They are placed before a noun or pronoun, forming a phrase that modifies another word in the sentence. *Prepositional phrases* begin with a preposition and end with a noun or pronoun, the *object of the preposition. A pristine lake is* <u>near the store</u> *and* <u>behind the bank</u>.

Some commonly used prepositions are *about, after, anti, around, as, at, behind, beside, by, for, from, in, into, of, off, on, to,* and *with.*

Complex prepositions, which also come before a noun or pronoun, consist of two or three words such as *according to, in regards to,* and *because of.*

Conjunctions

Conjunctions are vital words that connect words, phrases, thoughts, and ideas. Conjunctions show relationships between components. There are two types:

Coordinating conjunctions are the primary class of conjunctions placed between words, phrases, clauses, and sentences that are of equal grammatical rank; the coordinating conjunctions are for, and, nor, but, or, yes, and so. A useful memorization trick is to remember that the first letter of these conjunctions collectively spell the word *fanboys*.

> I need to go shopping, *but* I must be careful to leave enough money in the bank.
> She wore a black, red, *and* white shirt.

Subordinating conjunctions are the secondary class of conjunctions. They connect two unequal parts, one *main* (or *independent*) and the other *subordinate* (or *dependent*). I must go to the store *even though* I do not have enough money in the bank.

> *Because* I read the review, I do not want to go to the movie.

Notice that the presence of subordinating conjunctions makes clauses dependent. *I read the review* is an independent clause, but *because* makes the clause dependent. Thus, it needs an independent clause to complete the sentence.

Interjections

Interjections are words used to express emotion. Examples include *wow*, *ouch*, and *hooray*. Interjections are often separate from sentences; in those cases, the interjection is directly followed by an exclamation point. In other cases the interjection is included in a sentence and followed by a comma. The punctuation plays a big role in the intensity of the emotion that the interjection is expressing. Using a comma or semicolon indicates less excitement than using an exclamation mark.

Recognizing Sentence Types and Purposes

Sentence Types

There are four ways in which we can structure sentences: simple, compound, complex, and compound-complex. Sentences can be composed of just one clause or many clauses joined together.

When a sentence is composed of just one clause (an independent clause), we call it a simple sentence. Simple sentences do not necessarily have to be short sentences. They just require one independent clause with a subject and a predicate. For example:

> Thomas marched over to Andrew's house.

> Jonah and Mary constructed a simplified version of the Eiffel Tower with Legos.

When a sentence has two or more independent clauses we call it a compound sentence. The clauses are connected by a comma and a coordinating conjunction—*and, but, or, nor, for*—or by a semicolon. Compound sentences do not have dependent clauses. For example:

> We went to the fireworks stand, and we bought enough fireworks to last all night.

> The children sat on the grass, and then we lit the fireworks one at a time.

When a sentence has just one independent clause and includes one or more dependent clauses, we call it a complex sentence:

> Because she slept well and drank coffee, Sarah was quite productive at work.

> Although Will had coffee, he made mistakes while using the photocopier.

When a sentence has two or more independent clauses and at least one dependent clause, we call it a compound-complex sentence:

> It may come as a surprise, but I found the tickets, and you can go to the show.

> Jade is the girl who dove from the high-dive, and she stunned the audience silent.

<u>Sentence Purposes</u>
There isn't an overabundance of absolutes in grammar, but here is one: every sentence in the English language falls into one of four categories.

- Declarative: a simple statement that ends with a period

  > The price of milk per gallon is the same as the price of gasoline.

- Imperative: a command, instruction, or request that ends with a period

  > Buy milk when you stop to fill up your car with gas.

- Interrogative: a question that ends with a question mark

  > Will you buy the milk?

- Exclamatory: a statement or command that expresses emotions like anger, urgency, or surprise and ends with an exclamation mark

  > Buy the milk now!

Declarative sentences are the most common type, probably because they are comprised of the most general content, without any of the bells and whistles that the other three types contain. They are, simply, declarations or statements of any degree of seriousness, importance, or information.

Imperative sentences often seem to be missing a subject. The subject is there, though; it is just not visible or audible because it is *implied*. Look at the imperative example sentence.

> Buy the milk when you fill up your car with gas.

You is the implied subject, the one to whom the command is issued. This is sometimes called *the understood you* because it is understood that *you* is the subject of the sentence.

Interrogative sentences—those that ask questions—are defined as such from the idea of the word *interrogation*, the action of questions being asked of suspects by investigators. Although that is serious business, interrogative sentences apply to all kinds of questions.

To exclaim is at the root of *exclamatory* sentences. These are made with strong emotions behind them. The only technical difference between a declarative or imperative sentence and an exclamatory one is the exclamation mark at the end. The example declarative and imperative sentences can both become an exclamatory one simply by putting an exclamation mark at the end of the sentences.

> The price of milk per gallon is the same as the price of gasoline!
> Buy milk when you stop to fill up your car with gas!

After all, someone might be really excited by the price of gas or milk, or they could be mad at the person that will be buying the milk! However, as stated before, exclamation marks in abundance defeat their own purpose! After a while, they begin to cause fatigue! When used only for their intended purpose, they can have their expected and desired effect.

English Grammar and Conventions of Edited American English

<u>Errors in Standard English Grammar, Usage, Syntax, and Mechanics</u>

Sentence Fragments
A *complete sentence* requires a verb and a subject that expresses a complete thought. Sometimes, the subject is omitted in the case of the implied *you*, used in sentences that are the command or imperative form—e.g., "Look!" or "Give me that." It is understood that the subject of the command is *you*, the listener or reader, so it is possible to have a structure without an explicit subject. Without these elements, though, the sentence is incomplete—it is a *sentence fragment.* While sentence fragments often occur in conversational English or creative writing, they are generally not appropriate in academic writing. Sentence fragments often occur when dependent clauses are not joined to an independent clause:

> *Sentence fragment*: Because the airline overbooked the flight.

The sentence above is a dependent clause that does not express a complete thought. What happened as a result of this cause? With the addition of an independent clause, this now becomes a complete sentence:

> *Complete sentence*: Because the airline overbooked the flight, several passengers were unable to board.

Sentences fragments may also occur through improper use of conjunctions:

> I'm going to the Bahamas for spring break. And to New York City for New Year's Eve.

> While the first sentence above is a complete sentence, the second one is not because it is a prepositional phrase that lacks a subject [I] and a verb [am going]. Joining the two together with the coordinating conjunction forms one grammatically-correct sentence:

> I'm going to the Bahamas for spring break and to New York City for New Year's Eve.

Run-ons
A *run-on* is a sentence with too many independent clauses that are improperly connected to each other:

> This winter has been very cold some farmers have suffered damage to their crops.

The sentence above has two subject-verb combinations. The first is "this winter has been"; the second is "some farmers have suffered." However, they are simply stuck next to each other without any punctuation or conjunction. Therefore, the sentence is a run-on.

Another type of run-on occurs when writers use inappropriate punctuation:

> This winter has been very cold, some farmers have suffered damage to their crops.

Though a comma has been added, this sentence is still not correct. When a comma alone is used to join two independent clauses, it is known as a **comma splice**. Without an appropriate conjunction, a comma cannot join two independent clauses by itself.

Run-on sentences can be corrected by either dividing the independent clauses into two or more separate sentences or inserting appropriate conjunctions and/or punctuation. The run-on sentence can be amended by separating each subject-verb pair into its own sentence:

> This winter has been very cold. Some farmers have suffered damage to their crops.

The run-on can also be fixed by adding a comma and conjunction to join the two independent clauses with each other:

> This winter has been very cold, so some farmers have suffered damage to their crops.

Parallelism
Parallel structure occurs when phrases or clauses within a sentence contain the same structure. Parallelism increases readability and comprehensibility because it is easy to tell which sentence elements are paired with each other in meaning.

> Jennifer enjoys cooking, knitting, and to spend time with her cat.

This sentence is not parallel because the items in the list appear in two different forms. Some are *gerunds,* which is the verb + ing: *cooking, knitting.* The other item uses the *infinitive* form, which is to + verb: *to spend.* To create parallelism, all items in the list may reflect the same form:

> Jennifer enjoys cooking, knitting, and spending time with her cat.

All of the items in the list are now in gerund forms, so this sentence exhibits parallel structure. Here's another example:

> The company is looking for employees who are responsible and with a lot of experience.

Again, the items that are listed in this sentence are not parallel. "Responsible" is an adjective, yet "with a lot of experience" is a prepositional phrase. The sentence elements do not utilize parallel parts of speech.

> The company is looking for employees who are responsible and experienced.

"Responsible" and "experienced" are both adjectives, so this sentence now has parallel structure.

Dangling and Misplaced Modifiers
Modifiers enhance meaning by clarifying or giving greater detail about another part of a sentence. However, incorrectly-placed modifiers have the opposite effect and can cause confusion. A *misplaced modifier* is a modifier that is not located appropriately in relation to the word or phrase that it modifies:

> Because he was one of the greatest thinkers of Renaissance Italy, John idolized Leonardo da Vinci.

In this sentence, the modifier is "because he was one of the greatest thinkers of Renaissance Italy," and the noun it is intended to modify is "Leonardo da Vinci." However, due to the placement of the modifier next to the subject, John, it seems as if the sentence is stating that John was a Renaissance genius, not Da Vinci.

> John idolized Leonard da Vinci because he was one of the greatest thinkers of Renaissance Italy.

The modifier is now adjacent to the appropriate noun, clarifying which of the two men in this sentence is the greatest thinker.

Dangling modifiers modify a word or phrase that is not readily apparent in the sentence. That is, they "dangle" because they are not clearly attached to anything:

> After getting accepted to college, Amir's parents were proud.

The modifier here, "after getting accepted to college," should modify who got accepted. The noun immediately following the modifier is "Amir's parents"—but they are probably not the ones who are going to college.

> After getting accepted to college, Amir made his parents proud.

The subject of the sentence has been change to Amir himself, and now the subject and its modifier are appropriately matched.

Inconsistent Verb Tense
Verb tense reflects when an action occurred or a state existed. For example, the tense known as *simple present* expresses something that is happening right now or that happens regularly:

> She *works* in a hospital.

Present continuous tense expresses something in progress. It is formed by to be + verb + -ing.

> Sorry, I can't go out right now. I *am doing* my homework.

Past tense is used to describe events that previously occurred. However, in conversational English, speakers often use present tense or a mix of past and present tense when relating past events because it gives the narrative a sense of immediacy. In formal written English, though, consistency in verb tense is necessary to avoid reader confusion.

> I traveled to Europe last summer. As soon as I stepped off the plane, I feel like I'm in a movie! I'm surrounded by quaint cafes and impressive architecture.

The passage above abruptly switches from past tense—*traveled, stepped*—to present tense—*feel, am surrounded.*

> I *traveled* to Europe last summer. As soon as I *stepped* off the plane, I *felt* like I was in a movie! I *was surrounded* by quaint cafes and impressive architecture.

All verbs are in past tense, so this passage now has consistent verb tense.

Split Infinitives

The *infinitive form* of a verb consists of "to + base verb"—e.g., to walk, to sleep, to approve. A *split infinitive* occurs when another word, usually an adverb, is placed between *to* and the verb:

> I decided *to simply walk* to work to get more exercise every day.

The infinitive *to walk* is split by the adverb *simply*.

> It was a mistake *to hastily approve* the project before conducting further preliminary research.

The infinitive *to approve* is split by *hastily*.

Although some grammarians still advise against split infinitives, this syntactic structure is common in both spoken and written English and is widely accepted in standard usage.

Subject-Verb Agreement

In English, verbs must agree with the subject. The form of a verb may change depending on whether the subject is singular or plural, or whether it is first, second, or third person. For example, the verb *to be* has various forms:

> I <u>am</u> a student.
>
> You <u>are</u> a student.
>
> She <u>is</u> a student.
>
> We <u>are</u> students.
>
> They <u>are</u> students.

Errors occur when a verb does not agree with its subject. Sometimes, the error is readily apparent:

> We is hungry.

Is is not the appropriate form of *to be* when used with the third person plural *we*.

> We are hungry.

This sentence now has correct subject-verb agreement.

However, some cases are trickier, particularly when the subject consists of a lengthy noun phrase with many modifiers:

> Students who are hoping to accompany the anthropology department on its annual summer trip to Ecuador needs to sign up by March 31st.

The verb in this sentence is *needs*. However, its subject is not the noun adjacent to it—Ecuador. The subject is the noun at the beginning of the sentence—students. Because *students* is plural, *needs* is the incorrect verb form.

> *Students* who are hoping to accompany the anthropology department on its annual summer trip to Ecuador *need* to sign up by March 31st.

This sentence now uses correct agreement between *students* and *need*.

Another case to be aware of is a *collective noun*. A collective noun refers to a group of many things or people but can be singular in itself—e.g., family, committee, army, pair team, council, jury. Whether or not a collective noun uses a singular or plural verb depends on how the noun is being used. If the noun refers to the group performing a collective action as one unit, it should use a singular verb conjugation:

> The family is moving to a new neighborhood.

The whole family is moving together in unison, so the singular verb form *is* is appropriate here.

> The committee has made its decision.

The verb *has* and the possessive pronoun *its* both reflect the word *committee* as a singular noun in the sentence above; however, when a collective noun refers to the group as individuals, it can take a plural verb:

> The newlywed pair spend every moment together.

This sentence emphasizes the love between two people in a pair, so it can use the plural verb *spend*.

> The council are all newly elected members.

The sentence refers to the council in terms of its individual members and uses the plural verb *are*.

Overall though, American English is more likely to pair a collective noun with a singular verb, while British English is more likely to pair a collective noun with a plural verb.

<u>Grammar, Usage, Syntax, and Mechanics Choices</u>

Colons and Semicolons
In a sentence, *colons* are used before a list, a summary or elaboration, or an explanation related to the preceding information in the sentence:

> There are two ways to reserve tickets for the performance: by phone or in person.

> One thing is clear: students are spending more on tuition than ever before.

As these examples show, a colon must be preceded by an independent clause. However, the information after the colon may be in the form of an independent clause or in the form of a list.

Semicolons can be used in two different ways—to join ideas or to separate them. In some cases, semicolons can be used to connect what would otherwise be stand-alone sentences. Each part of the sentence joined by a semicolon must be an independent clause. The use of a semicolon indicates that these two independent clauses are closely related to each other:

> The rising cost of childcare is one major stressor for parents; healthcare expenses are another source of anxiety.

> Classes have been canceled due to the snowstorm; check the school website for updates.

Semicolons can also be used to divide elements of a sentence in a more distinct way than simply using a comma. This usage is particularly useful when the items in a list are especially long and complex and contain other internal punctuation.

> Retirees have many modes of income: some survive solely off their retirement checks; others supplement their income through part time jobs, like working in a supermarket or substitute teaching; and others are financially dependent on the support of family members, friends, and spouses.

Its and It's

These pronouns are the some of the most confused in the English language as most possessives contain the suffix –'s. However, for *it*, it is the opposite. *Its* is a possessive pronoun:

> The government is reassessing *its* spending plan.

It's is a contraction of the words *it is*:

> *It's* snowing outside.

Saw and Seen

Saw and *seen* are both conjugations of the verb *to see*, but they express different verb tenses. *Saw* is used in the simple past tense. *Seen* is the past participle form of *to see* and can be used in all perfect tenses.

> I seen her yesterday.

This sentence is incorrect. Because it expresses a completed event from a specified point in time in the past, it should use simple past tense:

> I *saw* her yesterday.

This sentence uses the correct verb tense. Here's how the past participle is used correctly:

> I *have seen* her before.

The meaning in this sentence is slightly changed to indicate an event from an unspecific time in the past. In this case, present perfect is the appropriate verb tense to indicate an unspecified past experience. Present perfect conjugation is created by combining *to have* + past participle.

Then and Than

Then is generally used as an adverb indicating something that happened next in a sequence or as the result of a conditional situation:

> We parked the car and *then* walked to the restaurant.

> If enough people register for the event, *then* we can begin planning.

Than is a conjunction indicating comparison:

> This watch is more expensive *than* that one.

> The bus departed later *than* I expected.

They're, Their, and There
They're is a contraction of the words *they are*:

> *They're* moving to Ohio next week.

Their is a possessive pronoun:

> The baseball players are training for *their* upcoming season.

There can function as multiple parts of speech, but it is most commonly used as an adverb indicating a location:

> Let's go to the concert! Some great bands are playing *there*.

Insure and Ensure
These terms are both verbs. *Insure* means to guarantee something against loss, harm, or damage, usually through an insurance policy that offers monetary compensation:

> The robbers made off with her prized diamond necklace, but luckily it was *insured* for one million dollars.

Ensure means to make sure, to confirm, or to be certain:

> *Ensure* that you have your passport before entering the security checkpoint.

Accept and Except
Accept is a verb meaning to take or agree to something:

> I would like to *accept* your offer of employment.

Except is a preposition that indicates exclusion:

> I've been to every state in America *except* Hawaii.

Affect and Effect
Affect is a verb meaning to influence or to have an impact on something:

> The amount of rainfall during the growing season *affects* the flavor of wine produced from these grapes.

Effect can be used as either a noun or a verb. As a noun, *effect* is synonymous with a result:

> If we implement the changes, what will the *effect* be on our profits?

As a verb, *effect* means to bring about or to make happen:

> In just a few short months, the healthy committee has *effected* real change in school nutrition.

Writing Strategies

Prewriting Strategies

Recognizing Research-Based Strategies for Teaching the Writing Process
Current trends in education have recognized the need to cultivate writing skills that prepare students for higher education and professional careers. To this end, writing skills are being integrated into other subjects beyond the language arts classroom. The skills and strategies used in language arts class, then, should be adaptable for other learning tasks. In this way, students can achieve greater proficiency by incorporating writing strategies into every aspect of learning.

To teach writing, it is important that writers know the writing process. Students should be familiar with the five components of the writing process:

1. *Pre-writing*: The drafting, planning, researching, and brainstorming of ideas
2. *Writing*: The part of the project in which the actual, physical writing takes place
3. *Revising*: Adding to, removing, rearranging, or re-writing sections of the piece
4. *Editing*: Analyzing and correcting mistakes in grammar, spelling, punctuation, formatting, and word choice
5. *Publishing*: Distributing the finished product to the teacher, employer, or other students

The *writing workshop* is possibly the most common approach to teaching writing. It is an organized approach in which the student is guided by the teacher and usually contains the following components:

- *Short lesson* (~10 min) in which the teacher focuses on a particular aspect of the writing process—e.g., strategies, organization, technique, processes, craft—and gives explicit instructions for the task at hand

- *Independent writing time* (~30 min) in which the student engages in the writing activity and works through the process while receiving help from the teacher, writing in his/her own style on either a chosen topic or one assigned, and engaging with other students

- *Sharing* (~10 min) in which the student shares a piece of his or her work, either in a small group or as a class, and gains insight by listening to the work of other students

Another common strategy is *teacher modeling*, in which the student views the teacher as a writer and is therefore more apt to believe the teacher's instruction on the subject. To be a good writing teacher, the teacher must be a good writer. Therefore, it is important that the teacher practice his or her own writing on a somewhat regular basis through blogging, journaling, or creative writing, in order to keep his or her skills sharp. The following are some strategies for teacher writing:

- *Sharing written work*: This strategy is a good audio and/or visual learning technique. The teacher should frequently share personal writing with students so that the student recognizes the instructor as having authority on the subject. Many teachers also encourage feedback from the students to stimulate critical thinking skills.

- *Writing in front of students*: This strategy is very effective as a visual learning technique as the students watch as the teacher works through the writing process. This could include asking the students to provide a question or topic on which to write and then writing on blackboard or projector.

- *Encouraging real-world writing*: This is a kinesthetic teaching strategy in which the teacher urges students to write as frequently as possible and to share their written work with other students or an authentic audience. Teachers may also find it beneficial to show students their own blogs and other online media to demonstrate exactly how it's done. Students may also choose to model their writing after a published author, imitating his or her style, sentence structure, and word choices to become comfortable with the writing process.

Finally, a good thing for a student to have is a *writer's notebook*, which contains all the student's written work over the course of the curriculum, including warm-up assignments, drafts, brainstorming templates, and completed works. This allows the student to review previous writing assignment, learn from their mistakes, and see concrete evidence for improvement. Depending on the age group, many of the assignments could be performed on a word processor to encourage computer literacy.

Formal Elements of Writing

Organizational Structure within Informational Text

Informational text is specifically designed to relate factual information, and although it is open to a reader's interpretation and application of the facts, the structure of the presentation is carefully designed to lead the reader to a particular conclusion or central idea. When reading informational text, it is important that readers are able to understand its organizational structure as the structure often directly relates to an author's intent to inform and/or persuade the reader.

The first step in identifying the text's structure is to determine the thesis or main idea. The thesis statement and organization of a work are closely intertwined. *A thesis statement* indicates the writer's purpose and may include the scope and direction of the text. It may be presented at the beginning of a text or at the end, and it may be explicit or implicit.

Once a reader has a grasp of the thesis or main idea of the text, he or she can better determine its organizational structure. Test takers are advised to read informational text passages more than once in order to comprehend the material fully. It is also helpful to examine any text features present in the text including the table of contents, index, glossary, headings, footnotes, and visuals. The analysis of these features and the information presented within them, can offer additional clues about the central idea and structure of a text. The following questions should be asked when considering structure:

- How does the author assemble the parts to make an effective whole argument?
- Is the passage linear in nature and if so, what is the timeline or thread of logic?
- What is the presented order of events, facts, or arguments? Are these effective in contributing to the author's thesis?
- How can the passage be divided into sections? How are they related to each other and to the main idea or thesis?
- What key terms are used to indicate the organization?

Next, test takers should skim the passage, noting the first line or two of each body paragraph—the *topic sentences*—and the conclusion. Key *transitional terms*, such as *on the other hand, also, because, however, therefore, most importantly*, and *first*, within the text can also signal organizational structure. Based on these clues, readers should then be able to identify what type of organizational structure is being used. The following organizational structures are most common:

- *Problem/solution*—organized by an analysis/overview of a problem, followed by potential solution(s)

- *Cause/effect*—organized by the effects resulting from a cause or the cause(s) of a particular effect

- *Spatial order*—organized by points that suggest location or direction—e.g., top to bottom, right to left, outside to inside

- *Chronological/sequence order*—organized by points presented to indicate a passage of time or through purposeful steps/stages

- *Comparison/Contrast*—organized by points that indicate similarities and/or differences between two things or concepts

- *Order of importance*—organized by priority of points, often most significant to least significant or vice versa

Using Varied and Effective Transitions

Transitions are the glue that holds the writing together. They function to purposefully incorporate new topics and supporting details in a smooth and coherent way. Usually, transitions are found at the beginnings of sentences, but they can also be located in the middle as a way to link clauses together. There are two types of clauses: independent and dependent as discussed in the language use and vocabulary section.

Transition words connect clauses within and between sentences for smoother writing. "I dislike apples. They taste like garbage." is choppier than "I dislike apples because they taste like garbage." Transitions demonstrate the relationship between ideas, allow for more complex sentence structures, and can alert the reader to which type of organizational format the author is using. For example, the above selection on human evolution uses the words *first, another,* and *finally* to indicate that the writer will be listing the reasons why humans and apes are evolutionarily different.

Transition words can be categorized based on the relationships they create between ideas:

- *General order*: signaling elaboration of an idea to emphasize a point—e.g., *for example, for instance, to demonstrate, including, such as, in other words, that is, in fact, also, furthermore, likewise, and, truly, so, surely, certainly, obviously, doubtless*

- *Chronological order*: referencing the time frame in which main event or idea occurs—e.g., *before, after, first, while, soon, shortly thereafter, meanwhile*

- *Numerical order/order of importance*: indicating that related ideas, supporting details, or events will be described in a sequence, possibly in order of importance—e.g., *first, second, also, finally, another, in addition, equally important, less importantly, most significantly, the main reason, last but not least*

- *Spatial order*: referring to the space and location of something or where things are located in relation to each other—e.g., *inside, outside, above, below, within, close, under, over, far, next to, adjacent to*

- *Cause and effect order*: signaling a causal relationship between events or ideas—e.g., *thus, therefore, since, resulted in, for this reason, as a result, consequently, hence, for, so*

- *Compare and contrast order*: identifying the similarities and differences between two or more objects, ideas, or lines of thought—e.g., *like, as, similarly, equally, just as, unlike, however, but, although, conversely, on the other hand, on the contrary*

- *Summary order*: indicating that a particular idea is coming to a close—e.g., *in conclusion, to sum up, in other words, ultimately, above all*

Sophisticated writing also aims to avoid overuse of transitions and ensure that those used are meaningful. Using a variety of transitions makes the writing appear more lively and informed and helps readers follow the progression of ideas.

Revisions of Written Text

Organization

Good writing is not merely a random collection of sentences. No matter how well written, sentences must relate and coordinate appropriately with one another. If not, the writing seems random, haphazard, and disorganized. Therefore, good writing must be organized, where each sentence fits a larger context and relates to the sentences around it.

Transition Words

The writer should act as a guide, showing the reader how all the sentences fit together. Consider the seat belt example again:

> Seat belts save more lives than any other automobile safety feature. Many studies show that airbags save lives as well. Not all cars have airbags. Many older cars don't. Air bags aren't entirely reliable. Studies show that in 15% of accidents, airbags don't deploy as designed. Seat belt malfunctions are extremely rare.

There's nothing wrong with any of these sentences individually, but together they're disjointed and difficult to follow. The best way for the writer to communicate information is through the use of transition words. Here are examples of transition words and phrases that tie sentences together, enabling a more natural flow:

- To show causality: as a result, therefore, and consequently
- To compare and contrast: *however, but,* and *on the other hand*
- To introduce examples: *for instance, namely,* and *including*
- To show order of importance: *foremost, primarily, secondly,* and *lastly*

NOTE: This is not a complete list of transitions. There are many more that can be used; however, most fit into these or similar categories. The important point is that the words should clearly show the relationship between sentences, supporting information, and the main idea.

Here is an update to the previous example using transition words. These changes make it easier to read and bring clarity to the writer's points:

> Seat belts save more lives than any other automobile safety feature. Many studies show that airbags save lives as well; however, not all cars have airbags. For instance, some older cars don't. Furthermore, air bags aren't entirely reliable. For example, studies show that in 15% of

accidents, airbags don't deploy as designed, but, on the other hand, seat belt malfunctions are extremely rare.

Also be prepared to analyze whether the writer is using the best transition word or phrase for the situation. Take this sentence for example: "As a result, seat belt malfunctions are extremely rare." This sentence doesn't make sense in the context above because the writer is trying to show the contrast between seat belts and airbags, not the causality.

Logical Sequence
Even if the writer includes plenty of information to support their point, the writing is only coherent when the information is in a logical order. First, the writer should introduce the main idea, whether for a paragraph, a section, or the entire piece. Then they should present evidence to support the main idea by using transitional language. This shows the reader how the information relates to the main idea and to the sentences around it. The writer should then take time to interpret the information, making sure necessary connections are obvious to the reader. Finally, the writer can summarize the information in a closing section.

Though most writing follows this pattern, it isn't a set rule. Sometimes writers change the order for effect. For example, the writer can begin with a surprising piece of supporting information to grab the reader's attention, and then transition to the main idea. Thus, if a passage doesn't follow the logical order, don't immediately assume it's wrong. However, most writing usually settles into a logical sequence after a nontraditional beginning.

Introductions and Conclusions
Examining the writer's strategies for introductions and conclusions puts the reader in the right mindset to interpret the rest of the text. Look for methods the writer might use for introductions such as:

- Stating the main point immediately, followed by outlining how the rest of the piece supports this claim.

- Establishing important, smaller pieces of the main idea first, and then grouping these points into a case for the main idea.

- Opening with a quotation, anecdote, question, seeming paradox, or other piece of interesting information, and then using it to lead to the main point.

Whatever method the writer chooses, the introduction should make their intention clear, establish their voice as a credible one, and encourage a person to continue reading.

Conclusions tend to follow a similar pattern. In them, the writer restates their main idea a final time, often after summarizing the smaller pieces of that idea. If the introduction uses a quote or anecdote to grab the reader's attention, the conclusion often makes reference to it again. Whatever way the writer chooses to arrange the conclusion, the final restatement of the main idea should be clear and simple for the reader to interpret. Finally, conclusions shouldn't introduce any new information.

Precision
People often think of precision in terms of math, but precise word choice is another key to successful writing. Since language itself is imprecise, it's important for the writer to find the exact word or words to convey the full, intended meaning of a given situation. For example:

The number of deaths has gone down since seat belt laws started.

There are several problems with this sentence. First, the word *deaths* is too general. From the context, it's assumed that the writer is referring only to deaths caused by car accidents. However, without clarification, the sentence lacks impact and is probably untrue. The phrase "gone down" might be accurate, but a more precise word could provide more information and greater accuracy. Did the numbers show a slow and steady decrease of highway fatalities or a sudden drop? If the latter is true, the writer is missing a chance to make their point more dramatically. Instead of "gone down" they could substitute *plummeted, fallen drastically,* or *rapidly diminished* to bring the information to life. Also, the phrase "seat belt laws" is unclear. Does it refer to laws requiring cars to include seat belts or to laws requiring drivers and passengers to use them? Finally, *started* is not a strong verb. Words like *enacted* or *adopted* are more direct and make the content more real. When put together, these changes create a far more powerful sentence:

> The number of highway fatalities has plummeted since laws requiring seat belt usage were enacted.

However, it's important to note that precise word choice can sometimes be taken too far. If the writer of the sentence above takes precision to an extreme, it might result in the following:

The incidence of high-speed, automobile accident related fatalities has decreased 75% and continued to remain at historical lows since the initial set of federal legislations requiring seat belt use were enacted in 1992.

This sentence is extremely precise, but it takes so long to achieve that precision that it suffers from a lack of clarity. Precise writing is about finding the right balance between information and flow. This is also an issue of conciseness (discussed in the next section).

The last thing to consider with precision is a word choice that's not only unclear or uninteresting, but also confusing or misleading. For example:

The number of highway fatalities has become hugely lower since laws requiring seat belt use were enacted.

In this case, the reader might be confused by the word *hugely*. Huge means large, but here the writer uses *hugely* to describe something small. Though most readers can decipher this, doing so disconnects them from the flow of the writing and makes the writer's point less effective.

Conciseness

"Less is more" is a good rule to follow when writing a sentence. Unfortunately, writers often include extra words and phrases that seem necessary at the time, but add nothing to the main idea. This confuses the reader and creates unnecessary repetition. Writing that lacks conciseness is usually guilty of excessive wordiness and redundant phrases. Here's an example containing both of these issues:

> When legislators decided to begin creating legislation making it mandatory for automobile drivers and passengers to make use of seat belts while in cars, a large number of them made those laws for reasons that were political reasons.

There are several empty or "fluff" words here that take up too much space. These can be eliminated while still maintaining the writer's meaning. For example:

- "Decided to begin" could be shortened to "began"
- "Making it mandatory for" could be shortened to "requiring"
- "Make use of" could be shortened to "use"
- "A large number" could be shortened to "many"

In addition, there are several examples of redundancy that can be eliminated:

- "Legislators decided to begin creating legislation" and "made those laws"
- "Automobile drivers and passengers" and "while in cars"
- "Reasons that were political reasons"

These changes are incorporated as follows:

> When legislators began requiring drivers and passengers to use seat belts, many of them did so for political reasons.

There are many general examples of redundant phrases, such as "add an additional," "complete and total," "time schedule," and "transportation vehicle." If asked to identify a redundant phrase on the test, look for words that are close together with the same (or similar) meanings.

Editing Written Work

Revisions
Leaving a few minutes at the end to revise and proofread offers an opportunity for writers to polish things up. Putting one's self in the reader's shoes and focusing on what the essay actually says helps writers identify problems—it's a movement from the mindset of writer to the mindset of editor. The goal is to have a clean, clear copy of the essay. The following areas should be considered when proofreading:

1. Sentence fragments
2. Awkward sentence structure
3. Run-on sentences
4. Incorrect word choice
5. Grammatical agreement errors
6. Spelling errors
7. Punctuation errors
8. Capitalization errors

Purposes for Writing

No matter the genre or format, all authors are writing to persuade, inform, entertain, or express feelings. Often, these purposes are blended, with one dominating the rest. It's useful to learn to recognize the author's intent.

Persuasive writing is used to persuade or convince readers of something. It often contains two elements: the argument and the counterargument. The argument takes a stance on an issue, while the counterargument pokes holes in the opposition's stance. Authors rely on logic, emotion, and writer credibility to persuade readers to agree with them. If readers are opposed to the stance before reading, they are unlikely to adopt that stance. However, those who are undecided or committed to the same stance are more likely to agree with the author.

Informative writing tries to teach or inform. Workplace manuals, instructor lessons, statistical reports and cookbooks are examples of informative texts. Informative writing is usually based on facts and is often void of emotion and persuasion. Informative texts generally contain statistics, charts, and graphs. Though most informative texts lack a persuasive agenda, readers must examine the text carefully to determine whether one exists within a given passage.

Stories or narratives are designed to entertain. When you go to the movies, you often want to escape for a few hours, not necessarily to think critically. Entertaining writing is designed to delight and engage the reader. However, sometimes this type of writing can be woven into more serious materials, such as persuasive or informative writing to hook the reader before transitioning into a more scholarly discussion.

Emotional writing works to evoke the reader's feelings, such as anger, euphoria, or sadness. The connection between reader and author is an attempt to cause the reader to share the author's intended emotion or tone. Sometimes in order to make a piece more poignant, the author simply wants readers to feel emotion that the author has felt. Other times, the author attempts to persuade or manipulate the reader into adopting his stance. While it's okay to sympathize with the author, be aware of the individual's underlying intent.

Writing Applications

Common Types of Writing

Opinion/Argument

In the early elementary grades, students begin to write simple *opinion pieces*. Acting as a precursor to argumentative and persuasive writing, opinion pieces allow children to express how they feel on a certain subject based on preferences, express their likes and dislikes, and use personal knowledge, without relying too heavily on supporting evidence. Educators encourage children to write opinion pieces with the use of personal journals as well as reflective pieces, connecting personal experiences to various stories read.

In the middle school years and beyond, students will be required to write *argumentative* or *persuasive* pieces of writing, which must involve logical and relevant proof for a claim or an assertion. Regarded as a more sophisticated form of writing, argumentative or persuasive writing works to change the point of view of the readers or ignite a call-to-action response. This form of writing does not shy away from contradicting points of view but, instead, brings them to light and then works to disprove or discredit each opposing claim. Some examples of argumentative or persuasive writing include essays, reviews, and letters to the editor.

Informative

Informative writing comes in many forms, including directions, instructions, definitions, summaries, and more. *Informative writing* works to relay information and advance the reader's understanding of a given subject. If written correctly, the vast majority of informative writing is written in third person to distance the author from relying on personal bias, instead relying on objective facts, historical evidence, and statistics.

<u>Narrative</u>
Almost always written in first person, *narratives* include autobiographies, memoirs, and even fictional stories. Their general purpose is to entertain readers, but some also focus on morals, values, or life lessons. By conveying personal experiences on a given subject or by opening up one's life to the audience, narrative writers create a more intimate connection with readers.

Purpose, Key Components, and Subgenres of Writing

Effective writing, whether for the purpose of persuading, entertaining, or advancing a reader's knowledge, must be well planned and organized. In order to create a powerful piece of writing, authors must adhere to specific structural designs, apply a functional and logical order to their writing, and employ key elements.

The following chart outlines three types of writing and their respective purposes, the structural elements unique to each type of writing, and some examples of subgenres:

	Opinion/Persuasive	**Narrative**	**Informative**
Purpose	To persuade, influence, or prompt a call-to-action response	To entertain or to share a moral when writing fictional narratives To share factual information when writing nonfiction narratives	To convey information and advance a reader's knowledge of a given topic
Key components	Opening statement and point of view Well organized paragraphs with supportive evidence and/or examples Strong concluding statement that reinforces point of view	Fictional narratives: plot, characters, setting, point of view, tone Nonfictional Narratives: introductory paragraph Body: including details and descriptions of events and individuals Conclusion	Introduction Headings and Subheadings Body Conclusion Works Cited
Subgenres	Speeches, letters, reviews, advertisements, essays	Fictional narratives: folktales, fantasy, science-fiction, mystery, drama Nonfictional narratives: autobiographies, biographies, memoirs	How-to books, cookbooks, instructional manuals, textbooks

Effectiveness of Writing Samples

The ultimate goal in every English language arts classroom is to advance students' ability to write coherently and effectively with relative ease. The process of writing begins in the very primary stages and continues throughout a student's academic career. With each passing year, students who receive effective writing instruction and constructive feedback will be able to practice and apply their writing skills to more complex writing assignments. To help students advance in their writing skills, evaluation and assessment of a student's writing should be ongoing and occur during and after instruction of each writing unit.

In order to evaluate the effectiveness of a student's writing, educators should continuously focus on formative and summative assessments that outline clear expectations for the student and the educator.

Formative assessments allow both the student and the educator to monitor the student's writing progress with ongoing feedback, discussion, and guidance. For example, after formative assessments, educators may recognize that some students need further instruction on a given skill or would benefit from a modified writing assignment. Summative assessments should only be employed at the very end of an instructional unit and should be used to evaluate how well the student was able to apply specific writing skills to the assigned and completed task. Praising each student's writing progress and allowing time for one-to-one conferences are also valuable instructional techniques that build a student's confidence in the writing process.

The following are examples of assessment practices that help drive instruction and strengthen a student's understanding and application of writing skills for different types of writing.

Effective writing assessments:

- Rating scales and rubrics
- Student logs: student evaluation of writing exercises
- Small groups and peer evaluations
- POWER method: Plan, Organize, Write, Edit, Rewrite (self-assessment)
- Standardized and diagnostic assessments
- Formative assessments
- Summative assessments

Educators who give clear expectations at the beginning, throughout, and at the end of a writing task help students advance their writing skills and become more proficient writers across a number of disciplines and genres. Since there are different types of writing, and considering that writing occurs in all subjects and disciplines, all educators should plan and develop several opportunities for students to practice various types of writing. For example, depending on the students' age and grade level, short, creative, daily writing exercises at the beginning or end of class can be used as an effective opening or closing routine. One day, students can practice narrative writing and the next, persuasive. Teachers can offer an author's chair in which children can read excerpts of their informative, persuasive, or narrative writing, and answer questions from peers relevant to their writing.

Dedicating time to the writing process—with a variety of writing exercises and assignments that occur in every discipline—is paramount to a child's writing acquisition. Effective instructional and assessment practices help foster an appreciation of writing that will continue throughout a student's lifetime.

Interpreting Words and Phrases Used in Text and Analyzing and Describing Text Structure

Interpreting Words and Phrases
Words can have different meanings depending on how they are used in a text. There are several methods for helping students decipher word meanings:

- Dictionary: Students should be taught to effectively use a dictionary and a thesaurus, including digital dictionaries and resources. Students need to know how to read the dictionary so they understand that there can be more than one meaning for a particular word. Dictionaries also help teach word pronunciation and syllables. A thesaurus teaches antonyms and synonyms. Once students know the correct meaning and pronunciation, they are able to better understand the context of the word in the text.

- Word Parts: Dissecting words into their word parts, (i.e., root word, prefix, suffix) will help determine the meaning of a word as a whole. It's beneficial to teach high-frequency Greek and Latin root words, since they comprise the majority of the English language. Some methods for teaching word parts include the following techniques:

  - Analogies
  - Word Play
  - Word Association
  - Syllabication
  - Spelling Patterns
  - Reading Context
  - Writing Context
  - Inventive Writing

- Context Clues: Students can look at other words in the same or surrounding sentences to help determine the meaning of an unknown word by the way it is used in the same sentence or paragraph. This kind of search provides context clues.

- Author's Purpose: Authors use words differently depending on what they want the reader to glean from the text. Some ways writers use words are as follows:

  - Literal — the exact meaning or definition of the word
  - Figurative — metaphorical language and figures of speech
  - Technical — in-depth writing about specific subjects such as math or music
  - Connotative — showing an opinion or suggestion within text as a secondary meaning

Determining Text Structures

There are different text structures used for various purposes in writing. Each text structure has key words and elements that help identify it. It is important to teach text structure because students who do not have much prior knowledge on a topic depend on structure to help assimilate new information. Readers use text structure to help find information within a text. Summarizing requires knowledge of the text structure of a piece of writing. Some common text structures include:

- Chronological Order — Time order or sequence from one point to another. Dates and times might be used, or bullets and numbering. Possible key words: *first, next, then, after, later, finally, before, preceding, following*

- Cause and Effect — Showing how causes come before effects and how one leads to the other. Time order may also clarify cause and effect. Possible key words: *cause, effect, consequently, as a result, due to, in order to, because of, therefore, so, leads to, if ... then*

- Problem and Solution — Outlines a particular problem in detail and suggests one or more solutions to the problem and the pros and cons of solutions. Possible key words: *difficulty, problem, solve, solution, possible, therefore, if ... then, challenge*

- Compare and Contrast — Describes how objects, people, places, and ideas are similar or different from one another. Possible key words: *like, unlike, similar to, in contrast, on the other hand, whereas, while, although, either or, opposed to, different from, instead*

- Description — Explains a topic, including the main idea and details. Possible key words: *for example, such as, for instance, most importantly, another, such as, next to, on top of, besides*

Workplace and Community Documents

Workplace and *community* documents help employers to communicate within the business world and foster positive community relations outside of it. Workplace communications typically craft a specific message to a targeted audience while community documents send a broader or more generic message to a wider range of recipients.

Workplace Documents

Even though workplace-related documents are generated in a multitude of paper and electronic formats—memorandums, bulletin boards, presentations, web conferencing, instant messaging, and e-mails—in general all effective business communications share relevant information concisely, accurately, and purposefully. Supervisors rely on workplace documents to communicate expectations to subordinates (downward communication), and subordinates rely on workplace documents to submit progress reports, ask questions, and address concerns with their supervisors (upward communication).

- Memorandums: Designed to communicate information to a wide audience, memorandums inform staff of company-wide policy changes. Similar to an e-mail, a memorandum has a header near the top which identifies the intended audience, the author of the memo, the subject of the memo, and the date it was issued. Unlike an e-mail, though, memorandums are longer, can be submitted in paper or electronic form, and contain an introduction that identifies the topic or problem, a body that expands on the topic, and a conclusion that suggests a course of action or solution.

- Bulletin Boards: Regardless of whether they are in paper or electronic form, bulletin boards provide a less formal setting for supervisors and staff to communicate. Bulletin boards are a perfect medium to post federal and state regulations, employee incentive initiatives, volunteer opportunities, and company news. While paper bulletin boards are limited to a specific office and personnel, electronic bulletin boards have the capability of broadcasting information nationally and even globally.

- Presentations: Presentations can be created with a variety of software—*PowerPoints, GoogleSlides*, and *Prezi*—and are given extemporaneously. Typically, presentations have an introductory slide, informational slides, and a concluding slide that gives the presenter's audience the opportunity to ask questions or create a dialogue. Presentations relay information in a media-rich format: graphics, tables, and hyperlinked documents and videos are easily imbedded within the slides.

- Web Conferencing: Web conferencing allows for employees to collaborate on projects and tasks. Employees are able to talk or videoconference from different locations, making it possible for remote workers from around the globe to participate simultaneously in one meeting. Web conferencing can be done via telephone with visuals (*PowerPoint* or *Microsoft Word* documents) or via video camera programs like *WebEx®, PGI GlobalMeet®*, and *Skype®*.

- Instant Messaging: Many staff outside of centralized locations who cannot communicate verbally with coworkers or supervisors rely, instead, on instant messaging programs. Instant messaging programs can deliver messages one-on-one or in circles and groups, and some software even provides screen-sharing capabilities. Since instant messaging is faster than e-mail, for many employees it has become the preferred method of communicating over long distances.

- E-Mails: In today's fast-paced business world, e-mails are heavily relied upon because they provide a platform that is perfect for quickly communicating brief, concise messages to targeted audiences. E-mails not only detail who the sender and receiver are but also provide a date, time, and subject line. Unlike a memorandum, sender and receiver can communicate back and forth, and, more importantly, they may do so over long distances. Many businesses today rely on *Google, Yahoo,* and *Outlook* mail severs.

Community Documents

Where business documents target a specific audience and often contain a higher level of proprietary, confidential, or sensitive information, community documents invite larger groups to discuss business matters in a less restrictive environment. Because community documents often help bridge the gap between businesses and community, an effective newsletter, discussion board, blog, website, and app have the power to influence public perception of private companies.

- Newsletters: Newsletters are used to provide the public information about the business. It can be used to generate excitement, inform or persuade staff or consumers, or give tips on how the public can contact or work with businesses. Newsletters can be mailed or sent electronically. Generally, newsletters are sent weekly, monthly, or quarterly. They can be interactive, providing the community a glance at what is going on with a business that they interact with, and, moreover, newsletters can communicate a company's mission, values, and priorities.

- Discussion Boards: Discussion boards offer a place to go to share information on a specific topic. Discussion boards are organized on menus, submenus, and discussion threads. People visit discussion boards to find out more about a topic. Discussion board members are granted greater access to the site and have greater power to publish and comment, but, still, visitors are welcome, and they often get difficult or obscure questions resolved.

- Blogs: A blog, which is usually centered on a specific topic or theme, is a website where individuals post and update information constantly. Blogs tend to feature the newest posts first while archiving older ones. Articles, editorials, images, videos, surveys, and social media (just to name a few) can all be imbedded within blogs. Menus, sidebars, recent posts, and search boxes help visitors wade through a dizzying array of media formats and topics. Though individuals can hire a web designer to create a blog for them, most people use existing platforms like *WordPress®, Blogger®,* and *Tumbler®.*

- Websites: As the world becomes more technologically savvy, a website can be used to house community documents, giving consumers instant access to tools they will need to interact with the business. It can house forms, contact information, discussion boards, surveys, and blogs. It is a one-stop-shop that can assist in the interaction between the business and the consumer.

Websites are advantageous because they can be accessed via computer, tablet, or mobile phone.

- Apps: Similar to a website, an application (app) gives businesses yet another method to reach individuals or segments of a community. Apps provide instant access to forms and other documentation. Designed to be downloaded on tablets or mobile phones, apps are streamlined and intuitive, allowing consumers on the go to access information at their convenience. The primary operating systems for apps include *iOS®* and *Android®*.

Non-Written Communication

Non-Written Genres and Traditions

<u>Engaging Oral Presentations</u>
Oral presentations can cause panic in a classroom as children scramble to figure out how, when, where, why, and what to speak about. However, if given proper guidance, appropriate time, and constructive feedback, the panic will soon fade, and in turn, students will learn how to give powerful oral presentations.

In order to be effective, educators should follow best practices, including sharing a well-designed rubric with the class, discussing the importance of each skill listed, answering any questions the children might have, and providing ongoing and constructive feedback while children develop their presentations.

Key areas to develop oral presentations:

Volume
Children should consider where the presentation would be held. Will it be indoors, outdoors, in an auditorium, or in the classroom? Learning to match the volume of the presentation with the location and size of the audience will greatly improve the presentation.

Articulation
Pronouncing words clearly is another aspect of effective communication, especially during an oral presentation. Slurred words, rushed words, mumbling, or leaving out the beginning or ending of sentences will have a negative impact on the message, and the presenter risks losing the interest of the audience.

Awareness of Audience
Facing the audience at all times is paramount to the success of an oral presentation. If possible, walking around the room and maintaining eye contact with the audience have proven to be effective techniques. Welcoming questions from the audience, restating questions for everyone to hear, and providing honest and thoughtful responses, also play a key role in ensuring a successful oral presentation.

<u>Storytelling and Poetry Recitations</u>
Before language was ever put down on paper, poets had been reciting verses in front of audiences for thousands of years. Epic poems, especially, were popular forms of entertainment in Greek culture for their oral storytelling appeal. The storyteller was known as a "rhapsode" and sometimes played a lyre while reciting verse or song. The content of epic poetry was mixed with the myth and folklore of Greek culture. The two most popular epic poems we know of today are *The Iliad* and *The Odyssey*. Another oral poetry tradition that began in Greece is known as the lyric, made famous by the Greek poet Sappho.

Lyrics are close in content and form to modern music: they reflect confessional or personal events or emotions and they are shorter in length than an epic poem.

Language Development Stages

There are many factors that influence a child's language acquisition. A child's physical age, level of maturity, home and school experiences, general attitudes toward learning, and home languages are just some of the many influences on a child's literacy development. However, a child's *language acquisition* progresses through the following generalized stages:

Stage	Examples	Age
Preproduction	does not verbalize/ nods yes and no	zero to six months
Early production	one to two word responses	six to twelve months
Speech emergence	produces simple sentences	one to three years
Intermediate fluency	simple to more complex sentences	three to five years
Advanced fluency	near native level of speech	five to seven years

While this applies to language acquisition in one's home language, the very same stages apply to English language learners (ELLs). Since effective communication in any given language requires much more than a mere collection of vocabulary words that one can accurately translate, paying particular attention to each stage in language acquisition is imperative. In addition to vocabulary knowledge, language acquisition involves the study and gradual mastery of intonation, a language's dialects—if applicable— and the various nuances in a language regarding word use, expression, and cultural contexts. With time, effort, patience, and effective instructional approaches, both students and educators will begin to see progress in language acquisition.

Second language acquisition does not happen overnight. When educators take the time to study each stage and implement a variety of effective instructional approaches, progress and transition from one stage to the next will undoubtedly be less cumbersome and more consistent. In the early stages of language acquisition, children are often silently observing their new language environment. At these early stages, listening comprehension should be emphasized with the use of read alouds, music, and visual aids. Educators should be mindful of their vocabulary usage by consciously choosing to speak slowly and to use shorter, less complex vocabulary. Modeling during these beginning stages is also very effective. If the educator has instructed the class to open a book for instance, they can open a book as a visual guide. If it is time to line up, the educator can verbally state the instruction and then walk to the door to begin the line.

During the *pre-production stage*, educators and classmates may assist ELLs by restating words or sentences that were uttered incorrectly, instead of pointing out errors. When modeling the correct language usage instead of pointing out errors, ELL learners may be less intimidated to practice their new language.

As students progress into the *early production stage*, they will benefit from exercises that challenge them to produce simple words and sentences with the assistance of visual cues. The educator should ask students to point to various pictures or symbols and produce words or sentences to describe the images they see. At the early production and speech emergent stages, ELL students are now ready to answer more diverse questions as they begin to develop a more complex vocabulary. Working in heterogeneous pairs and small groups with native speakers will help ELL students develop a more advanced vocabulary.

At the *beginning and intermediate fluency stages*, ELLs may be asked questions that require more advanced cognitive skills. Asking for opinions on a certain subject or requiring students to brainstorm and find ways to explain a given phenomenon are other ways to strengthen language proficiency and increase vocabulary.

When a child reaches the *advanced fluency stage*, he or she will be confident in social and academic language environments. This is an opportune time to introduce and/or increase his or her awareness of idiomatic expressions and language nuances.

World-Class Instructional Design and Assessment (WIDA) is a consortium of various departments of education throughout the United States that design and implement proficiency standards and assessments for English language learners and Spanish language learners. Primarily focusing on listening, speaking, reading, and writing, WIDA has designed and implemented English language development standards and offers professional development for educators, as well as educational research on instructional best practices. The five English language proficiency standards according to WIDA are as follows:

English Language Proficiency Standards—WIDA
1. Within a school environment, ELL students require communication skills for both social and instructional purposes.
2. Effective communication involving information, ideas, and concepts are necessary for ELL students to be academically successful in the area of Language Arts.
3. Effective communication involving information, ideas, and concepts are necessary for ELL students to be academically successful in the area of Mathematics.
4. Effective communication involving information, ideas, and concepts are necessary for ELL students to be academically successful in the area of Science.
5. Effective communication involving information, ideas, and concepts are necessary for ELL students to be academically successful in the area of Social Studies.

According to WIDA, mastering the understanding, interpretation, and application of the four language domains—listening, speaking, reading, and writing—is essential for language proficiency. Listening requires ELL students to be able to process, understand, interpret, and evaluate spoken language. Speaking proficiently allows ELL students to communicate their thoughts, opinions, and desires orally in a variety of situations and for a variety of audiences. The ability to read fluently involves the processing, understanding, interpreting, and evaluating of written language with a high level of accuracy, and writing proficiency allows ELL students to engage actively in written communication across a multitude of disciplines and for a variety of purposes.

Since language acquisition involves the ELL students, their families, their classmates, educators, principals and administrators, as well as test and curriculum developers, WIDA strives to ensure that the English Language Proficiency Standards reflect both the social and academic areas of language development.

Communicating with Diverse Partners

Communication is never one-sided. There are always at least two individuals engaged in a conversation, and both acts of speaking and listening are often interchangeable. In the classroom, educators communicate with all students, and students communicate with one another. Some forms of communication are intended for instructional purposes, while other forms may be solely for entertainment. To be an effective communicator, it is critical that the purpose for speaking is clear to both the presenter and the audience. It is also important that the mode of communication is culturally sensitive and age appropriate. The presenter should use language that best suits his or her audience. For example, if an educator wishes to speak to a primary class about the importance of homework, domain-specific language may not be appropriate, but that same conversation with educational colleagues may require domain-specific language. Here are some key techniques to consider when developing strong communication skills:

Effective Speaking	Effective Listening
Check for understanding and interest—ask key questions	Offer relevant information to the topic
Repeat important information in a variety of ways	Ask poignant questions, clarify understanding
Use nonverbal forms of communication—body language for effect	Use nonverbal forms of communication—body language for effect
Remain observant—maintain eye contact	Remain observant—maintain eye contact
Develop a healthy sense of humor	Develop a healthy sense of humor
Strive for honesty	Strive for honesty
Consider language choices	Develop active listening skills—not simply waiting to respond
Develop cultural sensitivity	Strengthen patience

Developing Skills Necessary for Speaking, Listening, and Presenting

Instructing Children to Enhance Their English Language Literacy Development
Speaking, listening, reading, and writing are all intimately connected as essential elements of literacy development. As social beings, children begin to recognize that with effective literacy skills, their social, emotional, and physical needs can be met, and their curiosity can be satisfied. They also begin to learn

that they can develop communication skills to answer questions that others pose. This can be an exciting and self-affirming realization for young children. In order to encourage literacy development, educators should ensure that all activities in the classroom involve meaningful language and literacy experiences. Each child learns at a unique pace and in a unique way. With this sensitivity in place, classroom activities should be as differentiated as possible.

Developing Listening Skills
Actively teaching good listening skills is essential in the classroom. Behaviors should not be expected that have not been taught. Students need to learn the difference between what an excellent listener does and what poor listening behaviors are. Good listening skills that should be taught include:

- Focusing on the speaker, looking them in the eye, and choosing not to interrupt.

- Looking at the speaker to indicate that the student is ready to hear what the speaker has to say and to pick up body language cues and facial expressions.

- Giving nonverbal signals that the student is listening (e.g., nods, smiles).

- Giving verbal signals that indicate interest in the speaker (e.g., repeating back what is heard to indicate understanding).

- Subtly matching the energy and emotional level of the speaker to indicate understanding.

- Choosing not to make side comments or to focus on other things occurring in the room.

Some strategies for teaching these skills in the classroom include, but are not limited to:

- Providing pre-listening activities, such as teaching new vocabulary words, outlining what students will be hearing, distributing study guides or pre-listening questions, and teaching students the objectives of the listening activity beforehand.

- Avoiding repeating directions multiple times. Teachers are often inclined to repeat steps and directions several times before allowing students to begin working. This is counterproductive because it teaches students that they do not have to listen the first time. Students should be taught that the teacher will say things only once and they are expected to listen, but they may ask for clarification. Students should also be taught to seek other sources of finding the instructions.

- Modeling good listening and speaking skills in the classroom because students learn by watching and emulating others. Teachers need to consistently model choosing not to interrupt and focusing their full attention on the speaker. They also need to model speaking clearly with proper grammar and foster an environment in the classroom of good peer modeling as well.

- Teaching students to take notes, write down questions, and report on or paraphrase what they have heard the speaker say. Students should be given active listening activities to complete during and after the listening task.

- Giving students multiple methods to contribute to conversations. Some students are not inclined to speak in front of others. In such cases, it may be helpful to allow them to give other signals of understanding such as "thumbs up," "thumbs sideways," "thumbs down," or sign language for "yes" and "no" answers.

- Encouraging the use of technology in the classroom to allow students to blog, tweet, or use quiz show-style games to indicate understanding of what they heard.

Developing Speaking Skills

Similar to listening skills, students also need to be taught speaking and presenting skills. Students need to learn such skills as:

- How to introduce themselves effectively
- How to make appropriate eye contact with listeners
- How to begin a conversation and keep it going
- How to interact with various types of audiences
- How to answer questions in an interview
- How to stand and deliver a speech with confidence
- How to ask for and answer questions during a presentation

The following strategies can help teach conversational and speaking skills:

- Students can be taught to use "conversation enhancers" when working with others. Some examples are: "Really?" "Wow!" "That's interesting" "Tell me more about …" "Can you say that in another way?" "Tell me what you are thinking …" and "Can you add to my idea?"

- Good conversational skills can be modeled as frequently as possible in one- to two-minute one-on-one dialogues with students. This is especially important for the introverted and shy students.

- A safe speaking environment can be fostered by teaching good manners to listeners, and by challenging students who are disrespectful listeners to act in a different way.

- Students should be asked open-ended questions that have no right or wrong answer and that invite lengthy answers instead of just "yes" or "no" responses.

- "I don't know" should not be accepted for an answer. Students should be taught that their thinking is valued rather than whether they *know* something.

- Students should be taught how to take turns in the classroom fairly and to not interrupt one another.

- Students should be instructed not to read their presentations word for word, and to speak toward the audience instead of toward the project or PowerPoint slide.

- Videos of good and poor presentations can be shown as models for students to critique.

- Students should be taught to build in humor and good non-verbal communication into their presentations.

- Students should be shown how to curb involuntary habits such as repeating themselves or saying "um" or "like" too much.

Task, Purpose, and Audience

Teaching students to present and speak to an audience involves teaching them how to structure a presentation so that it is appropriate for the task, purpose, and audience. *Task* is what the students are

63

required to do with their presentation. *Purpose* is the reason for the presentation and how it will achieve the outcome of the task. *Audience* is whom the presentation is for, the population it is trying to reach, and why it is specifically for that group. Some presentation tips that teachers should impart to students are as follows:

- During student preparation, students should ask themselves: "Why am I giving this presentation?" "What do I want people to take away from the presentation?" and "How much does my audience already know about the topic?"

- Presentations should be structured with an effective introduction, covering each item on their agenda succinctly, and wrapping up with a memorable conclusion.

- Presentations should be given with clarity and impact. The audience won't remember everything a student presents, so he or she needs to highlight the key points clearly and concisely and then expand and illustrate as needed.

- Visual aids should be used to enhance the presentation without causing distractions—such as useless images and animated transitions between slides—from the information.

- Presentations should be given without memorization. Students should be charged with becoming more familiar with their content and to "test drive" the presentation beforehand.

- Appropriate pauses should be used during presentations to help the audience better absorb the information.

- Various techniques can be employed if there is a "stumbling point" or a piece of information is forgotten during the presentation.

Dialects, Idiolects, and Changes in Standard Usage

<u>Identifying Variation in Dialect and Diction</u>
Language arts educators often seem to be in the position of teaching the "right" way to use English, particularly in lessons about grammar and vocabulary. However, all it takes is back-to-back viewings of speeches by the queen of England and the president of the United States or side-by-side readings of a contemporary poem and one written in the 1600s to come to the conclusion that there is no single, fixed, correct form of spoken or written English. Instead, language varies and evolves across different regions and time periods. It also varies between cultural groups depending on factors such as race, ethnicity, age, and socioeconomic status. Students should come away from a language arts class with more than a strictly prescriptive view of language; they should have an appreciation for its rich diversity.

It is important to understand some key terms in discussing linguistic variety.

Language is a tool for communication. It may be spoken, unspoken—as with body language—written, or codified in other ways. Language is symbolic in the sense that it can describe objects, ideas, and events that are not actually present, have not actually occurred, or only exist in the mind of the speaker. All languages are governed by systematic rules of grammar and semantics. These rules allow speakers to manipulate a finite number of elements, such as sounds or written symbols, to create an infinite number of meanings.

A *dialect* is a distinct variety of a language in terms of patterns of grammar, vocabulary, and/or *phonology*—the sounds used by its speakers—that distinguish it from other forms of that language. Two dialects are not considered separate languages if they are *mutually intelligible*—if speakers of each dialect are able to understand one another. A dialect is not a subordinate version of a language. Examples of English dialects include Scottish English and American Southern English.

By definition, *Standard English* is a dialect. It is one variety of English with its own usage of grammar, vocabulary, and pronunciation. Given that Standard English is taught in schools and used in places like government, journalism, and other professional workplaces, it is often elevated above other English dialects. Linguistically, though, there is nothing that makes Standard English more correct or advanced than other dialects.

A *pidgin* is formed when speakers of different languages begin utilizing a simplified mixture of elements from both languages to communicate with each other. In North America, pidgins occurred when Africans were brought to European colonies as slaves, leading to a mixture of African and European languages. Historically, pidgins also sprung up in areas of international trade. A pidgin is communication born of necessity and lacks the full complexity or standardized rules that govern a language.

When a pidgin becomes widely used and is taught to children as their native language, it becomes a *Creole*. An example is Haitian Creole, a language based on French and including elements of West African languages.

An *accent* is a unique speech pattern, particularly in terms of tone or intonation. Speakers from different regions tend to have different accents, as do learners of English from different native languages. In some cases, accents are mutually intelligible, but in other cases, speakers with different accents might have some difficulty in understanding one another.

Colloquial language is language that is used conversationally or familiarly—e.g., "What's up?"—in contrast to formal, professional, or academic language—"How are you this evening?"

Vernacular refers to the native, everyday language of a place. Historically, for instance, Bibles and religious services across Europe were primarily offered in Latin, even centuries after the fall of the Roman Empire. After the revolution of the printing press and the widespread availability of vernacular translations of the Bible in the fifteenth and sixteenth centuries, everyday citizens were able to study from Bibles in their own language without needing specialized training in Latin.

A *regionalism* is a word or expression used in a particular region. In the United States, for instance, examples of regionalisms might be *soda*, *pop*, or *Coke*—terms that vary in popularity according to region.

Jargon is vocabulary used within a specialized field, such as computer programming or mechanics. Jargon may consist of specialized words or of everyday words that have a different meaning in this specialized context.

Slang refers to non-standard expressions that are not used in elevated speech and writing. Slang creates linguistic in-groups and out-groups of people, those who can understand the slang terms and those who can't. Slang is often tied to a specific time period. For example, "groovy" and "far out" are connected to the 1970s, and "as if!" and "4-1-1-" are connected to the 1990s.

A language arts classroom should demonstrate the history and evolution of language, rather than presenting fixed, unchangeable linguistic regulations. Particularly for students who feel intimidated or excluded by Standard English, instructors can make lessons more relatable or inclusive by allowing students to share or explore their own patterns of language. Students can be encouraged to act as linguists or anthropologists by getting involved in projects. Some examples include asking them to identify and compare slang in their generation to slang from their parents' generation, to exchange information about their dialect with students who come from different cultural backgrounds, or to conduct a linguistic survey of their friends, family, or neighbors. Language arts class can also be integrated with history topics by having students research unfamiliar slang or words that have shifted in meaning from the past until now—a type of study particularly useful when reading a text from a past era.

Understanding Dialect and its Appropriateness

While students should come away from class feeling supported in their linguistic diversity, the reality is that certain forms of language are viewed differently depending on the context. Lessons learned in the classroom have a real-life application to a student's future, so he or she should know where, when, and how to utilize different forms of language.

For students preparing for college, knowledge of the conventions of Standard English is essential. The same is true for students who plan to enter professional job fields. Without necessarily having a word for it, many students are already familiar with the concept of *code-switching*—altering speech patterns depending upon context. For example, a person might use a different accent or slang with neighborhood friends than with coworkers or pick up new vocabulary and speech patterns after moving to a new region, either unconsciously or consciously. In this way, speakers have an innate understanding of how their language use helps them fit into any given situation.

Instructors can design activities that help students pay attention to their language use in a given context. When discussing a novel in class, students might be encouraged to spend a few minutes freewriting in a journal to generate ideas and express their unedited thoughts. Later, though, students will then be asked to present those thoughts in a formal writing assignment that requires adherence to Standard English grammar, employing academic vocabulary and expressions appropriate to literary discussions. Alternatively, students might design an advertisement that appeals to teenagers and another one that appeals to adults, utilizing different language in each. In this way, students can learn how to reformulate their thoughts using the language appropriate to the task at hand.

Awareness of dialect can also help students as readers, too. Many writers of literary fiction and nonfiction utilize dialect and colloquialisms to add verisimilitude to their writing. This is especially true for authors who focus on a particular region or cultural group in their works, also known as *regionalism* or *local color literature*. Examples include Zora Neale Hurston's *Their Eyes Were Watching God* and the short stories of Kate Chopin. Students can be asked to consider how the speech patterns in a text affect a reader's understanding of the characters—how the pattern reflects a character's background and place in society. They might consider a reader's impression of the region—how similar or different it is from the reader's region or what can be inferred about the region based on how people speak. In some cases, unfamiliar dialect may be very difficult for readers to understand on the page but becomes much more intelligible when read aloud—as in the reading of Shakespeare.

Reading passages together in class and then finding recordings or videos of the dialect presented in the text can help familiarize students with different speech patterns. And of course, students should also consider how use of dialect affects the audience or if it is directed to a specific audience. Who was the intended audience for *Their Eyes Were Watching God*, a novel that recreates the speech patterns of African Americans in early 1900s Florida? How might the novel be understood differently by readers who recognize that dialect than by readers who are encountering it for the first time? What would be lost if the characters didn't converse in their local dialect? Being alert to these questions creates students who are attuned to the nuances of language use in everyday life.

Collaborative Discussions with Diverse Partners

Once an appropriate topic has been chosen, discussions should be monitored to facilitate appropriate behavior. It is very important to stress that all perspectives will be welcome and respected and to make sure that student inquiries and responses are in alignment with that principle. The following are suggestions for facilitating appropriate discussion behavior in a group setting:

- Cultivating an environment of inclusion and mutual respect

    o Students should introduce themselves and be encouraged to address each other by name. "Icebreaker" games are an effective way to get students to know each other before engaging in any discussions.

    o Allowing enough time for students to think about the topic and thoughtfully contribute to the discussion will encourage inclusion.

    o The use of insulting or disrespectful language, tone, or body language should not be permitted.

    o Students should be made aware of differences in cultural and social perspectives.

    o Students should be encouraged to be mindful of the language they are using.

    o Teachers should not make assumptions on how students will respond or behave based on their cultural, racial, or religious backgrounds.

    o Everyone should have a chance to speak—e.g., teachers should not show favoritism towards a particular student or set of students or allow more tenacious students to dominate the discussion.

    o Particular perspectives or ideas should not be verbally or nonverbally discouraged. Instead, students should be encouraged to think critically about what is being discussed and what they are saying.

    o It's important not to rush students or make any student feel as though his or her comments and ideas are not important.

    o Facilitators should not display a sense of superiority.

- Keeping discussions productive

    o Teachers should be explicit about the expectations or goals of the discussion and guide students back towards the topic if they get off track.

    o Demonstrating what disrespectful behavior looks like at the start of the discussion can help establish clear expectations. Students should be reminded not to take things personally or to identify with any emotions they may experience from the discussion and, instead, approach the topics with logic.

- Ideas or counterarguments should be related to personal experiences or backed with evidence. Students should validate each other's ideas first before arguing in a respectful way, such as "I respect what you are saying," or "I understand where you are coming from."

- Stereotyping and sweeping generalizations should be identified when used and subsequently avoided.

- If a student goes off on a tangent, he or she should be guided back to the primary topic or purpose by asking him/her to summarize what he/she is saying.

- If the discussion becomes heated or emotional, students should be encouraged to explore the real issue that is causing the emotions. The teacher might say, "I think there is a greater issue here that we should discuss openly and respectfully." Alternatively, students can be asked if they would like to take break and resume the discussion later. A teacher may also wish to bring up the differing values that are being displayed in the conference in an unbiased way so that students can recognize what they're truly arguing about.

- It's important that teachers avoid arguing with a student if the student attacks them. Acknowledging this kind of behavior only validates it.

- Encouraging participants/guiding the flow of discussion

    - For shy students, it's helpful to call on them by name and ask if they have any thoughts/feedback, while being nonjudgmental if they admit they don't know or don't have anything to say.

    - Asking questions and requesting examples when students make a comment or present an idea helps guide the discussion flow.

    - Writing student comments down and asking for other participants to elaborate on them will encourage more participation.

    - Depending on the exercise, giving the students a topic or asking a student to present one will elicit participation.

    - For students who have trouble participating in large groups, breaking up discussion into smaller groups will help them feel more comfortable.

Ensuring Accountability

One of the most challenging things about group discussions is ensuring that the students have prepared for it. For a discussion to be as productive as possible, students should be held accountable for completing their due preparation, such as homework, pre-class readings, or research. This can be done in numerous ways, such as by requiring the students to complete an at-home assignment and submit it electronically by midnight the previous night or on the day before. This assignment could be worth a significant grade to encourage students to complete it, and it could be in the following forms: responding to a question on an online discussion board, completing quizzes in reading comprehension, or answering true or false questions.

To ensure accountability during the discussion, students should be encouraged to participate by asking questions and asked to elaborate when something is unclear. Letting them take notes and leaving plenty of time for the formulation of thoughts and follow-up questions will increase accountability. After the discussion has ended, passing out a handout that students can fill out or having them summarize the discussion online are two beneficial strategies for accountability.

<u>Evaluating the Effectiveness of Specific Strategies for Students Initiating and Participating Effectively in Discussions</u>

To increase student participation in discussion, teachers should consider the following strategies:

- Asking students what they know about the topic and writing their responses on the white or blackboard, which creates an outline of what the students do and don't know as well as increases their self-esteem.

- Having an anonymous question box where students can write down questions that can be read before or during the discussion, being careful not to react negatively to any questions, verbally or non-verbally, so as not to damage self-esteem

- Allowing students to teach each other, proven as the most effective way to learn something is to teach someone else what has been learned—e.g., writing their own tests or homework, conducting one-on-one conferences

- Dividing the class into smaller groups if students seem non-responsive, which helps shy students feel less intimidated and more comfortable in smaller settings

- Allowing students to work together, which encourages them to interact with others and allows them to feel more comfortable with doing so when it comes time for group discussion

- Asking students to create a topic to get them to initiate the conversation

- Using games to make the discussion fun and motivate students to participate

The effectiveness of these strategies will depend entirely on the class. Teachers should use the assessment tools discussed previously to determine whether the techniques have been effective and adjust the teaching style accordingly.

Many of the above strategies can be used for one-on-one discussions as well. The most important things to keep in mind in keeping a student engaged and comfortable during a one-on-one discussion are as follows:

- Asking follow-up questions
- Clarifying any unclear or obscure questions or statements
- Never making the student feel unintelligent or inadequate
- Being as reassuring as possible, particularly if a student expresses insecurity in his or her abilities
- Being patient and allowing time for the student to sort out thoughts and ask necessary questions

Research to Build and Present Knowledge

Research Process

The following list depicts the steps relevant to the research process. Each step should be performed in chronological order, as they depend on each other for optimal work. For example, without the "Revise and edit" step, step 8 would be a poorly written first draft.

- Step 1: Decide on a topic to research
- Step 2: Set the purpose of the research
- Step 3: Locate sources of information—print, digital, experts
- Step 4: Evaluate the sources
- Step 5: Summarize information and cite sources
- Step 6: Write draft
- Step 7: Revise and edit
- Step 8: Publish writing

Primary and Secondary Sources

Primary sources refer to first-hand accounts of events, a subject matter, an individual, or a time period. Primary sources also include original works of art. They can also be non-interpretive, factual pieces of information. Some examples include diaries, journals, letters, government records, maps, plays, novels, and songs.

Secondary sources refer to the analysis or interpretation of primary sources and are, therefore, usually considered more subjective than objective. In other words, researchers may discover contradictory information on the same subject from different secondary sources. Some examples include literary and film reviews, newspaper articles, and biographies.

Both primary and secondary sources of information are useful. They both offer invaluable insight that helps the writer learn more about the subject matter. However, researchers are cautioned to examine the information closely and to consider the time period as well as the cultural, political, and social climate in which accounts were given. Learning to distinguish between reliable sources of information and questionable accounts is paramount to a quality research report.

Reliable and Unreliable Sources

When conducting research, students must be able to distinguish between reliable and unreliable sources in order to develop a well-written research report. When choosing print sources, typically published works that have been edited and clearly identify the author or authors are considered credible sources. Peer-reviewed journals and research conducted by scholars are likewise considered to be credible sources of information.

When deciding on what Internet sources to use, it is also a sound practice for researchers to look closely at each website's universal resource locator, the *URL*. Generally speaking, websites with.edu, .gov, or .org as the Top Level Domain are considered reliable, but the researcher must still question any possible political or social bias. Personal blogs, tweets, personal websites, online forums, and any site that clearly demonstrates bias, strong opinions, or persuasive language are considered unreliable sources.

Paraphrasing and Plagiarizing

Paraphrasing: The restating of one's own words, text, passage, or any information that has already been heard, read, or researched

Plagiarizing: The copying of a text, passage, or any other information in print or digital format, and claiming the work as one's own

Credible Print and Digital Sources

Credible print sources are those that have been edited and published, reveal the author or authors, and clearly identify their expertise on the subject matter. Scholarly reviews are typically very reliable sources as they are written by experts in the field and, more often than not, have been evaluated by their respective peers. Credible digital sources may sometimes prove a little more difficult to discern, and researchers must employ due diligence to ensure the sources are reliable. Distinguishing between biased and unbiased websites, objective versus subjective information, as well as informative versus persuasive writing can prove confusing at times. By paying attention to a website's URL and carefully considering the language and tone applied to the writing, researchers should be able to evaluate the website's reliability.

Learning how to locate key information within sources requires a basic understanding of written structure. If the source of information is written well, there should be titles, subtitles, headings, and subheadings that researchers can use to zero in on key information. Additionally, informational texts often employ the use of an index and table of contents, which helps them locate specific information. Similarly, digital sources often employ titles, subtitles, headings, and subheadings, and they will generally offer a search box to look for specific information or key terms within the website.

Citing sources at the end of a research paper is critical to the overall quality of work. If sources are not cited or poorly cited, a researcher's work risks losing credibility. There are various accepted methods to use when citing information. The method used often depends on the preferences of the authority that has assigned the research. The most generally accepted methods for citing sources are MLA, APA, and Chicago style. Although each citation format is distinct in structure, order, and requirements, they all identify key information. Citation formats also ensure that published authors of given works receive full credit.

Effective and Ethical Research Practices

Identifying Relevant Information During Research on a Given Topic

Relevant information is that which is pertinent to the topic at hand. Particularly when doing research online, it is easy for students to get overwhelmed with the wealth of information available to them. Before conducting research, then, students need to begin with a clear idea of the question they want to answer.

For example, a student may be interested in learning more about marriage practices in Jane Austen's England. If that student types "marriage" into a search engine, he or she will have to sift through thousands of unrelated sites before finding anything related to that topic. Narrowing down search parameters, then, can aid in locating relevant information.

When using a book, students can consult the table of contents, glossary, or index to discover whether the book contains relevant information before using it as a resource. If the student finds a hefty volume on Jane Austen, he or she can flip to the index in the back, look for the word *marriage* and find out how many page references are listed in the book. If there are few or no references to the subject, it is probably not a relevant or useful source.

In evaluating research articles, students may also consult the title, abstract, and keywords before reading the article in its entirety. Referring to the date of publication will also determine whether the research contains up-to-date discoveries, theories, and ideas about the subject or is outdated.

Evaluating the Credibility of a Print or Digital Source

There are several additional criteria that need to be examined before using a source for a research topic. The following questions will help determine whether a source is credible:

- Author
- Who is he or she?
- Does he or she have the appropriate credentials—e.g., M.D, PhD?
- Is this person authorized to write on the matter through his/her job or personal experiences?
- Is he or she affiliated with any known credible individuals or organizations?
- Has he or she written anything else?
- Publisher
- Who published/produced the work? Is it a well-known journal, like National Geographic, or a tabloid, like The National Enquirer?
- Is the publisher from a scholarly, commercial, or government association?
- Do they publish works related to specific fields?
- Have they published other works?
- If a digital source, what kind of website hosts the text? Does it end in .edu, .org, or .com?
- Bias
- Is the writing objective? Does it contain any loaded or emotional language?
- Does the publisher/producer have a known bias, such as Fox News or CNN?
- Does the work include diverse opinions or perspectives?
- Does the author have any known bias—e.g., Michael Moore, Bill O'Reilly, or the Pope? Is he or she affiliated with any organizations or individuals that may have a known bias—e.g., Citizens United or the National Rifle Association?
- Does the magazine, book, journal, or website contain any advertising?
- References
- Are there any references?
- Are the references credible? Do they follow the same criteria as stated above?
- Are the references from a related field?
- Accuracy/reliability
- Has the article, book, or digital source been peer reviewed?
- Are all of the conclusions, supporting details, or ideas backed with published evidence?
- If a digital source, is it free of grammatical errors, poor spelling, and improper English?
- Do other published individuals have similar findings?
- Coverage
- Are the topic and related material both successfully addressed?
- Does the work add new information or theories to those of their sources?
- Is the target audience appropriate for the intended purpose?

Identifying Effective Research Practices

The purpose of all research is to provide an answer to an unknown question. Therefore, all good research papers pose the topic in the form of a question, which they will then seek to answer with clear ideas, arguments, and supporting evidence.

A *research question* is the primary focus of the research piece, and it should be formulated on a unique topic. To formulate a research question, writers begin by choosing a general topic of interest and then research the literature to determine what sort of research has already been done—the *literature review*. This helps them narrow the topic into something original and determine what still needs to be asked and researched about the topic. A solid question is very specific and avoids generalizations. The following question is offered for evaluation:

> *What is most people's favorite kind of animal?*

This research question is extremely broad without giving the paper any particular focus—it could go any direction and is not an exceptionally unique focus. To narrow it down, the question could consider a specific population:

> *What is the favorite animal of people in Ecuador?*

While this question is better, it does not address exactly why this research is being conducted or why anyone would care about the answer. Here's another possibility:

> *What does the animal considered as the most favorite of people in different regions throughout Ecuador reveal about their socioeconomic status?*

This question is extremely specific and gives a very clear direction of where the paper or project is going to go. However, sometimes the question can be too limited, where very little research has been conducted to create a solid paper, and the researcher most likely does not have the means to travel to Ecuador and travel door-to-door conducting a census on people's favorite animals. In this case, the research question would need to be broadened. Broadening a topic can mean introducing a wider range of criteria. Instead of people in Ecuador, the topic could be opened to include the population of South America or expanded to include more issues or considerations.

Identifying the Components of a Citation

Citation styles vary according to which style guide is consulted. Examples of commonly-used styles include MLA, APA, and Chicago/Turabian. Each citation style includes similar components, although the order and formatting of these components varies.

MLA Style

For an MLA style citation, components must be included or excluded depending on the source, so writers should determine which components are applicable to the source being cited. Here are the basic components:

- Author—last name, first name
- Title of source
- Title of container—e.g., a journal title or website
- Other contributors—e.g., editor or translator
- Version
- Number

- Publisher
- Publication date
- Location—e.g., the URL or DOI
- Date of Access—optional

APA Style

The following components can be found in APA style citations. Components must be included or excluded depending on the source, so writers should determine which components are applicable to the source being cited. The basic components are as follows:

- Author—last name, first initial, middle initial
- Publication date
- Title of chapter, article, or text
- Editor— last name, first initial, middle initial
- Version/volume
- Number/issue
- Page numbers
- DOI or URL
- Database—if article is difficult to locate
- City of publication
- State of publication, abbreviated
- Publisher

Chicago/Turabian Style

Chicago/Turabian style citations are also referred to as note systems and are used most frequently in the humanities and the arts. Components must be included or excluded depending on the source, so writers should determine which components are applicable to the source being cited. They contain the following elements:

- Author—last name, first name, middle initial
- Title of chapter or article—in quotation marks
- Title of source
- Editor—first name, last name
- Page numbers
- Version/volume
- Number/issue
- Page numbers
- Date of access
- DOI
- Publication location—city and state abbreviation/country
- Publisher
- Publication Date

Citing Source Material Appropriately

The following information contains examples of the common types of sources used in research as well as the formats for each citation style. First lines of citation entries are presented flush to the left margin, and second/subsequent details are presented with a hanging indent. Some examples of bibliography entries are presented below:

Book
- MLA
  Format: Last name, First name, Middle initial. *Title of Source.* Publisher, Publication Date.
  Example: Sampson, Maximus R. *Diaries from an Alien Invasion.* Campbell Press, 1989.
- APA
  Format: Last name, First initial, Middle initial. (Year Published) *Book Title.* City, State: Publisher.
  Example: Sampson, M. R. (1989). *Diaries from an alien invasion.* Springfield, IL: Campbell Press.
- Chicago/Turabian
  Format: Last name, First name, Middle initial. *Book Title.* City, State: Publisher, Year of publication.
  Example: Sampson, Maximus R. *Diaries from an Alien Invasion.* Springfield, IL: Campbell Press, 1989.

A Chapter in an Edited Book
- MLA
  Format: Last name, First name, Middle initial. "Title of Source." *Title of Container*, Other Contributors, Publisher, Publication Date, Location.
  Example: Sampson, Maximus R. "The Spaceship." *Diaries from an Alien Invasion*, edited by Allegra M. Brewer, Campbell Press, 1989, pp. 45-62.
- APA
  Format: Last name, First Initial, Middle initial. (Year Published) Chapter title. In First initial, Middle initial, Last Name (Ed.), *Book title* (pp. page numbers). City, State: Publisher.
  Example: Sampson, M. R. (1989). The Spaceship. In A. M. Brewer (Ed.), *Diaries from an Alien Invasion* (pp. 45-62). Springfield, IL: Campbell Press.
- Chicago/Turabian
  Format: Last name, First name, Middle initial. "Chapter Title." In Book Title, edited by Editor's Name (First, Middle In. Last), Page(s). City: Publisher, Year Published.
  Example: Sampson, Maximus R. "The Spaceship," in *Diaries from an Alien Invasion*, edited by Allegra M. Brewer, 45-62. Springfield: Campbell Press, 1989.

Article in a Journal
- MLA
  Format: Last name, First name, Middle initial. "Title of Source." *Title of Journa*, Number, Publication Date, Location.
  Example: Rowe, Jason R. "The Grief Monster." *Strong Living*, vol. 9, no. 9, 2016, pp 25-31.
- APA
  Format: Last name, First initial, Middle initial. (Year Published). Title of article. *Name of Journal, volume*(issue), page(s).
  Example: Rowe, J. R. (2016). The grief monster. *Strong Living, 9*(9), 25-31.
- Chicago/Turabian:
  Format: Last name, First name, Middle initial. "Title of Article." *Name of Journal* volume, issue (Year Published): Page(s).
  Example: Rowe, Jason, R. "The Grief Monster." *Strong Living* 9, no. 9 (2016): 25-31.

Page on a Website
- MLA
  Format: Last name, First name, Middle initial. "Title of Article." *Name of Website*, date published (Day Month Year), URL. Date accessed (Day Month Year).
  Example: Rowe, Jason. "The Grief Monster." *Strong Living Online*, 9 Sept. 2016. http://www.somanylosses.com/the-grief-monster/html. Accessed 13 Sept. 2016.
- APA
  Format: Last name, First initial. Middle initial. (Date Published—Year, Month Day). Page or article title. Retrieved from URL
  Example: Rowe, J. W. (2016, Sept. 9). The grief monster. Retrieved from http://www.somanylosses.com/ the-grief-monster/html
- Chicago/Turabian
  Format: Last Name, First Name, Middle initial. "Page Title." *Website Title*. Last modified Month day, year. Accessed month, day, year. URL.
  Example: Rowe, Jason. "The Grief Monster." Strong Living Online. Last modified September 9, 2016. Accessed September 13, 2016. http://www.somany osses.com/the-grief-monster/html.

In-Text Citations
Most of the content found in a research paper will be supporting evidence that must be cited in-text, i.e., directly after the sentence that makes the statement. In-text citations contain details that correspond to the first detail in the bibliography entry—usually the author.

- MLA style - In-text citations will contain the author and the page number (if the source has page numbers) for direct quotations. Paraphrased source material may have just the author.
  - According to Johnson, liver cancer treatment is "just beyond our reach" (976).
  - The treatment of liver cancer is not within our reach, currently (Johnson).
  - The narrator opens the story with a paradoxical description: "It was the best of times, it was the worst of times" (Dickens 1).
- APA Style - In text citations will contain the author, the year of publication, and a page marker—if the source is paginated—for direct quotations. Paraphrased source material will include the author and year of publication.
  - According to Johnson (1986), liver cancer treatment is "just beyond our reach" (p. 976).
  - The treatment of liver cancer is not within our reach, currently (Johnson, 1986).
- Chicago Style - Chicago style has two approaches to in-text citation: notes and bibliography or author-date.
  - Notes – There are two options for notes: endnotes—provided in a sequential list at the end of the paper and separate from bibliography—or footnotes provided at the bottom of a page. In either case, the use of superscript indicates the citation number.
    - Johnson states that treatment of liver cancer is "just beyond our reach." [1]
    - 1. Robert W. Johnson, Oncology in the Twenty-first Century (Kentville, Nova Scotia: Kentville Publishing, 1986), 159.
  - Author-Date – The author-date system includes the author's name, publication year, and page number.
    - Johnson states that treatment of liver cancer is "just beyond our reach" (1986, 159).

<u>Integrating Information from Source Material to Maintain the Flow of Ideas</u>
It can be daunting to integrate so many sources into a research paper while still maintaining fluency and coherency. Most source material is incorporated in the form of quotations or paraphrases, while citing the source at the end of their respective references. There are several guidelines to consider when integrating a source into writing:

- The piece should be written in the author's voice. Quotations, especially long ones, should be limited and spaced evenly throughout the paper.

- All paragraphs should begin with the author's own words and end with his or her own words; quotations should never start or end a paragraph.

- Quotations and paraphrases should be used to emphasize a point, give weight to an idea, and validate a claim.

- Supporting evidence should be introduced in a sentence or paragraph, and then explained afterwards: *According to Waters (1979)* [signal phrase], *"All in all, we're just another brick in the wall" (p.24). The wall suggests that people are becoming more alienated, and the bricks symbolize a paradoxical connection to that alienation* [Explanation].

- When introducing a source for the first time, the author's name and a smooth transition should be included: *In Pink Floyd's groundbreaking album The Wall, Roger Waters argues that society is causing people to become more alienated.*

- There should be an even balance between quotations and paraphrases.

- Quotations or paraphrases should never be taken out of context in a way that alters the original author's intent.

- Quotations should be syntactically and grammatically integrated.

- Quotations should not simply be copied and pasted in the paper. Rather, they should be introduced into a paper with natural transitions

- As argued in Johnson's article...
- Evidence of this point can be found in Johnson's article, where she asserts that...
- The central argument of John's article is...

Effective Speech and Presentation Delivery

<u>Identifying Characteristics of Effective Delivery of a Speech or Presentation</u>
Good public speakers all have several characteristics in common. It is not enough to simply write a speech, but it must also be delivered in a manner that is both engaging and succinct. The following qualities are inherent to good public speaking.

Confidence is possibly the most important attribute a speaker can have. It instills trust in the listener that the person knows what he or she is talking about and that he or she is credible and competent. Confidence is displayed by making brief eye contact—about 2-3 seconds—with different members of the audience to demonstrate that the speaker is engaged. It is also displayed in his or her tone of voice—strong, light-hearted, and natural. A nervous speaker can easily be identified by a small, quivering voice. Confidence is also conveyed by the speaker facing the audience; turning one's back may demonstrate insecurity.

Authenticity is another quality of an effective speaker, as it makes a person more relatable and believable to the audience. Speeches that are memorized word-for-word can give the impression of being inauthentic as the monologue does not flow quite naturally, especially if the speaker accidentally fumbles or forgets. Memorizing speeches can also lead to a monotonous tone, which is sure to put the audience to sleep, or worse, a misinterpreted tone, which can cause the audience to stop listening entirely or even become offended. Therefore, speeches should be practiced with a natural intonation and not be memorized mechanically.

Connection with the audience is another important aspect of public speaking. Speakers should engage with their listeners by the use of storytelling and visual or auditory aids, as well as asking questions that the audience can participate in. Visual and auditory aids could range from an interesting PowerPoint presentation to a short video clip to physical objects the audience can pass around to a soundtrack. The use of appropriate humor also allows the audience to connect with the speaker on a more personal level and will make the speech sound more like a conversation than a one-sided lecture. Speakers who are passionate about their subject inspire their listeners to care about what they're saying; they transfer their energy into the audience. This level of connection will encourage their listeners to want to be there.

Succinctness and *purposeful repetition* ensures that the audience's attention remains focused on the message at hand. Repeating the overall point of the speech in different ways helps listeners remember what the speaker is trying to tell them, even when the speech is over. A speech that is longer than necessary will cause listeners to become bored and stop absorbing information. Keeping the speech short and sweet and leaving more time for questions at the end will ensure that the audience stays engaged.

There are many different styles a speaker can utilize, but the most important thing speakers should keep in mind is maintaining a connection with the audience. This will help ensure that the audience will remain open and focused enough to hear and absorb the message.

Evaluating the Advantages and Disadvantages of Using Different Media to Present Ideas

Each visual aid has its advantages and disadvantages and should be used sparingly to avoid distracting the audience. Visual aids should be used to emphasize a presentation's message, not overwhelm it.

Microsoft PowerPoint is currently the most commonly used visual aid. It allows for pictures, words, videos, and music to be presented on the same screen and is essentially just a projection of a computer screen, allowing easy and quick access to all forms of media as well as the Internet. However, a PowerPoint presentation should not be overwhelmed with information, such as text-heavy slides, as audience members will spend more time reading the slides than listening to the speaker. Conversely, they may avoid reading it entirely, and the presentation will serve no purpose. A PowerPoint presentation that uses too many animations and visual elements may also detract from the presence of the speaker.

Handouts are a great way for the audience to feel more involved in a presentation. They can present lots of information that may be too much for a PowerPoint, and they can also be taken home and reviewed later. The primary disadvantage of handouts is that the audience may choose to read rather than to listen, thus missing the main points the speaker is trying to make, or they may decide not to read it at all. The best handouts are those that do not contain all the information of a presentation, but allow for the audience to take notes and complete the handout by listening or asking questions.

Whiteboards and *blackboards* are excellent for explaining difficult concepts by allowing the audience to follow along with a process and copy down their own version of what is being written on the board. This visual aid is best used to explain concepts in mathematics and science. The main problem with the board, however, is that there can be limited space, and if the presenter runs out of room, he or she will have to erase the content written on the board and will be unable to refer back to it later. He or she may also have to wait for the entire audience to write the information down, which slows down the presentation.

Overhead projectors are wonderful in that a speaker can use a prepared transparency and draw images or add words to emphasize or explain concepts. They can also erase these additions but still keep the original content if they wish to alter their method to fit the audience or provide further explanations. Similar to PowerPoint presentations, overhead projections should limit the amount of text to keep the audience focused on listening.

Physical objects are a useful way to connect with the audience and allow them to feel more involved. Because people interact with the physical world, physical objects can help solidify understanding of difficult concepts. However, they can be distracting if not properly introduced. If they are presented too early or are visible during the presentation, the audience will focus on the objects, wondering what purpose they may serve instead of listening to the speaker. Objects should instead be hidden until it is time to show them and then collected when they are no longer useful.

Videos are a great way to enliven a presentation by giving it sound, music, flow, and images. They are excellent for emphasizing points, providing evidence for ideas, giving context, or setting tone. The major issue with videos is that the presenter is unable to speak at this point, so this form of media should be used sparingly and purposefully. Also, overly-long videos may lose the audience's attention.

Effective public speakers are aware of the advantages and disadvantages of all forms of media and often choose to utilize a combination of several different types to keep the presentations lively and the audience engaged.

Determining Whether Information is Presented Clearly, Concisely, and Logically

All information should be presented with a clear beginning, middle, and end. Distinct organization always makes any work more clear, concise, and logical. For a presentation, this should involve choosing a primary topic and then discussing it in the following format:

- Introducing the speaker and the main topic
- Providing evidence, supporting details, further explanation of the topic in the main body
- Concluding it with a firm resolution and repetition of the main point

The beginning, middle, and end should also be linked with effective transitions that make the presentation flow well. For example, a presentation should always begin with an introduction by the speaker, including what he/she does and what he/she is there to present. Good transitional introductions may begin with statements such as *For those who do not know me, my name is..., As many of you know, I am...* or *Good morning everyone, my name is ___, and I am the new project manager.* A good introduction grabs the attention and interest of the audience.

After an introduction has been made, the speaker will then want to state the purpose of the presentation with a natural transition, such as *I am here to discuss the latest editions to our standard of procedure...* or *This afternoon, I would like to present the results of our latest findings*. Once the purpose has been identified, the speaker will want to adhere to the main idea announced. The presenter should be certain to keep the main idea to one sentence as too much information can confuse an audience; an introduction should be succinct and to the point.

Supporting information should always be presented in concise, easy-to-read formats such as bullet points or lists—if visual aids are presented during the presentation. Good transitions such as *Let's begin with...* or *Now to look at...* make the presentation flow smoothly and logically, helping listeners to keep ideas organized as they are presented. Keeping the material concise is extremely important in a presentation, and visual aids should be used only to emphasize points or explain ideas. All the supporting information should relate back to the main idea, avoiding unnecessary tangents.

Finally, a firm conclusion involves repeating the main point of the presentation by either inspiring listeners to act or by reiterating the most important points made in the speech. It should also include an expression of gratitude to the audience as well as transition to opening the floor for questions.

Integrating Technology, Multimedia, and Visual Displays

Teachers are learning to adapt their writing instruction to integrate today's technology standards and to enhance engagement in the writing process. The key is to still build a strong foundation of the fundamentals of writing while using current technology. Gone are the days when writing relied solely on handwritten pieces and when the tools of the trade were pencils, paper, hardback dictionaries, and encyclopedias. Online resources are now the backbone of the writing experience. It is now possible to integrate photo, video, and other interactive components into a completed project to provide a well-rounded engagement with media. In order to have an education conducive to college and career readiness and success, students need online research and digital media writing skills.

There are many compelling reasons to teach students to be digitally aware and prudent users of technology when it comes to their writing. With current digital technology, the writing process has become a much more collaborative experience. In higher education and in career settings, collaborative skills are essential. Publishing and presenting are now simplified such that completed work is often read by a wide variety of audiences. Writing can be instantly shared with parents, peers, educators, and the general public, including experts in the field. Students are more apt to take an interest in the writing process when they know that others are reading their writing. Feedback is also simplified because so many platforms allow comments from readers. Teachers can be interactive with the students throughout the process, allowing formative assessment and integration of personalized instruction. Technology is simply a new vehicle for human connection and interactivity.

A student may be exposed to a plethora of technology, but this does not mean that she or he necessarily knows how to use it for learning. The teacher is still responsible for guiding, monitoring, and scaffolding the students toward learning objectives. It is critical that educators teach students how to locate credible information and to reliably cite their sources using bibliographies. Platforms and apps for online learning are varied and plentiful. Here are some ideas for how to use technology for writing instruction in the classroom:

- Use a projector with a tablet to display notes and classwork for the group to see. This increases instructional time because notes are already available rather than having to be written in real-time. This also provides the ability to save, email, and post classwork and notes for students and parents to access on their own time. A student can work at his or her own pace and still keep up with instruction. Student screens can be displayed for peer-led teaching and sharing of class work.

- More technology in class means less paperwork. Digital drop-boxes can be used for students to turn in assignments. Teachers can save paper, keep track of student revisions of work, and give feedback electronically.

- Digital media can be used to differentiate instruction for multiple learning styles and multiple skill levels. Instead of using standardized textbook learning for everyone, teachers can create and collect resources for individualizing course content.

- Inquiry- and problem-based learning is easier with increased collaborative capabilities provided by digital tools.

- Digital textbooks and e-readers can replace hardback versions of text that are prone to damage and loss. Students can instantly access definitions for new words, as well as annotate and highlight useful information without ruining a hardbound book.

- Library databases can be used to locate reliable research information and resources. There are digital tools for tracking citation information, allowing annotations for internet content, and for storing internet content.

- Mobile devices may be used in the classroom to encourage reading and writing when students use them to text, post, blog, and tweet.

- PowerPoint and other presentation software can be used to model writing for students and to provide a platform for presenting their work.

- Students can create a classroom blog, review various blog sites, and use blogs as they would diaries or journals. They can even write from the perspective of the character in a book or a famous historical person.

- Web quests can be used to help guide students on research projects. They can get relevant information on specific topics and decide what pieces to include in their writing.

- Students can write about technology as a topic. They can "teach" someone how to use various forms of technology, specific learning platforms, or apps.

- Students can create webpages, make a class webpage, and then use it to help with home-school communication.

- Online feedback and grading systems can be used. There are many to choose from. This may allow students to see the grading rubric and ask questions or receive suggestions from the teacher.

- Students and teachers can use email to exchange ideas with other schools or experts on certain topics that are being studied in the classroom.

- Game show-style reviews can be created for units of study to use on computers or on an overhead projector.

- A wiki website can be created that allows students to collaborate, expand on each other's work, and do peer editing and revision.

- Publishing tools can be used to publish student work on the web or in class newspapers or social media sites.

Reading Comprehension and Analysis

Reading Literature

Understanding the Characteristics of Literary Genres

Fictional Prose

Fiction written in prose can be further broken down into *fiction genres*—types of fiction. Some of the more common genres of fiction are as follows:

- *Classical Fiction*—a work of fiction considered timeless in its message or theme, remaining noteworthy and meaningful over decades or centuries—e.g., Charlotte *Brontë's Jane Eyre*, Mark Twain's *Adventures of Huckleberry Finn*

- *Fables*— short fiction that generally features animals, fantastic creatures, or other forces within nature that assume human-like characters and has a moral lesson for the reader—e.g., Aesop's Fables

- *Fairy tales*—children's stories with magical characters in imaginary, enchanted lands, usually depicting a struggle between good and evil, a sub-genre of folklore—e.g., Hans Christian Anderson's *The Little Mermaid*, *Cinderella* by the Brothers Grimm

- *Fantasy*—fiction with magic or supernatural elements that cannot occur in the real world, sometimes involving medieval elements in language, usually includes some form of sorcery or witchcraft and sometimes set on a different world—e.g., J.R.R. Tolkien's *The Hobbit*, J.K. Rowling's *Harry Potter and the Sorcerer's Stone*, George R.R. Martin's *A Game of Thrones*

- *Folklore*—types of fiction passed down from oral tradition, stories indigenous to a particular region or culture, with a local flavor in tone, designed to help humans cope with their condition in life and validate cultural traditions, beliefs, and customs—e.g., William Laughead's *Paul Bunyan and The Blue Ox*, the Buddhist story of "The Banyan Deer"

- *Mythology*—closely related to folklore but more widespread, features mystical, otherworldly characters and addresses the basic question of why and how humans exist, relies heavily on allegory and features gods or heroes captured in some sort of struggle—e.g., Greek myths, Genesis I and II in the *Bible*, Arthurian legends

- *Science fiction*—fiction that uses the principle of *extrapolation*—loosely defined as a form of prediction—to imagine future realities and problems of the human experience—e.g., Robert Heinlein's *Stranger in a Strange Land*, Ayn Rand's *Anthem*, Isaac Asimov's *I, Robot*, Philip K. Dick's *Do Androids Dream of Electric Sheep?*

- *Short stories*—short works of prose fiction with fully-developed themes and characters, focused on mood, generally developed with a single plot, with a short period of time for settings—e.g., Edgar Allan Poe's "Fall of the House of Usher," Shirley Jackson's "The Lottery," Isaac Bashevis Singer's "Gimpel the Fool"

Drama

Drama is fiction that is written to be performed in a variety of media, intended to be performed for an audience, and structured for that purpose. It might be composed using poetry or prose, often straddling the elements of both in what actors are expected to present. Action and dialogue are the tools used in drama to tell the story. Please see the section called "Types of Drama" to see a more comprehensive list.

Poetry

Poetry is fiction in verse that has a unique focus on the rhythm of language and focuses on intensity of feeling. It is not an entire story, though it may tell one; it is compact in form and in function. Poetry can be considered as a poet's brief word picture for a reader. Poetic structure is primarily composed of lines and stanzas. Together, poetic structure and devices are the methods that poets use to lead readers to feeling an effect and, ultimately, to the interpretive message. Please see the section called "Types of Poetry" for a more comprehensive list, and the section "Poetry Techniques" for more information on the genre of poetry.

Nonfiction and Common Organizational Features of Nonfiction

Nonfiction is prose writing that is based on facts. It can be about real-life events, people, places, or things. Biographies, autobiographies, "how-to" books, memoirs, and essays are examples of nonfiction writing. There are many common features of nonfiction writing, including the use of chronological order, compare and contrast, illustration, captions, and keys. Review some of these features below:

Types of Nonfiction

Biography

A *biography* is a work written about a real person (historical or currently living). It involves factual accounts of the person's life, often in a re-telling of those events based on available, researched factual information. The re-telling and dialogue, especially if related within quotes, must be accurate and reflect reliable sources. A biography reflects the time and place in which the person lived, with the goal of creating an understanding of the person and his/her human experience. Examples of well-known biographies include *The Life of Samuel Johnson* by James Boswell and *Steve Jobs* by Walter Isaacson.

Autobiography

An *autobiography* is a factual account of a person's life written by that person. It may contain some or all of the same elements as a biography, but the author is the subject matter. An autobiography will be told in first person narrative. Examples of well-known autobiographies in literature include *Night* by Elie Wiesel and *Margaret Thatcher: The Autobiography* by Margaret Thatcher.

Memoir

A *memoir* is a historical account of a person's life and experiences written by one who has personal, intimate knowledge of the information. The line between memoir, autobiography, and biography is often muddled, but generally speaking, a memoir covers a specific timeline of events as opposed to the other forms of nonfiction. A memoir is less all-encompassing. It is also less formal in tone and tends to focus on the emotional aspect of the presented timeline of events. Some examples of memoirs in literature include *Angela's Ashes* by Frank McCourt and *All Creatures Great and Small* by James Herriot.

Journalism

Some forms of *journalism* can fall into the category of literary non-fiction—e.g., travel writing, nature writing, sports writing, the interview, and sometimes, the essay. Some examples include Elizabeth Kolbert's "The Lost World, in the Annals of Extinction series for *The New Yorker* and Gary Smith's "Ali and His Entourage" for *Sports Illustrated*.

Identifying Major Literary Works and Authors of U.S. Literature

Literature refers to a collection of written works that are the distinctive voices of peoples, time periods, and cultures. The world has gained great insight into human thought, vices, virtues, and desires through the written word. As the work pertains to the author's approach to these insights, literature can be classified as fiction or non-fiction.

The CSET Multiple Subjects test assumes test takers will have a familiarity with a wide range of American, British, World, and Young Adult literary works. In most cases, the test taker will be presented with a quoted literary passage and be required to answer one or more questions about it. This may involve having to identify the literary work presented from a list of options.

The ability of the test taker to demonstrate familiarity of major literary works is key in success when taking this exam. The following chart offers some examples of major works in addition to those listed elsewhere in this guide, but the list not exhaustive.

<u>American</u>
Fictional Prose
- Harriet Beecher Stowe | *Uncle Tom's Cabin*
- Ernest Hemingway | *For Whom the Bell Tolls*
- Jack London | *The Call of the Wild*
- Toni Morrison | *Beloved*
- N. Scott Momaday | *The Way to Rainy Mountain*
- J.D. Salinger | *Catcher in the Rye*
- John Steinbeck | *Grapes of Wrath*
- Alice Walker | *The Color Purple*

Drama
- Edward Albee | *Who's Afraid of Virginia Woolf?*
- Lorraine Hansberry | *A Raisin in the Sun*
- Amiri Baraka | *Dutchman*
- Eugene O'Neill |*Long Day's Journey into Night*
- Sam Shephard | *Buried Child*
- Thornton Wilder I *Our Town*
- Tennessee Williams | *A Streetcar Named Desire*

Poetry
- Anne Bradstreet | "In Reference to her Children, 23 June 1659"
- Emily Dickinson | "Because I could not stop for Death"
- Sylvia Plath | "Mirror"
- Langston Hughes | "Harlem"
- Edgar Allen Poe | "The Raven"
- Phillis Wheatley | "On Being Brought from Africa to America"
- Walt Whitman | "Song of Myself"

Literary Non-fiction
- Maya Angelou | I Know Why the Caged Bird Sings
- Truman | Capote In Cold Blood

- Frederick Douglass | My Bondage and My Freedom
- Archie Fire | Lame Deer The Gift of Power: The Life and Teachings of a Lakota Medicine Man
- Helen Keller | The Story of My Life
- Dave Pelzer | A Child Called "It"

Literature from Classical and Contemporary Periods

<u>British</u>
Fictional Prose
- John Bunyan | The Pilgrim's Progress
- Joseph Conrad | Heart of Darkness
- Charles Dickens | Tale of Two Cities
- George Eliot | Middlemarch
- George Orwell | 1984
- Mary Shelley | Frankenstein

Drama
- Samuel Beckett |Waiting for Godot
- Caryl Churchill | Top Girls
- William Congreve | The Way of the World
- Michael Frayn | Noises Off
- William Shakespeare | Macbeth
- Oscar Wilde | The Importance of Being Earnest

Poetry
- Elizabeth Barrett Browning | "How Do I Love Thee? (Sonnet 43)"
- Robert Burns | "A Red, Red Rose"
- Samuel Taylor Coleridge | "Rime of the Ancient Mariner"
- T.S. Eliot | "Love Song of J. Alfred Prufrock"
- John Milton | "Paradise Lost"

Literary Non-fiction
- Vera Brittain | Testament of Youth
- T. E. Lawrence | Seven Pillars of Wisdom
- Doris Lessing | Going Home
- Brian Blessed | Absolute Pandemonium: The Autobiography
- Virginia Woolf | A Room of One's Own

Recognizing Literature of Other Cultures

Literature from other cultures can vary based on an author's purpose. Stories can be passed down from one generation to the next through different types of literature. Fables, folktales, poetry, drama, fiction, and nonfiction texts often represent cultural themes from country to country. Readers may use literature from other cultures to compare and contrast cultural groups or time periods or even educate themselves on their own heritage.

In the tables below, review various types of literature from both Western and Eastern cultures. All literature listed has been published within the past one hundred years.

Western Culture:

Title	Author	Country	Genre	Year
The Hobbit	J.R.R. Tolkien	England	Fantasy	1937
Animal Farm	George Orwell	England	Political allegory/satire	1945
1984	George Orwell	England	Dystopia novel/fiction	1949
The Catcher in the Rye	J.D. Salinger	United States	Fiction	1951
The Old Man and the Sea	Ernest Hemingway	United States	Fiction	1952
Lolita	Vladimir Nabokov	Russia	Fiction	1955
To Kill a Mockingbird	Harper Lee	United States	Southern Gothic/fiction	1960
White Teeth	Zadie Smith	England	Fiction	2000
Atonement	Ian McEwan	England	Metafiction	2001
Half a Yellow Sun	Chimamanda Ngozi Adichie	Nigeria	Historical fiction	2006
Wolf Hall	Hilary Mantel	England	Biographical fiction	2010

Eastern Culture:

Title	Author	Country	Genre	Year
The Home and the World	Rabindranath Tagore	India	Historical fiction	1916
Rickshaw Boy	Lao She	China	Fiction	1937
An Insular Possession	Timothy Mo	Hong Kong	Historical fiction	1986
Wild Swans: Three Daughters of China	Jung Chang	China	Biography	1991
To Live	Yu Hua	China	Novel	1993
A Fine Balance	Rohinton Mistry	Canada	Historical novel	1995
The God of Small Things	Arundhati Roy	India	Fiction/coming of age	1997
Frog	Mo Yan	China	Fiction	2009

Elements in Fiction

There is no one, final definition of what literary elements are. They can be considered features or characteristics of fiction, but they are really more of a way that readers can unpack a text for the purpose of analysis and understanding the meaning. The elements contribute to a reader's literary interpretation of a passage as to how they function to convey the central message of a work. The most common literary elements used for analysis are the presented below.

Point of View

The *point of view* is the position the narrator takes when telling the story in prose. If a narrator is incorporated in a drama, the point of view may vary; in poetry, point of view refers to the position the speaker in a poem takes.

First Person

The first person point of view is when the writer uses the word "I" in the text. Poetry often uses first person, e.g., William Wordsworth's "I Wandered Lonely as a Cloud." Two examples of prose written in first person are Suzanne Collins' *The Hunger Games* and Anthony Burgess's *A Clockwork Orange*.

Second Person

The second person point of view is when the writer uses the pronoun "you." It is not widely used in prose fiction, but as a technique, it has been used by writers such as William Faulkner in *Absalom, Absalom!* And Albert Camus in *The Fall*. It is more common in poetry—e.g., Pablo Neruda's "If You Forget Me."

Third Person

Third person point of view is when the writer utilizes pronouns such as him, her, or them. It may be the most utilized point of view in prose as it provides flexibility to an author and is the one with which readers are most familiar. There are two main types of third person used in fiction. *Third person omniscient* uses a narrator that is all-knowing, relating the story by conveying and interpreting thoughts/feelings of all characters. In *third person limited,* the narrator relates the story through the perspective of one character's thoughts/feelings, usually the main character.

Plot

The *plot* is what happens in the story. Plots may be singular, containing one problem, or they may be very complex, with many sub-plots. All plots have exposition, a conflict, a climax, and a resolution. The *conflict* drives the plot and is something that the reader expects to be resolved. The plot carries those events along until there is a resolution to the conflict.

Tone

The *tone* of a story reflects the author's attitude and opinion about the subject matter of the story or text. Tone can be expressed through word choice, imagery, figurative language, syntax, and other details. The emotion or mood the reader experiences relates back to the tone of the story. Some examples of possible tones are humorous, somber, sentimental, and ironic.

Setting

The *setting* is the time, place, or set of surroundings in which the story occurs. It includes time or time span, place(s), climates, geography—man-made or natural—or cultural environments. Emily Dickinson's poem "Because I could not stop for Death" has a simple setting—the narrator's symbolic ride with Death through town towards the local graveyard. Conversely, Leo Tolstoy's *War and Peace* encompasses numerous settings within settings in the areas affected by the Napoleonic Wars, spanning 1805 to 1812.

Characters

Characters are the story's figures that assume primary, secondary, or minor roles. *Central* or *major* characters are those integral to the story—the plot cannot be resolved without them. A central character can be a *protagonist* or hero. There may be more than one protagonist, and he/she doesn't always have to possess good characteristics. A character can also be an *antagonist*—the force against a protagonist.

Dynamic characters change over the course of the plot time. *Static* characters do not change. A *symbolic* character is one that represents an author's idea about society in general—e.g., Napoleon in Orwell's *Animal Farm. Stock* characters are those that appear across genres and embrace stereotypes—e.g., the cowboy of the Wild West or the blonde bombshell in a detective novel. A *flat* character is one that does not present a lot of complexity or depth, while a *rounded* character does. Sometimes, the *narrator* of a story or the *speaker* in a poem can be a character—e.g., Nick Carraway in F. Scott Fitzgerald's *The Great Gatsby* or the speaker in Robert Browning's "My Last Duchess." The narrator might also function as a character in prose, though not be part of the story—e.g., Charles Dickens' narrator of *A Christmas Carol.*

Types of Poetry

Different poetic structures and devices are used to create the various major forms of poetry. Some of the most common forms are discussed in the following chart.

Type	Poetic Structure	Example
Ballad	A poem or song passed down orally which tells a story and in English tradition usually uses an ABAB or ABCB rhyme scheme	William Butler Yeats' "The Ballad Of Father O'Hart"
Epic	A long poem from ancient oral tradition which narrates the story of a legendary or heroic protagonist	Homer's The Odyssey Virgil's The Aeneid
Haiku	A Japanese poem of three unrhymed lines with five, seven, and five syllables (in English) with nature as a common subject matter	Matsuo Bashō An old silent pond... A frog jumps into the pond, splash! Silence again.
Limerick	A five-line poem written in an AABBA rhyme scheme, with a witty focus	From Edward Lear's Book of Nonsense— "There was a Young Person of Smyrna Whose grandmother threatened to burn her…"
Ode	A formal lyric poem that addresses and praises a person, place, thing, or idea	Edna St. Vincent Millay's "Ode To Silence"
Sonnet	A fourteen-line poem written in iambic pentameter	Shakespeare's Sonnets 18 and 130
Lyric	A lyric poem expresses the personal and emotional feelings of the author	Emily Dickinson "I Felt a Funeral in my Brain"
Narrative	A narrative poem tells a story	Edgar Allan Poe "The Raven"
Dramatic Monologue	A dramatic monologue is a poem where a character speaks to an auditor for the entire poem	Robert Browning "My Last Duchess"

Poetic Techniques

Poetic Devices

Rhyme is the poet's use of corresponding word sounds in order to create an effect. Most rhyme occurs at the ends of a poem's lines, which is how readers arrive at the *rhyme scheme*. Each line that has a corresponding rhyming sound is assigned a letter—A, B, C, and so on. When using a rhyme scheme, poets will often follow lettered patterns.

Robert Frost's *"The Road Not Taken"* uses the ABAAB rhyme scheme:

Two roads diverged in a yellow wood,	A
And sorry I could not travel both	B
And be one traveler, long I stood	A
And looked down one as far as I could	A
To where it bent in the undergrowth;	B

Another important poetic device is *rhythm*—metered patterns within poetry verses. When a poet develops rhythm through *meter*, he or she is using a combination of stressed and unstressed syllables to create a sound effect for the reader.

Rhythm is created by the use of *poetic feet*—individual rhythmic units made up of the combination of stressed and unstressed syllables. A line of poetry is made up of one or more poetic feet. There are five standard types in English poetry, as depicted in the chart below.

Foot Type	Rhythm	Pattern
Iamb	buh Buh	Unstressed/stressed
Trochee	Buh buh	Stressed/unstressed
Spondee	Buh Buh	Stressed/stressed
Anapest	buh buh Buh	Unstressed/unstressed/stressed
Dactyl	Buh buh buh	Stressed/unstressed/unstressed

Structure

Poetry is most easily recognized by its structure, which varies greatly. For example, a structure may be strict in the number of lines it uses. It may use rhyming patterns or may not rhyme at all. There are three main types of poetic structures:

- *Verse*—poetry with a consistent meter and rhyme scheme
- *Blank verse*—poetry with consistent meter but an inconsistent rhyme scheme
- *Free verse*—poetry with inconsistent meter or rhyme

Verse poetry is most often developed in the form of *stanzas*—groups of word lines. Stanzas can also be considered *verses*. The structure is usually formulaic and adheres to the protocols for the form. For example, the English *sonnet* form uses a structure of fourteen lines and a variety of different rhyming patterns. The English *ode* typically uses three ten-line stanzas and has a particular rhyming pattern.

Poets choose poetic structure based on the effect they want to create. Some structures—such as the ballad and haiku—developed out of cultural influences and common artistic practice in history, but in more modern poetry, authors choose their structure to best fit their intended effect.

Types of Drama

Drama refers to a form of literature written for the purpose of performance for an audience. Like prose fiction, drama has several genres. The following are the most common ones:

- *Comedy*—a humorous play designed to amuse and entertain, often with an emphasis on the common person's experience, generally resolved in a positive way—e.g., Richard Sheridan's *School for Scandal*, Shakespeare's *Taming of the Shrew*, Neil Simon's *The Odd Couple*

- *History*—a play based on recorded history where the fate of a nation or kingdom is at the core of the conflict—e.g., Christopher Marlowe's *Edward II*, Shakespeare's *King Richard III*, Arthur Miller's *The Crucible*

- *Tragedy*—a serious play that often involves the downfall of the protagonist, in modern tragedies, the protagonist is not necessarily in a position of power or authority—e.g., Jean Racine's *Phèdre*, Arthur Miller's *Death of a Salesman*, John Steinbeck's *Of Mice and Men*

- *Melodrama*—a play that is emphasizes heightened emotion and sensationalism, generally with stereotypical characters in exaggerated or realistic situations and with moral polarization—e.g., Jean-Jacques Rousseau's *Pygmalion*

- *Tragi-comedy*—a play that has elements of both tragedy—a character experiencing a tragic loss—and comedy—the resolution is often positive with no clear distinctive mood for either— e.g., Shakespeare's *The Merchant of Venice*, Anton Chekhov's *The Cherry Orchard*

Major Works in Children's Literature

<u>Young Adult</u>
Fictional Prose
- Jodi Lynn Anderson | *Tiger Lily*
- Lois Lowry | *The Giver*
- Scott O'Dell | *Island of the Blue Dolphins*
- Katherine Paterson Jacob | *Have I Loved*
- Antoine de Saint-Exupéry | *The Little Prince*
- Ellen Raskin | *The Westing Game*
- P. L. Travers | *Mary Poppins*
- Marcus Zusak | *The Book Thief*

Drama
- Peter Dee | Voices from the High School
- William Gibson | The Miracle Worker
- Poetry
- Sandra Cisneros | "Eleven"
- Eamon Grennan | "Cat Scat"
- Tom Junod | "My Mother Couldn't Cook"
- Tupac Shakur | "The Rose that Grew from Concrete"

Literary Non-fiction
- Sherman Alexie | The Absolutely True Diary of a Part-Time Indian
- Anne Frank | The Diary of Anne Frank
- Philip Hoose | The Boys who Challenged Hitler
- Cynthia Levinson | We've Got a Job
- Malala Yousafzai and Christina Lamb | I am Malala

Genres of Children's Literature

There are seven main genres of children's literature. The genres include fiction (realistic, historical, and science fiction), nonfiction (biography, autobiography, and informational texts), poetry, fantasy, mystery or suspense, folklore and fairy tales, and myths. Review each genre independently:

Fiction
Fiction is a type of literature based on imaginary events, people, or places. Fiction texts are not real, although they can appear to be real. Realistic fiction is a make-believe story about someone or something in an authentic setting. Fiction texts may also be based on historical events or science; however, details may be fabricated.

Nonfiction
Nonfiction texts are fact based. They represent real-life events, people, places, and things. Nonfiction texts include biography (a story about a person written by another person), autobiography (a story about someone written by themselves), and informational text (a text written to educate readers about a topic).

Poetry
Poetry is a piece of literary work meant to express feelings and ideas through rhythm and rhyme; however, not all poems rhyme. There are seven poetry forms: sonnet (short rhyming poem with 14 lines), limerick (5-line poem with rhythm), haiku (3-line poem following line-by-line syllable patterns), narrative (poem that tells a short story), epic (long poem usually featuring a hero or adventure), couplet (2-line rhyming poem), and finally, free verse (poem that does not follow any poetry rules).

Fantasy
In the fantasy genre, characters, places, and events are completely fictional. In no way, shape, or form could these things exist in real life.

Mystery or Suspense
The mystery or suspense genre is a fictional story involving some sort of crime or suspenseful event that needs to be solved. It can take place in a novel or a series of short stories.

Folklore and Fairy Tales
Folklore and fairy tales are stories that are told and passed down among generations. This genre usually includes animals, songs, cultural myths, and jokes. Fairy tales are also folkloric texts that may include magical creatures like dragons, giants, witches, or fairies.

Myths
Myths are fictional legendary stories incorporating heroic characters.

Major Themes Associated with Children's Literature

Children's literature tends to have overlapping themes throughout different genres. A theme is the overall subject or message in a story. Common themes in children's literature are family, friendship, growing up, self-esteem, and morality.

Family
Family tends to be a common theme in children's literature. Authors provide readers with examples of relationships such as father/son, mother/daughter, grandparent/grandchild, and cousin/cousin. These relationships may display positive or negative feelings of love, joy, pain, or sadness. They can also find strengths or weaknesses in family communication or togetherness. One popular children's book centered on family is *A Chair for My Mother* by Vera B. Williams. In this story, a family works hard to save money to buy their mother a special chair after all of her furniture is lost in a fire. The tale of hard work, sacrifice, and love teaches many lessons to students of all ages.

Friendship
Another common theme in children's literature is friendship. Children are greatly influenced by friends. Texts may portray positive or negative choices among friends leading to a great or poor outcome. Throughout friendship-themed literature, children learn all sorts of valuable lessons like compromise, coping skills, togetherness, caring for others, inclusion, and adversity. One popular children's book centered on friendship is *Charlotte's Web* by E.B. White. In this story, unlikely friendships occur in many forms. A young girl and a pig, a pig and a spider, and a goose and a horse all celebrate one another's differences and support each other's decisions through this children's tale.

Growing Up
Growing up is another common theme in children's literature. Children's literature has countless texts of kids going through different scenarios as they get older. Overlapping themes include friendship, puberty, judgment calls, overcoming challenges, and accepting responsibilities. For example, the children's book, *Alice in Wonderland,* by Lewis Carroll, demonstrates concepts such as the challenges of being big and small, as well as decision-making.

Self-Esteem
Self-esteem is the emotional feelings one has about himself or herself. Self-esteem–themed children's literature tries to demonstrate positive feelings and emotions to build self-esteem. Acceptance, love, learning opportunities, goal setting, pride, and trying new things are common subjects in self-esteem–themed texts. For example, the children's book, *I Like Myself,* by Karen Beaumont, discusses how to be proud and confident regardless of physical appearances.

Morality
Morality is the judgment of right from wrong. Children always have choices. Morality-themed children's books share the principles and outcomes of good and poor choices. Themes such as honesty, friend choices, respect, and sharing are common in morality-themed children's texts. For example, the children's book series, *The Berenstain Bears,* by Stan and Jan Berenstain, always reveals a predicament where the kids or adults need to use problem-solving skills to solve the issue. One of the books in the series, *The Berenstain Bears and the Truth,* discusses how to feel proud of telling the truth and how important truth telling is.

Rhetorical and Literary Devices in Children's Literature

Rhetorical devices are techniques and language used by authors to influence readers' perspectives of texts. *Literary devices* are methods that authors use to create special effects in literature. Both devices are commonly used in children's literature to create visual representations and examples for young readers. Four commonly used devices are analogies, similes, metaphors, and symbolism. Review each device individually below.

Analogies

Analogies compare two objects that are different yet share similar characteristics. When comparing two objects, the goal is to demonstrate how the objects relate to one another. Analogies often use similes and metaphors to compare objects. For example, in the simile "Her hands were as cold as ice," "her hands" are clearly not made of ice; however, the reference to "ice" tells the reader that her hands were extremely cold. Let's review the differences between similes and metaphors below.

Similes

A simile compares two objects using the words "like" or "as." For example, in the sentence, "The muffin was as hard as a rock," "the muffin" is clearly not a rock; however, the word "rock" creates a visual image for the reader that the muffin was very hard.

Metaphors

Metaphors compare two unlike objects by replacing one word with another word. For example, in the sentence, "The students were angels for the substitute teacher," "the students" are not actually angels; however, the term "angels" portrays good behavior, leading the reader to understand that the students were well behaved for the substitute teacher.

Symbolism

Metaphors use symbolism. Symbolism uses symbolic images, people, places, or things to represent them as something completely different. It provides a deeper meaning to literary works. For example, in the fairy tale, "Beauty and the Beast," a curse was cast on a prince, turning him into a beast. The prince needed to find true love and acceptance despite his new appearance as a beast. A single rose symbolized the amount of time the beast had to find true love, acceptance, and beauty in all things (including an ugly beast). As the rose wilted, the beast had less time and may have indefinitely remained a beast. Fortunately, the beast found true love, acceptance, and beauty in all things before the final rose petal fell, and the spell was broken.

Different Styles and Communicative Purposes in Children's Literature

Children's literature is an important teaching tool both inside and outside the classroom. No child has the same experience as another. Children are from different cultures, socioeconomic status, and families, yet they may all be in the same classroom expected to read and learn the same material. For this reason, it is important to expose all readers to a variety of texts to gain, or relate to, different outlooks and experiences. It is also vital to allow readers time to respond to what they have read and form their own opinions or summaries of texts in order to gain complete understanding.

Children's texts allow young readers to use their imaginations to build visual maps of stories in their heads or out loud in group settings. Children's literature also allows students to deal with personal situations by learning and relating to characters, settings, or problem-solving solutions. Review the chart below examining suggested book categories according to age groups. Remember, every child is different and may read above or below the suggested styles.

Suggested Age-Based Literature Categories:

Age	Category	Definition
Zero to 5 (Pre-readers)	Picture books	Combinations of visual images and short narratives to convey a message
5 to 7	Early readers	Short stories intended to help build reading skills
7 to 12	Chapter books: short (ages 7 to 9), long (ages 9 to 12)	Longer books with multiple chapters that build a story line
12 to 18	Young adult fiction	Story lines requiring critical thinking or focus on overcoming challenges

Each category has a variety of texts to communicate varying purposes. From picture books to chapter books, authors intend to strengthen language, fluency, and critical thinking skills. The exposure to new vocabulary words, phrases, tone, and dilemmas provides students with opportunities to activate their prior knowledge on topics as well as expand their thoughts further. One way teachers and parents can help young readers interpret text meaning is by doing a "picture walk." A picture walk is when students review the text's pictures to determine the meaning of the story. It is a great way to introduce stories or unfamiliar context to young readers. Picture walking also allows young readers to think about what may happen next or as a result of a previous action. Engaging students in the story, whether by interpreting pictures or recapping chapters, is key to successfully understanding literature. Simply put, any style of children's literature sparks discussions of all kinds.

Criteria for Evaluating Children's Literature

Children learn in different ways. What may interest one student may be a complete bore to another. Educationally, students are on all different levels. It is important for teachers and parents to expose students to a variety of texts to properly evaluate the type of literature they should be reading. Remember, students should be engaged while reading. Therefore, they need literature that they take interest in, or on their own level. If the content of the text is over their heads or uninteresting, what will the students learn or take away from the text? When evaluating children's literature, parents and teachers should consider reading level, literary quality, richness in vocabulary, student interests, illustrations, and gender and cultural bias. Below, review each evaluation topic individually.

Reading Level
Reading levels evaluate the difficulty of texts for students. Teachers and parents can assess students' reading levels by simply assessing their reading skills. There are four major reading-level assessment tests:

- The Lexile Framework for Reading
- Fountas and Pinnell
- Reading Recovery
- Developmental Reading Assessment (DRA)

Each of these assessments focuses on phonemic awareness, word blends, segmenting, syllabication, fluency, and comprehension to help target students' reading level. Once students' reading levels are determined, parents and teachers can guide students to books they will understand yet remained challenged.

Literary Quality
Another thing to consider when evaluating children's literature is the text quality. Is the story written well? Is the text engaging for the intended audience? Does the story use proper grammar and syntax to make the story readable for the age in which the story was written? Literary quality should represent a variety of perspectives; however, texts should also be well written and easy to understand. Poorly written or vague texts are confusing to readers. It is important for parents and teachers to properly evaluate the literary quality of texts to ensure that they are suitable for their students.

Richness in Vocabulary
Texts are word rich. Students learn new words and meanings through exposure. It is important for teachers and parents to provide text-rich literature to help children's vocabulary grow. If students read the same words over and over, their vocabulary will not expand. Exposing students to word meanings, synonyms, and antonyms will increase their overall literacy skills.

Student Interests
Teachers and parents must consider their audience when selecting literature for students. Children have different interests. Allowing students to choose their own texts is one option, as long as parents and/or teachers review the texts to ensure other aspects such as reading level and text quality are on target. Teachers or parents may also provide a variety of topics in their library. This allows students to find an interesting topic to read about. Teachers and parents may want to consider the use of "book bags." Book bags are designed for each student. Every individual bag contains books that are interesting to the intended reader and on the reader's level.

When evaluating student interests in children's literature, it is also important to make sure parents and teachers choose texts that are not embarrassing. Remember, the point of properly evaluating children's literature is to encourage reading, not to embarrass readers.

Illustrations
Illustrations are pictures used in a book to clarify text. Illustrations should tell stories of their own. Before teachers or parents read a children's book to students, they often ask, "What do you see on the cover? What do you think this story is about?" Pictures help students form thoughts and opinions on what the text is, or might be, about. Illustrations engage readers further into texts and make stories more understandable.

Evaluating illustrations in children's literature is important because teachers and parents should make sure that the illustrations help build story lines and critical thinking skills, not just make the cover or pages look pretty.

Gender and Cultural Bias
Finally, when evaluating children's literature, it is important to consider and assess gender and cultural bias in texts. Teachers and parents should check the story lines to make sure there is not any implicit or explicit race, gender, or cultural bias, unless that is the specific study topic. Character portrayal, settings, and language used in children's literature should be authentic, not generic.

Children's Literature in Relation to Style, Theme, or Voice

Style, theme, and voice are three influential factors on a reader's perspective of text. The way a reader interprets language, settings, characters, and plots is subjective to the author's purpose. If an author's style, theme, or voice is inconsistent in a text, what they are reading may confuse readers. Review each of the terms below.

Style
In literature, style is the way in which an author writes. It influences how readers understand the storyline and perceive the text itself. Authors must decide if they are going to write in the first or third person to portray the story line, the role(s) each character will play throughout the story's development, the key focus per page or chapter, and the setting of the story (including past or present tense as well as location(s)). All of these factors affect the clarity of the text. As long as authors are consistent with their style, readers should be able to unambiguously follow the plot.

Theme
Theme is the centralized topic of a text. Common themes in children's literature include friendship, family, growing up, acceptance, morality, and self-esteem. Each theme attempts to educate and influence readers and keeps the story line fluid. Some authors carry a theme through a series of texts with prequels and sequels.

Voice
Voice is the way in which the narrator conveys his or her message of a given text. The voice in a text grabs a reader's attention. It makes the text relatable and expressive. There are two main types of voices: author's voice and character's voice. When using an author's voice, the author uses his or her own language style and flow to influence how the text is interpreted. When the author uses a character's voice, he or she uses the main character of the text to portray a message. First- and third-person perspectives are commonly used in a character's voice.

Uses of Children's Literature

Children's literature is mainly used to model reading and writing skills. Beyond its basic purpose, children's literature opens the eyes and minds of young readers to the world much bigger than they know it. It is a way for children to learn about experiences that they may have yet to encounter but may cross paths with in the future. Children's literature allows young readers to engage and visualize word meanings through rich and deep language and illustrations.

Teachers and parents can use children's literature to help children "connect the dots" between varieties of subject matter. In classrooms, teachers can utilize children's literature to enhance other areas of the curriculum. In classrooms and homes, teachers and parents can use children's literature to foster cross-cultural understanding. Review ways in which teachers and parents use children's literature inside and outside classrooms and homes.

Other Areas of the Curriculum
Children's literature has a wide range of themes and topics for all ages. All major curricula subjects can utilize children's literature to reinforce material being taught in classrooms or in homes. For example, young learners begin their literacy and mathematical adventures with the alphabet and numbers. Teachers and parents can teach letters and numbers one way and then present a fun and engaging children's book reiterating the same concepts.

Using children's literature is not just for pre-readers or young readers. Social studies and science teachers often use informational children's literature to recap or introduce content. Nonfiction texts, including biographies, autobiographies, how-to books, and journal articles, are commonly used across social studies and science curricula.

Cross-Cultural Understanding
Children's literature celebrates how people, places, and things are different. Stories that range in topics addressing gender, race, and socioeconomic status are presented in a way that is easy for children to understand. Children's literature teaches moral lessons such as acceptance, perseverance, and kindness, often through relatable words and imagery.

Cross-cultural children's books help students understand their own cultures and discover information about their peers' cultures as well. It is important for teachers and parents to provide texts that are representative of the classroom population. Children come from all different backgrounds and experiences. Therefore, cross-cultural understanding should be fostered through multicultural books.

Reading Informational Text

Informational Texts

Informational texts are a category of texts within the genre of nonfiction. Their intent is to inform, and while they do convey a point of view and may include literary devices, they do not utilize other literary elements, such as characters or plot. An informational text also reflects a *thesis*—an implicit or explicit statement of the text's intent and/or a *main idea*—the overarching focus and/or purpose of the text, generally implied. Some examples of informational texts are informative articles, instructional/how-to texts, factual reports, reference texts, and self-help texts.

Organizational Structure within Informational Text
When reading informational text, it is important that readers are able to understand its organizational structure as the structure often directly relates to an author's intent to inform and/or persuade the reader. Informational text is specifically designed to relate factual information, and although it is open to a reader's interpretation and application of the facts, the structure of the presentation is carefully designed to lead the reader to a particular conclusion.

The first step in identifying the text's structure is to determine the thesis or main idea. The thesis statement and organization of a work are closely intertwined. *A thesis statement* indicates the writer's purpose and may include the scope and direction of the text. It may be presented at the beginning of a text or at the end, and it may be explicit or implicit.

Once a reader has a grasp of the thesis or main idea of the text, he or she can better determine its organizational structure. Test takers are advised to read informational text passages more than once in order to comprehend the material fully. The following questions should be considered when considering structure:

- How does the author assemble the parts to make an effective whole argument?
- Is the passage linear in nature and if so, what is the timeline or thread of logic?
- What is the presented order of events, facts, or arguments? Are these effective in contributing to the author's thesis?

- How can the passage be divided into sections? How are they related to each other and to the main idea or thesis?
- What key terms are used to indicate the organization?

Next, test takers should skim the passage, noting the first line or two of each body paragraph—the *topic sentences*—and the conclusion. Key *transitional terms*, such as *on the other hand, also, because, however, therefore, most importantly,* and *first,* within the text can also signal organizational structure. Based on these clues, readers should then be able to identify what type of organizational structure is being used. The following organizational structures are most common:

- *Problem/solution*—organized by an analysis/overview of a problem, followed by potential solution(s)

- *Cause/effect*—organized by the effects resulting from a cause or the cause(s) of a particular effect

- *Spatial order*—organized by points that suggest location or direction—e.g., top to bottom, right to left, outside to inside

- *Chronological/sequence order*—organized by points presented to indicate a passage of time or through purposeful steps/stages

- *Comparison/Contrast*—organized by points that indicate similarities and/or differences between two things or concepts

- *Order of importance*—organized by priority of points, often most significant to least significant or vice versa

Textual Evidence Support in Informational Text

Once a reader has determined an author's thesis or main idea, he or she will need to understand how textual evidence supports interpretation of that thesis or main idea. Test takers will be asked direct questions regarding an author's main idea and may be asked to identify evidence that would support those ideas. This will require test takers to comprehend literal and figurative meanings within the text passage, be able to draw inferences from provided information, and be able to separate important evidence from minor supporting detail. It's often helpful to skim test questions and answer options prior to critically reading informational text; however, test takers should avoid the temptation to solely look for the correct answers. Just trying to find the "right answer" may cause test takers to miss important supporting textual evidence. Making mental note of test questions is only helpful as a guide when reading.

After identifying an author's thesis or main idea, a test taker should look at the supporting details that the author provides to back up his or her assertions, identifying those additional pieces of information that help expand the thesis. From there, test takers should examine that additional information and related details for credibility, the author's use of outside sources, and be able to point to direct evidence that supports the author's claims. It's also imperative that test takers be able to identify what is strong support and what is merely additional information that is nice to know but not necessary. Being able to make this differentiation will help test takers effectively answer questions regarding an author's use of supporting evidence within informational text.

Inference in Informational Text

Inference refers to the reader's ability to understand the unwritten text, i.e., "read between the lines" in terms of an author's intent or message. The strategy asks that a reader not take everything he or she reads at face value but instead, add his or her own interpretation of what the author seems to be trying to convey. A reader's ability to make inferences relies on his or her ability to think clearly and logically about the text. It does not ask that the reader make wild speculation or guess about the material but demands that he or she be able to come to sound conclusion about the material.

An author's use of less literal words and phrases requires readers to make more inference when they read. Since inference involves *deduction*—deriving conclusions from ideas assumed to be true—there's more room for interpretation. Still, critical readers who employ inference, if careful in their thinking, can still arrive at the logical, sound conclusions the author intends.

Word Choice in Informational Text

An author's choice of words—also referred to as *diction*—helps to convey his or her meaning in a particular way. Through diction, an author can convey a particular tone—e.g., a humorous tone, a serious tone—in order to support the thesis in a meaningful way to the reader.

One aspect of understanding an author's word choice is understanding connotation and denotation.

Connotation is when an author chooses words or phrases that invoke ideas or feelings other than their literal meaning. An example of the use of connotation is the word *cheap*, which suggests something is poor in value or negatively describes a person is reluctant to spend money. When something or someone is described this way, the reader is more inclined to have a particular image or feeling about it or him/her. Thus, connotation can be a very effective language tool in creating emotion and swaying opinion.

Denotation refers to words or phrases that mean exactly what they say. It is helpful when a writer wants to present hard facts or vocabulary terms with which readers may be unfamiliar. Some examples of denotation are the words *inexpensive* and *frugal*. *Inexpensive* refers to the cost of something, not its value, and *frugal* indicates that a person is conscientiously watching his or her spending. These terms do not elicit the same emotions that *cheap* does.

Authors sometimes choose to use both, but what they choose and when they use it is what critical readers need to differentiate. One method isn't inherently better than the other; however, one may create a better effect, depending upon an author's intent. If, for example, an author's purpose is to inform, to instruct, and to familiarize readers with a difficult subject, his or her use of connotation may be helpful. However, it may also undermine credibility and confuse readers. An author who wants to create a credible, scholarly effect in his or her text would most likely use denotation, which emphasizes literal, factual meaning and examples.

Lastly, test takers and critical readers alike should be very aware of technical language used within informational text. *Technical language* refers to terminology that is specific to a particular industry and is best understood by those specializing in that industry. This language is fairly easy to differentiate, since it will most likely be unfamiliar to readers. It's critical to be able to define technical language either by the author's written definition, through the use of an included glossary—if offered—or through context clues that help readers clarify word meaning.

Text Complexity

Measuring Text Complexity

When selecting texts for classroom reading, it is imperative that educators consider the three main factors that measure complexity, which will best predict a child's reading success:

- Quantitative
- Qualitative
- Reader and Task

Quantitative Measures
When selecting appropriate texts for the classroom, educators must consider the type of words used throughout the text, the number of syllables in each word, and the spelling complexity of the words. Educators should also ask themselves if the text mostly contains decodable words or a significant number of sight word vocabulary. Finally, educators must consider the sentence lengths and the level of sentence complexity, since sentences vary from simple sentences to compound-complex sentences that may be too advanced for the students.

Qualitative Measures
Educators must also take into account the age of their students and whether or not certain subject matter is developmentally appropriate. Do children tend to have background knowledge in the subject, or will they likely be introduced to this new concept for the first time? Does the author employ the use of explicit language or figurative language that may be too complicated for younger students?

Reader and Task Measures
When educators go a step further in their planning by considering the needs of their individual students, reading instruction will be more effective. Educators should consider the various reader variables, such as level of reading fluency, the number of reluctant and motivated readers in the classroom, and the degree of home support for reading.

All of these factors combined significantly impact the type of text, level of complexity, and the tasks children are given to accomplish based on the reading material. Considering these factors that measure text complexity will also assist educators in choosing instruction and evaluation techniques.

Providing a Wide Range of Literary and Informational Texts

By reading multiple genres of text, students are exposed to a variety of words and word usage. Students not only begin to internalize how various authors use words, but they also gain vocabulary, learn the rules of academic language, and build concept and background knowledge. This will help students to develop a love of reading and motivate them to independently seek increasingly challenging reading levels.

Promoting a Wide Range of Formal and Informal Texts of Increasingly Challenging Levels

Since there's a positive correlation between a student's exposure to text and their academic success, students should be given ample opportunities for independent reading.

In order to read independently, students must be able to readily recognize frequently used words or quickly and accurately decode new words. Thus, before independent reading, students must be able to confidently execute strategies presented within Competency 9.

Once students become fluent readers, independent reading begins with *scaffolded opportunities*. Scaffolded opportunities occur when a teacher helps students by giving them support, suggesting strategies, and offering immediate feedback. Less scaffolding is required as a student becomes a more independent reader.

Students who don't yet display automaticity may need to read aloud or whisper to themselves during independent reading time. Independent silent reading accompanied by comprehension accountability is an appropriate strategy for students who demonstrate automaticity in their decoding skills.

Developing Knowledge of Language that Supports Comprehension

Developing a knowledge of syntax aids the development of student word knowledge and language structures. *Syntactic awareness* is the ability to change the order of words within a sentence without losing the meaning of the original sentence. It contributes to the process of inferring the meaning of new words from the context of a sentence or paragraph. Syntactic awareness has been shown to increase reading comprehension and writing skills. The following strategies can be used to develop syntactic awareness:

- Combining sentences requires students to develop the ability to write compound sentences. This process develops word choice and the use of transition words.

- Re-ordering and reconstructing sentences builds understanding of the importance of word order.

- The identification of signal words can cue a text's structure.

Through direct instruction and discussion, students become more conscious of word use and how proper grammar and punctuation are used to fit words together.

Cohesion and coherence in written and oral language is achieved through a full understanding of syntax, semantics, grammar, and punctuation. *Coherence* is the way language is comprehended by a reader based on the semantic configuration of the words and concepts, sentences, paragraphs, and sections of a piece of writing. *Cohesion* is the formal grammatical and lexical relationships between different elements of a text that hold it together. Cohesion includes formal linguistic features such as repetition, reference, conjunction, and substitution.

World History

Ancient Civilizations

Ancient Greece

Ancient Greece formed from scattered farming communities between 800 BCE and 500 BCE. In this early era of Greece, the polis, or city-state, held all of the political power locally. City-states were self-ruling and self-sufficient. The idea of a self-governing state had an enduring effect on the government of Greece and would result in the demokratia (rule by the people), which would spread and influence the world. As farming villages grew and marketplaces were built, a government with laws, an organized army, and tax collection took shape.

Each city-state was different from one another, but some unifying traits included a common language, a shared belief system, an agriculturally based economy, and rule by several wealthy citizens instead of rule by a king or queen. However, these few aristocratic rulers, known as *oligarchs,* often owned the best and most land, which created tension as the population grew. As a result, many citizens moved to less populated or newly conquered areas. By 800 BCE, there were over 1500 city-states, each with its own rulers and rules. Greek city-states were concentrated on the coast, resulting in greater contact with other civilizations through trade. City-states' governments and culture continued to diverge as time progressed. For example, in the fifth century BCE, Athens became the first direct democracy in the world, and Athenian citizens would vote directly on legislation. Only adult, male, landowning citizens could vote, but it was a remarkable departure from all contemporary forms of government to provide for direct democracy, especially relative to other city-states' oligarchies. Another world-renowned example is Sparta, which based its entire social system and constitution on military training and ability.

The Greek religion was polytheistic. Every city-state had a temple dedicated to a particular god or goddess; however, the whole of ancient Greece believed that Zeus, residing in Mount Olympus, was the most powerful of the gods. The physical presence of the temple, the rituals and festivals that dotted the Greek year, and the widespread belief in the gods controlling every aspect of human life heavily influenced their agricultural economy, government, and interactions with other ancient civilizations.

The ancient Greeks were known for their citizen-soldiers, known as *hoplites.* No ancient civilization could field a professional military due to economic restraints, such as a lack of a banking system and the need for agricultural laborers, but the hoplites were famous in ancient times for their tactics and skill. Hoplites were armed with spears and large shields, and they would fight in a phalanx formation. The Romans would later adopt many of the Greek military principles. Greek city-states fought numerous wars among each other, the largest being the Peloponnesian War, as well as wars against Persia. Fought between 499 BCE and 449 BCE, the Greco-Persian Wars pitted the Greek city-states against the mighty Persian Empire after the latter invaded. Although ancient sources are difficult to authenticate, it is certain that the Persian forces vastly outnumbered the Greeks who historically struggled to unite, even against a common enemy. This conflict included the legendary Battle of Thermopylae where three hundred Spartans, led by the Spartan king Leonidas, held off the elite contingent of the Persian army, the Immortals, for two days. After several setbacks and disastrous turns, the Greeks eventually defeated the Persian fleet at the naval Battle of Mycale and forced the Persians out of Europe. Greek unification did not last beyond this victory, and by 404 BCE, Sparta crushed Athens in the Peloponnesian War. Athens would never again attain its status as the leading city-state.

Roman Empire

Although already one of the world's most powerful civilizations, Rome began to strain under political pressure and domestic unrest in the mid-first century BCE. In 48 BCE, Gaius Julius Caesar seized power over the republic, but his assassination in 44 BCE on the Ides of March threw the republic back into turmoil. Caesar's great-nephew turned son adopted by will, Octavian, eventually emerged as the sole leader of Rome, and historians define this point as the beginning of the Roman Empire. Octavian would serve as the first emperor under the name Augustus. His rule would be one of the most peaceful and prosperous in Roman history, often referred to as the *Pax Romana* or *Pax Augusta*. Although the Roman Empire did not adhere to the republic's democratic principles and separations of powers, the Roman Empire would be the vehicle that enabled Rome to conquer and administer enormous territory.

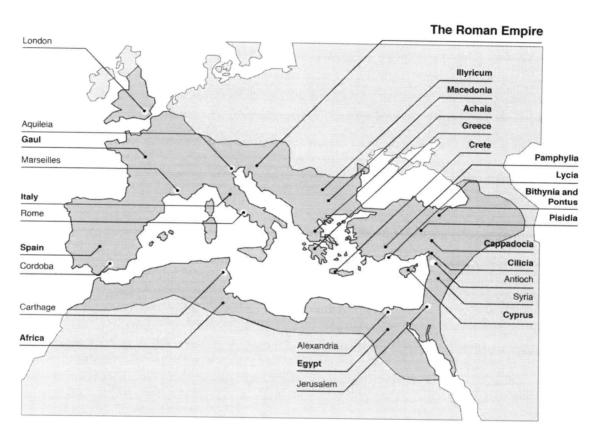

As Rome became an empire, its influence both in the ancient world and in the modern world began to take shape. Rome's ability to absorb and adapt the cultural achievements of Greece and push them on conquered cultures was a key to their success. Rome was highly influenced by Greek culture, religions, ideas, literature, and politics but kept at its roots the Roman ideals of simplicity, honesty, and loyalty. Rome was able to hold together a government that included multiple races, languages, and cultures in peace through the successful use of these ideas. In addition, Rome applied concepts developed by the Persians in the administration and political organization of its territories. By the time Rome became an empire, the government was highly structured with a complex civil service that addressed and administrated localized affairs.

Rome's decline began well before its eventual fall. There are many aspects to Rome's demise, including social, political, moral, religious, and economic. Each took their toll on the strength of the empire, and by 400 A.D., Rome collapsed under public unrest and religious discord, along with the invasion of the Huns of Mongolia and Germanic tribes. Although ultimately defeated, Rome's legacy extends all the way through to the present day. The Roman Republic's democratic elements and robust civil service would be the model for much of the West, especially the United States. That is to say nothing of the advancements in literature, technology, architecture, urban planning, and hygiene across the empire that influenced every future Western civilization.

Persian Empire

The Persian Empire consisted of multiple countries, religions, languages, and races governed by a central government. Cyrus the Great was known for his social and political acumen. He was able to navigate the empire's diversity with his "carrot or stick" approach. Cyrus the Great would offer foreign civilizations some degree of home rule, as long as they paid tribute to Persia and adopted some of its norms, or else the might of the legendary Persian military would crush them. As long as the citizens of Persia paid taxes and were peaceful, they were allowed to keep their own religious customs, local culture, and local economies. It was not until his successors that this political policy began to wan with the onset of multiple rebellions that weakened the centralized government.

The government of Persia delegated power among four governing capitals. Each state had a satrap, or governor. The satrapy government allowed for regional self-governance with a military leader and an official record-keeper that reported to the central government. The empire was also innovative in its road construction and postal systems. By allowing some degree of regional autonomy, Persia was able to rule over an unprecedented territory in ancient history. For example, Babylon even requested to be part of Persia because of its unique policies. The empire's enormity and vast scope influenced world history for centuries. Persian scholars and political philosophers would later influence rulers in the Renaissance and Enlightenment eras.

Maurya Empire

The Maurya Empire established a centralized government to govern its vast territories, and it specialized in tax collection, administration, and the military. It was modeled after the Greek and Persian governments, who, through trade and invasion, had influenced Chandragupta's government layout. Previously, regional chieftains and small armies governed India, which led to continuous skirmishes and wars. Chandragupta cleared out the chieftains and imposed regulated laws and tax reforms. The centralized form of government allowed for a period of peace, scientific advancement, and religious growth.

The centralized government was made up of four provinces organized under one capital. Each emperor had a cabinet of ministers known as a *Mantriparishad,* or Council of Ministers, to help guide him—an idea that is still used in governments across the world. Princes, or Kumaras, likewise oversaw each province, with a council of ministers called the *Mahamatyas.* A civil service was developed to govern many aspects of life and infrastructure, including waterworks, roads, and international trade. The army was expanded into one of the largest in the world at the time. Trade became a major source of revenue as other empires sought spices, food, and cloth from India.

India's three main religions flourished in this period. Hinduism, a blend of multiple beliefs, appeared in the Epic Age and became a central religion. Buddhism appeared as a consequence of the harsh social structure that had left a wide gap in the social and economic freedoms of the people. Chandragupta later accepted Jainism, a religion of total peace and unity with the world. Overall, the Maurya Empire featured a balance of religions that promoted peace as foundational and sought social harmony. The centralized government discouraged the infamous Indian caste system, which organized society by social status and led to discrimination against the lower castes.

<u>Chinese Empire</u>

Between 1000 BCE and 500 A.D., ancient China was unified under three successive dynasties: the Zhou Dynasty, the Qin Dynasty, and the Han Dynasty, in respective chronological order. The Zhou Dynasty was the longest dynasty in Chinese history and began after the fall of the Shang Dynasty. Originally, the Zhou Dynasty had moved away from the Shang Empire, created their own government, and formed alliances with enemies of the Shang. When war eventually broke, the people of Shang, so angered by their own government's foolishness, put up little resistance against the rebellion.

Under the Zhou Dynasty, the kingdom's ruler legitimized their power through the Mandate of Heaven, meaning they believed the rulers of the land were put in place by a higher being that could not be disposed. The Zhou claimed that the Shang Dynasty had forfeited their claim due to their mismanagement of the kingdom. This would be a common theme for dynasty takeovers. A centralized government was established, but the Zhou Dynasty never achieved complete centralized control across the kingdom. The economy was heavily agricultural and organized based on feudalism, an economical system in which a wealthy, landowning class rules the peasant class. These aristocratic rulers retained considerable power and regularly rebelled against the central government.

The Qin Dynasty was the first imperial dynasty, originally organized under Emperor Qin Shi Huangdi. The imperial state had a more centralized government, which limited the aristocratic landowners' power, stabilized the economy, and boosted the army. The Qin Dynasty formed a political structure that allowed China to start seriously building projects like the Great Wall of China. Its form of government would be adopted by many dynasties in China's history. The Qin Dynasty was short-lived and ended when Emperor Qin Shi Huangdi died prematurely, and rebel leaders fought for control of the kingdom. Liu Bang of Han defeated Xiang Yu of Chu at the Battle of Gaixia in 202 BCE, establishing the Han Dynasty.

Like the previous imperial dynasty, power was consolidated under a single emperor who dominated the Han Dynasty's centralized government. Under the emperor, a cabinet of ministers and chosen nobility acted as advisors who retained limited power. The Han dynasty was a golden era of Chinese innovation and technology, all driven by the tremendous growth in commerce and trade. To facilitate commerce, the Han Dynasty issued one of the world's earliest currencies under a money economy. Han coinage would remain the dominant currency from its introduction in 119 BCE until the Tang Dynasty in 618 A.D. A uniform currency was an essential part of the legendary Silk Road, which began under the Han Dynasty.

Medieval and Early Modern Times

World History in Western Civilization

<u>Development of Early Western Civilization</u>

There were a number of powerful civilizations during the classical period. Mesopotamia was home to one of the earliest civilizations between the Euphrates and the Tigris rivers in the Near East. The rivers provided water and vegetation for early humans, but they were surrounded by desert. This led to the beginning of irrigation efforts to expand water and agriculture across the region, which resulted in the area being known as the Fertile Crescent.

The organization necessary to initiate canals and other projects led to the formation of cities and hierarchies, which would have considerable influence on the structure of later civilizations. For instance, the new hierarchies established different classes within the societies, such as kings, priests, artisans, and workers. Over time, these city-states expanded to encompass outside territories, and the city of Akkad became the world's first empire in 2350 BCE. In addition, Mesopotamian scribes developed systemized drawings called pictograms, which were the first system of writing in the world; furthermore, the creation of wedge-shaped cuneiform tablets preserved written records for multiple generations.

Later, Mesopotamian kingdoms made further advancements. For instance, Babylon established a sophisticated mathematical system based on numbers from one to sixty; this not only influenced modern concepts, such as the number of minutes in each hour, but also created the framework for math equations and theories. In addition, the Babylonian king Hammurabi established a complex set of laws, known as the Code of Hammurabi, which would set a precedent for future legal systems.

Meanwhile, another major civilization began to form around the Nile River in Africa. The Nile's relatively predictable nature allowed farmers to use the river's water and the silt from floods to grow many crops along its banks, which led to further advancements in irrigation. Egyptian rulers mobilized the kingdom's population for incredible construction projects, including the famous pyramids. Egyptians also improved pictographic writing with their more complex system of hieroglyphs, which allowed for more diverse styles of writing. The advancements in writing can be seen through the Egyptians' complex system of religion, with documents such as the *Book of the Dead* outlining not only systems of worship and pantheons of deities but also a deeper, more philosophical concept of the afterlife.

While civilizations in Egypt and Mesopotamia helped to establish class systems and empires, other forms of government emerged in Greece. Despite common ties between different cities, such as the Olympic Games, each settlement, known as a polis, had its own unique culture. Many of the cities were oligarchies, in which a council of distinguished leaders monopolized the government; others were dictatorships ruled by tyrants. Athens was a notable exception by practicing an early form of democracy in which free, landholding men could participate, but it offered more freedom of thought than other systems.

Taking advantage of their proximity to the Mediterranean Sea, Greek cities sent expeditions to establish colonies abroad that developed their own local traditions. In the process, Greek merchants interacted with Phoenician traders, who had developed an alphabetic writing system built on sounds instead of pictures. This diverse network of exchanges made Greece a vibrant center of art, science, and philosophy. For example, the Greek doctor Hippocrates established a system of ethics for doctors called the Hippocratic Oath, which continues to guide the modern medical profession. Complex forms of literature were created, including the epic poem "The Iliad," and theatrical productions were also developed. Athens in particular sought to spread its vision of democratic freedom throughout the world, which led to the devastating Peloponnesian War between allies of Athens and those of oligarchic Sparta from 431 to 404 BCE.

Alexander the Great helped disseminate Greek culture to new regions, also known as *diffusion*. Alexander was in fact an heir to the throne of Macedon, which was a warrior kingdom to the north of Greece. After finishing his father's work of unifying Greece under Macedonian control, Alexander successfully conquered Mesopotamia, which had been part of the Persian Empire. The spread of Greek institutions throughout the Mediterranean and Near East led to a period of Hellenization, during which various civilizations assimilated Greek culture; this allowed Greek traditions, such as architecture and philosophy, to endure into the present day.

Greek ideas were later assimilated, along with many other concepts, into the Roman Empire. Located west of Greece on the Italian peninsula, the city of Rome gradually conquered its neighbors and expanded its territories abroad; by 44 BCE, Rome had conquered much of Western Europe, northern Africa, and the Near East. Romans were very creative, and they adapted new ideas and innovated new technologies to strengthen their power. For instance, Romans built on the engineering knowledge of Greeks to create arched pathways, known as aqueducts, to transport water for long distances and devise advanced plumbing systems.

One of Rome's greatest legacies was its system of government. Early Rome was a republic, a democratic system in which leaders are elected by the people. Although the process still heavily favored wealthy elites, the republican system was a key inspiration for later institutions such as the United States. Octavian "Augustus" Caesar later made Rome into an empire, and the senate had only a symbolic role in the government. The new imperial system built on the examples of earlier empires to establish a vibrant dynasty that used a sophisticated legal code and a well-trained military to enforce order across vast regions. Even after Rome itself fell to barbarian invaders in fifth century A.D., the eastern half of the empire survived as the Byzantine Empire until 1453 A.D. Furthermore, the Roman Empire's institutions continued to influence and inspire later medieval kingdoms, including the Holy Roman Empire; even rulers in the twentieth century called themselves Kaiser and Tsar, titles which stem from the word "Caesar."

In addition, the Roman Empire was host to the spread of new religious ideas. In the region of Israel, the religion of Judaism presented a new approach to worship via monotheism, which is the belief in the existence of a single deity. An offshoot of Judaism called Christianity spread across the Roman Empire and gained popularity. While Rome initially suppressed the religion, it later backed Christianity and allowed the religious system to endure as a powerful force in medieval times.

Middle Ages
Early Middle Ages
The Middle Ages refers to the period from the fifth century to the fifteenth century, beginning with the fall of the Roman Empire and ending with the Renaissance and Age of Exploration. Sharp population decline, intensely localized governance, frequent invasions, famine, and disease defined the early Middle Ages and explain why it is sometimes referred to as the *Dark Ages*. Manorialism and feudalism were the dominant economic systems of the period. Peasants would rent patches of land to farm on enormous manors of aristocrats, while knights and lower nobles would exchange military service with the aristocracy in exchange for control over a manor. In addition, much of the knowledge gained during the Age of Antiquity was lost during this period.

High Middle Ages
During the High Middle Ages, signs of revival began to emerge. Christians began to see the need to live out the fundamental convictions of Christianity and also saw the need for the clergy to exemplify Christ. After several reforms, religious orders developed, such as the Franciscans and Dominicans. The orders protected the knowledge and texts of the church, becoming a strong intellectual body. As a consequence, there was a revival in learning in the monasteries that trickled out to the cathedrals and then to schools.

Around 570 A.D., the Islamic prophet Muhammad was born in Mecca. Muhammad was a trade merchant who, coming into contact with Christian and Jewish traders, blended their religions with his own religious experience in which he believed that Allah was the one true god. He believed that Allah had called him to preach the Islamic religion. At first, he met with little success, as most Arabs believed in many and differing gods. However, in a few years, he was able to unite the nomadic tribes under Islam.

After Muhammad's death, his successors, known as *caliphs,* developed the religion of Islam into a system of government and spread the faith and government control into the Middle East, North Africa, Spain, and southern France. At one point, the Islamic Empire was larger than the Roman Empire. With invasion, Islam spread the Arabic language and embraced Greek science and Indian mathematics. From 900 A.D. to 1100 A.D., Islam experienced a golden age.

In 1095, European Christians launched military strikes against Muslims in the Holy Land, and the entire series of armed religious conflicts is known as the *Crusades*. During the Crusades, Italy's trade flourished because the movement of people facilitated commerce and communication with the Middle East and Africa. In the High Middle Ages, Italy expanded trade into Europe, and merchants across Europe began to settle in areas with good trade routes. Others who had a trade to sell settled in these areas, forming towns and local governments. The development of commerce would be the impetus for the Renaissance.

Age of Exploration
The traveling merchants, the Crusades, the conquests of foreign lands, and the writings of ancient Greece expanded the known world of Europeans to include Europe, northern Africa, the Middle East, and Asia. Early explorers such as Marco Polo brought back amazing stories and exotic goods from Asia, while ports in the Middle East and around the Mediterranean spread cultures through trade. However, the very existence of America and Australia was unknown to the ancient and medieval world. Likewise, there was very little knowledge of sub-Saharan Africa until the late Renaissance era.

In an effort to find better trade routes to China, explorers discovered unknown lands that would change the world in dramatic fashion. Over a two hundred year period from 1450 to 1650, the great explorers of the age would discover new lands, unknown people, and better trade routes to the silks, spices, precious metals, and other sought-after goods Europe was eager to own.

Portugal and Spain funded the first explorations and, along with Italy, dominated the discovery of new lands and trade routes for the first one hundred years of exploration. In 1488, Portuguese explorer Bartolomeu Dias became the first European to sail around the Cape of Good Hope in South Africa and the first European to sail from the Atlantic Ocean to the Indian Ocean. On a voyage lasting from 1497 to 1499, Vasco da Gama, another Portuguese explorer, followed the route of Dias and became the first European to reach India by sea.

Portuguese explorers' success led to Portugal's dominance over trade with Africa and Asia. In West Africa, the Portuguese traded for slaves, and in east Africa, they captured city-states and opened trading posts. The coastal trading posts were utilized to launch further exploration and trade farther east with China and Japan. During a voyage launched in 1500, Dias went on to reach Brazil after his ship was blown off course to Africa. Brazil would later become Portugal's most lucrative colony due to the sugar plantations farmed by African slaves and indigenous people.

By the 1530s, France, England, the Netherlands, and Scotland were beginning to send explorers on their own expeditions. In 1534, the king of France sent Jacques Cartier to discover a western passage to the Asian markets, and during his voyage in 1534, Cartier became the first European to travel down the Saint Lawrence River and explore Canada, which Cartier named after Iroquois settlements that he encountered. Englishman Francis Drake was the first European to successfully circumnavigate the world, completing the three-year voyage in 1580. Another Englishman, Henry Hudson, was hired by the Dutch

East India Company to find a northwest passage to India, and he explored the modern New York metropolitan area in the early seventeenth century. The Dutch would use this knowledge to colonize the area around the Hudson River, including New Amsterdam.

Even more devastating than the loss of their land, contact by Europeans exposed the indigenous people of America to devastating new diseases. Without any type of immunization, mild European diseases decimated the populations of the natives. Often the illness and death of natives made conquering the areas swift, and with it the loss of the culture, traditions, and languages of the native people. However, diseases such as syphilis and cholera were brought back from expeditions, ravaging European countries. The high death toll from disease, coupled with the deaths from native-born slave labor, caused a labor shortage that the Spanish replenished with slaves from their trade deals in West Africa. These slaves were mainly brought to the Caribbean Islands, though they were shipped to other Spanish colonies. The British colonies would later import millions of slaves to the modern-day American South to harvest cotton.

The Italian Renaissance

The Renaissance, meaning *rebirth*, began in the fourteenth century in Italy and spread throughout Europe during the fifteenth century. Its philosophy was humanism, or the study of man and his relationship with the world. It was a time when reason and knowledge were highly valued. The Roman Catholic Church kept pace with Europe's focus on mankind and nature, instead of heaven and heavenly beings. Popes sponsored educational enhancements and were, in some instances, as is the case with Pope Pius II, trained as classical scholars. In the early 1500s, Julius II had masters such as Michelangelo create artistic masterpieces that celebrated humans. Indeed, the arts moved toward a more realistic and proportional style with Italian painters such as Leonardo da Vinci, Raphael, and Titian leading the way.

The literary greats of the age were writing in their own vernacular, or language, instead of Latin. This was one of the greatest leaps forward; it not only built their native language, but it also allowed the Italian people to learn and grow in literacy. This and the advances in printing made the written word more accessible and widely dispersed than ever before. The dissemination of knowledge to larger groups of people would change the world, especially as the Renaissance spread to other European nations.

Renaissance in Northern Europe

The ideas in Italy began to spread northward, allowing the arts to flourish in Germany, such as Albrecht Dürer, and in the Netherlands, like Johannes Vermeer and Rembrandt. England began a long history of great literature with Geoffrey Chaucer's *The Canterbury Tales* and Edmund Spenser's *The Faerie Queene*. The highest literary achievements of the Renaissance came from two English playwrights, Christopher Marlowe and his better-known contemporary, William Shakespeare. But the Renaissance did not stray far from religious themes; instead, they humanized them, as is the case of Italian works of art. It was also an early changing point in Christianity, as theologians like Meister Eckhart, Thomas à Kempis, and Sir Thomas More began to use humanism to question the need for priestly intervention, favoring instead direct worship of God.

The invention of movable type by Johannes Gutenberg in 1439 started a revolution in printing that saw the expansion of books go from approximately 100,000 laboriously hand-copied books in Europe to over 9 million by 1500. The literacy rate in Europe improved vastly, as did the printing of religious writings. News could now travel to distant places, allowing for unprecedented communication both locally and globally. Movable type would be one of the major inventions of the Renaissance, heavily influencing the Reformation and Enlightenment.

The Reformation

In 1517, Martin Luther, a German monk and professor of theology, nailed his famous *Ninety-Five Theses,* or *Disputation on the Power of Indulgences,* to the door of the cathedral in Wittenberg, Germany. Pope Leo X demanded Luther to rescind, but Luther stood his ground, which launched the Protestant Reformation. There were serious problems in the Catholic Church, including clergy accepting simony, or the sale of church offices; pluralism, or having multiple offices; and the violation of vows. In addition, the worldly behavior of the church leaders and the biblical ignorance of the lower clergy prompted Luther to ignite a fire that could not be swept away or cleared up. The Roman Catholic Church could not weather this call for reform like it had done before. This was instead a call to cast off the Catholic faith for Protestantism. Many church denominations were formed under Protestantism, the first being Lutheranism, which gained strength in Germany and Switzerland.

Shortly after, the Roman Catholic Church issued a Counter Reformation in an attempt to quell the spread of Protestantism by addressing some of the complaints. In its initial stages, the Counter Reformation had little effect, and many Germans adopted Lutheranism as its officially recognized religion. By 1555, the Catholic Church recognized Lutheranism under the Peace of Augsburg, which allowed rulers to decide on which religion their kingdom would follow. In Germany there was peace, but civil wars broke out in France and the Netherlands. The Spanish-ruled Netherlands' struggle was as political as it was social, with other countries joining the fight against Catholic Spain.

In the 1600s, the peace in Germany faded as the country allied itself with either the Protestant Union or the Catholic League. The Thirty Years' War broke out in 1618 and became one of the most destructive wars in European history. It was a war of political and religious hostility that would involve Germany, Denmark, France, Austria, Spain, and Sweden, to some degree. Though it ended in 1648 with the Peace of Westphalia, France and Spain would wage war until 1659. The Treaty of Westphalia emphasized national self-determination, which directly led to the development of the nation-state. For the first time in human history, local people controlled the right to build a nation-state with the accompanying legitimacy to control their region. The new states, most of which were carved out of the Holy Roman Empire, were allowed to determine their religion, including Catholicism, Lutheranism, and Calvinism.

The Enlightenment

In the Enlightenment, also known as the *Age of Reason,* that followed the Renaissance, Europe began to move toward a view that men were capable of improving the world, including themselves, through rational thinking. The Enlightenment placed a heavy emphasis on individualism and rationalism. During the Renaissance, scholars looked at the Middle Ages as a lost period and considered their own time as modern and new. The Enlightenment, building on the foundations of humanism, began a prolific era of literature, philosophy, and invention.

By the 1700s, Europe had entered the High Enlightenment Age, where events started to take place as a result of the rational thought promoted by the first half of the age. The idea that everything in the universe could be reasoned and cataloged became a theme that set Diderot to work at the first encyclopedia and inspired Thomas Paine and Thomas Jefferson during the initial political unrest in the American colonies.

In the later years of the Enlightenment, the ideal vision that society could be reborn through reason was tested in the French Revolution of 1789. Instead of becoming a leader in rational thinking and orderly government, the revolution turned into the Reign of Terror that saw the mass execution of French citizens and opened the way for the rise of Napoleon.

American Revolution

The American Revolution occurred as a result of changing values in the Thirteen Colonies that broke from their traditional relationship with England. Early on in the colonization of North America, the colonial social structure tried to mirror the stratified order of Great Britain. In England, the landed elites were seen as intellectually and morally superior to the common man, which led to a paternalistic relationship. This style of governance was similarly applied to the colonial system; government was left to the property-owning upper class, and the colonies as a whole could be seen as a child dutifully serving "Mother England."

However, the colonies' distance from England meant that actual, hereditary aristocrats from Britain only formed a small percentage of the overall population and did not even fill all the positions of power. By the mid-eighteenth century, much of the American upper class consisted of local families who acquired status through business rather than lineage. Despite this, representatives from Britain were appointed to govern the colonies. As a result, a rift began to form between the colonists and British officials.

Uncertain about whether they should remain loyal to Britain, representatives from twelve colonies formed the First Continental Congress in 1774 to discuss what they should do next. When Patriot militiamen at Lexington and Concord fought British soldiers in April 1775, the Revolutionary War began. While the rebel forces worked to present the struggle as a united, patriotic effort, the colonies remained divided throughout the war. Thousands of colonists, known as Loyalists or Tories, supported Britain. Even the revolutionaries proved to be significantly fragmented, and many militias only served in their home states. The Continental Congress was also divided over whether to reconcile with Britain or push for full separation. These issues hindered the ability of the revolutionary armies to resist the British, who had superior training and resources at their disposal.

Even so, the Continental Army, under General George Washington, gradually built up a force that utilized Prussian military training and backwoods guerrilla tactics to make up for their limited resources. Although the British forces continued to win significant battles, the Continental Army gradually reduced Britain's will to fight as the years passed. Furthermore, Americans appealed to the rivalry that other European nations had with the British Empire. The support was initially limited to indirect assistance, but aid gradually increased. After the American victory at the Battle of Saratoga in 1777, France and other nations began to actively support the American cause by providing much-needed troops and equipment.

In 1781, the primary British army under General Cornwallis was defeated by an American and French coalition at Virginia, which paved the way for negotiations. The Treaty of Paris in 1783 ended the war, recognized the former colonies' independence from Great Britain, and gave America control over territory between the Appalachian Mountains and Mississippi River. However, the state of the new nation was still uncertain. The new nation's government initially stemmed from the state-based structure of the Continental Congress and was incorporated into the Articles of Confederation in 1777.

French Revolution

Unlike the United States' revolution against a ruler across the ocean, the French Revolution was an internal fight. In 1789, tension between the lower class (peasants) and middle class(bourgeois) and the extravagant wealthy upper class of France came to a head. The Old Regime, headed by the monarchy, was overthrown, and the Third Estate, made up of the bourgeois class, seized power. The American Revolution, overtaxation, years of bad harvests, drastic income inequality, and the Enlightenment influenced the French Revolution. In August 1789, the National Constituent Assembly, a democratic assembly formed during the French Revolution, passed the Declaration of the Rights of Man and of the Citizen, which defined the natural right of men to be free and equal under the law.

Napoleon

France radically changed the government from a monarchy to a democracy with provisions for civil rights, religious freedoms, and decriminalization of various morality crimes, like same-sex relationships. Two political powers emerged: liberal republicans called *Girondists* and radical revolutionaries, known as *Jacobins*. Conflict between the parties resulted in the Reign of Terror—a period of mass executions— and eventually the rise of Napoleon who set up a nationalist military dictatorship. During the revolution, Napoleon Bonaparte consolidated power after becoming famous for his heroism during the revolutionary wars against Britain, Austria, and other monarchies that sought to retain their right of royal rule. However, by 1804, Napoleon declared himself emperor and remilitarized France, and he conquered most of Europe in a series of global conflicts collectively known as the *Napoleonic Wars,* starting in 1803 and continuing until Napoleon's defeat at the Battle of Waterloo in 1815.

After the chaos sparked by the French Revolution that fanned across Europe during the revolutionary wars, European powers met at the Congress of Vienna in November 1814 to June 1815 to rebalance power and restore old boundaries. The Congress of Vienna carved out new territories, changing the map of Europe. France lost all of its conquered territories, while Prussia, Austria, and Russia expanded their own. With the restoration of a balance of power, Europe enjoyed nearly fifty years of peace.

Latin American Wars of Independence

Fueled by the successful American Revolution, Napoleon's rise to power, and the writings of the Enlightenment, a spirit of revolution swept across the Americas. The French colony in Haiti was the first major revolution occurring in 1791. The Haitian Revolution was the largest slave uprising since the Roman Empire, and it holds a unique place in history because it is the only slave uprising to establish a slave-free nation ruled by nonwhites and former slaves. In 1804, the Haitians achieved independence and became the first independent nation in Latin America. When Napoleon conquered Spain in 1808, Latin American colonies refused to recognize his elder brother, Joseph Bonaparte, as the new Spanish monarch and advocated for their own independence. Known as the *Latin American Wars of Independence,* Venezuela, Colombia, Ecuador, Argentina, Uruguay, Paraguay, Chile, Peru, and Bolivia all achieved independence between 1810 and 1830. In 1824, Mexico declared itself a republic when, after several attempts by the lower classes of Mexico to revolt, the wealthier classes joined and launched a final and successful revolt. When Napoleon overtook Portugal, King John VI fled to Brazil and set up court. Later he left his son Pedro behind to rule. Pedro launched a revolution that saw him crowned emperor.

By the mid-1800s, the revolutions of Latin America ceased, and only a few areas remained under European rule. The U.S. President James Monroe issued the Monroe Doctrine, which stated that the Americas could no longer be colonized. It was an attempt to stop European nations, especially Spain, from colonizing areas or attempting to recapture areas. England's navy contributed to the success of the doctrine, as they were eager to increase trade with the Americas and establish an alliance with the United States.

First World War

The onset of World War I began with the precarious balance of power and the geographic divisions written by the Napoleonic Wars' Vienna Congress.

Austria-Hungary's large empire was diverse in culture and included various peoples of several races, languages, and beliefs. However, minorities in their lands in the Balkans grew tired of foreign control. This was especially true in Bosnia, which was all but under control by the nationalistic secret military society, the Black Hand. This nationalistic sentiment grew until, in 1914, Gavrilo Princip, a Serb patriot and member of the Black Hand, assassinated Archduke Franz Ferdinand, heir presumptive to the throne of Austria-Hungary. In response, Emperor Franz Joseph I of Austria-Hungary declared war on the kingdom of Serbia, officially launching the First World War.

Europe had tied itself into a tangled web of alliances and mutual protection pacts. Germany and Austria-Hungary were allies. Russia promised protection to France and Serbia, and England maintained a tacit support to its past allies throughout the mainland. Each of the Allies soon mobilized to support each other. Germany had already planned for declarations of war, however, and was nervous about fighting a two-border war against both France and Russia, so it developed the Schlieffen Plan—a strategy to quickly demolish French resistance before turning around to fight Russia on the Eastern Front. However, this plan relied on the neutrality of England; after Germany invaded Belgium to attack France, England's declaration of war ensured that a long war would be inevitable.

The Great War lasted from 1914 to 1918 and was the deadliest war in European history until World War II, with approximately 16 million combatants and civilians dying in the conflict. The carnage was largely a result of technological innovation outpacing military tactics. World War I was the first military conflict to deploy millions of soldiers and the first war to involve telephones, tanks, aircrafts, chemical weapons, and heavy artillery. These twentieth-century technological innovations were deployed alongside outdated military tactics, particularly trench warfare. As a result, hundreds of thousands of troops would die during battles without achieving any meaningful strategic gains. Countries were devastated by the loss of the male population and struggled to cope with a depleted workforce, and widows and orphans struggled to regain any degree of normalcy.

Due to the high death tolls, the Allies' need of the financial support, and the anger associated with the war, the Treaty of Versailles harshly punished Germany, who the Allies blamed for the war. The Allies coerced Germany into signing the treaty that was a death sentence to their country's economy. It contained a "guilt clause," which, unlike the Congress of Vienna's terms for the similarly belligerent France, made oppressive demands on Germany. The treaty took German lands, enforced a heavy reparations debt that was impossible to pay, and stripped Germany of its colonies. After suffering enormous losses during the war itself, the Treaty of Versailles ensured that no national recovery would be possible.

In the aftermath, Russia, Italy, and Germany turned to totalitarian governments, and colonies of Europe started to have nationalistic, anticolonial movements. The Russian Revolution of 1917 led to a civil war in which the Bolsheviks, or Communists, took control under the guidance of Communist revolutionary Vladimir Lenin and established the Soviet Union. The Communist government turned into a dictatorship when Stalin emerged as leader in 1924. Stalin ruled with an iron fist and executed all of his political opponents, including the Bolsheviks. Dissatisfaction with the treaty in Italy led to the rise of fascist leader Benito Mussolini. Germany suffered through several small revolutions, splintering political parties, and class division; this, combined with wartime debt and hyperinflation—a result of the Treaty of Versailles—caused many to become desperate, especially during the throes of the Great Depression. Adolf Hitler, a popular leader in the National Socialist German Workers' Party (Nazi Party), organized street violence against Communists. In the 1932 parliamentary elections, the Nazis emerged as the largest party in the *Reichstag* (German Parliament), but the Nazis did not have enough votes to name Hitler as chancellor. The street violence against Communists and Jews continued unabated, and on

January 30, 1933, political pressure led to President von Hindenburg naming Adolf Hitler the chancellor of Germany. Hitler immediately expelled Communists, the second most popular political party, from the *Reichstag*, and coerced the *Reichstag* to pass the Enabling Act of 1933, effectively creating a dictatorship.

Second World War

Nazi Germany had risen to power through the 1920s and 1930s, with Hitler's belief that Germany would only recover its honor if it had a resounding military victory over Europe. Nazi ideology adhered to an extreme nationalism advocating for the superiority of the German people and the necessity of expanding their lands into an empire. Jews, Communists, and other nonconformists were banned from political and social participation.

In 1936, German troops violated the Treaty of Versailles by moving outside Germany's borders, with a remilitarization of the Rhineland. The Rome-Berlin Axis, an alliance between Germany and Italy, was forged in the same year. Germany was the only European power to support Italy's invasion and annexation of Ethiopia, and in exchange, Italy supported Germany's annexation of Austria. In 1936, a civil war broke out in Spain between Spanish nationalist rebels and the government of the Spanish Republic. Mussolini and Hitler supported the Spanish nationalist general Francisco Franco and used the Spanish Civil War as a testing ground for their new alliance. The Allies did not respond to these actions, and when Germany demanded the return of the Sudetenland, a territory in Czechoslovakia, France and Great Britain agreed in hopes of an appeasement despite the protests of the Czech government. Hitler then moved into more areas farther afield, which prompted the Soviet Union to sign a nonaggression pact with Germany. On September 1, 1939, Germany invaded Poland, and on September 3, 1939, France and Great Britain declared war on Germany, jumpstarting the deadliest conflict in world history.

Although less discussed than the Holocaust, the Japanese military committed similar war crimes across Asia, executing between three and ten million Chinese and Koreans, among others, between 1937 and 1945. In one event, the Rape of Nanking, Japanese soldiers captured Nanking and brutally murdered 300,000 civilians. An additional twenty thousand women, children, and elderly were raped during the massacre. Japanese newspapers closely covered a contest between two Japanese officers to see who could kill more people with a sword during the Rape of Nanking. Stalin also committed heinous war crimes during World War II, with estimates ranging from four to ten million deaths as a result of executions and sentences to the Gulag. The United States has also faced criticism for its decision to drop two nuclear bombs on the Japanese cities of Hiroshima and Nagasaki, killing more than 129,000 civilians, leveling both cities, and ending the war. The American government justified the use of nuclear weapons as the only way to avoid a ground invasion of Japan that would have cost more Japanese and American lives than the bombs.

Towns and cities had been leveled, civilian and soldier death tolls were crippling to economies, and countries struggled well into the 1950s to recover economically. It became a breeding ground for Communism, and in China, the end of the war meant a reprisal of the civil war between Mao Zedong's Communists and nationalists that had been interrupted by world war. Another result of the war was a changed map of the world, as countries were divided or newly formed, and the end of most of Britain's colonialism occurred as a result of the empire's economic and military losses. Following the war, Great Britain, France, Portugal, Belgium, Italy, the Netherlands, and Japan had either granted freedom to colonies or lost areas during the war. Many African and Middle Eastern countries would be granted their independence; however, the newly formed countries' borders were drawn according to those of the former colonies, creating ethnic and religious tensions that still exist today.

In an effort to stop a world war from occurring again, the Allies created the United Nations to be a safeguard and upholder of peace. This proved especially important, yet difficult, as the world was divided between a capitalist Western bloc and a Communist Eastern bloc. Germany was divided between the United States and Soviet Union to maintain peace and to better control the reconstruction of Germany; occupation zones were established, with East Germany occupied by the Soviet Union and West Germany occupied by Great Britain, France, and the United States.

Industrialization, Nationalism, Immigration, and Globalization in Modern World History

Industrialization

In the modern world, industrialization is the initial key to modernization and development. For developed nations, the process of industrialization took place centuries ago. England, where the *Industrial Revolution* began, actually began to produce products in factories in the early 1700s. Later, the United States and some nations of Western Europe followed suit, using raw materials brought in from their colonies abroad to make finished products. For example, cotton was spun into fabric on elaborate weaving machines that mass-produced textiles. As a result, nations that perfected the textile process were able to sell their products around the world, which produced enormous profits. Over time, those nations were able to accumulate wealth, improve their nation's infrastructure, and provide more services for their citizens. Similar to the events of the eighteenth and nineteenth centuries, nations throughout the world are undergoing the same process in today's world. China exemplifies this concept. In China, agriculture was once the predominant occupation, and although it is true that agriculture is still a dominant sector of the Chinese economy, millions of Chinese citizens are flocking to major cities like Beijing, Shanghai, and Hangzhou, due to the availability of factory jobs that allow its workers a certain element of *social mobility*, or the ability to rise up out of one's socioeconomic situation.

Nationalism and Imperialism

With most revolutions, nationalism, or the devotion to one's country, plays a central role. The American and French revolutions, along with the revolutions of Latin America, were fought with the desire to improve the prosperity and position of its civilians. After the Napoleonic Wars and the Congress of Vienna, the years of undisturbed peace resulted in a buildup of nationalism. Countries like Italy and Poland resented Austrian and Russian rule as much as they had disliked French occupation. A rise in nationalism in Germany was a constant threat to Austria, as it tried to govern multiple cultures and languages across a wide geographic area. The precarious situation would remain hostile to some degree until the outbreak of World War I. The Industrial Revolution had made the lower and middle classes restless for change and improvements. By 1848, uprisings began to spring up all over Europe, beginning with France. Many who had nationalistic leanings toward a country that was either no longer in existence or had been forced into another country were able to separate from other nations. The Hungarians broke with Vienna, though they were forced back soon after, the Romanians split from papal power, and the Italians threatened rebellion.

The development of imperialism began in the mid-nineteenth century and lasted until the twentieth century, with much of the imperialized world gaining freedom after World Wars I and II. The spread of imperialism that was to follow the revolutions of the eighteenth and nineteenth centuries can be traced, in part, to the idea of nationalism. Some countries believed they were doing a good, and even a moral, thing by conquering and colonizing new territory to spread their culture, traditions, religion, and government. However, a darker side of nationalism—the feeling of superiority and right—caused the takeover of areas and the enforcement of foreign rules and laws.

Globalization

The world economy also became increasingly interconnected during the post-World War II era. This accelerated the process of globalization, which is the integration of ideas and products from different cultures. This benefitted the United States economically because businesses, such as McDonald's and Coca-Cola, found many consumers around the world who were eager to consume American goods. However, the process works both ways, and many aspects of foreign culture, such as Japanese cartoons and animation, have become very popular in the United States. Many critics also point out that globalization has hurt the American economy in recent decades because manufacturing jobs have gone overseas to countries in South America and Asia where wages are low.

Immigration

Immigration has changed the demographics of countries and can have positive and negative effects. Migration and immigration have occurred due to famine, warfare, and lack of economic prospects. Immigration can aid countries struggling to maintain a workforce, and it can also bring in needed medical professionals, scientists, and others with special training. However, immigration also puts strain on developed economies to support migrants who arrive without the necessary education and training to thrive in the advanced economies. Until recently, immigrants were encouraged, or in some cases, forced to assimilate and take on the customs and culture of their new country. For example, in the United States, legislation was passed to force German immigrants to learn English. More recently, developed countries have struggled to assimilate new arrivals to their countries, such as the recent surge of refugees into Europe. Unfortunately, the failure to adequately assimilate immigrants has created greater inequality and prevalence of radical behavior.

United States History

Early Exploration, Colonial Era, and the War for Independence

Age of Exploration

When examining how Europeans explored what would become the United States of America, one must first examine why Europeans came to explore the New World as a whole. In the fifteenth century, tensions increased between the Eastern and Mediterranean nations of Europe and the expanding Ottoman Empire to the east. As war and piracy spread across the Mediterranean, the once-prosperous trade routes across Asia's Silk Road began to decline, and nations across Europe began to explore alternative routes for trade.

Italian explorer Christopher Columbus proposed a westward route. Contrary to popular lore, the main challenge that Columbus faced in finding backers was not proving that the world was round. Much of Europe's educated elite knew that the world was round; the real issue was that they rightly believed that a westward route to Asia, assuming a lack of obstacles, would be too long to be practical. Nevertheless, Columbus set sail in 1492 after obtaining support from Spain and arrived in the West Indies three months later.

Spain launched further expeditions to the new continents and established *New Spain*. The colony consisted not only of Central America and Mexico, but also the American Southwest and Florida. France claimed much of what would become Canada, along with the Mississippi River region and the Midwest. In addition, the Dutch established colonies that covered New Jersey, New York, and Connecticut. Each nation managed its colonies differently, and thus influenced how they would assimilate into the United States. For instance, Spain strove to establish a system of Christian missions throughout its territory, while France focused on trading networks and had limited infrastructure in regions such as the Midwest.

Even in cases of limited colonial growth, the land of America was hardly vacant, because a diverse array of Native American nations and groups were already present. Throughout much of colonial history, European settlers commonly misperceived native peoples as a singular, static entity. In reality, Native Americans had a variety of traditions depending on their history and environment, and their culture continued to change through the course of interactions with European settlers; for instance, tribes such as the Cheyenne and Comanche used horses, which were introduced by white settlers, to become powerful warrior nations. However, a few generalizations can be made: many, but not all, tribes were matrilineal, which gave women a fair degree of power, and land was commonly seen as belonging to everyone. These differences, particularly European settlers' continual focus on land ownership, contributed to increasing prejudice and violence.

The Americas During the Colonial Period

Interactions Among American Indians
Native Americans played an important role in the early history of Britain's North American colonies. Squanto was an Algonquian Indian who helped English settlers in Massachusetts survive by teaching them how to plant native crops. Some Native American tribes were friendly towards the colonists and traded with them.

However, Native Americans and Europeans often came into conflict, frequently over land disputes. The Native Americans and Europeans had very different concepts of land use and ownership. Native Americans did not understand the concept of landownership or sale. When they entered into agreements with the colonists, Native Americans thought they were allowing the settlers to farm the land temporarily, rather than retain it in perpetuity. On the other hand, colonists were frustrated when Native Americans continued to hunt and fish on lands they had "sold." These, and other disagreements, eventually led to bloody conflicts that gradually weakened Native American tribes.

Native Americans were also vulnerable to diseases to which the Europeans had developed immunity. These diseases included bubonic plague, cholera, chicken pox, pneumonic plague, influenza, measles, scarlet fever, typhus, smallpox, and tuberculosis. These diseases killed millions of Native Americans and were sometimes used as a biological weapon. Historians estimate that as much as 80 percent of the Native American population died through disease and warfare.

The southern colonies, including Virginia, Maryland, the Carolinas, and Georgia, were also organized by county. The southern economy focused on labor-intensive crops such as tobacco and rice, and as a result, landowners relied on indentured servants and African slaves. Slaves were present in most colonies, but were more common in the south.

Establishment of the Thirteen Colonies
News of his success sparked a number of other expeditions and the British, French, Dutch, Spanish, and Portuguese all eventually laid claim to lands in the New World. Columbus himself made three more voyages to the Americas. The French and Dutch focused mostly on the lucrative fur trade in North America. The Spanish and Portuguese sought gold in Central and South America but also tried to convert Native Americans to Christianity. British settlers also sought economic opportunity and created the first British colony at Jamestown, Virginia, in 1607. However, the Puritans who landed at Plymouth Rock in 1620 left for the New World in order to establish their ideal religious community.

Connecticut, New Hampshire, Massachusetts, and Rhode Island were considered the "New England colonies." The settlements in New England were based around an economy focused on fishing and lumber. These colonies maintained puritanical and Congregationalist religious beliefs. While English Puritans mostly settled in New England, a wide variety of colonists settled in the mid-Atlantic region. English, Scottish, Dutch, and Swedish settlers came to Delaware, New York, New Jersey, and Pennsylvania. As a result, the mid-Atlantic colonies were more religiously diverse and tolerant than the settlements in New England. Agriculture was the foundation of the economy in mid-Atlantic colonies. This meant that settlements were more dispersed. Government and administration were based on counties instead of towns.

Political power was also distributed differently among the colonies. Some colonies, such as New York and Virginia, were royal colonies ruled directly by the king. Pennsylvania was a proprietary colony—the king allowed William Penn to appoint officials and govern the colony as he saw fit. Corporate colonies, such as Rhode Island and Connecticut, were administered by a group of investors. But, by the early 1700s, the king had revoked the charters of most proprietary and corporate colonies and assumed direct control himself.

Development of Colonial Society
Situated on the Atlantic Coast, the Thirteen Colonies that would become the United States of America constituted only a small portion of North America. Even those colonies had significant differences that stemmed from their different origins. For instance, the Virginia colony under John Smith in 1607 started

with male bachelors seeking gold, whereas families of Puritans settled Massachusetts. As a result, the Thirteen Colonies—Virginia, Massachusetts, Connecticut, Maryland, New York, New Jersey, Pennsylvania, Delaware, Rhode Island, New Hampshire, Georgia, North Carolina, and South Carolina— had different structures and customs that would each influence the United States.

Britain continued to hold onto its other colonies, such as Canada and the West Indies, which reflects the continued power of multiple nations across North America, even as the United States began to expand across the continent. Many Americans advocated expansion regardless of the land's current inhabitants, but the results were often mixed. Still, events both abroad and within North America contributed to the growth of the United States. For instance, the rising tumult in France during the French Revolution and the rise of Napoleon led France to sell the Louisiana Purchase, a large chunk of land consisting not only of Louisiana but also much of the Midwest, to the United States in 1803. Meanwhile, as Spanish power declined, Mexico claimed independence in 1821, but the new nation became increasingly vulnerable to foreign pressure. In the Mexican-American War from 1846 to 1848, Mexico surrendered territory to the United States that eventually became California, Nevada, Utah, and New Mexico, as well as parts of Arizona, Colorado, and Wyoming.

Even as the United States sought new inland territory, American interests were also expanding overseas via trade. As early as 1784, the ship *Empress of China* traveled to China to establish trading connections. American interests had international dimensions throughout the nation's history. For instance, during the presidency of Andrew Jackson, the ship *Potomac* was dispatched to the Pacific island of Sumatra in 1832 to avenge the deaths of American sailors. This incident exemplifies how U.S. foreign trade connected with imperial expansion.

This combination of continental and seaward growth adds a deeper layer to American development, because it was not purely focused on western expansion. For example, take the 1849 Gold Rush; a large number of Americans and other immigrants traveled to California by ship and settled western territories before more eastern areas, such as Nevada and Idaho. Therefore, the United States' early history of colonization and expansion is a complex network of diverse cultures.

Revolutionary Era

Competition among several imperial powers in eastern areas of North America led to conflicts that would later bring about the independence of the United States. The Seven Years' War from 1756 to 1763, also known as the French and Indian War, ended with Great Britain claiming France's Canadian territories as well as the Ohio Valley. The same war was costly for all the powers involved, which led to increased taxes on the Thirteen Colonies. In addition, the new lands to the west of the colonies attracted new settlers, and they came into conflict with Native Americans and British troops that were trying to maintain the traditional boundaries. These growing tensions with Great Britain, as well as other issues, eventually led to the American Revolution, which ended with Britain relinquishing its control of the colonies.

A number of political acts by the British monarchy also led to more discontent among the colonies. After the French and Indian War ended in 1763, the king declared that the colonists could not settle west of the Appalachian Mountains. This was known as the Proclamation of 1763. Many colonists were frustrated because they had expected this territory would be open for expansion after the French had been defeated.

Additionally, taxes were imposed in an effort to help reduce the debt Britain amassed during the French and Indian War. In 1764, Parliament passed the Sugar Act, which reduced the tax on molasses but also provided for greater enforcement powers. Some colonists protested by organizing boycotts on British goods. One year later, in 1765, Parliament passed the Quartering Act, which required colonists to provide housing and food to British troops. This law was also very unpopular and led to protests in the North American colonies.

The Stamp Act of 1765 required the colonists to pay a tax on legal documents, newspapers, magazines and other printed materials. Colonial assemblies protested the tax and petitioned the British government in order to have it repealed. Merchants also organized boycotts and established correspondence committees in order to share information. Eventually, Parliament repealed the Stamp Act but simultaneously reaffirmed the Crown's right to tax the colonies.

In 1767, Parliament introduced the Townshend Acts, which imposed a tax on goods the colonies imported from Britain, such as tea, lead, paint, glass, and paper. The colonies protested again and British imperial officials were assaulted in some cases. The British government sent additional troops to North America to restore order. The arrival of troops in Boston only led to more tension that eventually culminated in the Boston Massacre in 1770, where five colonists were killed and eight were wounded. Except for the duty on tea, most of Townshend Act taxes were repealed after the Boston Massacre.

Parliament passed the Tea Act in 1773 and, although it actually reduced the tax on tea, it was another unpopular piece of legislation. The Tea Act allowed the British East India Company to sell its products directly, effectively cutting out colonial merchants and stirring more Anglo-American anger and resentment. This resulted in the Boston Tea Party in 1773, an incident in which colonial tea merchants disguised themselves as Indians before storming several British ships that were anchored in Boston harbor. Once aboard, the disguised colonists dumped more than 300 chests of tea into the water.

Because the British government was unable to identify the perpetrators, Parliament passed a series of laws that punished the entire colony of Massachusetts. These acts were known as the Coercive or Intolerable Acts. The first law closed the port of Boston until the tea had been paid for (an estimated $1.7 million in today's currency). The second act curtailed the authority of Massachusetts' colonial government. Instead of being elected by colonists, most government officials were now appointed by the king. In addition, the act restricted town meetings, the basic form of government in Massachusetts, and limited most villages to one meeting per year. This act angered colonists throughout the thirteen colonies because they feared their rights could be stripped away as well. A third act allowed for British soldiers to be tried in Britain if they were accused of a crime. The fourth act once again required colonists to provide food and shelter to British soldiers.

Colonists responded by forming the First Continental Congress in 1774, and all the colonies except for Georgia sent delegates. The delegates sought a compromise with the British government instead of launching an armed revolt. The First Continental Congress sent a petition to King George III affirming their loyalty but demanding the repeal of the Intolerable Acts. The delegates organized a boycott of imports from and exports to Britain until their demands were met.

The colonists began to form militias and gather weapons and ammunition. The first battle of the revolution began at Lexington and Concord in April 1775 when British troops tried to seize a supply of gunpowder and were confronted by about eighty Minutemen. A brief skirmish left eight colonists dead and ten wounded. Colonial reinforcements poured in and harassed the British force as they retreated to Boston. Although the battle did not result in many casualties, it marked the beginning of war.

A month later, the Second Continental Congress convened in Philadelphia. The delegates formed an army and appointed George Washington as commander in chief. Delegates were still reluctant to repudiate their allegiance to King George III and did not do so until they issued the Declaration of Independence on July 4, 1776. The Declaration drew on the ideas of the Enlightenment and declared that the colonists had the right to life, liberty, and the pursuit of happiness. The Declaration stated that the colonists had to break away from Britain because King George III had violated their rights.

After the Battle of Lexington and Concord, British troops retreated to Boston and the colonial militias laid siege to the city. Colonists built fortifications on Bunker Hill outside the city and British troops attacked the position in June 1775. The colonists inflicted heavy casualties on the British and killed a number of officers. However, the defenders ran out of ammunition and British troops captured Bunker Hill on the third assault. Although it was a defeat for the colonists, the Battle of Bunker Hill demonstrated that they could stand and fight against the disciplined and professional British army.

The British army initially had the upper hand and defeated colonial forces in a number of engagements. The Americans did not achieve a victory until the Battle of Trenton in December 1776. Washington famously crossed the Delaware River on Christmas Day and launched a surprise attack against Hessian mercenaries. They captured more than 1,000 soldiers and suffered very minimal casualties. The victory at Trenton bolstered American morale and showed that they could defeat professional European soldiers.

The Battle of Saratoga in New York in the fall of 1777 was an important turning point in the American War for Independence. American troops surrounded and captured more than 6,000 British soldiers. This victory convinced the French king to support the revolutionaries by sending troops, money, weapons, and ships to the American continent. French officers who fought alongside the Patriots brought back many ideas with them that eventually sparked a revolution in France in 1789.

The Development of the Constitution and the Early Republic

Constitutional Era and the Early Republic

America's first system of government was actually laid out in the Articles of Confederation, and not the Constitution. The Articles of Confederation were ratified during the Revolutionary War and went into effect in 1781. The Articles of Confederation created a relatively weak central government and allowed individual states to retain most of the power. Under this system, the national government did not have a president or judiciary. Each state had only one vote in the Confederation Congress and most major decisions required unanimous approval by all thirteen states. Despite this requirement, the Confederation Congress did pass some important legislation, including the Northwest Ordinance, which organized the land west of Appalachian Mountains. The territories eventually became the states of Ohio, Indiana, Michigan, Illinois, Wisconsin, and Minnesota. However, Congress did not have the power to tax and could only request money from the states without any way to enforce its demands. A Revolutionary War veteran named Daniel Shays led an armed insurrection in western Massachusetts in 1787. Although Shay's Rebellion was defeated, it drew attention to the weaknesses of the Articles of Confederation.

The Constitutional Convention met in Philadelphia a few months after the rebellion in order to create a stronger federal government. However, delegates disagreed over how to structure the new system. The Virginia Plan was one proposal that included a bicameral legislature where states were awarded representation based on their population size. This would benefit more populous states at the expense of smaller states. The other main proposal was the New Jersey Plan, which retained many elements of the Articles of Confederation, including a unicameral legislature with one vote per state. This plan would put states on an equal footing regardless of population.

Eventually, delegates agreed to support the Connecticut Compromise (also known as the Great Compromise), which incorporated elements from both the Virginia and New Jersey Plans. Under the new Constitution, Congress would be a bicameral body. In the House of Representatives, states would be allocated seats based on population, but in the Senate each state would have two votes. The Constitution also included a president and judiciary that would each serve to check the power of other branches of government. In addition, Congress had the power to tax and had more enforcement powers.

Slavery was another contentious issue during the Constitutional Convention. Slavery was more common in the Southern states and less common in the North. The Southern states wanted slaves to be counted when calculating representation in Congress but not when it came to assessing taxes. Northern states wanted the opposite and eventually the two sides agreed to the Three-Fifths Compromise where slaves were counted as three-fifths of a person for the purposes of both taxation and representation. The Constitution also included a provision that allowed slave owners to recover slaves who had escaped and permitted the international slave trade to continue until 1808.

Once the Constitution had been drafted, nine of the thirteen states had to ratify it. Vigorous debate erupted over whether or not the Constitution should be approved. Two different political factions emerged. The Federalists supported the Constitution because they felt a stronger central government was necessary in order to promote economic growth and improve national security. Several leading federalists, including Alexander Hamilton, John Jay, and James Madison, published a series of articles urging voters to support the Constitution. However, the Anti-Federalists, including Thomas Jefferson and Patrick Henry, felt that the Constitution took too much power away from the states and gave it to the national government. They also thought there weren't enough protections for individual rights and lobbied for the addition of a Bill of Rights that guaranteed basic liberties. Ultimately, the Constitution was ratified in 1788 and the Bill of Rights was approved a year later.

The Electoral College unanimously elected George Washington as the nation's first president in 1789. Despite this appearance of unity, deep political divisions led to the formation of the nation's first party system. Washington supported the Federalist ideology and appointed several Federalists to his cabinet, including Alexander Hamilton as secretary of the treasury. The Anti-Federalist faction evolved into the Democratic-Republican Party and favored stronger state governments instead of a powerful federal government. As settlers moved into the new Northwest Territories, Washington helped pacify Indians who opposed further expansion. He also successfully put down a rebellion in western Pennsylvania by farmers opposed to a federal tax on whiskey.

Washington declined to seek a third term and another Federalist, John Adams, became our second president. Adams signed the Alien and Sedition Acts, which made it a criminal offense to criticize the government, and allowed the president to deport aliens suspected of treason. Adams and the Federalists argued that the laws were necessary in order to improve security as Europe became embroiled in a war against the new French republic. Jefferson and the Democratic-Republicans said the laws restricted free speech. Jefferson made the acts an important topic in 1800 when he successfully ran for president.

Jefferson's victory marked a turning point in the political system because the Democratic-Republicans gained more power while the Federalists went into decline. He repealed the Alien and Sedition Acts when he was elected. The Federalists were further weakened when Hamilton was killed in a duel in 1804.

Jefferson accomplished several significant achievements during his presidency, and one of the most important was the Louisiana Purchase in 1803. For $15 million, Jefferson bought French territory west of the Mississippi River that doubled the size of the United States. He then appointed Meriwether Lewis and William Clark to lead an expedition to explore the vast new territory and study its geography, vegetation, and plant life. Clark also brought his African-American slave, York, on the journey. York helped hunt and even saved Clark's life during a flood. The expedition was also aided by Sacagawea, a Shoshone woman, who acted as a guide and interpreter. The explorers also established relations with Native American tribes and set the stage for further western expansion in the 1800s.

Civil War and Reconstruction

American Civil War and Reconstruction

Civil War

The First Battle of Bull Run (also known as the First Battle of Manassas) in 1861 was the first major infantry engagement of the Civil War. Both the Northern and Southern troops were inexperienced and although they had equal numbers, the Confederates emerged victorious. Many had thought the war would be short, but it continued for another four years.

The Union navy imposed a blockade on the Confederacy and captured the port of New Orleans in 1862. The Union navy was much stronger than the Confederate fleet and prevented the Southern states from selling cotton to foreign countries or buying weapons.

In 1862, Union forces thwarted a Confederate invasion of Maryland at the Battle of Antietam. This engagement was the single bloodiest day of the war and more than 23,000 men on both sides were killed or wounded. Union troops forced the Confederates to retreat, and that gave Lincoln the political capital he needed to issue the Emancipation Proclamation in 1863. This declaration did not abolish slavery, but it did free slaves in Southern territory. It also allowed African Americans to join the Union navy and about 200,000 did so. The 54th Massachusetts Infantry was a famous unit of African American soldiers who led an assault on Fort Wagner in South Carolina in 1863. Although the attack failed, the 54th Massachusetts witnessed African American troops fighting bravely under fire.

The Siege of Vicksburg in 1863 was a major Union victory because they gained control of the Mississippi River and cut the Confederacy in half. This made it difficult the Confederacy to move troops around and communicate with their forces. Grant commanded the Northern forces in the siege and eventually became the Union army's top general.

The Battle of Gettysburg in 1863 marked the turning point of the Civil War. Robert E. Lee led Confederate troops into Pennsylvania, but in three days of heavy fighting, the Union army forced them to retreat. The victory bolstered Northern morale and weakened Southern resolve. Never again would Confederate forces threaten Northern territory.

In 1864, Union general William T. Sherman captured Atlanta and then marched more than 200 miles to Savannah. Along the way, he destroyed anything that could support the Southern war effort, such as railroads and cotton mills. At this point, the Southern economy was beginning to collapse. The North had more manpower than the South and could afford to sustain more casualties. The North also had more industrial capacity to produce weapons and supplies and more railroads to transport men and equipment.

Eventually, Robert E. Lee surrendered to Ulysses S. Grant at Appomattox, Virginia, on April 9, 1865. Five days later, John Wilkes Booth assassinated Lincoln in Washington D.C. Vice President Andrew Johnson, a Democrat, succeeded him and soon came into conflict with Republicans in Congress about how to reintegrate Southern states into the nation. This process was known as Reconstruction and lasted from 1865 to 1877.

Reconstruction Era

Johnson opposed equal rights for African Americans and pardoned many Confederate leaders. However, many Congressional Republicans wanted to harshly punish Southerners for their attempts to secede from the Union. They were known as Radical Republicans because they also wanted to give former slaves equal rights.

Johnson vetoed bills that were designed to protect the rights of freed slaves, but Congress overrode his vetoes. This led to increasing conflict between Johnson and Congress, which eventually caused Radical Republicans to impeach him. Although Johnson was acquitted in 1868, he had very little power, and Radical Republicans took control of the Reconstruction process.

Republicans passed three important constitutional amendments as part of the Reconstruction process. The 13th amendment was ratified in 1865, and it abolished slavery throughout the country. The 14th Amendment was ratified in 1868 and gave equal rights to all citizens. The 15th Amendment was ratified in 1870 and specifically granted all men the right to vote regardless of race.

Southerners resisted these demands and passed laws that prohibited freed slaves from owning weapons or testifying against whites. They also formed militias and vigilante groups, such as the Ku Klux Klan, in order to intimidate African Americans who tried to vote. Congress sent federal troops into Southern states in order to enforce the law and prevent vigilante violence.

After the much-disputed election of 1876, the Democrats offered to let the Republicans have the White House if they agreed to end Reconstruction. After the Republicans agreed, federal troops were withdrawn and African Americans in the South were subjected to discrimination until the Civil Rights movement of the 1960s. Scholars often consider the Reconstruction era the beginning of Jim Crow and a transition into a new form of "institutionalized racism" that still pervades much of modern U.S. society.

The Rise of Industrial America

Industrialization and Urbanization

Industrialization

After the end of the Civil War, America experienced a period of intense industrialization, immigration, and urbanization, and all three trends were interrelated. The process of industrialization had begun before the Civil War but expanded into more sectors of the economy in the later part of the century. This era is often called the Second Industrial Revolution and included growth in the chemical, petroleum, iron, steel, and telecommunications industries. For example, the Bessemer process made it much easier to produce high quality steel by removing impurities during the smelting process.

The writer Mark Twain called the late 19th century the Gilded Age because the era was also one of extreme social inequality. Some corporations expanded and began to control entire industries. For example, by 1890, the Standard Oil Company produced 88 percent of all the refined oil in the nation. This made a few individuals, such as John D. Rockefeller who owned Standard Oil, extremely wealthy. On the other hand, many workers earned low wages and began to form labor unions, such as the American Federation of Labor in 1886, in order to demand better working conditions and higher pay. Strikes were one of the most common ways workers could express their dissatisfaction, and the Pullman Strike of 1894 was one of the largest such incidents in the 19th century. Workers went on strike after the Pullman Company, which manufactured railroad cars, cut wages by about 25 percent. More than 125,000 workers around the country walked off the job and attacked workers hired to replace them. Federal troops were sent in to end the strike, and more than eighty workers were killed or wounded during confrontations. The strike was unsuccessful, but Congress passed a law making Labor Day a federal holiday in order to placate union members.

Immigration also played an important part in the economic and social changes that occurred during the late 19th century. Immigration patterns changed during this time and immigrants from Southern and Eastern Europe, such as Italy and Poland, began to surpass the number of arrivals from Northern and Western Europe. The immigrants sought economic opportunity in the United States because wages for unskilled workers were higher than in their home countries. Some Americans resented the influx of immigrants because they spoke different languages and practiced Catholicism. In 1924, Congress passed a law that restricted immigration from Southern and Eastern Europe.

Increased urbanization was the last factor that contributed to the rapid changes of the Gilded Age. Factories were located near cities in order to draw upon a large pool of potential employees. Immigrants flooded into cities in search of work, and new arrivals often settled in the same neighborhoods where their compatriots lived. Between 1860 and 1890, the urbanization rate increased from about 20 percent to 35 percent. Cities struggled to keep up with growing populations, and services such as sanitation and water often lagged behind demand. Immigrants often lived in crowded living conditions that facilitated the spread of diseases.

Urbanization

Factories were located near cities in order to draw upon a large pool of potential employees. Immigrants flooded into cities in search of work, and new arrivals often settled in the same neighborhoods where their compatriots lived. Between 1860 and 1890, the urbanization rate increased from about 20 percent to 35 percent. Cities struggled to keep up with growing populations, and services such as sanitation and water often lagged behind demand. Immigrants often lived in crowded living conditions that facilitated the spread of diseases.

California History

The Pre-Columbian Period Through the Gold Rush

Impact of California's Physical Geography on History

California is not only one of the most diverse states in terms of demographics; it is one of the most diverse with regard to physical geography and climate. In fact, it may be argued that the physical and climatic diversity of California has paved the way to its cultural and demographic diversity. As one of the largest states, California offers a breadth of unique geological and ecological features. It is home to the lowest point in the United States (Death Valley) and the highest peak in the contiguous states (Mount Whitney), making it home to both snowy peaks and arid deserts. It is also home to foggy redwood forests and sunny southern coastlands. As one of the westernmost states in the Union, California has benefited, historically speaking, from its remote position which, for the most part, helped it avoid the revolutionary upheavals, international battles, and civil wars of the nineteenth century. Its remoteness has also helped create an escapist aura that surrounds California history. Its remote geography has helped make it a home for outlaws, gold miners, bandits, religious outcasts, Dust Bowl refugees, wanderlust-struck travelers, Hollywood hopefuls, down-and-out homeless citizens, documented and undocumented immigrants, civically engaged hipsters, and drug-induced hippies. The character of California's geographic landscape has helped make it a frontier of the American dream, its ideas, and its downfalls.

Geography, Economic Activities, Folklore, and Religion of California's American Indian Peoples

Isolated in their own right by the geographic remoteness of California, and specifically the geographic remoteness caused by separation from the rest of the American continent by the Sierra Nevada mountains, the earliest American Indians in California remained alienated for several centuries before European colonization. Tribes scattered along the coasts and Central Valley of California "lived close to the soil," meaning they were primarily hunters and gatherers rather than traditional agriculturalists. These various tribes—which included the Hupa and Yurok—fed their families with acorns, snails, caterpillars, crickets, grubs, seafood, shellfish, cacti, roots, and game. Their weapons and gear were not as advanced as their European counterparts. They used pelts, skins, and moccasins to cover themselves when it was too cold to be naked. These tribes constructed primitive dwellings where they would barbecue and smoke meats and seafood. Their economy was mostly self-sustaining and built upon the backbone of bartering systems. They were governed by family structures and loose bonds with neighbors and were generally nomadic, wandering from place to place in search of food and shelter. Thus, their roving bands never reached the socio-governmental complexity of other early American Indian civilizations. In terms of religion and folklore, they believed the world was created by a flood, one that wiped out many creatures, and a supreme being only allowed the chosen ones to survive.

Spanish Exploration and Colonization

California transferred hands from the Spanish Crown to the Mexican Republic in 1821 when revolutionary leader Augustine Iturbide successfully led a revolt. Iturbide declared himself the emperor of the new Mexican government on May 19, 1822. Following this declaration, he began using the California region of North America as a dumping ground for those who went against the new revolutionary government. During this transition, the Mexican government disbanded the Spanish-Catholic missionary system in favor of a new secular system of governance. All officers from the presidios and all padres from the mission houses were obligated to pledge an oath of allegiance to the new Mexican Republic. California avoided the vortex of the revolutionary struggle for the most part but absorbed much of the tumult and uncertainty of its aftermath. The era of Mexican control in California was consequently wrought with aggravated local tensions. During this era, residents witnessed periodic challenges to gubernatorial leadership. The era even created a cultural rift between Northern and Southern California that continues—to a certain degree—to this day. The era was also ripe with American infiltration, as settlers from the east flocked to the fruits of the Wild West. The tumult and rifts of this era thus paved the way to the eventual cessation of the California territory following the Mexican-American War.

War Between Mexico and the United States

The war between the Mexican Republic and the United States was catalyzed by the American desire to carry forth its so-called Manifest Destiny to conquer all lands between the Atlantic Ocean and Pacific Ocean. The Mexican-American War was, first and foremost, a war of expansion—the U.S. government and its citizens honed in on Texas and California as possible lands for American annexation and/or Mexican cessation. Both territories had already witnessed an impressive infiltration of Anglo-American settlers that stirred U.S. sympathies. The Mexican-American War was also a war over resources—the U.S. government had its sights set on the cotton plantations of Texas and the gold, timber, crops, and minerals of California. Lastly, the Mexican-American War was a war that displaced domestic sectional tensions—the United States, on the eve of its own civil war, looked westward and southwestward in an attempt to solve the sectionalism ingrained in the American fiber. The new territories that were sought after became key players in the battle over slavery and abolition. In terms of consequences, the Mexican-American War opened up California for a brief Bear Flag Revolt that witnessed the declaration of an independent California Republic. The Bear Flag Republic was more romanticism than reality, however, and William Ide, the leader of the incipient skirmish, remains just a footnote in U.S. and California history. With the signing of the Treaty of Guadalupe-Hidalgo on February 2, 1848, the Mexican-American War officially ended, and the California region officially became a part of the United States. The California territory remained unsettled following the war, as government power slipped from the hands of Latinos into the hands of Anglo-Americans. As a result, Hispanic culture slowly slipped into isolated shadows, only to be revealed in more vibrant colors in later decades. The ensuing gold rush brought even more white settlers to cities like Los Angeles and San Francisco, paving the way to a new era of U.S. occupation.

The Discovery of Gold in California

Native Americans discovered gold in California years before the Anglo-American discovery of gold there. Nevertheless, the American historical mythos traditionally points to January 24, 1848, as the paradigm-shifting date of gold discovery on the North American continent. On this date, Scotsman James Wilson Marshall gathered up and inspected gold nuggets and flakes for the first time at Johann Sutter's infamous sawmill. This "discovery" set into motion decades of movement west from the urban corridors of the Northeast and Midwest to the gold mines of the Sierra Nevada mountains. The discovery was even applauded by President James K. Polk in a presidential address on December 5, 1848, creating more of a romantic allure about the California gold rush. By 1849, hundreds of thousands of settlers and immigrants flocked to the Golden Gate of San Francisco, California, to try their luck in mining and/or entrepreneurship. Culturally speaking, states like California quickly became hubs of diversity, serving as the homes of thousands of Chinese, Mexican, black, and American Indian laborers. Socially, however, these diversities created racial tensions, leading to the persecution of "racial others" by white settlers. Wars ensued between U.S. citizens and American Indians in the West, paving the way to the creation of more reservations. These racialized others were also exploited for railroad construction. Chinese immigrants eventually became demonized by white U.S. politicians, leading to the passage of the xenophobic (i.e., prejudice against foreigners) exclusion acts in the late nineteenth century. The Chinese Exclusion Act of 1882 is famous, for example, for embedding xenophobic sentiments into U.S. law. Mexican nationals also struggled to find their place as Anglicized politics and economics pushed them further to the sociocultural margins. All residents—white or nonwhite—were affected by the boom-and-bust atmosphere of the gold rush. Very few residents became rich; many became broke in this staunchly capitalist tycoon environment.

Economic, Political, and Cultural Development Since the 1850's

California Constitution

The California Constitution was first ratified on November 13, 1849, after convention members toiled for nearly a month to create and edit the document. One of the earliest debates of the first California constitutional convention was over the state line of demarcation—some convention members wanted the state of California to extend into the deserts surrounding the Salt Lake Basin; others wanted the state to use the crest of the Sierra Nevada mountain range as a boundary. Eventually, convention members decided to place the line of demarcation just east of the Sierra Crest. Another crucial debate was over whether or not California would be admitted into the Union as a free or slave state. Following the infamous Compromise of 1850, convention members, influenced by the lobbying miners and gold rushers who were staunchly abolitionist, chose to make California a free state. On September 9, 1850, its statehood became official. The California Constitution of 1849, which pushed the region into statehood, was considered fundamental law in the region for nearly thirty years. It was finally revised on September 28, 1878. The second constitutional convention included 152 convention delegates. Most delegates were either lawyers or farmers. Many felt the pressure of labor demands in this era, focusing their efforts on the rise of violence and the exploitation of railroad companies. The Constitution of 1879 was also riddled with xenophobic sentiments, offering many anti-Asian clauses and condemning the act of Asiatic "coolieism" (i.e., contracted labor) as slavery. On the flip side, the Constitution of 1879 paved the way to the foundation of the University of California public university system. After 157 days of deliberation, it was ratified as a cataloged code of laws. Since 1879, the California Constitution has been amended over four hundred times. A lot of these amendments came during the Progressive Era of the early twentieth century. Women did not receive suffrage, for example, until 1911, and many of the restraints on corporations did not fully come into effect until this Progressive Era. These Progressive politicians, however, still fueled Californians' xenophobia by reinforcing Asian exclusionary laws. These laws were not repealed until later decades.

The California Constitution is built upon the same principles of liberty, justice, and equality as the U.S. Constitution. However, the two constitutions differ in three major ways. First, the California Constitution limits state Supreme Court terms to just twelve years; the U.S. Constitution appoints judges who serve for life. Second, the California Constitution does not allow the state to ratify treaties like the U.S. Constitution allows the federal government to ratify treaties. Third, the California Constitution requires a term limit for its congressional delegates, while the U.S. Constitution does not. They are similar, however, in that they both restrict their executive leadership to two terms.

Patterns of Immigration to California

Immigration has always been a key factor in the demographic growth and cultural diversity in California. This historical trend began in the mid-to-late nineteenth century with the gold rush years that brought hundreds of thousands of new immigrants to the Pacific coast. Cultural hubs like San Francisco and Los Angeles played host to Irish, German, and Italian immigrants, leading to an impressive urban growth that reached well into the Progressive Era. Initially, thousands of Chinese and Southeast Asian immigrants flocked to the railroad industry through the Golden Gate of California, but this demographic shift eventually brought about cultural xenophobia and exclusionary politics. California witnessed even more growth during the era of the Dust Bowl and the Great Depression in the 1930s, as hundreds of thousands of migrants from the Midwest and Great Plains made their way to the "Land of Milk and Honey." These new migrants added to the diversity of California. World War II and the postwar era witnessed yet another immigrant surge, as thousands of Mexican farmers and laborers flocked to Southern California to escape Depression economics in favor of the rising prospects of the military industrial complex and agribusiness. The end of Asian exclusion and the opening of immigration channels via the Immigration Act of 1965 helped bring hundreds of thousands of Vietnamese, Korean, Japanese, Chinese, Filipino, and Pacific Islander immigrants to Los Angeles and San Francisco. This influx helped chip away at the Judeo-Christian order, introducing East Asian religions to Californians. Latinos continue to add to the diverse fiber of the Golden State. As of 2010, Latinos make up nearly 40 percent of the state population. Today, many undocumented Latino immigrants flock to California for the refuge and protection of sanctuary cities such as San Francisco. This trend has catalyzed an era of divisive politics concerning undocumented immigration.

Federal and State Law on the Legal Status of Immigrants

Federal as well as state laws have played a significant role in both excluding and integrating certain immigrant groups in U.S. and California culture. Both the U.S. Constitution and the California Constitution, for instance, have placed restrictions on the immigration of certain groups. In particular, both have had a long history of anti-Asian xenophobia; both have declared Chinese exclusion as official law. Additionally, both have opened up their gates to new immigrant groups, especially in the post-1960 era of American history. Today, nevertheless, a debate still wages on about "illegal immigration." To some degree, "illegal immigrants" are sometimes protected at the state and local levels in ways that they are not always protected at the federal level. Likewise, state and local scare tactics and extralegal responses sometimes undermine federal policies regarding the human rights of undocumented immigrants. Proponents at all levels point to America's history of accepting the poor, the tired, and the hungry. Opponents at all levels claim that illegal immigration places a strain on public funds at the expense of tax-paying citizens. Laws concerning the legal status of immigrants have long been complicated and controversial in California, dating back to colonial times.

Cultural Diversity in the United States and California

The United States and California are constantly being pulled by two historical forces: xenophobia and multiculturalism. Xenophobic citizens and residents see diversity as a threat to the American ethos and its Judeo-Christian underpinnings. Multiculturalists argue that diversity is the backbone of the American dream. The current debates over the dramatic spike in Latino immigrants in the United States and California are yet another historical display of this ongoing tension in American history. Proponents of Latino immigration point to the ways in which Mexican, Caribbean, Central American, and South American immigrants enhance the very fiber of the American dream. Opponents to Latino immigration lament the slow death of white Anglo-Saxon nationalism. Some argue that immigrants catalyze economic growth; others argue that immigrants "drain the system." Most recently, these debates have polarized the two-party system of American politics, as witnessed by the historical insurgence of Trump conservatism and Sanders's democratic-socialism.

Major Economic Activities in California

Since the initial years of the California gold rush in the late 1840s, mining has long been a cornerstone of the California economy. California's mining industry has annually called the Sierra Nevadas and the surrounding deserts its home. Large-scale agricultural has blessed California's Central Valley, Southern California, and coastal California since the Dust Bowl migrations of the 1930s and the wartime boom of the 1940s. California's Mediterranean climate has made it an ideal location for fruit farms, vineyards, and the olive oil and tree nut industries. Recreation, as an economic industry, is scattered throughout the state, though Los Angeles, and particularly Hollywood and Disneyland, have always been beacons of American film and leisure. Throughout the Cold War 1980s, and even in contemporary times, Silicon Valley has blossomed to become the epicenter of the global aerospace, electronics, and international trade industries. The entire Bay Area has skyrocketed its real estate prices due to this tech boom. Places like San Francisco have now become major players in the Asian-Pacific trade economy that spans from Tokyo to the California coast.

California's Water Delivery System

Migration and civilization in California would not be possible without the complex California water delivery system that has been built throughout the twentieth and twenty-first centuries. After a series of bills and multistate compacts were passed by the federal government and the western states of the United States in the early twentieth century, California began an impressive, multidecade initiative with dam and canal construction. One of the crown jewels of this initiative was the creation of the Hoover Dam, located in Boulder Canyon of the Colorado River system. The result was the creation of Lake Mead, a 242-mile-long artificial lake that serves as an aquatic hub for the corridor between modern Las Vegas and Los Angeles. Other dams, canals, and aqueducts followed, especially as a result of the California agricultural boom brought on by the Dust Bowl era of American history. Even today, California's farmers continue to soak up about 80 percent of the state's water delivery system. The system continues to sustain arid and semi-arid regions, as well as lush valleys. The delivery system has placed a strain not only on California's water resources, but also its entire geographic environment. Urban sprawl has contributed to droughts and subsequent wild fires. The system has carved the natural environment with concrete and metal, ingraining an artificial character onto the land. Today, conservationists are trying to stave off the destruction wrought by society and its insatiable thirst for water and resources in California.

Practice Questions

1. When children begin to negotiate the sounds that make up words in their language independently, what skill/s are they demonstrating?
    a. Phonological awareness
    b. Phonemes
    c. Phoneme substitution
    d. Blending skills

2. What is phonics?
    a. The study of syllabication
    b. The study of onsets and rimes
    c. The study of sound-letter relationships
    d. The study of graphemes

3. Word analysis skills are NOT critical for the development of what area of literacy?
    a. Vocabulary
    b. Reading fluency
    c. Spelling
    d. Articulation

4. What area of study involves mechanics, usage, and sentence formation?
    a. Word analysis
    b. Spelling conventions
    c. Morphemes
    d. Phonics

5. How do the majority of high-frequency sight words differ from decodable words?
    a. They do not rhyme.
    b. They do not follow the Alphabetic Principle.
    c. They do not contain onsets.
    d. They contain rimes.

6. Reading fluency involves what key areas?
    a. Accuracy, rate, and prosody
    b. Accuracy, rate, and consistency
    c. Prosody, accuracy, and clarity
    d. Rate, prosody, and comprehension

7. When students study character development, setting, and plot, what are they studying?
    a. Word analysis
    b. Points of view
    c. Literary analysis of fictional texts
    d. Fluency

8. The author's purpose, major ideas, supporting details, visual aids, and vocabulary are the five key elements of what type of text?
   a. Fictional texts
   b. Narratives
   c. Persuasive texts
   d. Informational texts

9. When students use inference, what are they able to do?
   a. Make logical assumptions based on contextual clues
   b. Independently navigate various types of text
   c. Summarize a text's main idea
   d. Paraphrase a text's main idea

10. Story maps, an effective instructional tool, do NOT help children in what way?
   a. Analyze relationships among characters, events, and ideas in literature
   b. Understand key details of a story
   c. Follow the story's development
   d. Read at a faster pace

11. Which text feature does NOT help a reader locate information in printed or digital text?
   a. Hyperlink
   b. Sidebar
   c. Glossary
   d. Heading

The next question is based on the following passage.

> A famous children's author recently published a historical fiction novel under a pseudonym; however, it did not sell as many copies as her children's books. In her earlier years, she had majored in history and earned a graduate degree in Antebellum American History, which is the time frame of her new novel. Critics praised this newest work far more than the children's series that made her famous. In fact, her new novel was nominated for the prestigious Albert J. Beveridge Award, but still isn't selling like her children's books, which fly off the shelves because of her name alone.

12. Which one of the following statements might be accurately inferred based on the above passage?
   a. The famous children's author produced an inferior book under her pseudonym.
   b. The famous children's author is the foremost expert on Antebellum America.
   c. The famous children's author did not receive the bump in publicity for her historical novel that it would have received if it were written under her given name.
   d. People generally prefer to read children's series than historical fiction.

Read the selection and answer questions 31 – 36.

> [1]I have to admit that when my father bought an RV, I thought he was making a huge mistake. [2]In fact, I even thought he might have gone a little bit crazy. [3]I did not really know anything about recreational vehicles, but I knew that my dad was as big a "city slicker" as there was. [4]On trips to the beach, he preferred to swim at the pool, and whenever he went hiking, he avoided touching

any plants for fear that they might be poison ivy. [5]Why would this man, with an almost irrational fear of the outdoors, want a 40-foot camping behemoth?

[6]The RV was a great purchase for our family and brought us all closer together. [7]Every morning we would wake up, eat breakfast, and broke camp. [8]We laughed at our own comical attempts to back The Beast into spaces that seemed impossibly small. [9]We rejoiced when we figured out how to "hack" a solution to a nagging technological problem. [10]When things inevitably went wrong and we couldn't solve the problems on our own, we discovered the incredible helpfulness and friendliness of the RV community. We even made some new friends in the process.

[11] Above all, owning the RV allowed us to share adventures travelling across America that we could not have experienced in cars and hotels. [12]Enjoying a campfire on a chilly summer evening with the mountains of Glacier National Park in the background, or waking up early in the morning to see the sun rising over the distant spires of Arches National Park are memories that will always stay with me and our entire family. [13]Those are also memories that my siblings and I have now shared with our own children.

13. How should the author change sentence 11?
    a. Above all, it will allow us to share adventures travelling across America that we could not have experienced in cars and hotels.
    b. Above all, it allows you to share adventures travelling across America that you could not have experienced in cars and hotels.
    c. Above all, it allowed us to share adventures travelling across America that we could not have experienced in cars and hotels.
    d. Above all, it allows them to share adventures travelling across America that they could not have experienced in cars and hotels.

14. Which of the following examples would make a good addition to the selection after sentence 4?
    a. My father is also afraid of seeing insects.
    b. My father is surprisingly good at starting a campfire.
    c. My father negotiated contracts for a living.
    d. My father isn't even bothered by pigeons.

15. Timed oral reading can be used to assess:
    a. Phonics
    b. Listening comprehension
    c. Reading rate
    d. Background knowledge

16. Word walls are used to:
    a. Allow students to share words they find interesting
    b. Present words utilized in a current unit of study
    c. Specify words that students are to utilize within writing assignments
    d. All of the above

17. Context clues assist vocabulary development by providing:
    a. A knowledge of roots, prefixes, and suffixes are used to determine the meaning a word
    b. Information within the sentence that surrounds an unknown word is used to determine the word's meaning
    c. Content learned in previous grades that serves as a bridge to the new term

d. Background knowledge to fill in a missing word within a sentence

Questions 18-19 are based upon the following passage:

This excerpt is adaptation from Abraham Lincoln's Address Delivered at the Dedication of the Cemetery at Gettysburg, November 19, 1863.

> Four score and seven years ago our fathers brought forth on this continent, a new nation, conceived in liberty, and dedicated to the proposition that all men are created equal.
>
> Now we are engaged in a great civil war, testing whether that nation, or any nation so conceived and so dedicated, can long endure. We are met on a great battlefield of that war. We have come to dedicate a portion of that field, as a final resting place for those who here gave their lives that this nation might live. It is altogether fitting and proper that we should do this.
>
> But, in a larger sense, we cannot dedicate—we cannot consecrate that we cannot hallow—this ground. The brave men, living and dead, who struggled here, have consecrated it, far above our poor power to add or detract. The world will little note, nor long remember what we say here, but it can never forget what they did here. It is for us the living, rather, to be dedicated here to the unfinished work which they who fought here have thus far so nobly advanced. It is rather for us to be here and dedicated to the great task remaining before us—that from these honored dead we take increased devotion to that cause for which they gave the last full measure of devotion—that we here highly resolve that these dead shall not have died in vain—that these this nation, under God, shall have a new birth of freedom—and that government of people, by the people, for the people, shall not perish from the earth.

18. What message is the author trying to convey through this address?
    a. The audience should consider the death of the people that fought in the war as an example and perpetuate the ideals of freedom that the soldiers died fighting for.
    b. The audience should honor the dead by establishing an annual memorial service.
    c. The audience should form a militia that would overturn the current political structure.
    d. The audience should forget the lives that were lost and discredit the soldiers.

19. Which rhetorical device is being used in the following passage?
    . . . we here highly resolve that these dead shall not have died in vain—that these this nation, under God, shall have a new birth of freedom—and that government of people, by the people, for the people, shall not perish from the earth.

    a. Antimetatabolee
    b. Antiphrasis
    c. Anaphora
    d. Epiphora

20. Read the following poem. Which option best expresses the symbolic meaning of the "road" and the overall theme?
    Two roads diverged in a yellow wood,
    And sorry I could not travel both

And be one traveler, long I stood
And looked down one as far as I could
To where it bent in the undergrowth;
Then took the other, as just as fair,
And having perhaps the better claim,
Because it was grassy and wanted wear;
Though as for that the passing there
Had worn them really about the same,
And both that morning equally lay
In leaves no step had trodden black.
Oh, I kept the first for another day!
Yet knowing how way leads on to way,
I doubted if I should ever come back.
I shall be telling this with a sigh
Somewhere ages and ages hence:
Two roads diverged in a wood, and I—
I took the one less traveled by,
And that has made all the difference—Robert Frost, "The Road Not Taken"

    a. A divergent spot where the traveler had to choose the correct path to his destination
    b. A choice between good and evil that the traveler needs to make
    c. The traveler's struggle between his lost love and his future prospects
    d. Life's journey and the choices with which humans are faced

21. Which option best exemplifies an author's use of *alliteration* and *personification*?
    a. Her mood hung about her like a weary cape, very dull from wear.
    b. It shuddered, swayed, shook, and screamed its way into dust under hot flames.
    c. The house was a starch sentry, warning visitors away.
    d. At its shoreline, visitors swore they heard the siren call of the cliffs above.

22. Read the following poem. Which option best depicts the rhyme scheme?
    A slumber did my spirit seal;
    I had no human fears:
    She seemed a thing that could not feel
    The touch of earthly years.—from William Wordsworth, "A Slumber Did My Spirit Seal"

    a. BAC BAC
    b. ABAB
    c. ABBA
    d. AB CD AB

23. Read the following poem. Which option describes its corresponding meter?
    Half a league, half a league
    Half a league onward,
    All in the valley of Death
    Rode the six hundred.
    'Forward, the Light Brigade!
    Charge for the guns!' he said:
    Into the valley of Death

Rode the six hundred.—Alfred Lord Tennyson *"The Charge of the Light Brigade"*

    a. Iambic (unstressed/stressed syllables)
    b. Anapest (unstressed/unstressed/stressed syllables)
    c. Spondee (stressed/stressed syllables)
    d. Dactyl (stressed/unstressed/unstressed syllables)

24. This work, published in 1922, was a modernist piece that was banned both in the United States and overseas for meeting the criteria of obscenity. Taking place in a single day (June 16th, 1904), the novel contains eighteen episodes reflecting the activities of character Leopold Bloom in Dublin, Ireland. Originally written as to portray an Odysseus figure for adults, the structure of the work is often viewed as convoluted and chaotic, as its author utilized the stream of consciousness technique. Its literary reception was vastly polarized and remains so to this day, although modern critics tend to hail the novel as addressing the vast panoramic of futility within contemporary history.

The above passage describes which famous literary work?
    a. James Joyce's *Ulysses*
    b. Anne Sexton's poem "45 Mercy Street"
    c. F. Scott Fitzgerald's *Tender is the Night*
    d. George Eliot's *Middlemarch: A Study of Provincial Life*

25. In 1889, Jerome K. Jerome wrote a humorous account of a boating holiday. Originally intended as a chapter in a serious travel guide, the work became a prime example of a comic novel. Read the passage below, noting the word/words in italics. Answer the question that follows.

> I felt rather hurt about this at first; it seemed somehow to be a sort of slight. Why hadn't I got housemaid's knee? Why this invidious reservation? After a while, however, less grasping feelings prevailed. I reflected that I had every other known malady in the pharmacology, and I grew less selfish, and determined to do without housemaid's knee. Gout, in its most malignant stage, it would appear, had seized me without my being aware of it; and *zymosis* I had evidently been suffering with from boyhood. There were no more diseases after *zymosis*, so I concluded there was nothing else the matter with me.—Jerome K. Jerome, *Three Men in a Boat*

Which definition best fits the word *zymosis*?
    a. Discontent
    b. An infectious disease
    c. Poverty
    d. Bad luck

26. Read the following poem. Which option best describes the use of the spider?
    The spider as an artist
    Has never been employed
    Though his surpassing merit
    Is freely certified
    By every broom and Bridget
    Throughout a Christian land.
    Neglected son of genius,
    I take thee by the hand—Emily Dickinson, "Cobwebs"

a. Idiom
b. Haiku
c. ABBA rhyming convention
d. Metaphor

27. Which type of map illustrates the world's climatological regions?
    a. Topographic Map
    b. Conformal Projection
    c. Isoline Map
    d. Thematic Map

28. In which manner is absolute location expressed?
    a. The cardinal directions (north, south, east, and west)
    b. Through latitudinal and longitudinal coordinates
    c. Location nearest to a more well-known location
    d. Hemispherical position on the globe

29. Which of these is NOT a true statement about culture?
    a. Culture derives from the beliefs, values, and behaviors of people in a community.
    b. All people are born into a certain culture.
    c. Cultures are stagnant and cannot be changed.
    d. Culture can be embedded within families, schools, businesses, social classes, and religions.

30. Latitudinal lines are used to measure distance in which direction?
    a. East to west
    b. North to south
    c. Between two sets of coordinates
    d. In an inexact manner

31. Which of the following civilizations developed the first democratic form of government?
    a. Roman Empire
    b. Ancient Greece
    c. Achaemenid Empire
    d. Zhou dynasty

32. Which of the following statements most accurately describes the Achaemenid Empire in Persia until the fourth century BCE?
    a. Islam was the official religion.
    b. Achaemenid emperors constructed the entire Silk Road network.
    c. The Achaemenid Empire successfully conquered Greece.
    d. None of the above

33. The Silk Roads had which of the following results?
    a. Spread of Buddhism from India to China
    b. Resulted in the devastation of European economies
    c. Introduction of the Bubonic Plague to the New World
    d. Resulted in the Great War

34. What caused the end of the Western Roman Empire in 476 CE?
    a. Invasions by Germanic tribes
    b. The Mongol invasion
    c. The assassination of Julius Caesar
    d. Introduction of Taoism in Rome

35. Which of the following statements most accurately describes the Mongol Empire?
    a. The Mongol army was largely a cavalry force.
    b. Mongol rulers did not tolerate other religions.
    c. Mongol rulers neglected foreign trade.
    d. The Mongol Empire is known for its discouragement of literacy and the arts.

36. What social consequence(s) did the Black Death have in Europe?
    a. It gave birth to the concept of absolute monarchy.
    b. It ignited the Protestant Reformation.
    c. It eroded serfdom.
    d. It gave rise to Child Labor Laws in England.

37. Which Supreme Court decision struck down the "separate but equal" doctrine?
    a. *Roe vs. Wade*
    b. *Brown vs. Board of Education*
    c. *Plessy vs. Ferguson*
    d. *Marbury vs. Madison*

38. Which of the following led to the American Revolution?
    a. The Stamp Act
    b. The Boston Massacre
    c. The Boston Tea Party
    d. All of the above

39. Which political concept describes a ruling body's ability to influence the actions, behaviors, or attitudes of a person or community?
    a. Authority
    b. Sovereignty
    c. Power
    d. Legitimacy

40. Which feature differentiates a state from a nation?
    a. Shared history
    b. Common language
    c. Population
    d. Sovereignty

41. Which political theorist considered violence necessary in order for a ruler to maintain political power and stability?
    a. John Locke
    b. Jean-Jacques Rousseau
    c. Karl Marx
    d. Niccolo Machiavelli

42. Which political theorist is considered the father of the social contract theory?
    a. John Stuart Mills
    b. Thomas Hobbes
    c. Aristotle
    d. Immanuel Kant

43. Which political orientation emphasizes maintaining traditions and stability over progress and change?
    a. Socialism
    b. Liberalism
    c. Conservatism
    d. Libertarianism

44. What was the name of the incipient revolt led by the oft-overlooked American settler, William Ide, in 1846, which led to the halfhearted creation of the "California Republic"?
    a. The Bear Flag Revolt
    b. The Asian Exclusionary Revolt
    c. The Mexican-American War
    d. The Dust Bowl

45. In what year did the Scottish-American settler James Wilson Marshall discover gold at Sutter's Mill?
    a. 1822
    b. 1848
    c. 1849
    d. 1879

46. Which of the following would be an example of a xenophobic policy in U.S. history that affected race relations in California history?
    a. The Immigration Act of 1965
    b. The Civil Rights Act of 1964
    c. The Swing-Johnson Bill of 1928
    d. The Chinese Exclusion Act of 1882

47. In 1849, what geographic landmark was designated as the eastern line of demarcation for the state of California?
    a. The Salt Lake Basin
    b. The Central Valley
    c. The Sierra Crest
    d. The Redwood forests

48. In what years did California host its two major constitutional conventions?
    a. 1822 and 1849
    b. 1849 and 1911
    c. 1849 and 1879
    d. 1879 and 1911

49. Why did migrants travel to California during the Dust Bowl of the 1930s?
    a. They wanted to participate in the expansion of the aerospace industry.
    b. They wanted to participate in the Silicon Valley tech boom of this era.
    c. They wanted to find work in leisure industries such as Disneyland.

d. They wanted to find work in the expanding agricultural economy of California.

50. The modern-day debate over illegal immigration in California is mostly a debate over which of the following categories?
    a. Politics
    b. Race relations and diversity
    c. Economics
    d. All of the above

51. Which of the following can be considered a shortcoming of Progressive Era politics in California and the United States in the early twentieth century?
    a. Progressive Era politics failed to bring about women's suffrage.
    b. Progressive Era politics failed to end Asian exclusionary laws.
    c. Progressive Era politics failed to support temperance and bring about prohibition.
    d. Progressive Era politics failed to attack urban plight.

52. California was ceded to the United States following what North American conflict?
    a. The Spanish-American War
    b. The American Civil War
    c. The Mexican Revolution
    d. The Mexican-American War

Answer Explanations

1. A: Phonological Awareness refers to a child's ability to understand and use familiar sounds in his or her social environment in order to form coherent words. Phonemes are defined as distinct sound units in any given language. Phonemic substitution is part of phonological awareness—a child's ability to substitute specific phonemes for others. Blending skills refers to the ability to construct or build words from individual phonemes by blending the sounds together in a unique sequence.

2. C: When children begin to recognize and apply sound-letter relationships independently and accurately, they are demonstrating a growing mastery of phonics. Phonics is the most commonly used method for teaching people to read and write by associating sounds with their corresponding letters or groups of letters, using a language's alphabetic writing system. Syllabication refers to the ability to break down words into their individual syllables. The study of onsets and rimes strives to help students recognize and separate a word's beginning consonant or consonant-cluster sound—the onset—from the word's rime—the vowel and/or consonants that follow the onset. A grapheme is a letter or a group of letters in a language that represent a sound.

3. D: Breaking down words into their individual parts, studying prefixes, suffixes, root words, rimes, and onsets, are all examples of word analysis. When children analyze words, they develop their vocabulary and strengthen their spelling and reading fluency.

4. B: Spelling conventions is the area of study that involves mechanics, usage, and sentence formation. Mechanics refers to spelling, punctuation, and capitalization. Usage refers to the use of the various parts of speech within sentences, and sentence formation is the order in which the various words in a sentence appear. Generally speaking, word analysis is the breaking down of words into morphemes and word units in order to arrive at the word's meaning. Morphemes are the smallest units of a written language that carry meaning, and phonics refers to the study of letter-sound relationships.

5. B: Although some high-frequency sight words are decodable, the majority of them are not, so they do not follow the Alphabetic Principle, which relies on specific letter-sound correspondence. High-frequency sight words appear often in children's literature and are studied and memorized in order to strengthen a child's spelling and reading fluency. High-frequency sight words, as well as decodable words, may or may not rhyme and may or may not contain onsets and rimes.

6. A: Reading fluency involves how accurately a child reads each individual word within a sentence, the speed at which a child reads, and the expression the child applies while reading. Therefore, accuracy, rate, and prosody are the three key areas of reading fluency.

7. C: Literary analysis of a fictional text involves several areas of study, including character development, setting, and plot. Although points of view refer to a specific area of study in literary analysis, it is only one area. Word analysis does not involve the study of elements within a fictional text.

8. D: Informational texts generally contain five key elements in order to be considered informative. These five elements include the author's purpose, the major ideas, supporting details, visual aids, and key vocabulary. Narratives are accounts—either spoken or written—of an event or a story. Persuasive texts, such as advertisements, use persuasive language to try to convince the reader to act or feel a certain way. Informational texts strive to share factual information about a given subject in order to advance a reader's knowledge.

9. A: When a person infers something, he or she is demonstrating the ability to extract key information and make logical assumptions based on that information. The information provided is not direct, but implied. Being able to navigate a variety of texts independently has nothing to do with inference; it demonstrates a student's reading comprehension and fluency. Successfully summarizing and paraphrasing texts are advanced literacy skills that demonstrate a student's reading comprehension and writing proficiency.

10. D: Story maps are a specific type of visual aid that helps younger children develop a clearer understanding of a story being read. Story maps may represent the beginning, middle, and ending of a story, or they may be used to develop a clearer picture of each character's personality and traits, unfold the story's plot, or establish the setting.

11. C: Informational texts organized with headings, subheadings, sidebars, hyperlinks and other features help strengthen the reader's reading comprehension and vocabulary knowledge. A glossary defines terms and words used within a text.

12. C: We are looking for an inference—a conclusion that is reached on the basis of evidence and reasoning—from the passage that will likely explain why the famous children's author did not achieve her usual success with the new genre (despite the book's acclaim). Choice *A* is wrong because the statement is false according to the passage. Choice *B* is wrong because, although the passage says the author has a graduate degree on the subject, it would be an unrealistic leap to infer that she is the foremost expert on Antebellum America. Choice *D* is wrong because there is nothing in the passage to lead us to infer that people generally prefer a children's series to historical fiction. In contrast, Choice *C* can be logically inferred since the passage speaks of the great success of the children's series and the declaration that the fame of the author's name causes the children's books to "fly off the shelves." Thus, she did not receive any bump from her name since she published the historical novel under a pseudonym, and Choice *C* is correct.

13. C: The sentence should be in the same tense and person as the rest of the selection. The rest of the selection is in past tense and first person. Choice *A* is in future tense. Choice *B* is in second person. Choice *D* is in third person. While none of these sentences are incorrect by themselves, they are written in a tense that is different from the rest of the selection. Only *Choice C* maintains tense and voice consistent with the rest of the selection.

14. A: Choices *B* and *D* go against the point the author is trying to make—that the father is not comfortable in nature. Choice *C* is irrelevant to the topic. Choice *A* is the only choice that emphasizes the father's discomfort with spending time in nature.

15. C: The most common measurement of reading rate includes the oral contextual timed readings of students. During a timed reading, the number of errors made within a given amount of time is recorded. This data can be used to identify if a student's rate is improving and if the rate falls within the recommended fluency rates for their grade level.

16. D: A love of words can be instilled when students share new and interesting words that they encounter through independent reading or that are taught by a teacher. These words can be kept in either word lists or word walls. Word lists and walls help to personalize vocabulary instruction while improving students' flexibility and fluency. Additionally, there are thousands of online word blogs and word clouds that encourage students to share the words they love. If a lack of technology is an issue, students can share new words on a word bank displayed on a wall within the classroom or a word list contained within a notebook. The list of new words should be referred to often in order to increase students' exposure to new words. Students should be required to utilize the words within writing activities and discussions.

17. B: When using contextual strategies, students are indirectly introduced to new words within a sentence or paragraph. Contextual strategies require students to infer the meaning(s) of new words. Word meaning is developed by utilizing semantic and contextual clues of the reading in which the word is located.

18. A: The audience should consider the death of the people that fought in the war as an example and perpetuate the ideals of freedom that the soldiers died fighting for. Lincoln doesn't address any of the topics outlined in Choices B, C, or D. Therefore, Choice A is the correct answer.

19. D: Choice D is the correct answer because of the repetition of the word *people* at the end of the passage. Choice A, *antimetatabolee*, is the repetition of words in a succession. Choice B, *antiphrasis*, is a form of denial of an assertion in a text. Choice C, *anaphora*, is the repetition that occurs at the beginning of sentences.

20. D: Choice D correctly summarizes Frost's theme of life's journey and the choices one makes. While Choice A can be seen as an interpretation, it is a literal one and is incorrect. Literal is not symbolic. Choice B presents the idea of good and evil as a theme, and the poem does not specify this struggle for the traveler. Choice C is a similarly incorrect answer. Love is not the theme.

21. B: Only Choice B uses both repetitive beginning sounds (alliteration) and personification—the portrayal of a building as a human crumbling under a fire. Choice A is a simile and does not utilize alliteration or the use of consistent consonant sounds for effect. Choice C is a metaphor and does not utilize alliteration. Choice D describes neither alliteration nor personification.

22. B: The correct answer is ABAB. Choice A is not a valid rhyme scheme. Choice C would require the second and third lines to rhyme, so it is incorrect. Choice D would require the first and fifth lines rhyme, then the second and sixth. This is also incorrect as the passage only contains four lines.

23. D: The correct answer is dactyl. If read with the combination of stressed and unstressed syllables as Tennyson intended and as the poem naturally flows, the reader will stumble upon the stressed/unstressed/unstressed rhythmic, dactyl meter similar to a waltz beat. Choices A, B, and C describe meters that do not follow the dactyl pattern.

24. A: The correct answer is A as it is the only option that utilizes stream of consciousness technique in a novel format. Choice B is a poem by poet Anne Sexton, not a novel. Although Ms. Sexton's works were often criticized for their intimate content, this answer does not meet the question's criteria. Choices C and D are both incorrect. Both are novels, but not of the appropriate time period, country, or literary content.

25. B: The correct answer is an infectious disease. By reading context, all other options can be eliminated since the author restates zymosis as disease.

26. D: The correct answer is metaphor. Choice A is incorrect because the poem does not contain an idiom. Choice B is incorrect since the poem is not haiku. Choice C is incorrect as it does not use the ABBA rhyming convention.

27. D: Thematic maps create certain themes in which they attempt to illustrate a certain phenomenon or pattern. The obvious theme of a climate map is the climates in the represented areas. Thematic maps are very extensive and can include thousands of different themes, which makes them quite useful for students of geography. Topographic maps (Choice A) are utilized to show physical features, conformal projections (Choice B) attempt to illustrate the globe in an undistorted fashion, and isoline maps (Choice C) illustrate differences in variables between two points on a map.

28. B: Latitudinal and longitudinal coordinates delineate absolute location. In contrast to relative location, which describes a location as compared to another, better-known place, absolute location provides an exact place on the globe through the latitude and longitude system. Choice A, cardinal directions (north, south, east, west) are used in absolute location, but coordinates must be added in order to have an absolute location. Using other, better known locations to find a location, Choice C, is referred to as relative location, and absolute location is far more precise than simply finding hemispherical position on the globe.

29. C: Each statement about culture is correct except for Choice C. Cultures often will adapt to the settings in which they are found. Some cultures derive from such settings and have continued on adapting to what works best to keep that culture.

30. B: Lines of latitude measure distance north and south. The Equator is zero degrees and the Tropic of Cancer is 23 ½ degrees north of the Equator. The distance between those two lines measures degrees north to south, as with any other two lines of latitude. Longitudinal lines, or meridians, measure distance east and west, even though they run north and south down the Globe. Latitude is not inexact, in that there are set distances between the lines. Furthermore, coordinates can only exist with the use of longitude and latitude.

31. B: Ancient Greeks created many of the cultural and political institutions that form the basis of modern western civilization. Athens was an important Greek democracy, and all adult men could participate in politics after they had completed their military service. The Roman Empire, Choice A, evolved from the Roman Republic, but it was not democratic. The Achaemenid Empire and Zhou Dynasty, Choices C and D, were imperial monarchies that did not allow citizens to have much, if any, political voice.

32. D: During the Achaemenid Empire, Persians practiced the Zoroastrian faith and worshipped two gods. Islam only came about one thousand years later. The Achaemenids built a Royal Road that stretched across their empire, but the Silk Roads expanded throughout Asia. The Achaemenids twice tried to conquer Greece but failed both times.

33. A: The Silk Roads were a network of trade routes between Asia and the Mediterranean. Merchants and Pilgrims traveled along the Silk Roads and brought new ideas and technologies, as well as trade goods. For example, Buddhism spread from India to China. Chinese technologies also spread westward, including gunpowder and the printing press. The Silk Roads also spread the Bubonic Plague to Europe, but it did not arrive in the New World until Columbus landed there in 1492.

34. A: Invasions by Germanic tribes. Large numbers of Franks, Goths, Vandals, and other Germanic peoples began moving south in the fifth century CE. They conquered Rome twice, and the Western Roman Empire finally disintegrated. The Mongol invasion, Choice B, pushed westward in the thirteenth century, long after the western Roman Empire was gone. The assassination of Julius Caesar, Choice C, led to the end of the Roman Republic and the birth of the Roman Empire. Taoism never spread to Rome, making Choice D incorrect.

35. A: The Mongol army was largely a cavalry force. The Mongols were a nomadic people who trained as horsemen from a young age. They used their highly mobile army to build a huge empire in Asia, the Middle East, and Eastern Europe. Mongol rulers were relatively tolerant of other religions because they wanted to reduce conflict within their empire, making Choice *B* incorrect. They also encouraged trade because they produced few of their own goods, making Choice *C* incorrect. The Mongol rulers also encouraged literacy and appreciated visual art, making Choice *D* incorrect.

36. C: It eroded serfdom. Millions of people died during the Black Death, but those who survived found that their standard of living had improved, especially serfs. Before the Black Death, serfs had few rights and were expected to work without pay for their lord. Because labor was in such short supply after the Black Death, serfs found they were in a much better bargaining position. The Protestant Reformation was a cultural phenomenon, and the rise of absolutism was a political change. Neither had any connection to the Black Death, making Choices *A* and *B* incorrect. Choice *D* is also incorrect; although Child Labor Laws came after the Black Death in the early 1800s, they weren't a direct result of the Black Death.

37. B: *Brown vs. Board of Education* ruled that separate schools for blacks and whites were inherently unequal and sparked demands for more civil rights. *Roe v. Wade* in 1973, Choice *A*, increased access to abortion. *Plessy vs. Ferguson*, Choice *C*, established the "separate but equal" doctrine. *Marbury vs. Madison* in 1803, Choice *D*, established the doctrine of judicial review.

38. D: All three events led to increasing tension and conflict between the colonists and the British government, which finally exploded at the Battle of Lexington and Concord in 1775. The Stamp Act of 1765 imposed a tax on documents. It was repealed after colonists organized protests. The Boston Massacre resulted in the death of five colonists in 1770. The Boston Tea Party was a protest in 1773 against a law that hurt colonial tea merchants. The British responded to the tea party by punishing the colony of Massachusetts, which created fear among the other colonies and united them against the British government.

39. C: Power is the ability of a ruling body or political entity to influence the actions, behavior, and attitude of a person or group of people. Authority, Choice *A*, is the right and justification of the government to exercise power as recognized by the citizens or influential elites. Similarly, legitimacy, Choice *D*, is another way of expressing the concept of authority. Sovereignty, Choice *B*, refers to the ability of a state to determine and control their territory without foreign interference.

40. D: Sovereignty is the feature that differentiates a state from a nation. Nations have no sovereignty, as they are unable to enact and enforce laws independently of their state. A state must possess sovereignty over the population of a territory in order to be legitimized as a state. Both a nation and a state must have a population, Choice *C*. Although sometimes present, shared history and common language are not requirements for a state, making Choices *A* and *B* incorrect.

41. D: In his book, *The Prince*, Niccolo Machiavelli advocated that a ruler should be prepared to do whatever is necessary to remain in power, including using violence and political deception as a means to coerce the people of a state or eliminate political rivals. John Locke, Choice *A*, contributed and advocated liberal principles, most prominently the right to life, liberty, and health. Jean-Jacques Rousseau, Choice *B*, heavily influenced the French Revolution and American Revolution by advocating individual equality, self-rule, and religious freedom. Karl Marx, Choice *C*, wrote that the struggle between the bourgeois (ruling class) and the proletariat (working class) would result in a classless society in which all citizens commonly owned the means of production.

42. B: Thomas Hobbes is considered the father of social contract theory. In his book *Leviathan,* Hobbes advocated for a strong central government and posited that the citizens of a state make a social contract with the government to allow it to rule them in exchange for protection and security. John Stuart Mills, Choice A, is most commonly associated with the political philosophy of utilitarianism. Aristotle, Choice C, believed that man could only achieve happiness by bettering their community through noble acts, while Immanuel Kant, Choice D, promoted democracy and asserted that states could only achieve lasting global peace through international cooperation.

43. C: Conservatism emphasizes maintaining traditions and believes political and social stability is more important than progress and reform. In general, Socialism, Choice A, seeks to establish a democratically elected government that owns the means of production, regulates the exchange of commodities, and distributes the wealth equally among citizens. Liberalism, Choice B, is based on individualism and equality, supporting the freedoms of speech, press, and religion, while Libertarian ideals, Choice D, emphasize individual liberties and freedom from government interference.

44. A: The answer is Choice A, the Bear Flag Revolt. The Bear Flag Revolt has long been the part of the historical mythos of California history; however, the skirmish, which was led by William Ide in 1846, affected the history of the state in only a minor way, paving the way to the engineering of California's infamous "Bear Flag," which still serves as the state flag. Choice B, the Asian Exclusionary Revolt, is a fictitious event meant to trick the test taker into latching onto California's long history of Asian exclusion. Choice C, the Mexican-American War, was a much larger North American conflict that led to the cession of California to the United States by Mexico. Choice D, the Dust Bowl, was not a military conflict, but rather an environmental disaster during the 1930s that brought many farmers and migrants to California's lush Central Valley.

45. B: The answer is Choice B, 1848. This is the year the Scottish-American settler James Wilson Marshall discovered gold at Sutter's Mill. Test takers may be tempted to choose Choice C, 1849, because of the association of the gold rush with the so-called forty-niners, but the discovery actually began a year prior to this rush. Choice A, 1822, is the year that California became a part of the new Mexican Republic. Choice D, 1879, is the year of the second California state constitutional convention.

46. D: The answer is Choice D, the Chinese Exclusion Act of 1882, a xenophobic law that restricted the immigration of Asians, and specifically Chinese Asians, to the United States based solely on U.S. citizens' prejudice and fears. Choices A and B, the Immigration Act of 1965 and the Civil Rights Act of 1964, are incorrect because they actually encouraged diversity and inclusion. The Immigration Act of 1965 opened the gates to more immigrants from Asia and other parts of the world. The Civil Rights Act of 1964 helped end legal segregation by protecting ethnic and racial minorities and their civil rights as citizens of the United States. Choice C, the Swing-Johnson Bill of 1928, is the furthest from the mark because it has nothing to do with immigration or civil rights. The Swing-Johnson Bill of 1928 helped make the construction of the Hoover Dam a reality.

47. C: The answer is Choice C, the Sierra Crest. The delegates at the first state constitutional convention in California debated whether the eastern line of demarcation should be placed along the Sierra Crest or the Salt Lake Basin (Choice A). Ultimately, they decided on the former, leaving the deserts to the east of the Sierra Nevada mountain range to the territory that would later become the state of Nevada. Choice B, the Central Valley, is the region in the center of the state known for its agricultural production. Choice D, the Redwood forests, are the ancient woodlands located along the northwest coast of California.

48. C: The answer is Choice C, 1849 and 1879. The initial state constitution was drafted and ratified in 1849, and it was later rewritten as an extended code of laws in 1879, as the railroad industry and rampant urbanization shifted the labor and political scenes in California. Choice A, 1822 and 1849, is incorrect because 1822 is the date when California fell under Mexican independence. Choices B and D are incorrect because they include the date 1911, which is the year suffrage was extended to women.

49. D: The answer is Choice D, "They wanted to find work in the expanding agricultural economy of California." The Dust Bowl of the 1930s devastated farmlands in the Midwest and Great Plains, forcing farmers and their families to move west to California, known as the "Land of Milk and Honey." In California, they became part of a burgeoning agricultural economy that avoided most of the environmental plight of the Depression era. Choices A, B, and C are incorrect because the leisure industries (i.e., Disneyland) and the aerospace industry did not take root in California until the economic boom of the early Cold War. The tech boom—Choice B—in the Silicon Valley did not occur until the advent of personal computers and the Internet in the 1980s and 1990s.

50. D: The answer is Choice D, all of the above. The modern-day debate over illegal immigration in California extends into all aspects of society, including politics (Choice A), race relations and diversity (Choice B), and economics (Choice C). Liberal political proponents of undocumented immigration point out the ways in which undocumented immigrants increase diversity structures in the United States and bolster the economy. Conservative political opponents of illegal immigration claim that illegal immigrants threaten the cultural character of the nation and place a strain on welfare and the economy.

51. B: The answer is Choice B, "Progressive Era politics failed to end Asian exclusionary laws." In fact, critics of Progressive politics claim that the Progressive Era fell short in its reforms by reinforcing xenophobia and racism in spite of the apparent moral and political gains. Choices A, C, and D are incorrect because Progressive Era politics actually helped bring about women's suffrage (Choice A) and temperance/prohibition (Choice C). Additionally, Progressive Era politics can be categorized as a direct response to the "ills" of urbanization and urban plight (Choice D).

52. D: The answer is Choice D, the Mexican-American War. Following this North American conflict, the California territory of the Mexican Republic fell into U.S. hands. Choice A—the Spanish-American War—also led to some territory changes in the Caribbean and the Pacific but occurred well after California statehood, at the turn of the twentieth century. Although California became a player in the divisive politics of the American Civil War (Choice B) as a "free state," it was already in U.S. hands by the time shots were fired between the Union and the Confederacy. The Mexican Revolution (Choice C) brought California under the control of the newly founded Mexican Republic, not the United States.

Constructed-Response Questions

Constructed-response questions allow CSET test takers to break free from the monotonous, restrictive limitations multiple-choice questions place on one's knowledge. They provide a platform for writers of any skill level to openly display their content knowledge and test-prep capabilities. Fortunately, test takers are assessed solely on subject matter knowledge and not writing skills, though it never hurts to brush up on writing techniques (i.e., grammar, style, syntax). These constructed-response questions demand, at the very least, a 100-to200-word short essay. The key to a successful response is to meticulously read each assignment and its directions. If time permits, test takers should outline their responses on scratch paper. CSET scorers will assess test-taker responses with rubrics that examine the following three categories: 1) Purpose, 2) Subject Matter Knowledge, and 3) Support. In assessing purpose, CSET scorers look for test takers to make connections between content knowledge and the specific parameters of the question. In assessing subject matter knowledge, CSET scorers will, quite literally, be comparing the subject matter applied in the essay to a checklist of necessary and expected CSET content specifications. In assessing support, CSET scorers will rate the quality of the supporting evidence. All three of these categories should be evidenced through the quality of a writer's organization (rather than the quality of grammar, style, and syntax). Nonetheless, most CSET test-prep experts will agree that streamlined and organized grammar, style, and syntax will assist test takers in appropriately communicating their points. Remember that the appropriate audience (i.e., the CSET scorers) will be professionals in the field of education, so it never hurts to practice answering questions on the "CSET: Multiple Subjects Test Guide" at www.ctcexams.nesinc.com.

Constructed-Response Assignment #1

Read the excerpt below from *The Chinese Exclusion Act (May 6, 1882)*; then, complete the exercise that follows.

An Act to Execute Certain Treaty Stipulations Relating to Chinese

SEC. 11. That any person who shall knowingly bring into or cause to be brought into the United States by land, or who shall knowingly aid or abet the same, or aid or abet the landing in the United States from any vessel of any Chinese person not lawfully entitled to enter the United States, shall be deemed guilty of a misdemeanor, and shall, on conviction thereof, be fined in a sum not exceeding $1,000, and imprisoned for a term not exceeding one year.

SEC. 12. That no Chinese person shall be permitted to enter the United States by land without producing to the proper officer of customs the certificate in this act required of Chinese persons seeking to land from a vessel...

SEC. 13. That this act shall not apply to diplomatic and other officers of the Chinese Government traveling upon the business of that government, whose credentials shall be taken as equivalent to the certificate in this act mentioned, and shall exempt them and their body and household servants from the provisions of this act as to other Chinese persons.

SEC. 14. That hereafter no State court or court of the United States shall admit Chinese to citizenship; and all laws in conflict with this act are hereby repealed.

SEC. 15. That the words "Chinese laborers," wherever used in this act, shall be construed to mean both skilled and unskilled laborers and Chinese employed in mining.

Approved, May 6, 1882.

Write a response in which you:

- Use the excerpt to describe the ways in which xenophobia is embedded into the sections of the document.
- Explain the ways in which common U.S. citizens were also affected by the Chinese Exclusion Act.

Be sure to cite specific evidence from the text.

Constructed-Response Assignment #2

A fifth-grade student attempts to list important dates in California history. Shown below are the student's answers on a matching section of the quiz. Write a quick response in which you correct student errors and provide feedback. Cite specific historical materials to support your conclusions.

WORD BANK
First California Constitutional Convention Women's Suffrage Second California Constitutional Convention "Discovery of Gold" at Sutter's Mill The Chinese Exclusion Act Creation of the Mexican Republic

Student Directions: Please use the word bank above to fill in the proper event to match the appropriate year.

1822	Creation of the Mexican Republic
1848	"Discovery of Gold" at Sutter's Mill
1849	The Chinese Exclusion Act
1879	First California Constitutional Convention
1882	Second California Constitutional Convention
1911	Women's Suffrage

Write a quick response in which you correct student errors and provide history-based feedback.

Constructed-Response Assignment #3

Complete the exercise that follows.

> In the 1920s and 1930s, the U.S. and California governments joined forces in public works projects to create an expansive water delivery system in the West.

Using your knowledge of U.S. and California history, prepare a response in which you:

- Identify three important causes that led to the creation of the water delivery system.
- Select one of the causes you have identified.
- Explain why this cause was a decisive factor in the creation of modern dams, canals, and aqueduct systems in California.

Constructed-Response Assignment #4

Complete the exercise that follows.

> In the twentieth and twenty-first centuries, Californians have become enmeshed in the ongoing debate over undocumented labor and illegal immigration.

Using your knowledge of California history, prepare a response in which you:

- Identify four important focal points (social, political, economic, cultural) of the ongoing debate over undocumented labor and illegal immigration.
- Select one of the focal points you have identified.
- Explain the contentious arguments (on both "sides" of the debate) that have stemmed from this particular focal point.

Physical Science

Structure and Properties of Matter

Structure of Matter

Elements, Compounds, and Mixtures
Everything that takes up space and has mass is composed of *matter*. Understanding the basic characteristics and properties of matter helps with classification and identification.

An *element* is a substance that cannot be chemically decomposed to a simpler substance, while still retaining the properties of the element.

Compounds are composed of two or more elements that are chemically combined. The constituent elements in the compound are in constant proportions by mass.

When a material can be separated by physicals means (such as sifting it through a colander), it is called a *mixture*. Mixtures are categorized into two types: *heterogeneous* and *homogeneous*. Heterogeneous mixtures have physically distinct parts, which retain their different properties. A mix of salt and sugar is an example of a heterogeneous mixture. With heterogenous mixtures, it is possible that different samples from the same parent mixture may have different proportions of each component in the mixture. For example, in the sugar and salt mixture, there may be uneven mixing of the two, causing one random tablespoon sample to be mostly salt, while a different tablespoon sample may be mostly sugar.

A homogeneous mixture, also called a *solution*, has uniform properties throughout a given sample. An example of a homogeneous solution is salt fully dissolved in warm water. In this case, any number of samples taken from the parent solution would be identical.

Atoms, Molecules, and Ions
The basic building blocks of matter are *atoms*, which are extremely small particles that retain their identity during chemical reactions. Atoms can be singular or grouped to form elements. Elements are composed of one type of atom with the same properties.

Molecules are a group of atoms—either the same or different types—that are chemically bonded together by attractive forces. For example, hydrogen and oxygen are both atoms but, when bonded together, form water.

Ions are electrically-charged particles that are formed from an atom or a group of atoms via the loss or gain of electrons.

Basic Properties of Solids, Liquids, and Gases
Matter exists in certain *states*, or physical forms, under different conditions. These states are called *solid*, *liquid*, or *gas*.

A solid has a rigid, or set, form and occupies a fixed shape and volume. Solids generally maintain their shape when exposed to outside forces.

Liquids and gases are considered fluids, which have no set shape. Liquids are fluid, yet are distinguished from gases by their incompressibility (incapable of being compressed) and set volume. Liquids can be transferred from one container to another, but cannot be forced to fill containers of different volumes via compression without causing damage to the container. For example, if one attempts to force a given volume or number of particles of a liquid, such as water, into a fixed container, such as a small water bottle, the container would likely explode from the extra water.

A gas can easily be compressed into a confined space, such as a tire or an air mattress. Gases have no fixed shape or volume. They can also be subjected to outside forces, and the number of gas molecules that can fill a certain volume vary with changes in temperature and pressure.

Basic Structure of an Atom

Atomic Models
Theories of the atomic model have developed over the centuries. The most commonly referenced model of an atom was proposed by Niels Bohr. Bohr studied the models of J.J. Thomson and Ernest Rutherford and adapted his own theories from these existing models. Bohr compared the structure of the atom to that of the Solar System, where there is a center, or nucleus, with various sized orbitals circulating around this nucleus. This is a simplified version of what scientists have discovered about atoms, including the structures and placements of any orbitals. Modern science has made further adaptations to the model, including the fact that orbitals are actually made of electron "clouds."

Atomic Structure: Nucleus, Electrons, Protons, and Neutrons
Following the Bohr model of the atom, the nucleus, or core, is made up of positively charged *protons* and neutrally charged *neutrons*. The neutrons are theorized to be in the nucleus with the protons to provide greater "balance" at the center of the atom. The nucleus of the atom makes up the majority (more than 99%) of the mass of an atom, while the orbitals surrounding the nucleus contain negatively charged *electrons*. The entire structure of an atom is incredibly small.

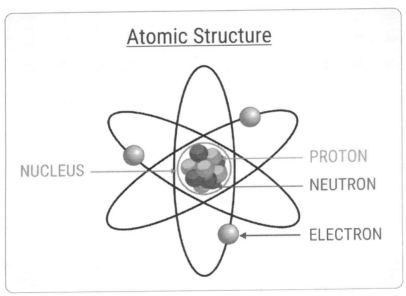

Atomic Number, Atomic Mass, and Isotopes
The *atomic number* of an atom is determined by the number of protons within the nucleus. When a substance is composed of atoms that all have the same atomic number, it is called an *element*. Elements are arranged by atomic number and grouped by properties in the *periodic table*.

An atom's *mass number* is determined by the sum of the total number of protons and neutrons in the atom. Most nuclei have a net neutral charge, and all atoms of one type have the same atomic number. However, there are some atoms of the same type that have a different mass number, due to an imbalance of neutrons. These are called *isotopes*. In isotopes, the atomic number, which is determined by the number of protons, is the same, but the mass number, which is determined by adding the protons and neutrons, is different due to the irregular number of neutrons.

Electron Arrangements

Electrons are most easily organized into distributions of subshells called *electron configurations*. Subshells fill from the inside (closest to the nucleus) to the outside. Therefore, once a subshell is filled, the next shell farther from the nucleus begins to fill, and so on. Atoms with electrons on the outside of a noble gas core (an atom with an electron inner shell that corresponds to the configuration of one of the noble gases, such as Neon) and pseudo-noble gas core (an atom with an electron inner shell that is similar to that of a noble gas core along with (n -1) d^{10} electrons), are called *valence* electrons. Valence electrons are primarily the electrons involved in chemical reactions. The similarities in their configurations account for similarities in properties of groups of elements. Essentially, the groups (vertical columns) on the periodic table all have similar characteristics, such as solubility and reactivity, due to their similar electron configurations.

Basic Characteristics of Radioactive Materials

Radioisotopes

As mentioned, an isotope is a variation of an element with a different number of neutrons in the nucleus, causing the nucleus to be unstable. When an element is unstable, it will go through decay or disintegration. All manmade elements are unstable and will break down. The length of time for an unstable element to break down is called the *half-life*. As an element breaks down, it forms other elements, known as daughters. Once a stable daughter is formed, the radioactive decay stops.

Characteristics of Alpha Particles, Beta Particles, and Gamma Radiation

As radioactive decay is occurring, the unstable element emits *alpha*, *beta*, and *gamma* radiation. Alpha and beta radiation are not as far-reaching or as powerful as gamma radiation. Alpha radiation is caused by the emission of two protons and two neutrons, while beta radiation is caused by the emission of either an electron or a positron. In contrast, gamma radiation is the release of photons of energy, not particles. This makes it the farthest-reaching and the most dangerous of these emissions.

Fission and Fusion

The splitting of an atom is referred to as fission, whereas the combination of two atoms into one is called fusion. To achieve fission and break apart an isotope, the unstable isotope is bombarded with high-speed particles. This process releases a large amount of energy and is what provides the energy in a nuclear power plant. Fusion occurs when two nuclei are merged to form a larger nucleus. The action of fusion also creates a tremendous amount of energy. To put the difference in the levels of energy between fission and fusion into perspective, the level of energy from fusion is what provides energy to the Earth's sun.

Basic Concepts and Relationships Involving Energy and Matter

The study of energy and matter, including heat and temperature, is called *thermodynamics*. There are four fundamental laws of thermodynamics, but the first two are the most commonly discussed.

First Law of Thermodynamics

The first law of thermodynamics is also known as the *conservation of energy*. This law states that energy cannot be created or destroyed, but is just transferred or converted into another form through a thermodynamic process. For example, if a liquid is boiled and then removed from the heat source, the liquid will eventually cool. This change in temperature is not because of a loss of energy or heat, but from a transfer of energy or heat to the surroundings. This can include the heating of nearby air molecules, or the transfer of heat from the liquid to the container or to the surface where the container is resting.

This law also applies to the idea of perpetual motion. A self-powered perpetual motion machine cannot exist. This is because the motion of the machine would inevitably lose some heat or energy to friction, whether from materials or from the air.

Second Law of Thermodynamics

The second law of thermodynamics is also known as the *law of entropy*. Entropy means chaos or disorder. In simple terms, this law means that all systems tend toward chaos. When one or more systems interacts with another, the total entropy is the sum of the interacting systems, and this overall sum also tends toward entropy.

Conservation of Matter in Chemical Systems

The conservation of energy is seen in the conservation of matter in chemical systems. This is helpful when attempting to understand chemical processes, since these processes must balance out. This means that extra matter cannot be created or destroyed, it must all be accounted for through a chemical process.

Kinetic and Potential Energy

The conservation of energy also applies to the study of energy in physics. This is clearly demonstrated through the kinetic and potential energy involved in a system.

The energy of motion is called *kinetic energy*. If an object has height, or is raised above the ground, it has *potential energy*. The total energy of any given system is the sum of the potential energy and the kinetic energy of the subject (object) in the system.

Potential energy is expressed by the equation:

$$PE = mgh$$

Where m equals the object's mass, g equals acceleration caused by the gravitational force acting on the object, and h equals the height of the object above the ground.

Kinetic energy is expressed by the following equation:

$$KE = \frac{1}{2} mv^2$$

Where m is the mass of the object and v is the velocity of the object.

Conservation of energy allows the total energy for any situation to be calculated by the following equation:

$$KE + PE$$

For example, a roller coaster poised at the top of a hill has all potential energy, and when it reaches the bottom of that hill, as it is speeding through its lowest point, it has all kinetic energy. Halfway down the hill, the total energy of the roller coaster is about half potential energy and half kinetic energy. Therefore, the total energy is found by calculating both the potential energy and the kinetic energy and then adding them together.

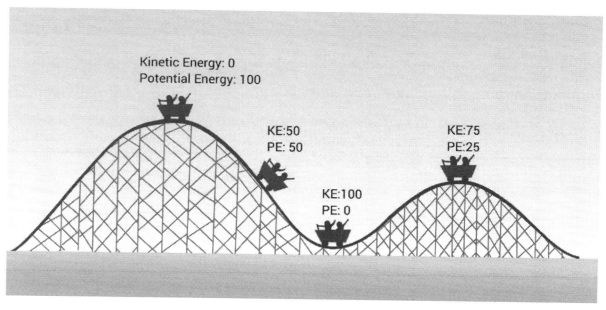

Transformations Between Different Forms of Energy

As stated by the conservation of energy, energy cannot be created or destroyed. If a system gains or loses energy, it is transformed within a single system from one type of energy to another or transferred from one system to another. For example, if the roller coaster system has potential energy that transfers to kinetic energy, the kinetic energy can then be transferred into thermal energy or heat released through braking as the coaster descends the hill. Energy can also transform from the chemical energy inside of a battery into the electrical energy that lights a train set. The energy released through nuclear fusion (when atoms are joined together, they release heat) is what supplies power plants with the energy for electricity. All energy is transferred from one form to another through different reactions. It can also be transferred through the simple action of atoms bumping into each other, causing a transfer of heat.

Differences Between Chemical and Physical Properties/Changes

A change in the physical form of matter, but not in its chemical identity, is known as a *physical change*. An example of a physical change is tearing a piece of paper in half. This changes the shape of the matter, but it is still paper.

Conversely, a *chemical change* alters the chemical composition or identity of matter. An example of a chemical change is burning a piece of paper. The heat necessary to burn the paper alters the chemical composition of the paper. This chemical change cannot be easily undone, since it has created at least one form of matter different than the original matter.

Temperature Scales

There are three main temperature scales used in science. The scale most often used in the United States is the *Fahrenheit* scale. This scale is based on the measurement of water freezing at 32° F and water boiling at 212° F. The Celsius scale uses 0° C as the temperature for water freezing and 100° C for water boiling. The accepted measurement by the International System of Units (from the French *Système international d'unités*), or SI, for temperature is the Kelvin scale. This is the scale employed in thermodynamics, since its zero is the basis for *absolute zero*, or the unattainable temperature, when matter no longer exhibits degradation.

The conversions between the temperature scales are as follows:

°Fahrenheit to °Celsius: $^0C = \frac{5}{9}(^0F - 32)$

°Celsius to °Fahrenheit: $^0F = \frac{9}{5}(^0C) + 32$

°Celsius to Kelvin: $K = {}^0C + 273.15$

Transfer of Thermal Energy and Its Basic Measurement
There are three basic ways in which energy is transferred. The first is through *radiation*. Radiation is transmitted through electromagnetic waves and it does not need a medium to travel (it can travel in a vacuum). This is how the sun warms the Earth, and typically applies to large objects with great amounts of heat or objects with a large difference in their heat measurements.

The second form of heat transfer is *convection*. Convection involves the movement of "fluids" from one place to another. (The term *fluid* does not necessarily apply to a liquid, but any substance in which the molecules can slide past each other, such as gases.) It is this movement that transfers the heat to or from an area. Generally, convective heat transfer occurs through diffusion, which is when heat moves from areas of higher concentrations of particles to those of lower concentrations of particles and less heat. This process of flowing heat can be assisted or amplified through the use of fans and other methods of forcing the molecules to move.

The final process is called *conduction*. Conduction involves transferring heat through the touching of molecules. Molecules can either bump into each other to transfer heat, or they may already be touching each other and transfer the heat through this connection. For example, imagine a circular burner on an electric stove top. The coil begins to glow orange near the base of the burner that is connected to the stove because it heats up first. Since the burner is one continuous piece of metal, the molecules are touching each other. As they pass heat along the coil, it begins to glow all the way to the end.

To determine the amount of heat required to warm the coil in the above example, the type of material from which the coil is made must be known. The quantity of heat required to raise one gram of a substance one degree Celsius (or Kelvin) at a constant pressure is called *specific heat*. This measurement can be calculated for masses of varying substances by using the following equation:

$$q = s \times m \times \Delta t$$

Where *q* is the specific heat, *s* is the specific heat of the material being used, *m* is the mass of the substance being used, and *Δt* is the change in temperature.

A calorimeter is used to measure the heat of a reaction (either expelled or absorbed) and the temperature changes in a controlled system. A simple calorimeter can be made by using an insulated coffee cup with a thermometer inside. For this example, a lid of some sort would be preferred to prevent any escaping heat that could be lost by evaporation or convection.

Applications of Energy and Matter Relationships

When considering the cycling of matter in ecosystems, the flow of energy and atoms is from one organism to another. The *trophic level* of an organism refers to its position in a food chain. The level shows the relationship between it and other organisms on the same level and how they use and transfer energy to other levels in the food chain. This includes consumption and decomposition for the transfer of energy among organisms and matter. The sun provides energy through radiation to the Earth, and plants convert this light energy into chemical energy, which is then released to fuel the organism's activities.

Naturally occurring elements deep within the Earth's mantle release heat during their radioactive decay. This release of heat drives convection currents in the Earth's magma, which then drives plate tectonics. The transfer of heat from these actions causes the plates to move and create convection currents in the oceans. This type of cycling can also be seen in transformations of rocks. Sedimentary rocks can undergo significant amounts of heat and pressure to become metamorphic rocks. These rocks can melt back into magma, which then becomes igneous rock or, with extensive weathering and erosion, can revert to sediment and form sedimentary rocks over time. Under the right conditions (weathering and erosion), igneous rocks can also become sediment, which eventually compresses into sedimentary rock. Erosion helps the process by redepositing rocks into sediment on the sea floor.

All of these cycles are examples of the transfer of energy from one type into another, along with the conservation of mass from one level to the next.

Periodicity and States of Matter

Periodic Table of the Elements
Using the periodic table, elements are arranged by atomic number, similar characteristics, and electron configurations in a tabular format. The columns, called *groups*, are sorted by similar chemical properties and characteristics such as appearance and reactivity. This can be seen in the shiny texture of metals,

the high melting points of alkali Earth metals, and the softness of post-transition metals. The rows are arranged by electron valance configurations and are called *periods*.

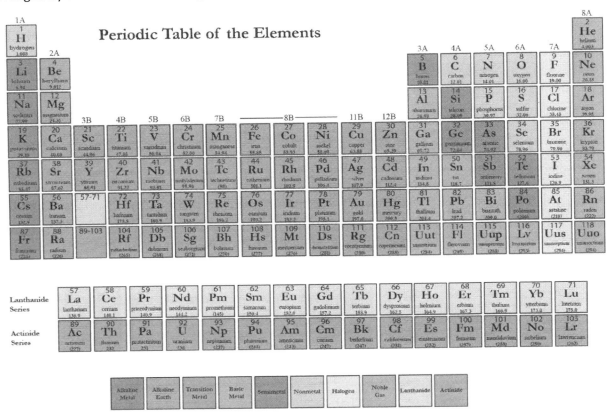

The elements are set in ascending order from left to right by atomic number. As mentioned, the atomic number is the number of protons contained within the nucleus of the atom. For example, the element helium has an atomic number of 2 because it has two protons in its nucleus.

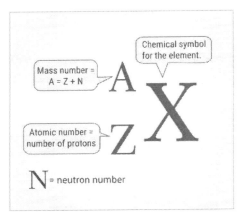

An element's mass number is calculated by adding the number of protons and neutrons of an atom together, while the atomic mass of an element is the weighted average of the naturally occurring atoms of a given element, or the relative abundance of isotopes that might be used in chemistry. For example, the atomic (mass) number of chlorine is 35; however, the atomic mass of chlorine is 35.5 amu (atomic mass unit). This discrepancy exists because there are many isotopes (meaning the nucleus could have 36 instead of 35 protons) occurring in nature. Given the prevalence of the various isotopes, the average of all of the atomic masses turns out to be 35.5 amu, which is slightly higher than chlorine's number on the periodic table. As another example, carbon has an atomic number of 12, but its atomic mass is 12.01 amu because, unlike chlorine, there are few naturally occurring isotopes to raise the average number.

Elements are arranged according to their valance electron configurations, which also contribute to trends in chemical properties. These properties help to further categorize the elements into blocks, including metals, non-metals, transition metals, alkali metals, alkali earth metals, metalloids, lanthanides, actinides, diatomics, post-transition metals, polyatomic non-metals, and noble gases. Noble gases (the far-right column) have a full outer electron valence shell. The elements in this block possess similar characteristics such as being colorless, odorless, and having low chemical reactivity. Another block, the metals, tend to be shiny, highly conductive, and easily form alloys with each other, non-metals, and noble gases.

The symbols of the elements on the periodic table are a single letter or a two-letter combination that is usually derived from the element's name. Many of the elements have Latin origins for their names, and their atomic symbols do not match their modern names. For example, iron is derived from the word *ferrum*, so its symbol is Fe, even though it is now called iron. The naming of the elements began with those of natural origin and their ancient names, which included the use of the ending "ium." This naming practice has been continued for all elements that have been named since the 1940s. Now, the names of new elements must be approved by the International Union of Pure and Applied Chemistry.

The elements on the periodic table are arranged by number and grouped by trends in their physical properties and electron configurations. Certain trends are easily described by the arrangement of the periodic table, which includes the increase of the atomic radius as elements go from right to left and from top to bottom on the periodic table. Another trend on the periodic table is the increase in ionization energy (or the tendency of an atom to attract and form bonds with electrons). This tendency increases from left to right and from bottom to top of the periodic table—the opposite directions of the trend for the atomic radius. The elements on the right side and near the bottom of the periodic table tend to attract electrons with the intent to gain, while the elements on the left and near the top usually lose, or give up, one or more electrons in order to bond. The only exceptions to this rule are the noble gases. Since the noble gases have full valence shells, they do not have a tendency to lose or gain electrons.

Chemical reactivity is another trend identifiable by the groupings of the elements on the periodic table. The chemical reactivity of metals decreases from left to right and while going higher on the table. Conversely, non-metals increase in chemical reactivity from left to right and while going lower on the table. Again, the noble gases present an exception to these trends because they have very low chemical reactivity.

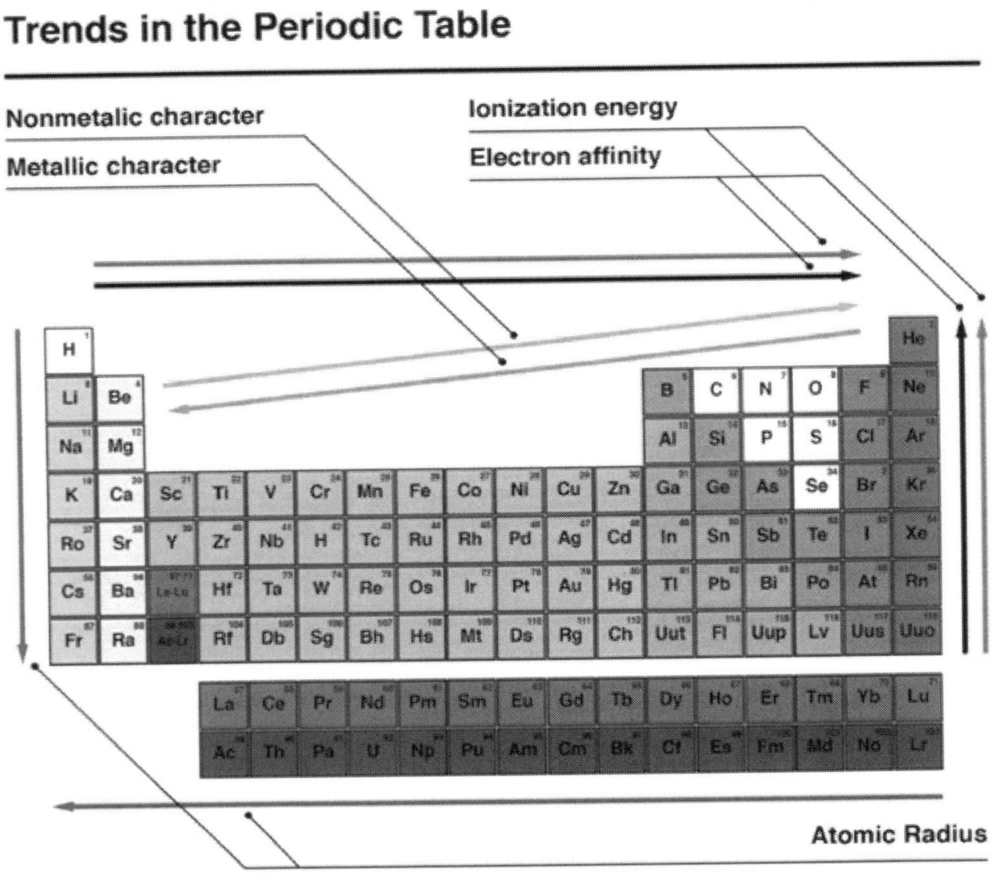

Trends in the Periodic Table

Nonmetalic character

Metallic character

Ionization energy

Electron affinity

Atomic Radius

States of Matter and Factors that Affect Phase Changes

Matter is most commonly found in three distinct states: solid, liquid, and gas. A solid has a distinct shape and a defined volume. A liquid has a more loosely defined shape and a definite volume, while a gas has no definite shape or volume. The *Kinetic Theory of Matter* states that matter is composed of a large number of small particles (specifically, atoms and molecules) that are in constant motion. The distance between the separations in these particles determines the state of the matter: solid, liquid, or gas. In gases, the particles have a large separation and no attractive forces. In liquids, there is moderate separation between particles and some attractive forces to form a loose shape. Solids have almost no separation between their particles, causing a defined and set shape. The constant movement of particles causes them to bump into each other, thus allowing the particles to transfer energy between each other. This bumping and transferring of energy helps explain the transfer of heat and the relationship between pressure, volume, and temperature.

The *Ideal Gas Law* states that pressure, volume, and temperature are all related through the equation: $PV = nRT$, where P is pressure, V is volume, n is the amount of the substance in moles, R is the gas constant, and T is temperature.

Through this relationship, volume and pressure are both proportional to temperature, but pressure is inversely proportional to volume. Therefore, if the equation is balanced, and the volume decreases in the system, pressure needs to proportionately increase to keep both sides of the equation balanced. In contrast, if the equation is unbalanced and the pressure increases, then the temperature would also increase, since pressure and temperature are directly proportional.

When pressure, temperature, or volume change in matter, a change in state can occur. Changes in state include solid to liquid (melting), liquid to gas (evaporation), solid to gas (sublimation), gas to solid (deposition), gas to liquid (condensation), and liquid to solid (freezing). There is one other state of matter called *plasma*, which is seen in lightning, television screens, and neon lights. Plasma is most commonly converted from the gas state at extremely high temperatures.

The amount of energy needed to change matter from one state to another is labeled by the terms for phase changes. For example, the temperature needed to supply enough energy for matter to change from a liquid to a gas is called the *heat of vaporization*. When heat is added to matter in order to cause a change in state, there will be an increase in temperature until the matter is about to change its state. During its transition, all of the added heat is used by the matter to change its state, so there is no increase in temperature. Once the transition is complete, then the added heat will again yield an increase in temperature.

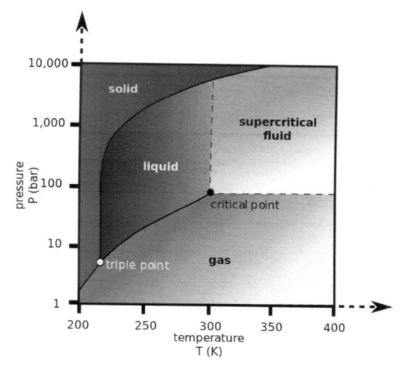

Each state of matter is considered to be a phase, and changes between phases are represented by phase diagrams. These diagrams show the effects of changes in pressure and temperature on matter. The states of matter fall into areas on these charts called *heating curves*.

Chemical Nomenclature, Composition, and Bonding

<u>Simple Compounds and Their Chemical Formulas</u>
Chemical formulas represent the proportion of the number of atoms in a chemical compound. Chemical symbols are used for the elements present and numerical values. Parentheses are also sometimes used to show the number of combinations of the elements in relation to their ionic charges. An element's

ionic charge can be determined by its location on the periodic table. This information is then used to correctly combine its atoms in a compound.

For example, the chemical formula for sodium chloride (table salt) is the combination of sodium (Na, ionic charge of +1) and chlorine (Cl, ionic charge of -1). From its placement on the periodic table, the electron valence of an outer shell can be determined: sodium has an ionic charge of +1, while chlorine has an ionic charge of -1. Since these two elements have an equal and opposite amount of charge, they combine in a neutral one-to-one ratio: NaCl. The naming of compounds depends mainly on the second element in a chemical compound. If it is a non-metal (such as chlorine), it is written with an "ide" at the end. The compound NaCl is called "sodium chloride."

If the elements forming a compound do not have equal and opposite ionic charges, there will be an unequal number of each element in the compound to balance the ionic charge. This situation happens with many elements, for example, in the combination of nickel and oxygen into nickel oxide (Ni_2O_3). Nickel has a +3 ionic charge and oxygen has a -2 ionic charge, so when forming a compound, there must be two nickel atoms for every three oxygen atoms (a common factor of 6) to balance the charge of the compound. This compound is called "nickel oxide."

A chemical formula can also be written from a compound's name. For instance, the compound carbon dioxide is formed by the combination of carbon and oxygen. The word "dioxide" means there are two oxygen atoms for every carbon atom, so it is written as CO_2.

To better represent the composition of compounds, structural formulas are used. The combination of atoms is more precisely depicted by lining up the electron configuration of the outer electron shell through a Lewis dot diagram.

The Lewis dot diagram, named for Gilbert N. Lewis, shows the arrangement of the electrons in the outer shell and how these electrons can pair/bond with the outer shell electrons of other atoms when forming compounds. The diagram is created by writing the symbol of an element and then drawing dots to represent the outer shell of valence electrons around what would be an invisible square surrounding the symbol. The placement of the first two dots can vary based on the school of teaching. For the given example, the first dot is placed on the top and then the next dot is placed beside it, since it represents the pair of electrons in the 1s valence shell. The next dots (electrons) are placed one at a time on each side—right, bottom, left, right bottom left, etc.—of the element symbol until all of the valence shell electrons are represented, or the structure has eight dots (electrons), which means it is full. This method gives a more specific picture of compounds, how they are structured, and what electrons are available for bonding, sharing, and forming new compounds. For example, the compound sodium chloride is written separately with sodium having one valence electron and chlorine having seven valence electrons. Then, combined with a total of eight electrons, it is written with two dots being shared between the two elements.

$$Na + \overset{\bullet\bullet}{\underset{\bullet\bullet}{\cdot \overset{}{C}l}} \colon \rightarrow Na^+ + \overset{\bullet\bullet}{\underset{\bullet\bullet}{\colon \overset{}{C}l}} \colon {}^-$$

Types of Chemical Bonding
A chemical bond is a strong attractive force that can exist between atoms. The bonding of atoms is separated into two main categories. The first category, *ionic bonding,* primarily describes the bonding that occurs between oppositely charged ions in a regular crystal arrangement. It primarily exists between salts, which are known to be ionic. Ionic bonds are held together by the electrostatic attraction

between oppositely charged ions. This type of bonding involves the transfer of electrons from the valence shell of one atom to the valence shell of another atom. If an atom loses an electron from its valence shell, it becomes a positive ion, or *cation*. If an atom gains an electron, it becomes a negative ion, or an *anion*. The Lewis electron-dot symbol is used to more simply express the electron configuration of atoms, especially when forming bonds.

The second type of bonding is covalent bonding. This bonding involves the sharing of a pair of electrons between atoms. There are no ions involved in covalent bonding, but the force holding the atoms together comes from the balance between the attractive and repulsive forces involving the shared electron and the nuclei. Atoms frequently engage is this type of bonding when it enables them to fill their outer valence shell.

Mole Concept and Its Applications

The calculation of mole ratios of reactants and products involved in a chemical reaction is called "stoichiometry." To find these ratios, one must first find the proportion of the number of molecules in one mole of a substance. This relates the molar mass of a compound to its mass and this relationship is a constant known as *Avogadro's number* (6.23×10^{23}). Since it is a ratio, there are no dimensions (or units) for Avogadro's number.

Molar Mass and Percent Composition

The molar mass of a substance is the measure of the mass of one mole of the substance. For pure elements, the molar mass is also known as the atomic mass unit (amu) of the substance. For compounds, it can be calculated by adding the molar masses of each substance in the compound. For example, the molar mass of carbon is 12.01 g/mol, while the molar mass of water (H_2O) requires finding the sum of the molar masses of the constituents ((1.01 x 2 = 2.02 g/mol for hydrogen) + (16.0 g/mol for oxygen) = 18.02 g/mol).

The percentage of a compound in a composition can be determined by taking the individual molar masses of each component divided by the total molar mass of the compound, multiplied by 100. Determining the percent composition of carbon dioxide (CO_2) first requires the calculation of the molar mass of CO_2.

molar mass of carbon = 12.01 x 1 atom = 12.01 g/mol

molar mass of oxygen = 16.0 × 2 atoms = 32.0 g/mol

molar mass of CO_2 = 12.01 g/mol + 32.0 g/mol = 44.01 g/mol

Next, each individual mass is divided by the total mass and multiplied by 100 to get the percent composition of each component.

12.01/44.01 = (0.2729 × 100) = 27.29% carbon

32.0/44.01 = (0.7271 × 100) = 72.71% oxygen

(A quick check in the addition of the percentages should always yield 100%.)

Chemical Reactions

Basic Concepts of Chemical Reactions

Chemical reactions rearrange the initial atoms of the reactants into different substances. These types of reactions can be expressed through the use of balanced chemical equations. A *chemical equation* is the symbolic representation of a chemical reaction through the use of chemical terms. The reactants at the beginning (or on the left side) of the equation must equal the products at the end (or on the right side) of the equation.

For example, table salt (NaCl) forms through the chemical reaction between sodium (Na) and chlorine (Cl) and is written as: $Na + Cl_2 \rightarrow NaCl$.

However, this equation is not balanced because there are two sodium atoms for every pair of chlorine atoms involved in this reaction. So, the left side is written as: $2Na + Cl_2 \rightarrow NaCl$.

Next, the right side needs to balance the same number of sodium and chlorine atoms. So, the right side is written as: $2Na + Cl_2 \rightarrow 2NaCl$. Now, this is a balanced chemical equation.

Chemical reactions typically fall into two types of categories: *endothermic* and *exothermic*.

An endothermic reaction absorbs heat, whereas an exothermic reaction releases heat. For example, in an endothermic reaction, heat is drawn from the container holding the chemicals, which cools the container. Conversely, an exothermic reaction emits heat from the reaction and warms the container holding the chemicals.

Factors that can affect the rate of a reaction include temperature, pressure, the physical state of the reactants (e.g., surface area), concentration, and catalysts/enzymes.

The formula $PV = nRT$ shows that an increase in any of the variables (pressure, volume, or temperature) affects the overall reaction. The physical state of two reactants can also determine how much interaction they have with each other. If two reactants are both in a fluid state, they may have the capability of interacting more than if solid. The addition of a catalyst or an enzyme can increase the rate of a chemical reaction, without the catalyst or enzyme undergoing a change itself.

Le Chatelier's principle describes factors that affect a reaction's equilibrium. Essentially, when introducing a "shock" to a system (or chemical reaction), a positive feedback/shift in equilibrium is often the response. In accordance with the second law of thermodynamics, this imbalance will eventually even itself out, but not without counteracting the effects of the reaction.

There are many different types of chemical reactions. A *synthesis reaction* is the combination of two or more elements into a compound. For example, the synthesis reaction of hydrogen and oxygen forms water.

$$2 H_2(g) + O_2(g) \rightarrow 2 H_2O(g)$$

A *decomposition reaction* is the breaking down of a compound into its more basic components. For example, the decomposition, or electrolysis, of water results in it breaking down into oxygen and hydrogen gas.

$$2 H_2O \rightarrow 2 H_2 + O_2$$

A *combustion reaction* is similar to a decomposition reaction, but it requires oxygen and heat for the reaction to occur. For example, the burning of a candle requires oxygen to ignite and the reaction forms carbon dioxide during the process.

$$CH_4(g) + 2O_2(g) \rightarrow CO_2(g) + 2H_2O(g)$$

There are also single and double replacement reactions where compounds swap components with each other to form new compounds. In the *single replacement reaction*, a single element will swap into a compound, thus releasing one of the compound's elements to become the new single element. For example, the reaction between iron and copper sulfate will create copper and iron sulfate.

$$1Fe(s) + 1CuSO_4(aq) \rightarrow 1FeSO_4(aq) + 1Cu(s)$$

In a *double replacement reaction*, two compounds swap components to form two new compounds. For example, the reaction between sodium sulfide and hydrochloric acid forms sodium chloride and hydrogen sulfide.

$$Na_2S + HCl \rightarrow NaCl + H_2S$$

An organic reaction is a chemical reaction involving the components of carbon and hydrogen.

Finally, there are oxidation/reduction (redox or half) reactions. These reactions involve the loss of electrons from one species (oxidation), and the gain of electrons to the other species (reduction). For example, the oxidation of magnesium is as follows:

$$2\ Mg(s) + O_2(g) \rightarrow 2\ MgO(s)$$

Acid-Base Chemistry

Simple Acid-Base Chemistry
If something has a sour taste, it is acidic, and if something has a bitter taste, it is basic. Unfortunately, it can be extremely dangerous to ingest chemicals in an attempt to classify them as an acid or a base. Therefore, acids and bases are generally identified by the reactions they have when combined with water. An acid will increase the concentration of the hydrogen ion (H^+), while a base will increase the concentration of the hydroxide ion (OH^-).

To better categorize the varying strengths of acids and bases, the pH scale is used. The pH scale provides a logarithmic (base 10) grading to acids and bases based on their strength. The pH scale contains values from 0 through 14, with 7 being neutral. If a solution registers below 7 on the pH scale, it is considered an acid. If it registers higher than 7, it is considered a base. To perform a quick test on a solution, litmus paper can be used. A base will turn red litmus paper blue, whereas an acid will turn blue litmus paper red. To gauge the strength of an acid or base, a test of phenolphthalein can be used. An acid will turn red phenolphthalein colorless, and a base will turn colorless phenolphthalein pink. As demonstrated with these types of tests, acids and bases neutralize each other. When acids and bases react with one another, they produce salts (also called ionic substances).

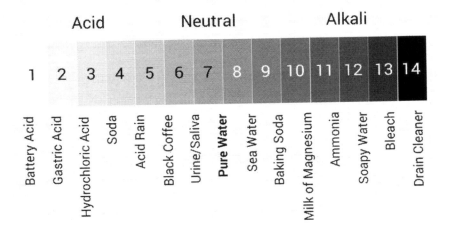

Solutions and Solubility

Different Types of Solutions

A *solution* is a homogenous mixture of more than one substance. A *solute* is another substance that can be dissolved into a substance called a *solvent*. If only a small amount of solute is dissolved in a solvent, the solution formed is said to be *diluted*. If a large amount of solute is dissolved into the solvent, then the solution is said to be *concentrated*. For example, water from a typical, unfiltered household tap is diluted because it contains other minerals in very small amounts.

Solution Concentration

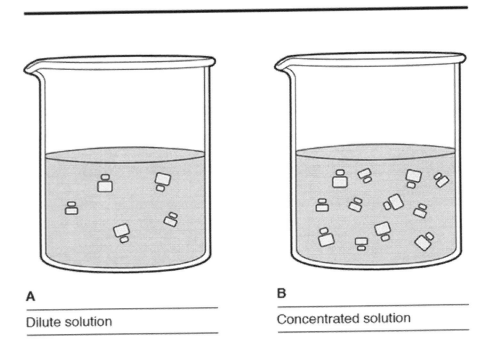

A

Dilute solution

B

Concentrated solution

If more solute is being added to a solvent, but not dissolving, the solution is called *saturated*. For example, when hummingbirds eat sugar-water from feeders, they prefer it as sweet as possible. When trying to dissolve enough sugar (solute) into the water (solvent), there will be a point where the sugar crystals will no longer dissolve into the solution and will remain as whole pieces floating in the water. At this point, the solution is considered saturated and cannot accept more sugar. This level, at which a solvent cannot accept and dissolve any more solute, is called its *saturation point*. In some cases, it is possible to force more solute to be dissolved into a solvent, but this will result in crystallization. The state of a solution on the verge of crystallization, or in the process of crystallization, is called a *supersaturated* solution. This can also occur in a solution that seems stable, but if it is disturbed, the change can begin the crystallization process.

Although the terms *dilute*, *concentrated*, *saturated*, and *supersaturated* give qualitative descriptions of solutions, a more precise quantitative description needs to be established for the use of chemicals. This holds true especially for mixing strong acids or bases. The method for calculating the concentration of a solution is done through finding its molarity. In some instances, such as environmental reporting, molarity is measured in parts per million (ppm). Parts per million, is the number of milligrams of a substance dissolved in one liter of water. To find the *molarity*, or the amount of solute per unit volume of solution, for a solution, the following formula is used:

$$c = \frac{n}{V}$$

In this formula, c is the molarity (or unit moles of solute per volume of solution), n is the amount of solute measured in moles, and V is the volume of the solution, measured in liters.

Example:

What is the molarity of a solution made by dissolving 2.0 grams of NaCl into enough water to make 100 mL of solution?

To solve this, the number of moles of NaCl needs to be calculated:

First, to find the mass of NaCl, the mass of each of the molecule's atoms is added together as follows:

23.0g (Na) + 35.5g (Cl) = 58.8g NaCl

Next, the given mass of the substance is multiplied by one mole per total mass of the substance:

2.0g NaCl × (1 mol NaCl/58.5g NaCl) = 0.034 mol NaCl

Finally, the moles are divided by the number of liters of the solution to find the molarity:

(0.034 mol NaCl)/(0.100L) = 0.34 M NaCl

To prepare a solution of a different concentration, the *mass solute* must be calculated from the molarity of the solution. This is done via the following process:

Example:

How would you prepare 600.0 mL of 1.20 M solution of sodium chloride?

To solve this, the given information needs to be set up:

1.20 M NaCl =1.20 mol NaCl/1.00 L of solution

0.600 L solution × (1.20 mol NaCl/1.00 L of solution) = 0.72 moles NaCl

0.72 moles NaCl × (58.5g NaCl/1 mol NaCl) = 42.12 g NaCl

This means that one must dissolve 42.12 g NaCl in enough water to make 600.0 L of solution.

Factors Affecting the Solubility of Substances and the Dissolving Process
Certain factors can affect the rate in dissolving processes. These include temperature, pressure, particle size, and agitation (stirring). As mentioned, the *ideal gas law* states that *PV = nRT*, where *P* equals pressure, *V* equals volume, and *T* equals temperature. If the pressure, volume, or temperature are affected in a system, it will affect the entire system. Specifically, if there is an increase in temperature, there will be an increase in the dissolving rate. An increase in the pressure can also increase the dissolving rate. Particle size and agitation can also influence the dissolving rate, since all of these factors contribute to the breaking of intermolecular forces that hold solute particles together. Once these forces are broken, the solute particles can link to particles in the solvent, thus dissolving the solute.

A *solubility curve* shows the relationship between the mass of solute that a solvent holds at a given temperature. If a reading is on the solubility curve, the solvent is *full* (*saturated*) and cannot hold anymore solute. If a reading is above the curve, the solvent is *unstable* (*supersaturated*) from holding more solute than it should. If a reading is below the curve, the solvent is *unsaturated* and could hold more solute.

If a solvent has different electronegativities, or partial charges, it is considered to be *polar*. Water is an example of a polar solvent. If a solvent has similar electronegativities, or lacking partial charges, it is considered to be *non-polar*. Benzene is an example of a non-polar solvent. Polarity status is important when attempting to dissolve solutes. The phrase "like dissolves like" is the key to remembering what will happen when attempting to dissolve a solute in a solvent. A polar solute will dissolve in a like, or polar solvent. Similarly, a non-polar solute will dissolve in a non-polar solvent. When a reaction produces a solid, the solid is called a *precipitate*. A precipitation reaction can be used for removing a salt (an ionic compound that results from a neutralization reaction) from a solvent, such as water. For water, this process is called ionization. Therefore, the products of a neutralization reaction (when an acid and base react) are a salt and water. Therefore, the products of a neutralization reaction (when an acid and base react) are a salt and water.

When a solute is added to a solvent to lower the freezing point of the solvent, it is called *freezing point depression*. This is a useful process, especially when applied in colder temperatures. For example, the addition of salt to ice in winter allows the ice to melt at a much lower temperature, thus creating safer road conditions for driving. Unfortunately, the freezing point depression from salt can only lower the melting point of ice so far, and is ineffectual when temperatures are too low. This same process, with a mix of ethylene glycol and water, is also used to keep the radiator fluid (antifreeze) in an automobile from freezing during the winter.

Principles of Motion and Energy

Mechanics

Description of Motion in One and Two Dimensions
The description of motion is known as *kinetics*, and the causes of motion are known as *dynamics*. Motion in one dimension is known as a *scalar* quantity. It consists of one measurement such as length (length or distance is also known as displacement), speed, or time. Motion in two dimensions is known as a *vector* quantity. This would be a speed with a direction, or velocity.

Velocity is the measure of the change in distance over the change in time. All vector quantities have a direction that can be relayed through the sign of an answer, such as -5.0 m/s or +5.0 m/s. The objects registering these velocities would be in opposite directions, where the change in distance is denoted by Δx and the change in time is denoted by Δt:

$$v = \frac{\Delta x}{\Delta t}$$

Acceleration is the measure of the change in an object's velocity over a change in time, where the change in velocity, $v_2 - v_1$, is denoted by Δv and the change in time, $t_1 - t_2$, is denoted by Δt:

$$a = \frac{\Delta v}{\Delta t}$$

The linear momentum, p, of an object is the result of the objects mass, m, multiplied by its velocity, v, and is described by the equation:

$$p = mv$$

This aspect becomes important when one object hits another object. For example, the linear momentum of a small sports car will be much smaller than the linear momentum of a large semi-truck. Thus, the semi-truck will cause more damage to the car than the car to the truck.

Newton's Three Laws of Motion
Sir Isaac Newton summarized his observations and calculations relating to motion into three concise laws.

First Law of Motion: Inertia
This law states that an object in motion tends to stay in motion or an object at rest tends to stay at rest, unless the object is acted upon by an outside force.

For example, a rock sitting on the ground will remain in the same place, unless it is pushed or lifted from its place.

The First Law also includes the relation of weight to gravity and force between objects relative to the distance separating them.

$$Weight = G\frac{Mm}{r^2}$$

In this equation, *G* is the gravitational constant, *M* and *m* are the masses of the two objects, and *r* is the distance separating the two objects.

Second Law of Motion: F = ma
This law states that the force on a given body is the result of the object's mass multiplied by any acceleration acting upon the object. For objects falling on Earth, an acceleration is caused by gravitational force (9.8 m/s^2).

Third Law of Motion: Action-Reaction
This law states that for every action there is an equal and opposite reaction. For example, if a person punches a wall, the wall exerts a force back on the person's hand equal and opposite to his or her punching force. Since the wall has more mass, it absorbs the impact of the punch better than the person's hand.

Mass, Weight, and Gravity
Mass is a measure of how much of a substance exists, or how much inertia an object has. The mass of an object does not change based on the object's location, but the weight of an object does vary with its location.

For example, a 15-kg mass has a weight that is determined by acceleration from the force of gravity here on Earth. However, if that same 15-kg mass were to be weighed on the moon, it would weigh much less, since the acceleration force from the moon's gravity is approximately one-sixth of that on Earth.

Weight = mass × acceleration

W_{Earth} = 15 kg × 9.8 m/s^2 > W_{Moon} = 15 kg × 1.62 m/s^2

W_{Earth} = 147N   >   24.3N

Analysis of Motion and Forces
Projectile Motion describes the path of an object in the air. Generally, it is described by two-dimensional movement, such as a stone thrown through the air. This activity maps to a parabolic curve. However, the definition of projectile motion also applies to free fall, or the non-arced motion of an object in a path straight up and/or straight down. When an object is thrown horizontally, it is subject to the same influence of gravity as an object that is dropped straight down. The farther the projectile motion, the farther the distance of the object's flight.

Friction is a force that opposes motion. It can be caused by a number of materials; there is even friction caused by air. Whenever two differing materials touch, rub, or pass by each other, it will create friction, or an oppositional force, unless the interaction occurs in a true vacuum. To move an object across a floor, the force exerted on the object must overcome the frictional force keeping the object in place. Friction is also why people can walk on surfaces. Without the oppositional force of friction to a shoe pressing on the floor, a person would not be able to grip the floor to walk—similar to the challenge of walking on ice. Without friction, shoes slip and are unable to help people propel forward and walk.

When calculating the effects of objects hitting (or colliding with) each other, several things are important to remember. One of these is the definition of momentum: the mass of an object multiplied by the object's velocity. As mentioned, it is expressed by the following equation:

$$p = mv$$

Here, p is equal to an object's momentum, m is equal to the object's mass, and v is equal to the object's velocity.

Another important thing to remember is the principle of the conservation of linear momentum. The total momentum for objects in a situation will be the same before and after a collision. There are two primary types of collisions: elastic and inelastic. In an elastic collision, the objects collide and then travel in different directions. During an inelastic collision, the objects collide and then stick together in their final direction of travel. The total momentum in an elastic collision is calculated by using the following formula:

$$m_1 v_1 + m_2 v_2 = m_1 v_1 + m_2 v_2$$

Here, m_1 and m_2 are the masses of two separate objects, and v_1 and v_2 are the velocities, respectively, of the two separate objects.

The total momentum in an inelastic collision is calculated by using the following formula:

$$m_1 v_1 + m_2 v_2 = (m_1 + m_2) v_f$$

Here, v_f is the final velocity of the two masses after they stick together post-collision.

Example:
If two bumper cars are speeding toward each other, head-on, and collide, they are designed to bounce off of each other and head in different directions. This would be an elastic collision.

If real cars are speeding toward each other, head-on, and collide, there is a good chance their bumpers might get caught together and their direction of travel would be together in the same direction.

An *axis* is an invisible line on which an object can rotate. This is most easily observed with a toy top. There is actually a point (or rod) through the center of the top on which the top can be observed to be spinning. This is called the axis.

When objects move in a circle by spinning on their own axis, or because they are tethered around a central point (also an axis), they exhibit circular motion. Circular motion is similar in many ways to linear (straight line) motion; however, there are a few additional points to note. A spinning object is always accelerating because it is always changing direction. The force causing this constant acceleration on or around an axis is called *centripetal force* and is often associated with centripetal acceleration.

Centripetal force always pulls toward the axis of rotation. An imaginary reactionary force, called *centrifugal force*, is the outward force felt when an object is undergoing circular motion. This reactionary force is not the real force; it just feels like it is there. For this reason, it has also been referred to as a "fictional force." The true force is the one pulling inward, or the centripetal force.

The terms *centripetal* and *centrifugal* are often mistakenly interchanged. If the centripetal force acting on an object moving with circular motion is removed, the object will continue moving in a straight line tangent to the point on the circle where the object last experienced the centripetal force. For example, when a traditional style washing machine spins a load of clothes to expunge the water from the load, it rapidly spins the machine barrel. A force is pulling in toward the center of the circle (centripetal force). At the same time, the wet clothes, which are attempting to move in a straight line, are colliding with the outer wall of the barrel that is moving in a circle. The interaction between the wet clothes and barrel wall cause a reactionary force to the centripetal force and this expels the water out of the small holes that line the outer wall of the barrel.

Conservation of Angular Momentum
An object moving in a circular motion also has momentum; for circular motion, it is called *angular momentum*. This is determined by rotational inertia, rotational velocity, and the distance of the mass from the axis or center of rotation. When objects exhibit circular motion, they also demonstrate the *conservation of angular momentum*, meaning that the angular momentum of a system is always constant, regardless of the placement of the mass. Rotational inertia can be affected by how far the mass of the object is placed with respect to the axis of rotation. The greater the distance between the mass and the axis of rotation, the slower the rotational velocity. Conversely, if the mass is closer to the axis of rotation, the rotational velocity is faster. A change in one affects the other, thus conserving the angular momentum. This holds true as long as no external forces act upon the system.

For example, ice skaters spinning in on one ice skate extends their arms out for a slower rotational velocity. When skaters bring their arms in close to their bodies (which lessens the distance between the mass and the axis of rotation), their rotational velocity increases and they spin much faster. Some skaters extend their arms straight up above their head, which causes an extension of the axis of rotation, thus removing any distance between the mass and the center of rotation, which maximizes their rotational velocity.

Another example is when a person selects a horse on a merry-go-round: the placement of their horse can affect their ride experience. All of the horses are traveling with the same rotational speed, but in order to travel along the same plane as the merry-go-round turns, a horse on the outside will have a greater linear speed because it is further away from the axis of rotation. Essentially, an outer horse has to cover a lot more ground than a horse on the inside in order to keep up with the rotational speed of the merry-go-round platform. Thrill seekers should always select an outer horse.

The center of mass is the point that provides the average location for the total mass of a system. The word "system" can apply to just one object/particle or to many. The center of mass for a system can be calculated by finding the average of the mass of each object and multiplying by its distance from an origin point using the following formula:

$$x_{centerofmass} = \frac{m_1 x_1 + m_2 x_2}{m_1 + m_2}$$

In this case, x is the distance from the point of origin for the center of mass and each respective object, and m is the mass of each object.

To calculate for more than one object, the pattern can be continued by adding additional masses and their respective distances from the origin point.

Simple Machines

A simple machine is a mechanical device that changes the direction or magnitude of a force. There are six basic types of simple machines: lever, wedge, screw, inclined plane, wheel and axle, and pulley.

Here is how each type works and an example:

- A lever helps lift heavy items higher with less force, such as a crowbar lifting a large cast iron lid.

- A wedge helps apply force to a specific area by focusing the pressure, such as an axe splitting a tree.

- An inclined plane, such as a loading dock ramp, helps move heavy items up vertical distances with less force.

- A screw is an inclined plane wrapped around an axis and allows more force to be applied by extending the distance of the plane. For example, a screw being turned into a piece of wood provides greater securing strength than hitting a nail into the wood.

- A wheel and axle allows the use of rotational force around an axis to assist with applying force. For example, a wheelbarrow makes it easier to haul large loads by employing a wheel and axle at the front.

- A pulley is an application of a wheel and axle with the addition of cords or ropes and it helps move objects vertically. For example, pulling a bucket out of a well is easier with a pulley and ropes.

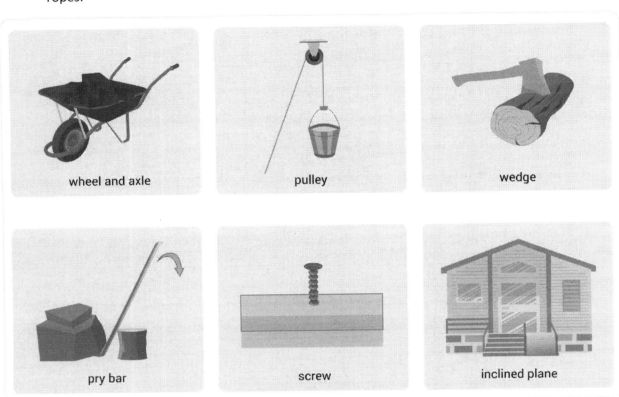

wheel and axle   pulley   wedge

pry bar   screw   inclined plane

Using a simple machine employs an advantage to the user. This is referred to as the mechanical advantage. It can be calculated by comparing the force input by the user to the simple machine with the force output from the use of the machine (also displayed as a ratio).

$$MechanicalAdvantage = \frac{output force}{input force}$$

$$MA = \frac{F_{out}}{F_{in}}$$

In the following instance of using a lever, it can be helpful to calculate the torque, or circular force, necessary to move something. This is also employed when using a wrench to loosen a bolt.

$$Torque = F \times distance of lever arm from the axis of rotation \ (called\ the\ moment\ arm)$$

$$T = F \times d$$

Electricity and Magnetism

<u>Electrical Nature of Common Materials</u>
Generally, an atom carries no net charge because the positive charges of the protons in the nucleus balance the negative charges of the electrons in the outer shells of the atom. This is considered to be electrically neutral. However, since electrons are the only portion of the atom known to have the freedom to "move," this can cause an object to become electrically charged. This happens either through a gain or a loss of electrons. Electrons have a negative charge, so a gain creates a net negative charge for the object. On the contrary, a loss of electrons creates a positive charge for the object. This charge can also be focused on specific areas of an object, causing a notable interaction between charged objects. For example, if a person rubs a balloon on a carpet, the balloon transfers some of is electrons to the carpet. So, if that person were to hold a balloon near his or her hair, the electrons in the "neutral" hair would make the hair stand on end. This is due to the electrons wanting to fill the deficit of electrons on the balloon. Unless electrically forced into a charged state, most natural objects in nature tend toward reestablishing and maintaining a neutral charge.

When dealing with charges, it is easiest to remember that *like charges repel* each other and *opposite charges attract* each other. Therefore, negatives and positives attract, while two positives or two negatives will repel each other. Similarly, when two charges come near each other, they exert a force on one another. This is described through *Coulomb's Law*:

$$F = k\frac{q_1 q_2}{r^2}$$

In this equation, *F* is equal to the force exerted by the interaction, *k* is a constant (*k* = 8.99 x 10^9 N m^2/C^2), q_1 and q_2 are the measure of the two charges, and *r* is the distance between the two charges.

When materials readily transfer electricity or electrons, or can easily accept or lose electrons, they are considered to be good conductors. The transferring of electricity is called *conductivity*. If a material does not readily accept the transfer of electrons or readily loses electrons, it is considered to be an *insulator*. For example, copper wire easily transfers electricity because copper is a good conductor. However, plastic does not transfer electricity because it is not a good conductor. In fact, plastic is an insulator.

<u>Basic Electrical Concepts</u>
In an electrical circuit, the flow from a power source, or the voltage, is "drawn" across the components in the circuit from the positive end to the negative end. This flow of charge creates an electric current (*I*), which is the time (*t*) rate of flow of net charge (*q*). It is measured with the formula:

$$I = \frac{q}{t}$$

Current is measured in amperes (amps). There are two main types of currents:

1. *Direct current* (DC): a unidirectional flow of charges through a circuit

2. *Alternating current* (AC): a circuit with a changing directional flow of charges or magnitude

Every circuit will show a loss in voltage across its conducting material. This loss of voltage is from resistance within the circuit and can be caused by multiple factors, including resistance from wiring and components such as light bulbs and switches. To measure the resistance in a given circuit, Ohm's law is used:

$$Resistance \; = \frac{Voltage}{current} = R \; = \frac{V}{I}$$

Resistance (R) is measured in Ohms (Ω).

Components in a circuit can be wired *in series* or *in parallel*. If the components are wired in series, a single wire connects each component to the next in line. If the components are wired in parallel, two wires connect each component to the next. The main difference is that the voltage across those in series is directly related from one component to the next. Therefore, if the first component in the series becomes inoperable, no voltage can get to the other components. Conversely, the components in parallel share the voltage across each other and are not dependent on the prior component wired to allow the voltage across the wire.

To calculate the resistance of circuit components wired in series or parallel, the following equations are used:

Resistance in series:

$$R_{total} = R_1 + R_2 + R_3 + \cdots$$

Resistance in parallel:

$$R_{total} = \frac{1}{R_1} + \frac{1}{R_2} + \frac{1}{R_3} + \cdots$$

To make electrons move so that they can carry their charge, a change in voltage must be present. On a small scale, this is demonstrated through the electrons traveling from the light switch to a person's finger. This might happen in a situation where a person runs his or her socks on a carpet, touches a light switch, and receives a small jolt from the electrons that run from the switch to the finger. This minor jolt is due to the deficit of electrons created by rubbing the socks on the carpet, and then the electrons going into the ground. The difference in charge between the switch and the finger caused the electrons to move.

If this situation were to be created on a larger and more sustained scale, the factors would need to be more systematic, predictable, and harnessed. This could be achieved through batteries/cells and generators. Batteries or cells have a chemical reaction that occurs inside, causing energy to be released and charges to be able to move freely. Batteries generally have nodes (one positive and one negative), where items can be hooked up to complete a circuit and allow the charge to travel freely through the item. Generators convert mechanical energy into electric energy using power and movement.

Basic Properties of Magnetic Fields and Forces

Consider two straight rods that are made from magnetic material. They will naturally have a negative end (pole) and a positive end (pole). These charged poles react just like any charged item: opposite charges attract and like charges repel. They will attract each other when arranged positive pole to negative pole. However, if one rod is turned around, the two rods will now repel each other due to the alignment of negative to negative and positive to positive. These types of forces can also be created and amplified by using an electric current. For example, sending an electric current through a stretch of wire creates an electromagnetic force around the wire from the charge of the current. This force exists as long as the flow of electricity is sustained. This magnetic force can also attract and repel other items with magnetic properties. Depending on the strength of the current in the wire, a greater or smaller magnetic force can be generated around the wire. As soon as the current is stopped, the magnetic force also stops.

Optics and Waves

Electromagnetic Spectrum

The movement of light is described like the movement of waves. Light travels with a wave front, has an amplitude (height from the neutral), a cycle or wavelength, a period, and energy. Light travels at approximately 3.00×10^8 m/s and is faster than anything created by humans thus far.

Light is commonly referred to by its measured wavelengths, or the distance between two successive crests or troughs in a wave. Types of light with the longest wavelengths include radio, TV, and micro, and infrared waves. The next set of wavelengths are detectable by the human eye and create the *visible spectrum*. The visible spectrum has wavelengths of 10^{-7} m, and the colors seen are red, orange, yellow, green, blue, indigo, and violet. Beyond the visible spectrum are shorter wavelengths (also called the *electromagnetic spectrum*) containing ultraviolet light, X-rays, and gamma rays. The wavelengths outside of the visible light range can be harmful to humans if they are directly exposed or are exposed for long periods of time. For example, the light from the Sun has a small percentage of ultraviolet (UV) light, which is mostly absorbed by the UV layer of the Earth's atmosphere. When this layer does not filter out the UV rays, the exposure to the wavelengths can be harmful to humans' skin. When there is an extra layer of pollutants, and the light from the sun is trapped by repeated reflection to the Earth (so that it is unable to bounce back into space), it creates another harmful condition for the Earth called the *greenhouse effect*. This is an overexposure to the Sun's light and contributes to *global warming* by increasing the temperature on Earth.

Basic Characteristics and Types of Waves

A *mechanical wave* is a type of wave that passes through a medium (solid, liquid, or gas). There are two basic types of mechanical waves: longitudinal and transverse.

A *longitudinal wave* has motion that is parallel to the direction of the wave's travel. This can best be visualized by compressing one side of a tethered spring and then releasing that end. The movement travels in a bunching/un-bunching motion across the length of the spring and back.

A *transverse wave* has motion that is perpendicular to the direction of the wave's travel. The particles on a transverse wave do not move across the length of the wave; instead, they oscillate up and down, creating peaks and troughs.

A wave with a combination of both longitudinal and transverse motion can be seen through the motion of a wave on the ocean—with peaks and troughs, and particles oscillating up and down.

Mechanical waves can carry energy, sound, and light, but they need a medium through which transport can occur. An electromagnetic wave can transmit energy without a medium, or in a vacuum.

A more recent addition in the study of waves is the *gravitational wave*. Its existence has been proven and verified, yet the details surrounding its capabilities are still somewhat under inquiry. Gravitational waves are purported to be ripples that propagate as waves outward from their source and travel in the curvature of space/time. They are thought to carry energy in a form of radiant energy called *gravitational radiation*.

Basic Wave Phenomena

When a wave crosses a boundary or travels from one medium to another, certain things occur. If the wave can travel through one medium into another medium, it experiences *refraction*. This is the bending of the wave from one medium to another due to a change in density of the mediums, and thus, the speed of the wave changes. For example, when a pencil is sitting in half of a glass of water, a side view of the glass makes the pencil appear to be bent at the water level. What the viewer is seeing is the refraction of light waves traveling from the air into the water. Since the wave speed is slowed in water, the change makes the pencil appear bent.

When a wave hits a medium that it cannot penetrate, it is bounced back in an action called *reflection*. For example, when light waves hit a mirror, they are reflected, or bounced, off the mirror. This can cause it to seem like there is more light in the room, since there is a "doubling back" of the initial wave. This same phenomenon also causes people to be able to see their reflection in a mirror.

When a wave travels through a slit or around an obstacle, it is known as *diffraction*. A light wave will bend around an obstacle or through a slit and cause what is called a *diffraction pattern*. When the waves bend around an obstacle, it causes the addition of waves and the spreading of light on the other side of the opening.

Dispersion is used to describe the splitting of a single wave by refracting its components into separate parts. For example, if a wave of white light is sent through a dispersion prism, the light appears as its separate rainbow-colored components, due to each colored wavelength being refracted in the prism.

When wavelengths hit boundaries, different things occur. Objects will absorb certain wavelengths of light and reflect others, depending on the boundaries. This becomes important when an object appears to be a certain color. The color of an object is not actually within that object, but rather, in the wavelengths being transmitted by that object. For example, if a table appears to be red, that means the table is absorbing all other wavelengths of visible light except those of the red wavelength. The table is reflecting, or transmitting, the wavelengths associated with red back to the human eye, and so it appears red.

Interference describes when an object affects the path of a wave, or another wave interacts with a wave. Waves interacting with each other can result in either *constructive interference* or *destructive interference*, based on their positions. With constructive interference, the waves are in sync with each other and combine to reinforce each other. In the case of deconstructive interference, the waves are out of sync and reduce the effect of each other to some degree. In *scattering*, the boundary can change the direction or energy of a wave, thus altering the entire wave. *Polarization* changes the oscillations of a wave and can alter its appearance in light waves. For example, polarized sunglasses remove the "glare" from sunlight by altering the oscillation pattern observed by the wearer.

When a wave hits a boundary and is completely reflected, or if it cannot escape from one medium to another, it is called *total internal reflection*. This effect can be seen in the diamonds with a brilliant cut. The angle cut on the sides of the diamond causes the light hitting the diamond to be completely reflected back inside the gem, making it appear brighter and more colorful than a diamond with different angles cut into its surface.

The *Doppler effect* applies to situations with both light and sound waves. The premise of the Doppler effect is that, based upon the relative position or movement of a source and an observer, waves can seem shorter or longer than they actually are. When the Doppler effect is noted with sound, it warps the noise being heard by the observer. This makes the pitch or frequency seem shorter or higher as the source is approaching, and then longer or lower as the source is getting farther away. The frequency/pitch of the source never actually changes, but the sound in respect to the observer makes it seem like the sound has changed. This can be observed when a siren passes by an observer on the road. The siren sounds much higher in pitch as it approaches the observer and then lower after it passes and is getting farther away.

The Doppler effect also applies to situations involving light waves. An observer in space would see light approaching as being shorter wavelengths than the light actually is, causing it to look blue. When the light wave gets farther away, the light would appear red because of the apparent elongation of the wavelength. This is called the *red-blue shift*.

Basic Optics
When reflecting light, a mirror can be used to observe a virtual (not real) image. A *plane mirror* is a piece of glass with a coating in the background to create a reflective surface. An image is what the human eye sees when light is reflected off the mirror in an unmagnified manner. If a *curved mirror* is used for reflection, the image seen will not be a true reflection. Instead, the image will either be enlarged or miniaturized compared to its actual size. Curved mirrors can also make the object appear closer or farther away than the actual distance the object is from the mirror.

Lenses can be used to refract or bend light to form images. Examples of lenses are the human eye, microscopes, and telescopes. The human eye interprets the refraction of light into images that humans understand to be actual size. *Microscopes* allow objects that are too small for the unaided human eye to be enlarged enough to be seen. *Telescopes* allow objects to be viewed that are too far away to be seen with the unaided eye. *Prisms* are pieces of glass that can have a wavelength of light enter one side and appear to be divided into its component wavelengths on the other side. This is due to the ability of the prism to slow certain wavelengths more than others.

Sound
Sound travels in waves and is the movement of vibrations through a medium. It can travel through air (gas), land, water, etc. For example, the noise a human hears in the air is the vibration of the waves as

they reach the ear. The human brain translates the different frequencies (pitches) and intensities of the vibrations to determine what created the noise.

A tuning fork has a predetermined frequency because of the length and thickness of its tines. When struck, it allows vibrations between the two tines to move the air at a specific rate. This creates a specific tone, or note, for that size of tuning fork. The number of vibrations over time is also steady for that tuning fork and can be matched with a frequency. All pitches heard by the human ear are categorized by using frequency and are measured in Hertz (cycles per second).

The level of sound in the air is measured with sound level meters on a decibel (dB) scale. These meters respond to changes in air pressure caused by sound waves and measure sound intensity. One decibel is 1/10th of a *bel*, named after Alexander Graham Bell, the inventor of the telephone. The decibel scale is logarithmic, so it is measured in factors of 10. This means, for example, that a 10 dB increase on a sound meter equates to a 10-fold increase in sound intensity.

Life Science

Structure of Living Organisms and Their Functions

Structure and Function of Animal and Plant Cell Organelles

Animal and plant cells contain many of the same or similar *organelles*, which are membrane enclosed structures that each have a specific function; however, there are a few organelles that are unique to either one or the other general cell type. The following cell organelles are found in both animal and plant cells, unless otherwise noted in their description:

- *Nucleus*: The nucleus consists of three parts: the nuclear envelope, the nucleolus, and chromatin. The *nuclear envelope* is the double membrane that surrounds the nucleus and separates its contents from the rest of the cell. The *nucleolus* produces ribosomes. *Chromatin* consists of DNA and protein, which form chromosomes that contain genetic information. Most cells have only one nucleus; however, some cells, such as skeletal muscle cells, have multiple nuclei.

- *Endoplasmic reticulum (ER)*: The ER is a network of membranous sacs and tubes that is responsible for membrane synthesis. It is also responsible for packaging and transporting proteins into vesicles that can move out of the cell. It folds and transports other proteins to the Golgi apparatus. It contains both smooth and rough regions; the rough regions have ribosomes attached, which are the sites of protein synthesis.

- *Flagellum*: Flagellum are found only in animal cells. They are made up of a cluster of microtubules projected out of the plasma membrane, and they aid in cell mobility.

- *Centrosome*: The centrosome is the area of the cell where *microtubules*, which are filaments that are responsible for movement in the cell, begin to be formed. Each centrosome contains two centrioles. Each cell contains one centrosome.

- *Cytoskeleton*: The cytoskeleton in animal cells is made up of microfilaments, intermediate filaments, and microtubules. In plant cells, the cytoskeleton is made up of only microfilaments and microtubules. These structures reinforce the cell's shape and aid in cell movement.

- *Microvilli*: Microvilli are found only in animal cells. They are protrusions in the cell membrane that increase the cell's surface area. They have a variety of functions, including absorption, secretion, and cellular adhesion. They are found on the apical surface of epithelial cells, such as in the small intestine. They are also located on the plasma surface of a female's eggs to help anchor sperm that are attempting fertilization.

- *Peroxisome*: A peroxisome contains enzymes that are involved in many of the cell's metabolic functions, one of the most important being the breakdown of very long chain fatty acids. Peroxisomes produces hydrogen peroxide as a byproduct of these processes and then converts the hydrogen peroxide to water. There are many peroxisomes in each cell.

- *Mitochondrion*: The mitochondrion is often called the powerhouse of the cell and is one of the most important structures for maintaining regular cell function. It is where aerobic cellular respiration occurs and where most of the cell's adenosine triphosphate (ATP) is generated. The number of mitochondria in a cell varies greatly from organism to organism, and from cell to cell. In human cells, the number of mitochondria can vary from zero in a red blood cell, to 2000 in a liver cell.

- *Lysosome*: Lysosomes are exclusively found in animal cells. They are responsible for digestion and can hydrolyze macromolecules. There are many lysosomes in each cell.

- *Golgi apparatus*: The Golgi apparatus is responsible for the composition, modification, organization, and secretion of cell products. Because of its large size, it was actually one of the first organelles to be studied in detail. There are many Golgi apparati in each cell.

- *Ribosomes*: Ribosomes are found either free in the cytosol, bound to the rough ER, or bound to the nuclear envelope. They manufacture proteins within the cell.

- *Plasmodesmata*: The plasmodesmata are found only in plant cells. They are cytoplasmic channels, or tunnels, that go through the cell wall and connect the cytoplasm of adjacent cells.

- *Chloroplast*: Chloroplasts are found only in plant cells. They are responsible for *photosynthesis*, which is the process of converting sunlight to chemical energy that can be stored and used later to drive cellular activities.

- *Central vacuole*: A central vacuole is found only in plant cells. It is responsible for storing material and waste. This is the only vacuole found in a plant cell.

- *Plasma membrane*: The plasma membrane is a phospholipid bilayer that encloses the cell.

- *Cell wall*: Cell walls are only present in plant cells. The cell wall is made up of strong fibrous substances including cellulose and other polysaccharides, and protein. It is a layer outside of the plasma membrane, which protects the cell from mechanical damage and helps maintain the cell's shape.

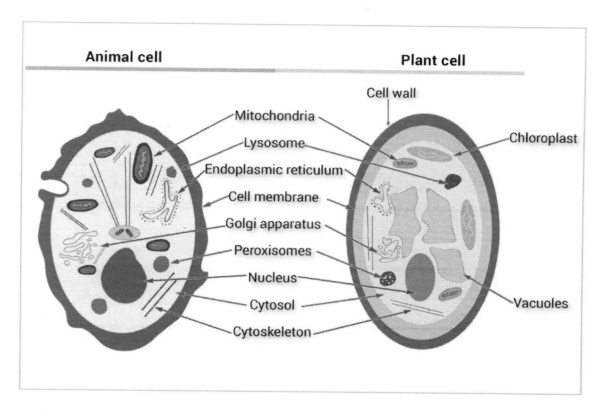

Levels of Organization

There are about two hundred different types of cells in the human body. Cells group together to form *biological* tissues, and tissues combine to form organs, such as the heart and kidneys. Organs that work together to perform vital functions of the human body form organ systems. There are eleven organ systems in the human body: skeletal, muscular, urinary, nervous, digestive, endocrine, reproductive, respiratory, cardiovascular, integumentary, and lymphatic. Although each system has its own unique function, they all rely on each other, either directly or indirectly, to operate properly.

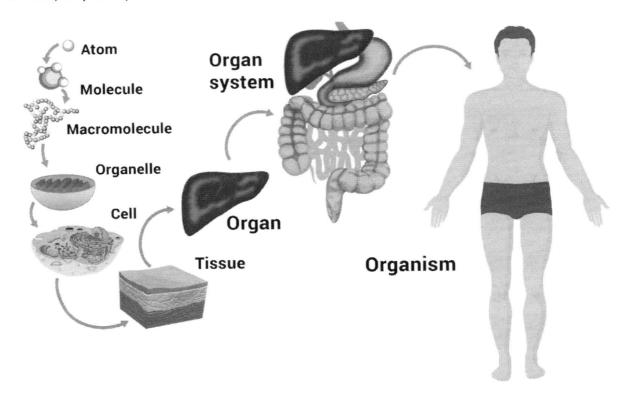

Major Features of Common Animal Cell Types

The most common animal cell types are blood, muscle, nerve, epithelial, and gamete cells. The three main blood cells are *red blood cells (RBCs), white blood cells (WBCs),* and *platelets*. RBCs transport oxygen and carbon dioxide through the body. They do not have a nucleus and they live for about 120 days in the blood. WBCs defend the body against diseases. They do have a nucleus and live for only three to four days in the human body. Platelets help with the formation of blood clots following an injury. They do not have a nucleus and live for about eight days after formation. *Muscle cells* are long, tubular cells that form muscles, which are responsible for movement in the body. On average, they live for about fifteen years, but this number is highly dependent on the individual body. There are three main types of muscle tissue: skeletal, cardiac, and smooth. *Skeletal muscle cells* have multiple nuclei and are the only voluntary muscle cell, which means that the brain consciously controls the movement of skeletal muscle. *Cardiac muscle cells* are only found in the heart; they have a single nucleus and are involuntary. *Smooth muscle cells* make up the walls of the blood vessels and organs. They have a single nucleus and are involuntary. *Nerve cells* conduct electrical impulses that help send information and instructions from the brain to the rest of the body. They contain a single nucleus and have a specialized membrane that allows for this electrical signaling between cells. *Epithelial* cells cover exposed surfaces, and line internal cavities and passageways. *Gametes* are specialized cells that are responsible for reproduction. In the human body, the gametes are the egg and the sperm.

Prokaryotes and Eukaryotes

There are two distinct types of cells that make up most living organisms: *prokaryotic* and *eukaryotic*. Both types of cells are enclosed by plasma membranes with cytosol on the inside. They both contain *ribosomes* and DNA. One major difference between these types of cells is that in eukaryotic cells, the cell's DNA is enclosed in a membrane-bound nucleus, whereas in prokaryotic cells, the cell's DNA is in a region—called the *nucleoid*—that is not enclosed by a membrane. Another major difference is that eukaryotic cells contain organelles, while prokaryotic cells do not have organelles.

Prokaryotic cells include *bacteria* and archaea. They do not have a nucleus or any membrane-bound organelles, are unicellular organisms, and are generally very small in size. Eukaryotic cells include animal, plant, fungus, and protist cells. *Fungi* are unicellular microorganisms such as yeasts, molds, and mushrooms. Their distinguishing characteristic is the chitin that is in their cell walls. *Protists* are organisms that are not classified as animals, plants, or fungi; they are unicellular; and they do not form tissues.

Classification Schemes

Taxonomy is the science behind the biological names of organisms. Biologists often refer to organisms by their Latin scientific names to avoid confusion with common names, such as with fish. Jellyfish, crayfish, and silverfish all have the word "fish" in their name, but belong to three different species. In the eighteenth century, Carl Linnaeus invented a naming system for species that included using the Latin scientific name of a species, called the *binomial*, which has two parts: the *genus*, which comes first, and the *specific epithet*, which comes second. Similar species are grouped into the same genus. The Linnean system is the commonly used taxonomic system today and, moving from comprehensive similarities to more general similarities, classifies organisms into their species, genus, family, order, class, phylum, kingdom, and domain. *Homo sapiens* is the Latin scientific name for humans.

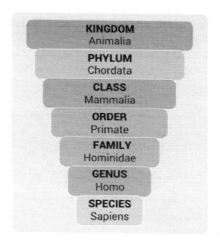

Phylogenetic trees are branching diagrams that represent the evolutionary history of a species. The branch points most often match the classification groups set forth by the Linnean system. Using this system helps elucidate the relationship between different groups of organisms. The diagram below is that of an empty phylogenetic tree:

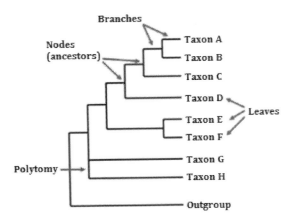

Each branch of the tree represents the divergence of two species from a common ancestor. For example, the coyote is known as Canis latrans and the gray wolf is known as Canis lupus. Their common ancestor, the Canis lepophagus, which is now extinct, is where their shared genus derived.

Characteristics of Bacteria, Animals, Plants, Fungi, and Protists

As discussed earlier, there are two distinct types of cells that make up most living organisms: prokaryotic and eukaryotic. Bacteria (and archaea) are classified as prokaryotic cells, whereas animal, plant, fungi, and protist cells are classified as eukaryotic cells.

Although animal cells and plant cells are both eukaryotic, they each have several distinguishing characteristics. *Animal cells* are surrounded by a plasma membrane, while *plant cells* have a cell wall made up of cellulose that provides more structure and an extra layer of protection for the cell. Animals use oxygen to breathe and give off carbon dioxide, while plants do the opposite—they take in carbon dioxide and give off oxygen. Plants also use light as a source of energy. Animals have highly developed sensory and nervous systems and the ability to move freely, while plants lack both abilities. Animals, however, cannot make their own food and must rely on their environment to provide sufficient nutrition, whereas plants do make their own food.

Fungal cells are typical eukaryotes, containing both a nucleus and membrane-bound organelles. They have a cell wall, similar to plant cells; however, they use oxygen as a source of energy and cannot perform photosynthesis. They also depend on outside sources for nutrition and cannot produce their own food. Of note, their cell walls contain *chitin.*

Protists are a group of diverse eukaryotic cells that are often grouped together because they do not fit into the categories of animal, plant, or fungal cells. They can be categorized into three broad categories: protozoa, protophyta, and molds. These three broad categories are essentially "animal -like," "plant-like," and "fungus-like," respectively. All of them are unicellular and do not form tissues. Besides this simple similarity, protists are a diverse group of organisms with different characteristics, life cycles, and cellular structures.

Types of Anatomy and Physiology

Anatomy is the study of external and internal body parts and structures, and their physical relationships to each other. Physiology is the study of the function of living organisms and their body parts. Understanding these areas of study is easier after learning the specific terms relating to the field.

Gross Anatomy: The study of large structures and features visible to the naked eye. It is also known as macroscopic anatomy.

Microscopic: The study of structures and their functions that can only be seen with magnification, such as through a magnifying glass or microscope.

Systemic: The study of a major organ system.

Developmental: The study of the physical changes that occur between conception and physical maturity. It includes gross anatomy, microscopic anatomy and physiology, because of the broad range of anatomical structures that undergo changes during this time.

Comparative: The study of structural organization and their functions among different types of animals. Animals that look different now but have the same internal structures with similar functions may have an evolutionary relationship.

Pathophysiology: The study of the effects of diseases on how an organ or organ system functions.

Integumentary System (Skin)

Skin consists of three layers: epidermis, dermis, and the hypodermis. There are four types of cells that make up the keratinized stratified squamous epithelium in the epidermis. They are keratinocytes, melanocytes, Merkel cells, and Langerhans cells. Skin is composed of many layers, starting with a basement membrane. On top of that sits the stratum germinativum, the stratum spinosum, the stratum granulosum, the stratum lucidum, and then the stratum corneum at the outer surface. Skin can be classified as thick or thin. These descriptions refer to the epidermis layer. Most of the body is covered with thin skin, but areas such as the palm of the hands are covered with thick skin. The dermis consists of a superficial papillary layer and a deeper reticular layer. The papillary layer is made of loose connective tissue, containing capillaries and the axons of sensory neurons. The reticular layer is a meshwork of tightly packed irregular connective tissue, containing blood vessels, hair follicles, nerves, sweat glands, and sebaceous glands. The hypodermis is a loose layer of fat and connective tissue. Since it is the third layer, if a burn reaches this third degree, it has caused serious damage.

Sweat glands and sebaceous glands are important exocrine glands found in the skin. Sweat glands regulate temperature, and remove bodily waste by secreting water, nitrogenous waste, and sodium salts to the surface of the body. Some sweat glands are classified as apocrine glands. Sebaceous glands are holocrine glands that secrete sebum, which is an oily mixture of lipids and proteins. Sebum protects the skin from water loss, as well as bacterial and fungal infections.

The three major functions of skin are protection, regulation, and sensation. Skin acts as a barrier and protects the body from mechanical impacts, variations in temperature, microorganisms, and chemicals. It regulates body temperature, peripheral circulation, and fluid balance by secreting sweat. It also contains a large network of nerve cells that relay changes in the external environment to the body.

Skeletal System

The skeletal system consists of the 206 bones that make up the skeleton, as well as the cartilage, ligaments, and other connective tissues that stabilize them. Bone is made of collagen fibers and calcium salts. The calcium salts are strong but brittle, and the collagen fibers are weak but flexible, so the combination makes bone resistant to shattering. There are two types of bone: compact and spongy. Compact bone has a basic functional unit, called the Haversian system. Osteocytes, or bone cells, are arranged in concentric circles around a central canal, called the Haversian canal, which contains blood vessels. While Haversian canals run parallel to the surface of the bone, perforating canals, also known as the canals of Volkmann, run perpendicularly between the central canal and the surface of the bone. The concentric circles of bone tissue that surround the central canal within the Haversian system are called lamellae. The spaces that are found between the lamellae are called lacunae. The Haversian system is a reservoir for calcium and phosphorus for blood. Spongy bone, in contrast to compact bone, is lightweight and porous. It covers the outside of the bone and it gives it a shiny, white appearance. It has a branching network of parallel lamellae, called trabeculae.

Although spongy bone forms an open framework around the compact bone, it is still quite strong. Different bones have different ratios of compact-to-spongy bone, depending on their functions. The outside of the bone is covered by a periosteum, which has four major functions. It isolates and protects bones from the surrounding tissue; provides a place for attachment of the circulatory and nervous system structures; participates in growth and repair of the bone; and attaches the bone to the deep fascia. An endosteum is found inside the bone, covers the trabeculae of the spongy bone and lines the inner surfaces of the central canals.

One major function of the skeletal system is to provide structural support for the entire body. It provides a framework for the soft tissues and organs to attach to. The skeletal system also provides a reserve of important nutrients, such as calcium and lipids. Normal concentrations of calcium and phosphate in body fluids are partly maintained by the calcium salts stored in bone. Lipids that are stored in yellow bone marrow can be used as a source of energy. Red bone marrow produces red blood cells, white blood cells, and platelets that circulate in the blood. Certain groups of bones form protective barriers around delicate organs. The ribs, for example, protect the heart and lungs, the skull encloses the brain, and the vertebrae cover the spinal cord.

Muscular System

The muscular system of the human body is responsible for all movement that occurs. There are approximately 700 muscles in the body that are attached to the bones of the skeletal system and that make up half of the body's weight. Muscles are attached to the bones through tendons. Tendons are made up of dense bands of connective tissue and have collagen fibers that firmly attach to the bone on one side and the muscle on the other. Their fibers are actually woven into the coverings of the bone and muscle so they can withstand the large forces that are put on them when muscles are moving. There are three types of muscle tissue in the body: Skeletal muscle tissue pulls on the bones of the skeleton and causes body movement; cardiac muscle tissue helps pump blood through veins and arteries; and smooth muscle tissue helps move fluids and solids along the digestive tract and contributes to movement in other body systems. All of these muscle tissues have four important properties in common: They are excitable, meaning they respond to stimuli; contractile, meaning they can shorten and pull on connective tissue; extensible, meaning they can be stretched repeatedly, but maintain the ability to contract; and elastic, meaning they rebound to their original length after a contraction.

Muscles begin at an origin and end at an insertion. Generally, the origin is proximal to the insertion and the origin remains stationary while the insertion moves. For example, when bending the elbow and moving the hand up toward the head, the part of the forearm that is closest to the wrist moves and the part closer to the elbow is stationary. Therefore, the muscle in the forearm has an origin at the elbow and an insertion at the wrist.

Body movements occur by muscle contraction. Each contraction causes a specific action. Muscles can be classified into one of three muscle groups based on the action they perform. Primary movers, or agonists, produce a specific movement, such as flexion of the elbow. Synergists are in charge of helping the primary movers complete their specific movements. They can help stabilize the point of origin or provide extra pull near the insertion. Some synergists can aid an agonist in preventing movement at a joint. Antagonists are muscles whose actions are the opposite of that of the agonist. If an agonist is contracting during a specific movement, the antagonist is stretched. During flexion of the elbow, the biceps' brachii muscle contracts and acts as an agonist, while the triceps' brachii muscle on the opposite side of the upper arm acts as an antagonist and stretches.

Skeletal muscle tissue has several important functions. It causes movement of the skeleton by pulling on tendons and moving the bones. It maintains body posture through the contraction of specific muscles responsible for the stability of the skeleton. Skeletal muscles help support the weight of internal organs and protect these organs from external injury. They also help to regulate body temperature within a normal range. Muscle contractions require energy and produce heat, which heats the body when cold.

Nervous System

Although the nervous system is one of the smallest organ systems in the human body, it is the most complex. It consists of all of the neural tissue, and is in charge of controlling and adjusting the activities of all of the other systems of the body. Neural responses to stimuli are often fast, but disappear quickly once the neural activity stops. Neural tissue contains two types of cells: neurons and neuroglia. Neurons, or nerve cells, are the main cells responsible for transferring and processing information in the nervous system. Neuroglia support the neurons by providing a framework around them and isolating them from the surrounding environment. They also act as phagocytes and protect neurons from harmful substances.

The nervous system is made of the central nervous system (CNS) and the peripheral nervous system (PNS). The CNS includes the brain and the spinal cord, while the PNS includes the rest of the neural tissue not included in the CNS. The CNS is where intelligence, memory, learning, and emotions are processed. It is responsible for processing and coordinating sensory data and motor commands. The PNS is responsible for relaying sensory information and motor commands between the CNS and peripheral tissues and systems. The PNS has two subdivisions, known as the afferent and efferent divisions. While the afferent division relays sensory information to the CNS, the efferent division transmits motor commands to muscles and glands. The efferent division consists of the somatic nervous system (SNS), which controls skeletal muscle contractions, and the autonomic nervous system (ANS), which regulates activity of smooth muscle, cardiac muscle, and glands.

Two types of pathways are used to communicate information between the brain and the peripheral tissues. Sensory pathways start in a peripheral system and end in the brain. Motor pathways carry information from the brain to peripheral systems. Motor commands often occur in response to the information transmitted through a sensory pathway. Processing in both pathways happens at several points along the way, where neurons pass the information to each other.

The nervous system is responsible for processing both general senses and specialized senses. General senses include temperature, pain, touch, pressure, vibration and proprioception. Specialized senses include olfaction (smell), gustation (taste), equilibrium, hearing, and vision. The information from each sense is processed through a specific receptor for that sense. A receptor that is sensitive to touch may not be responsive to chemical stimuli, for example. The specificity of the receptor is developed either from its individual structure or from accessory cells or structures creating a shield against other senses.

Endocrine System

The endocrine system is made of the ductless tissues and glands that secrete hormones into the interstitial fluids of the body. Interstitial fluid is the solution that surrounds tissue cells within the body. This system works closely with the nervous system to regulate the physiological activities of the other systems of the body to maintain homeostasis. While the nervous system provides quick, short-term responses to stimuli, the endocrine system acts by releasing hormones into the bloodstream that get distributed to the whole body. The response is slow but long-lasting, ranging from a few hours to a few weeks.

Hormones are chemical substances that change the metabolic activity of tissues and organs. While regular metabolic reactions are controlled by enzymes, hormones can change the type, activity, or quantity of the enzymes involved in the reaction. They bind to specific cells and start a biochemical chain of events that changes the enzymatic activity. Hormones can regulate development and growth, digestive metabolism, mood, and body temperature, among other things. Often small amounts of hormone will lead to large changes in the body.

Major Endocrine Glands

Hypothalamus: A part of the brain, the hypothalamus connects the nervous system to the endocrine system via the pituitary gland. Although it is considered part of the nervous system, it plays a dual role in regulating endocrine organs.

Pituitary Gland: A pea-sized gland found at the bottom of the hypothalamus. It has two lobes, called the anterior and posterior lobes. It plays an important role in regulating the function of other endocrine glands. The hormones released control growth, blood pressure, certain functions of the sex organs, salt concentration of the kidneys, internal temperature regulation, and pain relief.

Thyroid Gland: This gland releases hormones, such as thyroxine, that are important for metabolism, growth and development, temperature regulation, and brain development during infancy and childhood. Thyroid hormones also monitor the amount of circulating calcium in the body.

Parathyroid Glands: These are four pea-sized glands located on the posterior surface of the thyroid. The main hormone secreted is called parathyroid hormone (PTH) and helps with the thyroid's regulation of calcium in the body.

Thymus Gland: The thymus is located in the chest cavity, embedded in connective tissue. It produces several hormones important for development and maintenance of normal immunological defenses. One hormone promotes the development and maturation of lymphocytes, which strengthens the immune system.

Adrenal Gland: One adrenal gland is attached to the top of each kidney. It produces adrenaline and is responsible for the "fight or flight" reactions in the face of danger or stress. The hormones epinephrine and norepinephrine cooperate to regulate states of arousal.

Pancreas: The pancreas is an organ that has both endocrine and exocrine functions. The endocrine functions are controlled by the pancreatic islets of Langerhans, which are groups of beta cells scattered throughout the gland that secrete insulin to lower blood sugar levels in the body. Neighboring alpha cells secrete glucagon to raise blood sugar.

Pineal Gland: The pineal gland secretes melatonin, a hormone derived from the neurotransmitter serotonin. Melatonin can slow the maturation of sperm, oocytes, and reproductive organs. It also regulates the body's circadian rhythm, which is the natural awake/asleep cycle. It also serves an important role in protecting the CNS tissues from neural toxins.

Testes and Ovaries: These glands secrete testosterone and estrogen, respectively, and are responsible for secondary sex characteristics, as well as reproduction.

Circulatory System

The circulatory system is composed of the heart and blood vessels of the body. The heart is the main organ of the circulatory system. It acts as a pump and works to circulate blood throughout the body. Gases, nutrients, and waste are constantly exchanged between the circulating blood and interstitial fluid, keeping tissues and organs alive and healthy. The circulatory system is divided into the pulmonary and systemic circuits. The pulmonary circuit is responsible for carrying carbon dioxide-rich blood to the lungs and returning oxygen-rich blood to the heart. The systemic circuit transports the oxygen-rich blood to the rest of the body and returns carbon dioxide-rich blood to the heart.

Heart

The heart is located posterior to the sternum, on the left side, in the front of the chest. The heart wall is made of three distinct layers. The outer layer, the epicardium, is a *serous* membrane that is also known as the visceral pericardium. The middle layer is called the myocardium, and contains connective tissue, blood vessels, and nerves within its layers of cardiac muscle tissue. The inner layer is the endocardium, and is made of a simple squamous epithelium. This layer includes the heart valves, and is continuous with the endothelium of the attached blood vessels.

The heart has four chambers: the right atrium, the right ventricle, the left atrium, and the left ventricle. An interatrial septum, or wall, separates the right and left atria, and the right and left ventricles are separated by an interventricular septum. The atrium and ventricle on the same side of the heart have an opening between them that is regulated by a valve. The valve maintains blood flow in only one direction, moving from the atrium to the ventricle, and prevents backflow. The systemic circuit pumps oxygen-poor blood into the right atrium, then pumps it into the right ventricle. From there, the blood enters the pulmonary trunk and then flows into the pulmonary arteries, where it can become re-oxygenated. Oxygen-rich blood from the lungs flows into the left atrium and then passes into the left ventricle. From there, blood enters the aorta and is pumped to the entire systemic circuit.

Blood

Blood circulates throughout the body in a system of vessels that includes arteries, veins, and capillaries. It distributes oxygen, nutrients, and hormones to all the cells in the body. The vessels are muscular tubes that allow gas exchange to occur. Arteries carry oxygen-rich blood from the heart to the other tissues of the body. The largest artery is the aorta. Veins collect oxygen-depleted blood from tissues and organs, and return it to the heart. The walls of veins are thinner and less elastic than arteries, because the blood pressure in veins is lower than in arteries. Capillaries are the smallest of the blood vessels and do not function individually; instead, they work together in a unit, called a capillary bed. This network of capillaries provides oxygen-rich blood from arterioles to tissues and feeds oxygen-poor blood from tissues back to venules.

Blood comprises plasma and formed elements, which include red blood cells (RBCs), white blood cells (WBCs), and platelets. Plasma is the liquid matrix of the blood and contains dissolved proteins. RBCs transport oxygen and carbon dioxide. WBCs are part of the immune system and help fight diseases. Platelets contain enzymes and other factors that help with blood clotting.

Respiratory System

The respiratory system mediates the exchange of gas between the air and the blood, mainly by the act of breathing. This system is divided into the upper respiratory system and the lower respiratory system. The upper system comprises the nose, the nasal cavity and sinuses, and the pharynx. The lower respiratory system comprises the larynx (voice box), the trachea (windpipe), the small passageways leading to the lungs, and the lungs. The upper respiratory system is responsible for filtering, warming, and humidifying the air that gets passed to the lower respiratory system, protecting the lower respiratory system's more delicate tissue surfaces.

The Lungs

The right lung is divided into three lobes: superior, middle, and inferior. The left lung is divided into two lobes: superior and inferior. The left lung is smaller than the right, likely because it shares its space in the chest cavity with the heart. Together, the lungs contain approximately 1500 miles of airway passages. The bronchi, which carry air into the lungs, branch into bronchioles and continue to divide into smaller and smaller passageways, until they become alveoli, which are the smallest passages. Most of the gas exchange in the lungs occurs between the blood-filled pulmonary capillaries and the air-filled alveoli.

Functions of the Respiratory System

The respiratory system has many functions. Most importantly, it provides a large area for gas exchange between the air and the circulating blood. It protects the delicate respiratory surfaces from environmental variations and defends them against pathogens. It is responsible for producing the sounds that the body makes for speaking and singing, as well as for non-verbal communication. It also helps regulate blood volume, blood pressure, and body fluid pH.

Breathing

When a breath of air is inhaled, oxygen enters the nose or mouth, and passes into the sinuses, where the temperature and humidity of the air get regulated. The air then passes into the trachea and is filtered. From there, the air travels into the bronchi and reaches the lungs. Bronchi are tubes that lead from the trachea to each lung, and are lined with cilia and mucus that collect dust and germs along the way. Within the lungs, oxygen and carbon dioxide are exchanged between the air in the alveoli and the blood in the pulmonary capillaries. Oxygen-rich blood returns to the heart and is pumped through the systemic circuit. Carbon dioxide-rich air is exhaled from the body.

Breathing is possible due to the muscular diaphragm pulling on the lungs, increasing their volume and decreasing their pressure. Air flows from the external high-pressure system to the low-pressure system inside the lungs. When breathing out, the diaphragm releases its pressure difference, decreases the lung volume, and forces the stale air back out.

Digestive System

The digestive system is a group of organs that work together to transform food and liquids into energy, which can then be used by the body as fuel. Food is ingested and then passes through the alimentary canal, or GI tract, which comprises the mouth, pharynx, esophagus, stomach, small intestine, and large intestine. The digestive system has accessory organs, including the liver, gallbladder, and pancreas, that help with the processing of food and liquids, but do not have food pass directly through them. These accessory organs and the digestive system organs work together in the following functions:

Ingestion: Food and liquids enter the alimentary canal through the mouth.

Introductory Mechanical and Chemical Processing: Teeth grind the food and the tongue swirls it to facilitate swallowing. Enzymes in saliva begin chemical digestion.

Advanced Mechanical and Chemical Digestion: The muscular stomach uses physical force and enzymes, which function at low pH levels, to break down the food and liquid's complex molecules, such as sugars, lipids, and proteins, into smaller molecules that can be absorbed by the small intestine.

Secretion: Most of the acids, buffers, and enzymes that aid in digestion are secreted by the accessory organs, but some are provided by the digestive tract. Bile from the liver facilitates fat digestion.

Absorption: Vitamins, electrolytes, organic molecules, and water are absorbed by the villi and microvilli lining in the small intestine and are moved to the interstitial fluid of the digestive tract.

Compaction: Indigestible materials and organic wastes are dehydrated in the large intestine and compacted before elimination from the body.

Excretion: Waste products are excreted from the digestive tract.

Major Organs of the Alimentary Canal

Stomach: This organ stores food so the body has time to digest large meals. Its highly acidic environment and enzyme secretions, such as pepsin and trypsin, aid in digestion. It also aids in mechanical processing through muscular contractions.

Small Intestine: This organ is a thin tube that is approximately ten feet long. It secretes enzymes to aid in digestion and has many folds that increase its surface area and allows for maximum absorption of nutrients from the digested food.

Large Intestine: This organ is a long thick tube that is about five feet long. It absorbs water from the digested food and transports waste to be excreted from the body. It also contains symbiotic bacteria that further breaks down the waste products, allowing for any extra nutrients to be absorbed.

Major Accessory Organs

Liver: The liver produces and secretes bile, which is important for the digestion of lipids. It also plays a large role in the regulation of circulating levels of carbohydrates, amino acids, and lipids in the body. Excess nutrients are removed by the liver and deficiencies are corrected with its stored nutrients.

Gallbladder: This organ is responsible for storing and concentrating bile before it gets secreted into the small intestine. While the gallbladder is storing bile, it can regulate the bile's composition by absorbing water, thereby increasing the concentration of bile salts and other components.

Pancreas: The Pancreas has exocrine cells that secrete buffers and digestive enzymes. It contains specific enzymes for each type of food molecule, such as carbohydrases for carbohydrates, lipases for lipids, and proteinases for proteins.

Urinary System

The urinary system is made up of the kidneys, ureters, urinary bladder, and the urethra. It is the main system responsible for getting rid of the organic waste products, excess water and electrolytes are generated by the body's other systems. The kidneys are responsible for producing urine, which is a fluid waste product containing water, ions, and small soluble compounds. The urinary system has many important functions related to waste excretion. It regulates the concentrations of sodium, potassium, chloride, calcium, and other ions in the plasma by controlling the amount of each that is excreted in urine. This also contributes to the maintenance of blood pH. It regulates blood volume and pressure by controlling the amount of water lost in the urine, and releasing erythropoietin and renin. It eliminates toxic substances, drugs, and organic waste products, such as urea and uric acid. It also synthesizes calcitriol, which is a hormone derivative of vitamin D3 that aids in calcium ion absorption by the intestinal epithelium.

The Kidneys

Under normal circumstances, humans have two functioning kidneys. They are the main organs are responsible for filtering waste products out of the blood and transferring them to urine. Every day, the kidneys filter approximately 120 to 150 quarts of blood and produce one to two quarts of urine. Kidneys are made of millions of tiny filtering units, called nephrons. Nephrons have two parts: a glomerulus, which is the filter, and a tubule. As blood enters the kidneys, the glomerulus allows fluid and waste products to pass through it and enter the tubule. Blood cells and large molecules, such as proteins, do not pass through and remain in the blood. The filtered fluid and waste then pass through the tubule, where any final essential minerals are sent back to the bloodstream. The final product at the end of the tubule is called urine.

Waste Excretion

Once urine accumulates, it leaves the kidneys. The urine travels through the ureters into the urinary bladder, a muscular organ that is hollow and elastic. As more urine enters the urinary bladder, its walls stretch and become thinner so there is no significant difference in internal pressure. The urinary bladder stores the urine until the body is ready for urination, at which time the muscles contract and force the urine through the urethra and out of the body.

Reproductive System

The reproductive system is responsible for producing, storing, nourishing, and transporting functional reproductive cells, or gametes, in the human body. It includes the reproductive organs, also known as gonads, the reproductive tract, the accessory glands and organs that secrete fluids into the reproductive tract, and the perineal structures, which are the external genitalia. The human male and female reproductive systems are very different from each other.

The Male System

The male gonads are called testes. The testes secrete androgens, mainly testosterone, and produce and store 500 million sperms cells, which are the male gametes, each day. An androgen is a steroid hormone that controls the development and maintenance of male characteristics. Once the sperm are mature, they move through a duct system, where they mix with additional fluids secreted by accessory glands, forming a mixture called semen. The sperm cells in semen are responsible for fertilization of the female gametes to produce offspring.

The Female System

The female gonads are the ovaries. Ovaries generally produce one immature gamete, or oocyte, per month. They are also responsible for secreting the hormones estrogen and progesterone. When the oocyte is released from the ovary, it travels along the uterine tubes, or Fallopian tubes, and then into the uterus. The uterus opens into the vagina. When sperm cells enter the vagina, they swim through the uterus and may fertilize the oocyte in the Fallopian tubes. The resulting zygote travels down the tube and implants into the uterine wall. The uterus protects and nourishes the developing embryo for nine months until it is ready for the outside environment. If the oocyte is not fertilized, it is released in the uterine, or menstrual, cycle. The menstrual cycle occurs monthly and involves the shedding of the functional part of the uterine lining.

Mammary glands are a specialized accessory organ of the female reproductive system. The mammary glands are located in the breast tissue, and during pregnancy begin to grow, and the cells proliferate in preparation for lactation. After pregnancy, the cells begin to secrete nutrient-filled milk, which is transferred into a duct system and out through the nipple for nourishment of the baby.

Response to Stimuli and Homeostasis

A *stimulus* is a change in the environment, either internal or external, around an organism that is received by a sensory receptor and causes the organism to react. *Homeostasis* is the stable state of an organism. When an organism reacts to stimuli, it works to counteract the change in order to reach homeostasis again.

Exchange with the Environment

Animals exchange gases and nutrients with the environment through several different organ systems. The *respiratory system* mediates the exchange of gas between the air and the circulating blood, mainly through the act of breathing. It filters, warms, and humidifies the air that gets inhaled and then passes it into the blood stream. The main function of the *excretory system* is to eliminate excess material and fluids in the body. The kidneys and bladder work together to filter organic waste products, excess water, and electrolytes from the blood that are generated by the other physiologic systems, and excrete them from the body. The *digestive system* is a group of organs that work together to transform ingested food and liquid into energy, which can then be used by the body as fuel. Once all of the nutrients are absorbed, the waste products are excreted from the body.

Characteristics of Vascular and Nonvascular Plants

Plants that have an extensive vascular transport system are called *vascular plants*. Those plants without a transport system are called *nonvascular plants*. Approximately ninety-three percent of plants that are currently living and reproducing are vascular plants. The cells that comprise the vascular tissue in vascular plants form tubes that transport water and nutrients through the entire plant. Nonvascular plants include mosses, liverworts, and hornworts. They do not retain any water; instead, they transport water using other specialized tissue. They have structures that look like leaves, but are actually just single sheets of cells without a cuticle or stomata.

Structure and Function of Roots, Leaves, and Stems

Roots are responsible for anchoring plants in the ground. They absorb water and nutrients and transport them up through the plant. *Leaves* are the main location of photosynthesis. They contain *stomata*, which are pores used for gas exchange, on their underside to take in carbon dioxide and release oxygen. *Stems* transport materials through the plant and support the plant's body. They contain *xylem*, which conducts water and dissolved nutrients upward through the plant, and *phloem*, which conducts sugars and metabolic products downward through the leaves.

Living and Nonliving Components in Environments

Population Dynamics

Population dynamics is the study of the composition of populations, including size, age, and the biological and environmental processes that cause changes. These can include immigration, emigration, births, and deaths.

Growth Curves and Carrying Capacity

Population dynamics can be characterized by *growth curves*. Growth can either be *unrestricted*, which is modeled by an exponential curve, or *restricted*, which is modeled by a logistic curve. Population growth can be restricted by environmental factors such as the availability of food and water sources, habitat, and other necessities. The *carrying capacity* of a population is the maximum population size that an environment can sustain indefinitely, given all of the above factors.

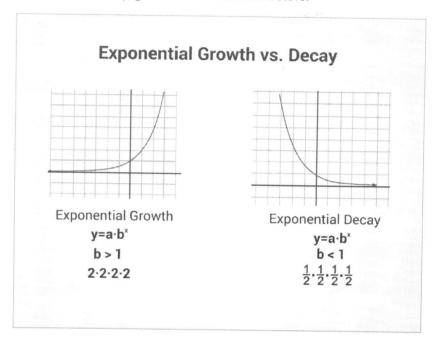

Behavior
Different species within a population can act differently regarding their environment. Some species display *territoriality*, which is a specific type of competition that excludes other species from a given area. It can be shown through specific animal calls, intimidating behavior, or marking an area with scents, and is often a display of defense.

Intraspecific Relationships
Intraspecific relationships is a term that describes the competition and cooperation between organisms that belong to the same species. They may compete for the same food sources, or for mates that are necessary for their personal survival and reproduction. Stronger organisms may display dominance that allows them to reside at the top of a social hierarchy and obtain better food and higher quality mates. However, organisms may also cooperate with each other in order to benefit the larger group; for instance, they may divide laborious activities among themselves.

Community Ecology

An *ecological community* is a group of species that interact and live in the same location. Because of their shared environment, they tend to have a large influence on each other.

Niche
An *ecological niche* is the role that a species plays in its environment, including how it finds its food and shelter. It could be a predator of a different species, or prey for a larger species.

Species Diversity
Species diversity is the number of different species that cohabitate in an ecological community. It has two different facets: *species richness*, which is the general number of species, and *species evenness*, which accounts for the population size of each species.

<u>Interspecific Relationships</u>

Interspecific relationships include the interactions between organisms of different species. The following list defines the common relationships that can occur:

- *Commensalism*: One organism benefits while the other is neither benefited nor harmed

- *Mutualism*: Both organisms benefit

- *Parasitism*: One organism benefits and the other is harmed

- *Competition*: Two or more species compete for limited resources that are necessary for their survival

- *Predation (Predator-Prey)*: One species is a food source for another species

Ecosystems

An *ecosystem* includes all of the living organisms and nonliving components of an environment (each community) and their interactions with each other.

<u>Biomes</u>

A *biome* is a group of plants and animals that are found in many different continents and have the same characteristics because of the similar climates in which they live. Each biome is composed of all of the ecosystems in that area. Five primary types of biomes are aquatic, deserts, forests, grasslands, and tundra. The sum total of all biomes comprises the Earth's biosphere.

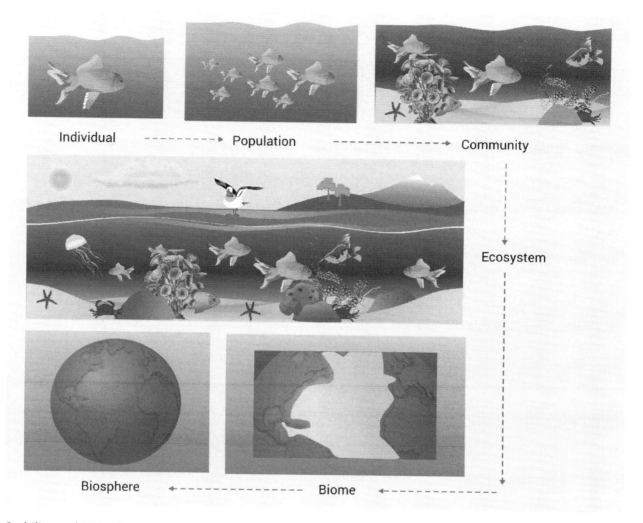

Stability and Disturbances

Ecological stability is the ability of an ecosystem to withstand changes that are occurring within it. With *regenerative stability*, an ecosystem may change, but then quickly return to its previous state. *Constant stability* occurs in ecosystems that remain unchanged despite the changes going on around them.

An *ecological disturbance* is a change in the environment that causes a larger change in the ecosystem. Smaller disturbances include fires and floods. Larger disturbances include the *climate change* that is currently occurring. Gas emissions from human activity are causing the atmosphere to warm up, which is changing the Earth's water systems and making weather more extreme. The increase in temperature is causing greater evaporation of the water sources on Earth, creating droughts and depleting natural water sources. This has also caused many of the Earth's glaciers to begin melting, which can change the salinity of the oceans.

Changes in the environment can cause an *ecological succession* to occur, which is the change in structure of the species that coexist in an ecological community. When the environment changes, resources available to the different species also change. For example, the formation of sand dunes or a forest fire would change the environment enough to allow a change in the social hierarchy of the coexisting species.

Energy Flow

Ecosystems are maintained by cycling the energy and nutrients that they obtain from external sources. The process can be diagramed in a *food web*, which represents the feeding relationship between species in a community. The different levels of the food web are called *trophic levels*. The first trophic level generally consists of plants, algae, and bacteria. The second trophic level consists of herbivores. The third trophic level consists of predators that eat herbivores. The trophic levels continue on to larger and larger predators. *Decomposers* are an important part of the food chain that are not at a specific trophic level. They eat decomposing things on the ground that other animals do not want to eat. This allows them to provide nutrients to their own predators.

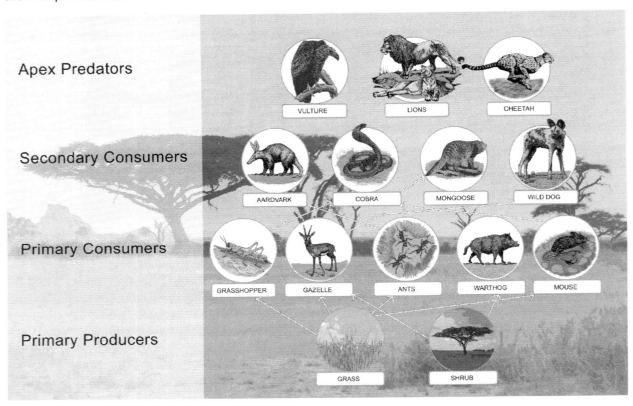

Biogeochemical Cycles

Biogeochemical cycles are the pathways by which chemicals move through the *biotic*, or biospheric, and *abiotic*, or atmospheric, parts of the Earth. The most important biogeochemical cycles include the water, carbon, and nitrogen cycles. *Water* goes through an evaporation, condensation, and precipitation cycle. *Nitrogen* makes up seventy-eight percent of the Earth's atmosphere and can affect the rate of many ecosystem processes, such as production of the primary producers at the first trophic level of the food web. The *carbon cycle* has many steps that are vitally important for sustaining life on Earth.

The water cycle:

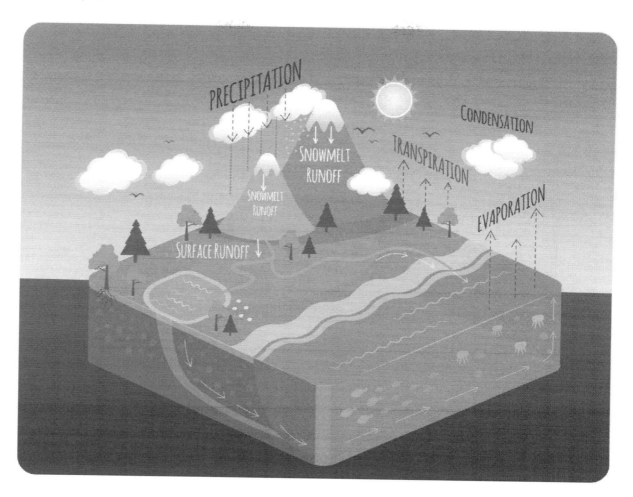

The nitrogen cycle:

The Nitrogen Cycle

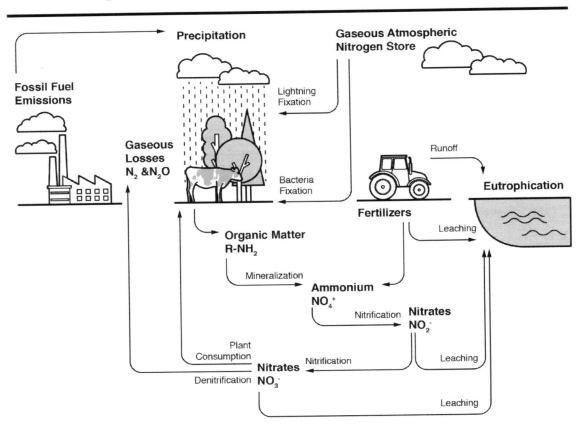

The carbon cycle:

The Carbon Cycle

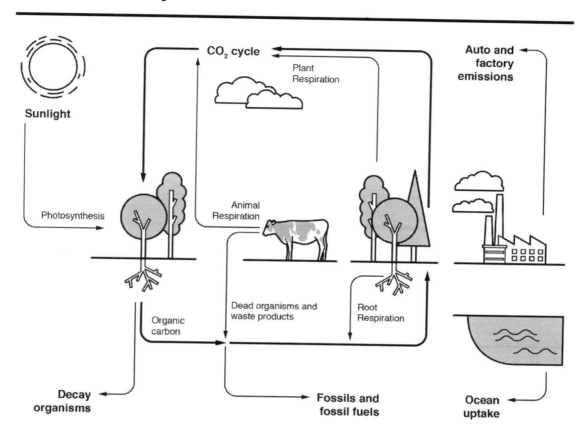

Climate Change and Greenhouse Gases

Greenhouse gases in the Earth's atmosphere include water vapor, carbon dioxide, methane, nitrous oxide, and *chlorofluorocarbons(CFCs)*, which trap heat between the surface of the Earth and the Earth's lowest atmospheric layer, the troposphere. The increase of these gases leads to warming or cooling trends that cause unpredictable or unprecedented meteorological shifts. These shifts can cause natural disasters, affect plant and animal life, and dramatically impact human health. *Water vapor* is a naturally found gas, but as the Earth's temperature rises, the presence of water vapor increases; as water vapor increases, the Earth's temperature rises. This creates a somewhat undesirable loop. *Carbon dioxide* is produced through natural causes, such as volcanic eruptions, but also is greatly affected by human activities, such as burning fossil fuels. A significant increase in the presence of atmospheric carbon dioxide has been noted since the Industrial Revolution; this is important as carbon dioxide is considered the most significant influencer of climate change on Earth. *Methane* is produced primarily from animal and agriculture waste and landfill waste. *Nitrous oxide* is primarily produced from the use of fertilizers and fossil fuels. CFCs are completely synthetic and were previously commonly found in aerosol and other high pressure containers; however, after being linked to ozone layer depletion, they have been stringently regulated internationally and are now in limited use. Scientists have stated that the climate shifts recorded since the Industrial Revolution cannot be attributed to natural causes alone, as the patterns do not follow those of climate shifts that took place prior to the Industrial Revolution.

Natural Greenhouse Effect vs. Human Influence

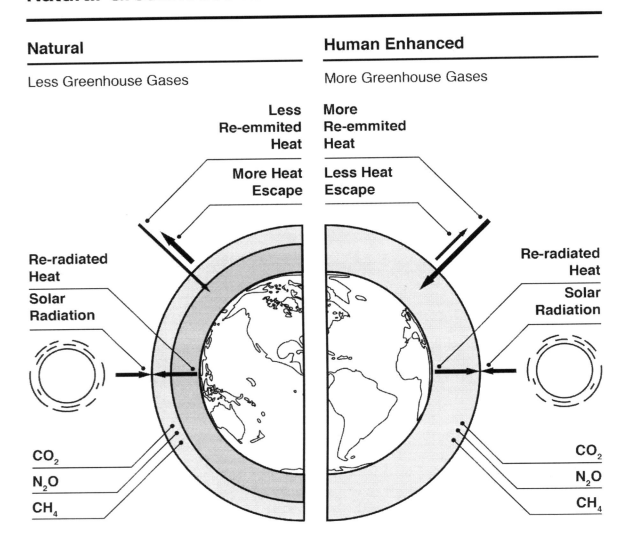

Located in the stratosphere, the *ozone layer* protects the Earth from excessive *ultraviolet B (UVB)* ray exposure. The last century has shown signification depletion of the ozone layer, especially over Antarctica; this region is known as the *ozone hole*, missing almost 70% of its ozone layer. Chlorine molecules are especially harmful to ozone molecules. CFCs have been a major contributor to the ozone layer's depletion due to their high concentration of chlorine molecules. Almost all CFC production was a result of industrialization and human activity. In 1996, most CFC production was banned; however, it is expected that atmospheric chlorine levels will remain high for the next couple of decades. Additionally, other effects of climate change may prevent the stratosphere from ever reaching the gas composition that existed before CFCs were utilized. While ozone depletion does not contribute to global warming directly, its impact on human health and disease is significant. The consequent increase in UVB exposure is linked to skin cancer in people, and ecosystem and food source disruption in animals. The effect on plants can lead to plant loss, which can indirectly impact the greenhouse effect, global warming, climate change, and human health.

Loss of Biodiversity

Biodiversity refers to the varied number of species on Earth—ranging from humans, to fish, to plants—and the way ecosystems are built within them. The biodiversity of an area strongly influences its air and soil quality, its energy availability, and how well its community thrives. Natural resources are currently being expended faster rate than they can be replaced, which is resulting in the extinction of species. As all species are interconnected in some way, the loss of an entire species can detrimentally impact the interactions and existence of other species. For example, if a particular animal feeds primarily on a plant species that becomes extinct, the animal species will have to radically change its feeding behaviors or it becomes prone to extinction. Decreasing supplies of water can impact the existence of plant and animal species as well, which, in turn, may affect how and what humans eat and grow. Plants are crucial to providing oxygen and reducing carbon dioxide—a greenhouse gas—on Earth. Additionally, many plants serve as ingredient sources in medicines; loss of plant life affects not only potential food sources but also medicinal sources. Overpopulation is likely the biggest threat to biodiversity, due to the inherent competing needs for land, water, and food production, as well as the risks of excess waste and pollution.

Waste Disposal and Landfills

Waste disposal is a serious human concern. Waste production has almost doubled in the United States in the last 50 years, with the average household producing over 6,000 pounds of trash per year. Over half of that waste is disposed of in man-made sites in the Earth's ground. Piling (and even burying) trash is an ancient tradition. *Dumps* are open pits of trash, susceptible to rot, stench, and animal infestations. *Landfills* are designed structures intended to create a distinct boundary between the trash and the Earth. This boundary may be made of plastic, or with clay and soil. These structures try to prevent contamination of aquifers and crop soil. As waste breaks down in a landfill, methane is released into the air. Environmental groups and government regulations are pushing lifestyle changes and new technologies to reduce human trash generation. These include repurposing waste, extracting valuable materials from waste, turning waste into a renewable energy source, and advocating green behaviors such as using reusable grocery bags, using fewer plastic goods, and having *compost bins* at home. Many items in landfills could be disposed of in compost bins. These are composed of organic materials that decay quickly, such as food rinds and plant detritus. Once decayed, this material can be used to enrich soil and plant life, limit erosion, and even retain extra groundwater. The average household throws away between 20 to 50 percent of items to landfills that are compostable.

Finally, businesses and landfills in many countries have experienced new regulations aimed to limit waste production. Some governments offer tax breaks to companies that utilize green behaviors and focus on waste reduction.

Energy Production and the Management of Natural Resources

As the Earth's human population grows, more energy and natural resources are required to sustain communities. This need is increasing at a rate of approximately two-to-three percent annually. The growth in human population and related energy needs presents energy production and management issues that need to be addressed.

Renewable and Non-Renewable Energy Sources

Renewable energy sources are those that cannot be depleted; they are able to replenish themselves (or humans are able to replenish what they use) after consumption. These include sources such as solar energy, wind energy, hydro energy from the ocean, and geothermal heat. To be considered a viable resource, these energy sources should be able to translate into usable electricity, heat, cooling, or transportation fuel. Some biomass sources, such as waste, can also technically be considered "renewable" due to the amount of waste that humans produce. This would allow humans to recycle materials, and become less dependent on foreign fossil fuels. Scientists are also examining ways to make energy out of more plentiful biomass sources such as algae. Out of all human energy consumption in 2016, approximately one-fifth was from renewable resources. Out of all human energy production in 2016, approximately one-fourth was from renewable resources. Most large developed nations are investing heavily in renewable energy resources.

Traditionally, energy has come from *non-renewable energy sources* such as *fossil fuels* (common fossil fuels include carbon, coal, petroleum, oil, and natural gas) and other non-renewable biomass sources, such as wood. Fossil fuel consumption makes up almost three-fourths of all global energy consumption, with the United States responsible for almost twenty-five percent of that consumption. Fossil fuels take over millions of years to form, and supplies are quickly dwindling. Additionally, the methods of extracting fossil fuels are considered to be environmentally detrimental as is the exceedingly high production of greenhouse gases that results from their use. Fossil fuels are also concentrated in certain geographic locations around the globe, which has led to extensive geopolitical tension and conflict. These reasons have all led to the increased global interest in developing and utilizing renewable energy resources. However, barriers to developing renewable energy sources include those that are similar to any new start-up venture. Permitting, regulating, marketing to consumers, training employees, examining long-term implications, and costs are all barriers that are still being examined and managed.

Recycling and Conservation

Recycling and conservation are two important tools for protecting the Earth's resources, but as relatively newer practices, they are not without issues. In general, the practice of *recycling* allows for the *conservation* of Earth's resources by reusing manufactured products, which limits the production and use of raw materials. This reduces landfill use, minimizes waste elimination practices that release greenhouse gas emissions, and is often more cost-effective for manufacturers. However, introducing new recycling centers to an area is often costly in the beginning, as it requires constructing and developing the facility and hiring and training workers. Recycling facilities are often dirty, due to the nature of the items that are recycled, which may have once contained food items, human waste, and other organic materials. These materials quickly rot, may attract vermin, and/or create an overall biological hazard. If the waste from recycled materials is improperly handled, it can cause a pollution problem. Additionally, recycled materials used to create new goods may not be high quality, which can be problematic for the consumer. Finally, recycling is a newer trend that has not yet been adopted on a global scale. Some researchers worry that the amount of recycling that occurs is on a scale that is too small to have a lasting impact, and therefore may be a cost-prohibitive practice.

Pros and Cons of Power Generation

All presently available energy resources have pros and cons to their utilization. Fossil fuels are a non-renewable resource created from organic sources (such as coal) that developed over millions of years. Two pros for using fossil fuels include the existence of systems that are already in place to use this form of energy, and that a fairly large resource of fossil fuel material still exists. However, burning this resource for energy is a primary contributor to greenhouse gas production and disrupts many ecosystems. Sources are concentrated in certain areas around the globe, which has led to geopolitical conflict and tension. Additionally, the current rate of expenditure is faster than the rate of replenishment. This fact has led to research and development in the alternative energy industry.

Alternative energy sources include any source of energy that protects the environment and can be used as an alternative to fossil fuels. The term usually refers to solar, wind, water, and biomass power, but additional options also exist. In general, alternative energy sources are considered to be sustainable and conserving measures. However, a major con is that the industry is relatively new, and research is ongoing to utilize these sources in the most productive, efficient, and wide-reaching ways. Specific pros and cons of different types of alternative energy sources are listed below.

Nuclear fuel is a renewable resource created by the splitting of uranium atoms. This source greatly limits air pollution, as greenhouse gas emissions are low. Nuclear fuel also enjoys a relatively low production cost. However, upfront costs to build safe facilities are high. Nuclear accidents are also likely to be catastrophic to life, and adequate and safe storage of radioactive waste is another issue yet to resolve.

Hydropower refers to a renewable resource created from fast-flowing water sources that may be natural or man-made. This source is cheap, helps with global irrigation, and can provide drinking water. Disadvantages to hydropower include its inevitable disruption to many ecosystems; facilities are costly and may displace residents; and finally, while the risk of flooding is moderate, the risk of pollution is high.

Wind power refers to a renewable resource created by harnessing air flow. This source is abundant, cheap, clean, and does not require water or large facilities to use. However, wind has to be moving swiftly in order to be harnessed, and it cannot be stored. Commercializing a resource that easily crosses man-made borders can become complicated from legal and business standpoints.

Solar power is a renewable resource that uses the sun's rays for energy. This source is abundant, easily accessible, receives capital funding from both government and private sources, and requires minimal maintenance. However, even with subsidizing, initial production can be costly. It requires land or roof space for cell panels, and utilizes large-scale batteries. These can be a major contributor to waste and pollution.

Finally, *geothermal power* is a renewable resource that uses the Earth's core temperature to generate energy. This resource does not involve combustion (therefore no greenhouse gas emission), yet is three-to-five times more efficient than other sources. It can be used to heat or cool any residential or commercial space. However, utilizing this resource has a high upfront cost. It also requires a large amount of water, and can cause underground and well water damage. Additionally, emergency events, such as geyser eruptions and landslides, have a high risk of being catastrophic to life.

The Use and Extraction of Earth's Resources

Extracting resources from the Earth is inherently damaging in its process. *Mining* for minerals and fossil fuels has vast environmental impacts. Surface damage, unnatural erosion, increases in sinkholes, disruption to ecosystems, unnatural animal migration, and pollution are all side effects of mining. *Deforesting* lands to use the land for commercial or residential use or to use the trees for raw materials significantly disrupts ecosystems, contributes to global warming from reduced carbon dioxide consumption, affects water levels, reduces biodiversity, and endangers wildlife. Many rainforests, such as the Amazon rainforest, are believed to have "tipping points" of damage, where the land will be unable to replenish itself and the overall climate will have changed so drastically that it will set off other climate feedback responses. For example, cutting down trees leads to increased atmospheric carbon dioxide in the area, which leads to higher temperatures, which decreases plant water availability, resulting in less vegetation (and the loop continues). *Land reclamation* often focuses on correcting negative impacts to natural resources (i.e., restoring deforested lands by planting indigenous vegetation, replacing sands near beaches that have eroded, and so forth).

Life Cycle, Reproduction, and Evolution

Cell Cycle

The *cell cycle* is the process by which a cell divides and duplicates itself. There are two processes by which a cell can divide itself: mitosis and meiosis. In *mitosis*, the daughter cells that are produced from parental cell division are identical to each other and the parent. *Meiosis* is a unique process that involves two stages of cell division and produces *haploid cells*, which are cells containing only one set of chromosomes, from *diploid parent cells*, which are cells containing two sets of chromosomes.

The Cell Cycle

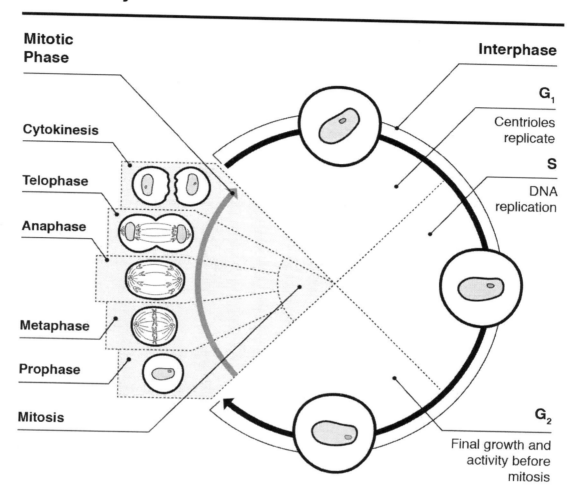

Mitosis

Mitosis can be broken down into five stages: prophase, prometaphase, metaphase, anaphase, and telophase.

- *Prophase*: During this phase, the mitotic spindles begin to form from centrosomes and microtubules. As the microtubules lengthen, the centrosomes move farther away from each other. The nucleolus disappears and the chromatin fibers begin to coil up and form chromosomes. Two sister chromatids, which are two copies of one chromosome, are joined together.

- *Prometaphase*: The nuclear envelope begins to break down and the microtubules enter the nuclear area. Each pair of chromatin fibers develops a *kinetochore*, which is a specialized protein structure in the middle of the adjoined fibers. The chromosomes are further condensed.

- *Metaphase*: In this stage, the microtubules are stretched across the cell and the centrosomes are at opposite ends of the cell. The chromosomes align at the *metaphase plate*, which is a plane that is exactly between the two centrosomes. The kinetochore of each chromosome is attached to the kinetochore of the microtubules that are stretching from each centrosome to the metaphase plate.

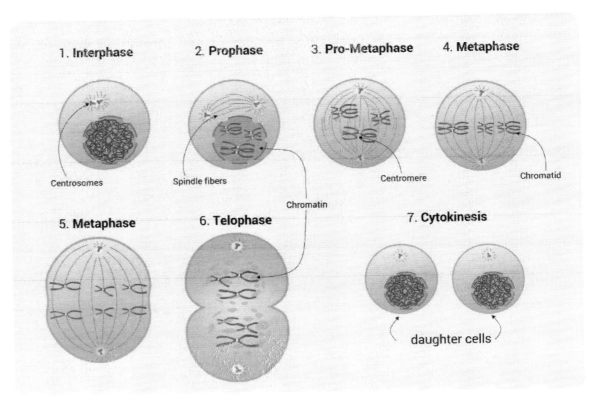

- *Anaphase*: The sister chromatids break apart, forming full-fledged chromosomes. The two daughter chromosomes move to opposite ends of the cell. The microtubules shorten toward opposite ends of the cell as well, and the cell elongates.

- *Telophase*: Two nuclei form at each end of the cell and nuclear envelopes begin to form around each nucleus. The nucleoli reappear and the chromosomes become less condensed. The microtubules are broken down by the cell and mitosis is complete.

Meiosis

Meiosis is a type of cell division in which the daughter cells have half as many sets of chromosomes as the parent cell. In addition, one parent cell produces four daughter cells. Meiosis has the same phases as mitosis, except that they occur twice—once in meiosis I and once in meiosis II. The diploid parent has two sets of chromosomes, set A and set B. During meiosis I, each chromosome set duplicates, producing a second set of A chromosomes and a second set of B chromosomes, and the cell splits into two. Each cell contains two sets of chromosomes. Next, during meiosis II, the two intermediate daughter cells divide again, producing four total haploid cells that each contain one set of chromosomes. Two of the haploid cells each contain one chromosome of set A and the other two cells each contain one chromosome of set B.

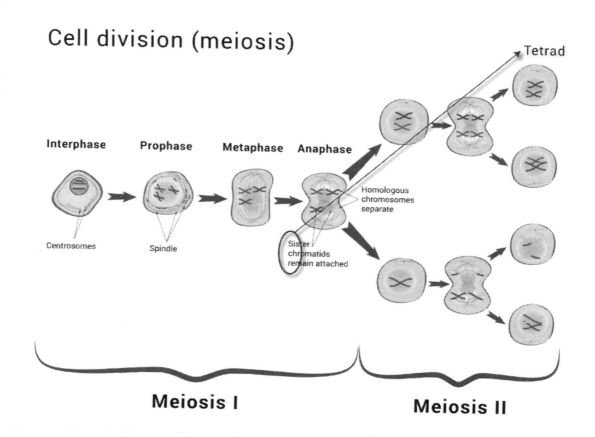

Cytokinesis

Cytokinesis is the division of cytoplasm that occurs immediately following the division of genetic material during cellular reproduction. The process of mitosis or meiosis, followed by cytokinesis, makes up the complete cell cycle.

Cellular Respiration

Cellular respiration is a set of metabolic processes that converts energy from nutrients into ATP, which is the molecule of useable energy for the cell. Respiration can either occur aerobically, using oxygen, or anaerobically, without oxygen. While prokaryotic cells carry out respiration in the cytosol, most of the aerobic respiration in eukaryotic cells occurs in the mitochondria. Glycolysis and ATP-PC (phosphocreatine system) take place in the cytosol.

Anaerobic Respiration

Some organisms do not live in oxygen-rich environments and must find alternate methods of respiration. *Anaerobic respiration* occurs in certain prokaryotic organisms, and while it does occur in eukaryotic organisms, it happens in them much less frequently. The organisms utilize an electron transport chain similar to that of the aerobic respiration pathway; the terminal acceptor molecule, however, is an electronegative substance that is not an oxygen molecule. Some bacteria, for example, use the sulfate ion (SO_4^{2-}) as the final electron accepting molecule and the resulting byproduct is hydrogen sulfide (H_2S), instead of water.

Aerobic Respiration

There are two main steps in *aerobic cellular respiration*: the *citric acid cycle*, also known as the *Krebs cycle*, and *oxidative phosphorylation*. A process called *glycolysis* converts glucose molecules into pyruvate molecules and those pyruvate molecules then enter the citric acid cycle. The pyruvate molecules are broken down to produce ATP, as well as NADH and $FADH_2$—molecules that are used energetically to drive the next step of oxidative phosphorylation. During this phase of aerobic respiration, an electron transport chain pumps electrons and protons across the inner mitochondrial matrix. The electrons are accepted by an oxygen molecule, and water is produced. This process then fuels *chemiosmosis*, which helps convert ADP molecules to ATP. The total number of ATP molecules generated through aerobic respiration can be as many as thirty-eight, if none are lost during the process. Aerobic respiration is up to fifteen times more efficient than anaerobic respiration.

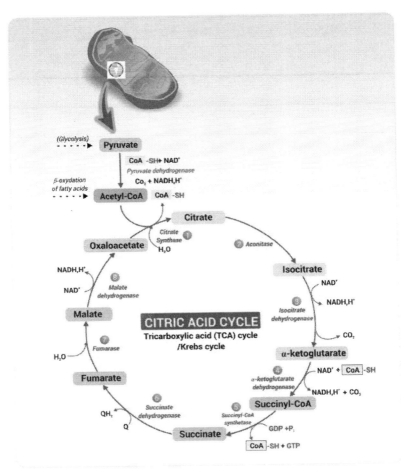

Photosynthesis

Photosynthesis is the process of converting light energy into chemical energy, which is then stored in sugar and other organic molecules. It can be divided into two stages called the *light reactions* and the *Calvin cycle*. The photosynthetic process takes place in the chloroplast in plants. Inside the chloroplast, there are membranous sacs called *thylakoids*. *Chlorophyll* is a green pigment that lives in the thylakoid membranes, absorbs photons from light, and starts an electron transport chain in order to produce energy in the form of ATP and NADPH. The ATP and NADPH produced from the light reactions are used as energy to form organic molecules in the Calvin cycle.

The Calvin cycle takes place in the *stroma*, or inner space, of the chloroplasts. The process consumes nine ATP molecules and six NADPH molecules for every one molecule of glyceraldehyde 3-phosphate (G3P) that it produces. The G3P that is produced can be used as the starting material to build larger organic compounds, such as glucose. The complex series of reactions that takes place in photosynthesis can be simplified into the following equation: $6CO_2 + 12\ H_2O + \text{Light Energy} \rightarrow C_6H_{12}O_6 + 6O_2 + 6H_2O$.

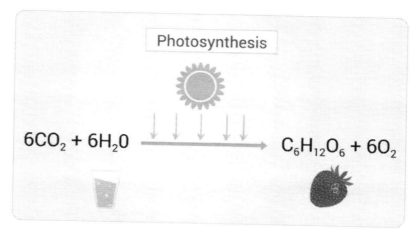

Basically, carbon dioxide and water mix with light energy inside the chloroplast to produce organic molecules, oxygen, and water. It is interesting to note that water is on both sides of the equation. Twelve water molecules are consumed during this process and six water molecules are newly formed as byproducts. Although the Calvin cycle itself is not dependent on light energy, both steps of photosynthesis usually occur during daylight because the Calvin cycle is dependent upon the ATP and NADPH that is produced by the light reactions.

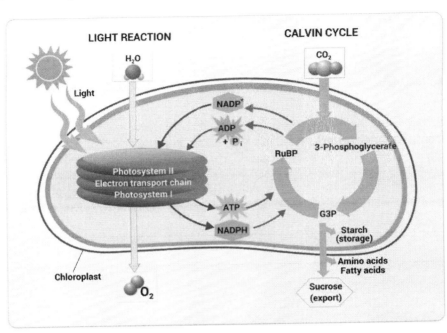

Biological Molecules

Repeating units of monomers (small molecules that bond with identical small molecules) that are linked together are called *polymers*. The most important polymers found in all living things can be divided into five categories: nucleic acids (such as DNA), carbohydrates, proteins, lipids, and enzymes. Carbon (C), hydrogen (H), oxygen (O), nitrogen (N), sulfur (S), and phosphorus (P) are the major elements of most biological molecules. Carbon is a common backbone of large molecules because of its ability to bond to four different atoms.

DNA and RNA
Nucleotides consist of a five-carbon sugar, a nitrogen-containing base, and one or more phosphate groups. *Deoxyribonucleic acid (DNA)* is made up of two strands of nucleotides coiled together in a double-helix structure. It plays a major role in enabling living organisms to pass their genetic information and complex components on to subsequent generations. There are four nitrogenous bases that make up DNA: adenine, thymine, guanine, and cytosine. Adenine always pairs with thymine, and guanine always

pairs with cytosine. *Ribonucleic acid (RNA)* is often made up of only one strand of nucleotides folded in on itself. Like DNA, RNA has four nitrogenous bases; however, in RNA, thymine is replaced by uracil.

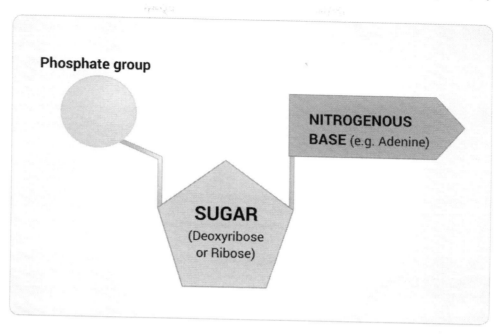

Carbohydrates

Carbohydrates consist of sugars and polymers of sugars, such as starches, which make up the cell walls of plants. The simplest sugar is called a *monosaccharide* and has the molecular formula of CH_2O, or a multiple of that formula. Monosaccharides are important molecules for cellular respiration. Their carbon skeleton can also be used to rebuild new small molecules. *Polysaccharides* are made up of a few hundred to a few thousand monosaccharides linked together.

Proteins

Proteins are essential for almost all functions in living beings. All proteins are made from a set of twenty *amino acids* that are linked in *unbranched polymers*. The amino acids are linked by *peptide bonds*, and polymers of amino acids are called *polypeptides*. These polypeptides, either individually or in linked combination with each other, fold up and form coils of biologically functional molecules.

There are four levels of protein structure: primary, secondary, tertiary, and quaternary. The *primary structure* is the sequence of amino acids, similar to the letters in a long word. The *secondary structure* comprises the folds and coils that are formed by hydrogen bonding between the slightly charged atoms of the polypeptide backbone. *Tertiary structure* is the overall shape of the molecule that results from the interactions between the side chains that are linked to the polypeptide backbone. *Quaternary structure* is the overall protein structure that occurs when a protein is made up of two or more polypeptide chains.

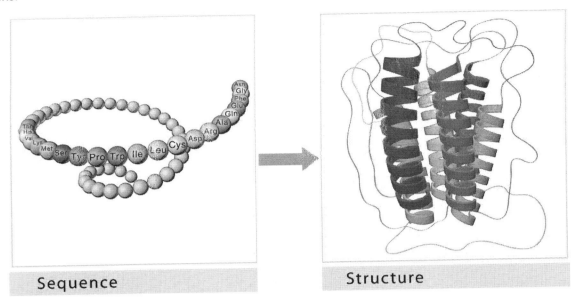

Sequence   Structure

Lipids

Lipids are a class of biological molecules that are *hydrophobic*, which means that they do not mix well with water. They are mostly made up of large chains of carbon and hydrogen atoms, termed *hydrocarbon chains*. The three most important types of lipids are fats, phospholipids, and steroids.

Fats are made up of two types of smaller molecules: three fatty acids and one glycerol molecule. Saturated fats do not have double bonds between the carbons in the fatty acid chain, such as glycerol, pictured below. They are fairly straight molecules and can pack together closely, so they form solids at room temperature. Unsaturated fats have one or more double bonds between carbons in the fatty acid chain. Since they cannot pack together as tightly as saturated fats, they take up more space and are called oils. They remain liquid at room temperature.

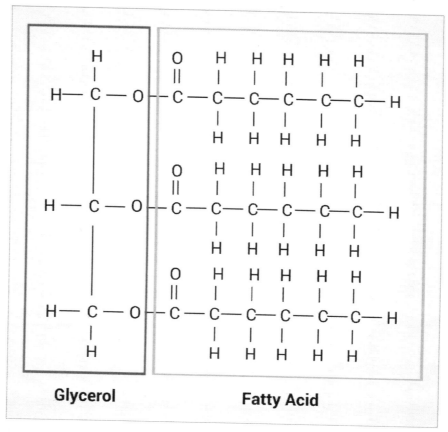

Glycerol   **Fatty Acid**

Phospholipids are made up of two fatty acid molecules linked to one glycerol molecule. When phospholipids are mixed with water, they inherently create double-layered structures, called *bilayers*, which shield their hydrophobic regions from the water molecules.

Steroids are lipids that consist of four fused carbon rings. They can mix in between the phospholipid bilayer cell membrane and help maintain its structure, as well as aid in cell signaling.

Enzymes

Enzymes are biological molecules that accelerate the rate of chemical reactions by lowering the activation energy needed to make the reaction proceed. Although most enzymes can be classified as proteins, some are ribonucleic acid (RNA) molecules. Enzymes function by interacting with a specific substrate in order to create a different molecule, or product. Most reactions in cells need enzymes to make them occur at rates fast enough to sustain life.

Structure and Function of DNA and RNA

DNA and RNA are made up of *nucleotides*, which are formed from a five-carbon sugar, a nitrogenous base, and one or more phosphate group. While DNA is made up of the sugar deoxyribose, RNA is made up of the sugar ribose. Deoxyribose has one fewer oxygen atom than ribose. DNA and RNA each comprise four nitrogenous bases, three of which they have in common: adenine, guanine, and cytosine. Thymine is found only in DNA and uracil is found only in RNA. Each base has a specific pairing formed by hydrogen bonds, and is known as a *base pair*. Adenine interacts with thymine or uracil, and guanine interacts only with cytosine. While RNA is found in a single strand, DNA is a double-stranded molecule that coils up to form a *double helix* structure.

The specific pairing of the nitrogenous bases allows for the hereditary information stored in DNA to be passed down accurately from parent cells to daughter cells. When chromosomes are *replicated* during cell division, the double-helix DNA is first uncoiled, each strand is replicated, and then two new identical DNA molecules are generated. DNA can also be used as a template for generating proteins. A *single-stranded* RNA is generated from the DNA during a process called *transcription*; proteins are then generated from this RNA in a process called *translation*.

Chromosomes, Genes, Alleles

Chromosomes are found inside the nucleus of cells and contain the hereditary information of the cell in the form of *genes*. Each gene has a specific sequence of DNA that eventually encodes proteins and results in inherited traits. *Alleles* are variations of a specific gene that occur at the same location on the chromosome. For example, blue and brown are two different alleles of the gene that encodes for eye color.

Dominant and Recessive Traits

In genetics, *dominant alleles* are mostly noted in capital letters (A) and *recessive alleles* are mostly noted in lower case letters (a). There are three possible combinations of alleles among dominant and recessive alleles: AA, Aa, and aa. Dominant traits are phenotypes that appear when at least one dominant allele is present in the gene. Dominant alleles are considered to have stronger phenotypes and, when mixed with recessive alleles, will mask the recessive trait. The recessive trait would only appear as the phenotype when the allele combination is "aa" because a dominant allele is not present to mask it.

Mendelian Inheritance

A monk named Gregor Mendel is referred to as the father of genetics. He was responsible for coming up with one of the first models of inheritance in the 1860s. His model included two laws to determine which traits are inherited. These laws still apply today, even after genetics has been studied much more in depth.

- *The Law of Segregation*: Each characteristic has two versions that can be inherited. When two parent cells form daughter cells, the two alleles of the gene segregate and each daughter cell can inherit only one of the alleles from each parent.

- *The Law of Independent Assortment*: The alleles for different traits are inherited independent of one another. In other words, the biological selection of one allele by a daughter cell is not linked to the biological selection of an allele for a different trait by the same daughter cell. The genotype that is inherited is the alleles that are encoded on the gene, and the phenotype is the outward appearance of the physical trait for that gene. For example, "A" is the dominant allele for brown eyes and "a" is the recessive allele for blue eyes; the phenotype of brown eyes would occur for two different genotypes: both "AA" and "Aa."

Punnett Squares

For simple genetic combinations, a *Punnett square* can be used to assess the phenotypic ratios of subsequent generations. In a 2 x 2 cell square, one parent's alleles are set up in columns and the other parent's alleles are set up in rows. The resulting allele combinations are shown in the four internal cells.

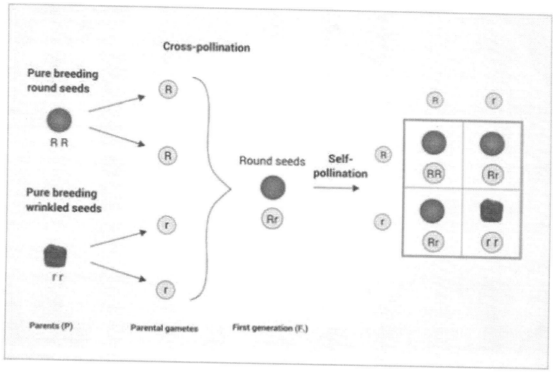

Pedigree

For existing populations where genetic crosses cannot be controlled, phenotype information can be collected over several generations and a *pedigree analysis* can be done to investigate the dominant and recessive characteristics of specific traits. There are several rules to follow when determining the pedigree of a trait. For dominant alleles:

- Affected individuals have at least one affected parent;
- The phenotype appears in every generation; and
- If both parents are unaffected, their offspring will always be unaffected.

For recessive alleles:

- Unaffected parents can have affected offspring; and
- Affected offspring are male and female.

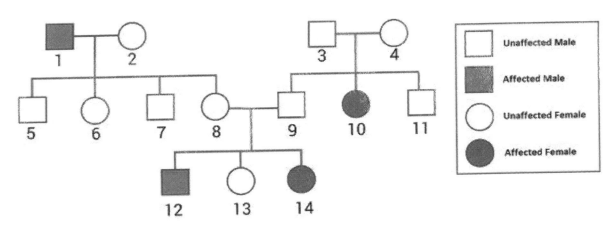

Mutations, Chromosomal Abnormalities, and Common Genetic Disorders

Mutations

Genetic *mutations* occur when there is a permanent alteration in the DNA sequence that codes for a specific gene. They can be small, affecting only one base pair, or large, affecting many genes on a chromosome. Mutations are classified as either hereditary, which means they were also present in the parent gene, or acquired, which means that they occurred after the genes were passed down from the parents. Although mutations are not common, they are an important aspect of genetics and variation in the general population.

Chromosomal Abnormalities and Common Genetic Disorders

Structural chromosomal abnormalities are mutations that affect a large chromosomal segment of more than one gene. This often occurs due to an error in cell division. Acute myelogenous leukemia is caused by a *translocation error*, which is when a segment of one chromosome is moved to another chromosome.

There can also be an abnormal number of chromosomes, which is referred to as *aneuploidy*. Down syndrome is an example of an aneuploidy in which there are three copies of chromosome 21 instead of two copies. Turner syndrome is another example of aneuploidy, in which a female is completely or partially missing an X chromosome. Without the second X chromosome, these females do not develop all of the typical female physical characteristics and are unable to bear children.

Mechanisms of Evolution

Evolution is the concept that there is one common ancestor for all living organisms, and, over time, genetic variation and mutations cause the development of different species. Charles Darwin came up with a scientific model of evolution based on the idea that individuals within a population can have longer lives (better survival) and higher reproduction rates based on certain specific traits that they have inherited, called *natural selection*. The variation of a trait that enhances survival and reproduction in the environment is the one that gets passed on. The survival and inheritance of these traits through many subsequent generations causes a change in the overall population. The traits that are more advantageous for survival and reproduction become more common in subsequent generations and increase the diversity of the population. For example, when there was a drought in the Galapagos Islands, the finches with large beaks became more populous because they were able to survive on the larger, rougher seeds that were remaining.

Speciation and Isolation Methods

Speciation is the method by which one species splits into two or more species due to either geographic separation, called allopatric speciation, or a reduction in gene flow between varying members of the population, called sympatric speciation. In *allopatric speciation*, one population is divided into two subpopulations. For example, if a drought occurs and a large lake becomes divided into two smaller lakes, each lake is left with its own population that cannot intermingle with the population of the other lake. When the genes of these two subpopulations are no longer mixing with each other, new mutations can arise and natural selection can take place.

In *sympatric speciation*, gene flow in the population is reduced by polyploidy, sexual selection, and habitat differentiation. *Polyploidy* is more common in plants than animals and results when cell division during reproduction creates an extra set of chromosomes. In *sexual selection*, organisms of one sex choose their mate of the opposite sex based on certain traits. If there is high selection for two extreme variations of a trait, sympatric speciation may occur. *Habitat differentiation* occurs when a subpopulation exploits a resource that is not used by the parent population. Both allopatric and sympatric speciation can occur quickly or slowly, and may involve just a few gene changes or many gene changes between the new species.

One important distinguishing factor in the formation of two species is their *reproductive isolation*. Species are characterized by their members' ability to breed and produce viable offspring. When speciation occurs and new species are formed, there must have been a biological barrier that prevented the two species from producing viable offspring.

Following speciation, there are two types of *reproductive barriers* that keep the two populations from mating with each other. These are classified as either prezygotic barriers or postzygotic barriers. *Prezygotic barriers* prevent fertilization via habitat isolation, temporal isolation, and behavioral isolation. Through habitat isolation, two species may inhabit the same area but don't often encounter each other. *Temporal isolation* is when species breed at different times of the day, during different seasons, or during different years, so their mating patterns never coincide. *Behavioral isolation* refers to mating rituals that prevent an organism from recognizing a different species as potential mate.

Other prezygotic barriers block fertilization after a mating attempt. *Mechanical isolation* occurs when anatomical differences prevent fertilization. *Gametic isolation* occurs when the gametes of two species are incompatible.

Supporting Evidence

<u>The Fossil Record</u>
Fossils are the preserved remains of animals and organisms from the distant past. They provide evidence of evolution and can elucidate the homology of both living and extinct species. Looking at the *fossil*

record over time can help identify how quickly or slowly evolutionary changes occurred, and can also help match those changes to environmental changes that were occurring concurrently.

Comparative Genetics

In *comparative genetics*, different organisms are compared at a genetic level to look for similarities and differences. DNA sequence, genes, gene order, and other structural features are among the features that may be analyzed in order to look for evolutionary relationships and common ancestors between the organisms. Comparative genetics was useful in elucidating the similarities between humans and chimpanzees and linking their evolutionary history.

Homology

Organisms that developed from a common ancestor often have similar characteristics that function differently. This similarity is known as *homology*. For example, humans, cats, whales, and bats all have bones arranged in the same manner from their shoulders to their digits. However, the bones form arms in humans, forelegs in cats, flippers in whales, and wings in bats, and these forelimbs are used for lifting, walking, swimming, and flying, respectively. The similarity of the bone structure shows a common ancestry, but the functional differences are the product of evolution.

Homologous Structures

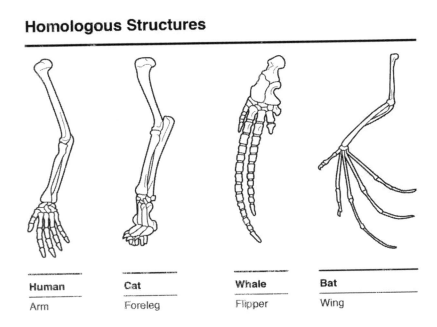

Human	Cat	Whale	Bat
Arm	Foreleg	Flipper	Wing

Asexual and Sexual Reproduction in Plants

Plants can generate future generations through both asexual and sexual reproduction. Asexually, plants can go through an artificial reproductive technique called *budding*, in which parts from two or more plants of the same species are joined together with the hope that they will begin to grow as a single plant.

Sexual reproduction of flowers can happen in a couple of ways. *Angiosperms* are flowering plants that have seeds. The flowers have male parts that make pollen and female parts that contain ovules. Wind, insects, and other animals carry the pollen from the male part to the female part in a process called *pollination*. Once the ovules are pollinated, or fertilized, they develop into seeds that then develop into new plants. In many angiosperms, the flowers develop into fruit, such as oranges, or even hard nuts, which protect the seeds inside of them.

Nonvascular plants reproduce by sexual reproduction involving *spores*. Parent plants send out spores that contain a set of chromosomes. The spores develop into sperm or eggs, and fertilization is similar to that in humans. Sperm travel to the egg through water in the environment. An embryo forms and then a new plant grows from the embryo. Generally, this happens in damp places.

Earth and Space Sciences

The Solar System and the Universe

Major Features of the Solar System

<u>Structure of the Solar System</u>
The *solar system* is an elliptical planetary system with a large sun in the center that provides gravitational pull on the planets. It was formed 4.568 billion years ago from the gravitational collapse of a region within a giant molecular cloud that likely birthed other suns. This region of collapse is called a *pre-solar nebula*. As it started to collapse in the center, the nebula accumulated more energy and became hotter and heavier, providing more gravitational energy to the rest of the cloud, eventually becoming the Sun. The planets likely formed in a similar fashion, starting as small clumps called *protoplanets* that revolved around the Sun and then smashed together to form larger planets and, eventually, the Solar System seen today.

<u>Laws of Motion</u>
Planetary motion is governed by three scientific laws called Kepler's laws:

1. The orbit of a planet is elliptical in shape, with the Sun as one focus.

2. An imaginary line joining the center of a planet and the center of the Sun sweeps out equal areas during equal intervals of time.

3. For all planets, the ratio of the square of the orbital period is the same as the cube of the average distance from the Sun.

The most relevant of these laws is the first. Planets move in elliptical paths because of gravity; when a planet is closer to the Sun, it moves faster because it has built up gravitational speed. As illustrated in the diagram below, the second law states that it takes planet 1 the same time to travel along the A1 segment as the A2 segment, even though the A2 segment is shorter.

Kepler's Laws of Planetary Motion

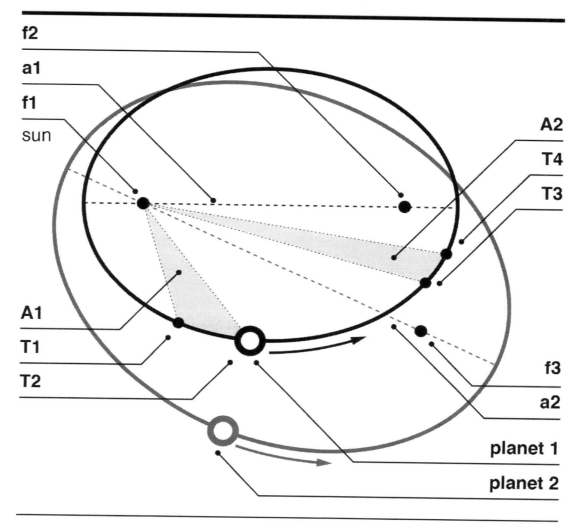

$$(T2 - T1) = (T4 - T3)$$

$$\Delta\, TA1 = \Delta\, TA2$$

Characteristics of the Sun, Moon, and Planets

The Sun is comprised mainly of hydrogen and helium. Metals make up only about 2% of its total mass. The Sun is 1.3 million kilometers wide, weighs 1.989×10^{30} kilograms, and has temperatures of 5,800 Kelvin (9980 °F) on the surface and 15,600,000 Kelvin (28 million °F) at the core. The Sun's enormous size and gravity give it the ability to provide sunlight. The gravity of the Sun compresses hydrogen and helium atoms together through nuclear fusion and releases energy and light.

The Moon has a distinct core, mantle, and crust. It has elevations and craters created by impacts with large objects in the solar system. The Moon makes a complete orbit around the Earth every 27.3 days. It's relatively large compared to other moons in the Solar System, with a diameter one-quarter of the Earth and a mass 1/81 of the Earth.

The eight planets of the Solar System are divided into four inner (or terrestrial) planets and four outer (or Jovian) planets. In general, terrestrial planets are small, and Jovian planets are large and gaseous. The planets in the Solar System are listed below from nearest to farthest from the Sun:

- Mercury: the smallest planet in the Solar System; it only takes about 88 days to completely orbit the Sun.

- Venus: around the same size, composition, and gravity as Earth and orbits the Sun every 225 days.

- Earth: the only known planet with life

- Mars: called the Red Planet due to iron oxide on the surface; takes around 365 days to complete its orbit

- Jupiter: the largest planet in the system; made up of mainly hydrogen and helium

- Saturn: mainly composed of hydrogen and helium along with other trace elements; has 61 moons; has beautiful rings, which may be remnants of destroyed moons

- Uranus: the coldest planet in the system, with temperatures as low as -224.2 °Celsius (-371.56 °F)

- Neptune: the last and third-largest planet; also, the second-coldest planet

Asteroids, Meteoroids, Comets, and Dwarf/Minor Planets
Several other bodies travel through the universe. *Asteroids* are orbiting bodies composed of minerals and rock. They're also known as *minor planets*—a term given to any astronomical object in orbit around the Sun that doesn't resemble a planet or a comet. *Meteoroids* are mini-asteroids with no specific orbiting pattern. *Meteors* are meteoroids that have entered the Earth's atmosphere and started melting from contact with greenhouse gases. *Meteorites* are meteors that have landed on Earth. *Comets* are composed of dust and ice and look like a comma with a tail from the melting ice as they streak across the sky.

Theories of Origin of the Solar System
One theory of the origins of the Solar System is the *nebular hypothesis*, which posits that the Solar System was formed by clouds of extremely hot gas called a *nebula*. As the nebula gases cooled, they became smaller and started rotating. Rings of the nebula left behind during rotation eventually condensed into planets and their satellites. The remaining nebula formed the Sun.

Another theory of the Solar System's development is the *planetesimal hypothesis*. This theory proposes that planets formed from cosmic dust grains that collided and stuck together to form larger and larger bodies. The larger bodies attracted each other, growing into moon-sized protoplanets and eventually planets.

Interactions of the Earth-Moon-Sun System

The Earth's Rotation and Orbital Revolution Around the Sun
Besides revolving around the Sun, the Earth also spins like a top. It takes one day for the Earth to complete a full spin, or rotation. The same is true for other planets, except that their "days" may be shorter or longer. One Earth day is about 24 hours, while one Jupiter day is only about nine Earth hours, and a Venus day is about 241 Earth days. Night occurs in areas that face away from the Sun, so one side of the planet experiences daylight and the other experiences night. This phenomenon is the reason that the Earth is divided into time zones. The concept of time zones was created to provide people around the world with a uniform standard time, so the Sun would rise around 7:00 AM, regardless of location.

Effect on Seasons
The Earth's tilted axis creates the seasons. When Earth is tilted toward the Sun, the Northern Hemisphere experiences summer while the Southern Hemisphere has winter—and vice versa. As the Earth rotates, the distribution of direct sunlight slowly changes, explaining how the seasons gradually change.

Phases of the Moon
The Moon goes through two phases as it revolves around Earth: waxing and waning. Each phase lasts about two weeks:

- Waxing—the right side of the Moon is illuminated
- New moon (dark): the Moon rises and sets with the Sun
- Crescent: a tiny sliver of illumination on the right
- First quarter: the right half the Moon is illuminated
- Gibbous: more than half of the Moon is illuminated
- Full moon: the Moon rises at sunset and sets at sunrise
- Waning—the left side of the Moon is illuminated
- Gibbous: more than half is illuminated, only here it is the left side that is illuminated
- Last quarter: the left half of the Moon is illuminated
- Crescent: a tiny sliver of illumination on the left
- New moon (dark)—the Moon rises and sets with the Sun

Effect on Tides
Although the Earth is much larger, the Moon still has a significant gravitational force that pulls on Earth's oceans. At its closest to Earth, the Moon's gravitation pull is greatest and creates high tide. The opposite is true when the Moon is farthest from the Earth: less pull creates low tide.

Solar and Lunar Eclipses
Eclipses occur when the Earth, the Sun, and the Moon are all in line. If the three bodies are perfectly aligned, a total eclipse occurs; otherwise, it's only a partial eclipse. A *solar eclipse* occurs when the Moon is between the Earth and the Sun, blocking sunlight from reaching the Earth. A *lunar eclipse* occurs when the Earth interferes with the Sun's light reflecting off the full moon. The Earth casts a shadow on the

Moon, but the particles of the Earth's atmosphere refract the light, so some light reaches the Moon, causing it to look yellow, brown, or red.

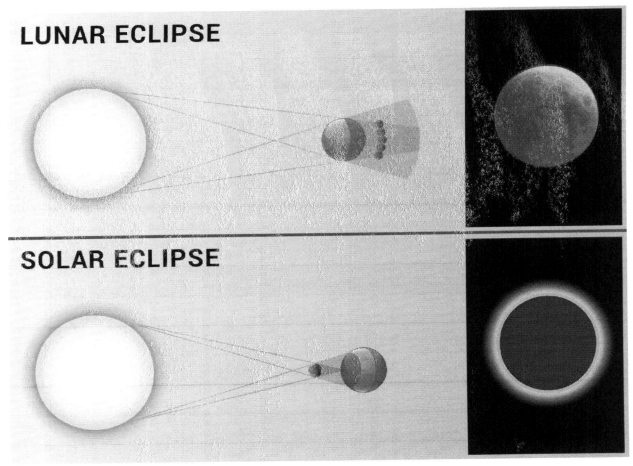

Time Zones
Longitudinal, or vertical, lines determine how far east or west different regions are from each other. These lines, also known as *meridians,* are the basis for time zones, which allocate different times to regions depending on their position eastward and westward of the prime meridian.

Effect of Solar Wind on the Earth
Solar winds are streams of charged particles emitted by the Sun, consisting of mostly electrons, protons, and alpha particles. The Earth is largely protected from solar winds by its magnetic field. However, the winds can still be observed, as they create phenomena like the beautiful Northern Lights (or Aurora Borealis).

Major Features of the Universe

Galaxies
Galaxies are clusters of stars, rocks, ice, and space dust. Like everything else in space, the exact number of galaxies is unknown, but there could be as many as a hundred billion. There are three types of galaxies: spiral, elliptical, and irregular. Most galaxies are *spiral galaxies*; they have a large, central galactic bulge made up of a cluster of older stars. They look like a disk with spinning arms. *Elliptical*

galaxies are groups of stars with no pattern of rotation. They can be spherical or extremely elongated, and they don't have arms. *Irregular galaxies* vary significantly in size and shape.

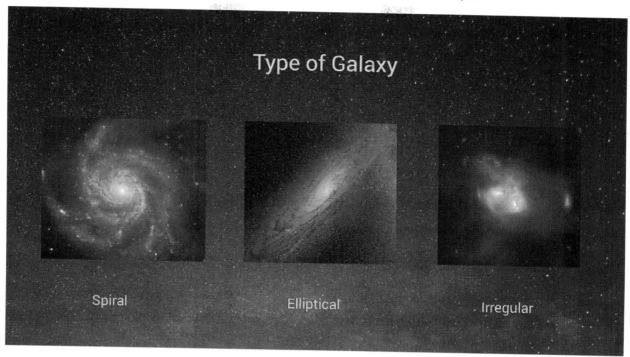

To say that galaxies are large is an understatement. Most galaxies are 1,000 to 100,000 parsecs in diameter, with one *parsec* equal to about 19 trillion miles. The Milky Way is the galaxy that contains Earth's Solar System. It's one of the smaller galaxies that has been studied. The diameter of the Milky Way is estimated to be between 31,000 to 55,000 parsecs.

Characteristics of Stars and Their Life Cycles
Life Cycle of Stars

All stars are formed from nebulae. Depending on their mass, stars take different pathways during their evolution. Low- and medium-mass stars start as nebulae and then become red giants and white dwarfs. High-mass stars become red supergiants, supernovas, and then either neutron stars or black holes. Official stars are born as red dwarves because they have plentiful amounts of gas—mainly hydrogen—to undergo nuclear fusion. Red dwarves mature into white dwarves before expending their hydrogen fuel source. When the fuel is spent, it creates a burst of energy that expands the star into a red giant. Red giants eventually condense to form white dwarves, which is the final stage of a star's life.

Stars that undergo nuclear fusion and energy expenditure extremely quickly can burst in violent explosions called *supernovas*. These bursts can release as much energy in a few seconds as the Sun can release in its entire lifetime. The particles from the explosion then condense into the smallest type of star—a neutron star—and eventually form a *blackhole*, which has such a high amount of gravity that not even light energy can escape. The Sun is currently a red dwarf, early in its life cycle.

Color, Temperature, Apparent Brightness, Absolute Brightness, and Luminosity

The color of a star depends on its surface temperature. Stars with cooler surfaces emit red light, while the hottest stars give off blue light. Stars with temperatures between these extremes, such as the Sun, emit white light. The *apparent brightness* of a star is a measure of how bright a star appears to an observer on the Earth. The *absolute brightness* is a measure of the intrinsic brightness of a star and is measured at a distance of exactly 10 parsecs away. The *luminosity* of a star is the amount of light emitted from its surface.

Hertzsprung-Russell Diagrams
Hertzsprung-Russell diagrams are scatterplots that show the relationship of a star's brightness and temperature, or color. The general layout shows stars of greater luminosity toward the top of the diagram. Stars with higher surface temperatures appear toward the left side of the diagram. The diagonal area from the top-left of the diagram to the bottom-right is called the *main sequence*. Stars may or may not follow the main sequence during their evolutionary period.

Dark Matter
Dark matter is an unidentified type of matter that comprises approximately 27% of the mass and energy in the observable universe. As the name suggests, dark matter is so dense and small that it doesn't emit or interact with electromagnetic radiation, such as light, making it electromagnetically invisible. Although dark matter has never been directly observed, its existence and properties can be inferred from its gravitational effects on visible objects as well as the cosmic microwave background. Patterns of movement have been observed in visible objects that would only be possible if dark matter exerted a gravitational pull.

Theories About the Origin of the Universe
The *Big Bang theory* is the most plausible cosmological model for the origin of the universe. It theorizes that the universe expanded from a high-density and high-temperature state. The theory offers comprehensive explanations for a wide range of astronomical phenomena, such as the cosmic microwave background and Hubble's Law. From detailed measurements of the expansion rate of the universe, it's estimated that the Big Bang occurred approximately 13.8 billion years ago, which is considered the age of the universe. The theory states that after the initial expansion, the universe cooled enough for subatomic particles and atoms to form and aggregate into giant clouds. These clouds coalesced through gravity and formed the stars and galaxies. If this theory holds true, it's predicted that the universe will reach a point where it will stop expanding and start to pull back toward the center due to gravity.

The Structure and Composition of the Earth

Types and Basic Characteristics of Rocks and Minerals and Their Formation Processes

The Rock Cycle
Although it may not always be apparent, rocks are constantly being destroyed while new ones are created in a process called the *rock cycle*. This cycle is driven by plate tectonics and the water cycle, which are discussed in detail later. The rock cycle starts with *magma*, the molten rock found deep within the Earth. As magma moves toward the Earth's surface, it hardens and transforms into igneous rock. Then, over time, igneous rock is broken down into tiny pieces called *sediment* that are eventually deposited all over the surface. As more and more sediment accumulates, the weight of the newer sediment compresses the older sediment underneath and creates sedimentary rock. As sedimentary rock is pushed deeper below the surface, the high pressure and temperature transform it into

metamorphic rock. This metamorphic rock can either rise to the surface again or sink even deeper and melt back into magma, thus starting the cycle again.

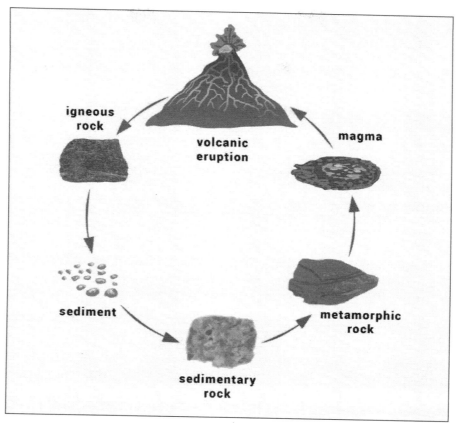

Characteristics of Rocks and Their Formation Processes
There are three main types of rocks: sedimentary, igneous, and metamorphic. Aside from physical characteristics, one of their main differences is how they are created. *Sedimentary rocks* are formed at the surface, on land and in bodies of water, through processes called deposition and cementation. They can be classified as clastic, biochemical, and chemical. *Clastic rocks*, such as sandstone, are composed of other pieces of inorganic rocks and sediment. *Biochemical rocks* are created from an organic material, such as coal, forming from dead plant life. *Chemical rocks* are created from the deposition of dissolved minerals, such as calcium salts that form stalagmites and stalactites in caves.

Igneous rocks are created when magma solidifies at or near the Earth's surface. When they're formed at the surface, (i.e. from volcanic eruption), they are *extrusive*. When they form below the surface, they're called *intrusive*. Examples of extrusive rocks are obsidian and tuff, while rocks like granite are intrusive.

Metamorphic rocks are the result of a transformation from other rocks. Based on appearance, these rocks are classified as foliated or non-foliated. *Foliated rocks* are created from compression in one direction, making them appear layered or folded like slate. *Non-foliated rocks* are compressed from all directions, giving them a more homogenous appearance, such as marble.

Characteristics of Minerals and Their Formation Processes
A *mineral*, such as gold, is a naturally occurring inorganic solid composed of one type of molecule or element that's organized into a crystalline structure. Rocks are aggregates of different types of minerals.

Depending on their composition, minerals can be mainly classified into one of the following eight groups:

- *Carbonates*: formed from molecules that have either a carbon, nitrogen, or boron atom at the center.

- *Elements*: formed from single elements that occur naturally; includes metals such as gold and nickel, as well as metallic alloys like brass.

- *Halides:* formed from molecules that have halogens; halite, which is table salt, is a classic example.

- *Oxides*: formed from molecules that contain oxygen or hydroxide and are held together with ionic bonds; encompasses the phosphates, silicates, and sulfates.

- *Phosphates*: formed from molecules that contain phosphates; the apatite group minerals are in this class.

- *Silicates*: formed from molecules that contain silicon, silicates are the largest class and usually the most complex minerals; topaz is an example of a silicate.

- *Sulfates*: formed from molecules that contain either sulfur, chromium, tungsten, selenium, tellurium, and/or molybdenum.

- *Sulfides*: formed from molecules that contain sulfide (S^{2-}); includes many of the important metal ores, such as lead and silver.

One important physical characteristic of a mineral is its *hardness*, which is defined as its resistance to scratching. When two crystals are struck together, the harder crystal will scratch the softer crystal. The most common measure of hardness is the Mohs Hardness Scale, which ranges from 1 to 10, with 10 being the hardest. Diamonds are rated 10 on the Mohs Hardness Scale, and talc, which was once used to make baby powder, is rated 1. Other important characteristics of minerals include *luster* or shine, *color,* and *cleavage*, which is the natural plane of weakness at which a specific crystal breaks.

Erosion, Weathering, and Deposition of Earth's Surface Materials and Soil Formation

Erosion and Deposition
Erosion is the process of moving rock and occurs when rock and sediment are picked up and transported. Wind, water, and ice are the primary factors for erosion. *Deposition* occurs when the particles stop moving and settle onto a surface, which can happen through gravity or involve processes such as precipitation or flocculation. *Precipitation* is the solidification or crystallization of dissolved ions that occurs when a solution is oversaturated. *Flocculation* is similar to coagulation and occurs when colloid materials (materials that aren't dissolved but are suspended in the medium) aggregate or clump until they are too heavy to remain suspended.

Chemical and Physical (Mechanical) Weathering
Weathering is the process of breaking down rocks through mechanical or chemical changes. Mechanical forces include animal contact, wind, extreme weather, and the water cycle. These physical forces don't alter the composition of rocks. In contrast, chemical weathering transforms rock composition. When water and minerals interact, they can start chemical reactions and form new or secondary minerals from

the original rock. In chemical weathering, the processes of oxidation and hydrolysis are important. When rain falls, it dissolves atmospheric carbon dioxide and becomes acidic. With sulfur dioxide and nitrogen oxide in the atmosphere from volcanic eruptions or burning fossil fuels, the rainfall becomes even more acidic and creates acid rain. Acidic rain can dissolve the rock that it falls upon.

Characteristics of Soil

Soil is a combination of minerals, organic materials, liquids, and gases. There are three main types of soil, as defined by their compositions, going from coarse to fine: sand, silt, and clay. Large particles, such as those found in sand, affect how water moves through the soil, while tiny clay particles can be chemically active and bind with water and nutrients. An important characteristic of soil is its ability to form a crust when dehydrated. In general, the finer the soil, the harder the crust, which is why clay (and not sand) is used to make pottery.

There are many different classes of soil, but the components are always sand, silt, or clay. Below is a chart used by the United States Department of Agriculture (USDA) to define soil types:

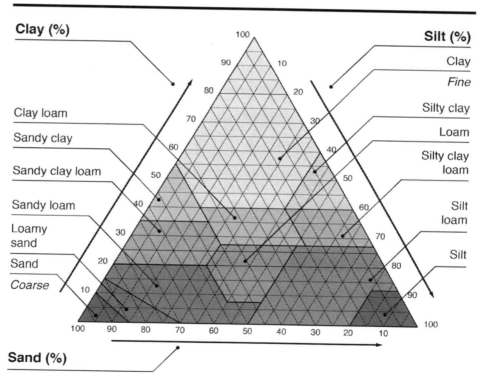

The United States Department of Agriculture's (USDA's) Soil Types

Loam is a term for soil that is a mixture of sand, silt, and clay. It's also the soil most commonly used for agriculture and gardening.

Porosity and Permeability

Porosity and permeability refer to how water moves through rock and soil underground. *Porosity* is a measure of the open space in a rock. This space can be between grains or within cracks and cavities in the rock. *Permeability* is a measure of the ease with which water can move through a porous rock. Therefore, rock that's more porous is also more permeable. When a rock is more permeable, it's less effective as a water purifier because dirty particles in the water can pass through porous rock.

Runoff and Infiltration

An important function of soil is to absorb water to be used by plants or released into groundwater. *Infiltration capacity* is the maximum amount of water that can enter soil at any given time and is regulated by the soil's porosity and composition. For example, sandy soils have larger pores than clays, allowing water to infiltrate them easier and faster. *Runoff* is water that moves across land's surface and may end up in a stream or a rut in the soil. Runoff generally occurs after the soil's infiltration capacity is reached. However, during heavy rainfalls, water may reach the soil's surface at a faster rate than infiltration can occur, causing runoff without soil saturation. In addition, if the ground is frozen and the soil's pores are blocked by ice, runoff may occur without water infiltrating the soil.

Earth's Basic Structure and Internal Processes

Earth's Layers

Earth has three major layers: a thin solid outer surface or *crust*, a dense *core*, and a *mantle* between them that contains most of the Earth's matter. This layout resembles an egg, where the eggshell is the crust, the mantle is the egg white, and the core is the yolk. The outer crust of the Earth consists of igneous or sedimentary rocks over metamorphic rocks. Together with the upper portion of the mantle, it forms the *lithosphere*, which is broken into tectonic plates.

Major plates of the lithosphere

The mantle can be divided into three zones. The *upper mantle* is adjacent to the crust and composed of solid rock. Below the upper mantle is the *transition zone*. The *lower mantle* below the transition zone is a layer of completely solid rock. Underneath the mantle is the molten *outer core* followed by the compact, solid *inner core*. The inner and outer cores contain the densest elements, consisting of mostly iron and nickel.

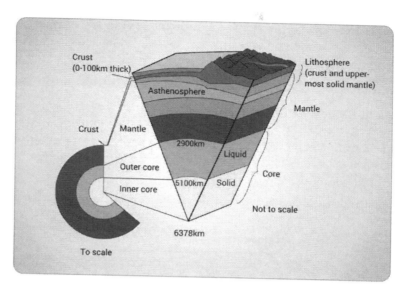

Shape and Size of the Earth

The Earth isn't a perfect sphere; it's slightly elliptical. From center to surface, its radius is almost 4,000 miles, and its circumference around the equator is about 24,902 miles. In comparison, the Sun's radius is 432,288 miles—over 1,000 times larger than the Earth's—and the Moon's radius is about 1,000 miles.

Geographical Features

The Earth's surface is dynamic and consists of various landforms. As tectonic plates are pushed together, *mountains* are formed. *Canyons* are deep trenches that are usually created by plates moving apart, but can also be created by constant weathering and erosion from rivers and runoff. *Deltas* are flat, triangular stretches of land formed by rivers that deposit sediment and water into the ocean. *Sand dunes* are mountains of sand located in desert areas or the bottom of the ocean. They are formed by wind and water movement when there's an absence of plants or other features that would otherwise hold the sand in place.

The Earth's Magnetic Field

The Earth's magnetic field is created by the magnetic forces that extend from the Earth's interior to outer space. It can be modeled as a magnetic dipole tilted about 10 degrees from the Earth's rotational axis, as if a bar magnet was placed at an angle inside the Earth's core. The geomagnetic pole located near Greenland in the northern hemisphere is actually the south pole of the Earth's magnetic field, and vice versa for the southern geomagnetic pole. The *magnetosphere* is the Earth's magnetic field, which extends tens of thousands of kilometers into space and protects the Earth and the atmosphere from damaging solar wind and cosmic rays.

Plate Tectonics Theory and Evidence

The theory of *plate tectonics* hypothesizes that the continents weren't always separated like they are today, but were once joined and slowly drifted apart. Evidence for this theory is based upon evolution and the fossil record. Fossils of one species were found in regions of the world now separated by an ocean. It's unlikely that a single species could have travelled across the ocean or that two separate species evolved into a single species.

Folding and Faulting

The exact number of tectonic plates is debatable, but scientists estimate there are around nine to fifteen major plates and almost 40 minor plates. The line where two plates meet is called a *fault*. The San Andreas Fault is where the Pacific and North American plates meet. Faults or boundaries are classified depending on the interaction between plates. Two plates collide at *convergent boundaries*. *Divergent boundaries* occur when two plates move away from each other. Tectonic plates can move vertically and horizontally.

Continental Drift, Seafloor Spreading, Magnetic Reversals

The movement of tectonic plates is similar to pieces of wood floating in a pool of water. They can bob up and down as well as bump, slide, and move away from each other. These different interactions create the Earth's landscape. The collision of plates can create mountain ranges, while their separation can create canyons or underwater chasms. One plate can also slide atop another and push it down into the Earth's hot mantle, creating magma and volcanoes, in a process called *subduction*.

Subduction

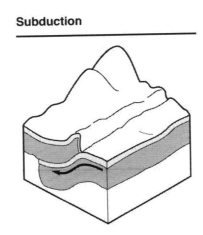

Unlike a regular magnet, the Earth's magnetic field changes over time because it's generated by the motion of molten iron alloys in the outer core. Although the magnetic poles can wander geographically, they do so at such a slow rate that they don't affect the use of compasses in navigation. However, at irregular intervals that are several hundred thousand years long, the fields can reverse, with the north and south magnetic poles switching places.

Characteristics of Volcanoes

Volcanoes are mountainous structures that act as vents to release pressure and magma from the Earth's crust. During an *eruption*, the pressure and magma are released, and volcanoes smoke, rumble, and throw ash and *lava*, or molten rock, into the air. *Hot spots* are volcanic regions of the mantle that are hotter than surrounding regions.

Characteristics of Earthquakes

Earthquakes occur when tectonic plates slide or collide as a result of the crust suddenly releasing energy. Stress in the Earth's outer layer pushes together two faults. The motion of the planes of the fault continues until something makes them stop. The *epicenter* of an earthquake is the point on the surface directly above where the fault is slipping. If the epicenter is located under a body of water, the earthquake may cause a *tsunami*, a series of large, forceful waves.

Seismic waves and Triangulation

Earthquakes cause *seismic waves*, which travel through the Earth's layers and give out low-frequency acoustic energy. Triangulation of seismic waves helps scientists determine the origin of an earthquake.

Historical Geology

Principle of Uniformitarianism

Uniformitarianism is the assumption that natural laws and processes haven't changed and apply everywhere in the universe. In geology, uniformitarianism includes the *gradualist model*, which states that "the present is the key to the past" and claims that natural laws functioned at the same rates as observed today.

Basic Principles of Relative Age Dating

Relative age dating is the determination of the relative order of past events without determining absolute age. The Law of Superposition states that older geological layers are deeper than more recent layers. Rocks and fossils can be used to compare one stratigraphic column with another. A *stratigraphic column* is a drawing that describes the vertical location of rocks in a cliff wall or underground. Correlating these columns from different geographic areas allows scientists to understand the relationships between different areas and strata. Before the discovery of radiometric dating, geologists used this technique to determine the ages of different materials. Relative dating can only determine the sequential order of events, not the exact time they occurred. The Law of Fossil Succession states that when the same kinds of fossils are found in rocks from different locations, the rocks are likely the same age.

Trace fossils   Remain   Layer Analysis

Absolute (Radiometric) Dating

Absolute or *radiometric dating* is the process of determining age on a specified chronology in archaeology and geology. It provides a numerical age by measuring the radioactive decay of elements (such as carbon-14) trapped in rocks or minerals and using the known rate of decay to determine how much time has passed. *Uranium-lead dating* can be used to date some of the oldest rocks on Earth, from 1 million to over 4.5 billion years old.

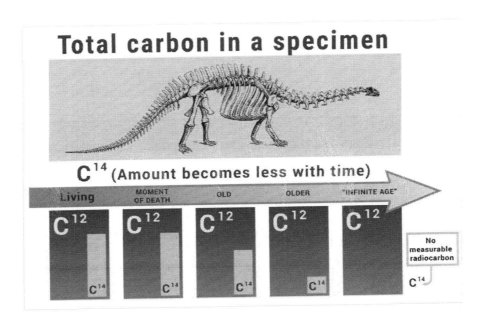

Total carbon in a specimen

C^{14} (Amount becomes less with time)

Living | MOMENT OF DEATH | OLD | OLDER | "INFINITE AGE"

C^{12} | C^{12} | C^{12} | C^{12} | C^{12}

No measurable radiocarbon

C^{14} | C^{14} | C^{14} | C^{14} | C^{14}

Geologic Time Scale

The *geological timescale* is a system that correlates geological strata to time. It's used by scientists to describe the timing and relationships of past natural events. Radiometric dating calculates that the Earth is around 4.55 billion years old. The geology of the Earth's past is organized into units following events that occurred in each period. The diagram below is geologic time scale represented in a clock-face format. The 12 o'clock position represents the formation of the Earth as well as present time. It shows important events in the Earth's history in relation to each other. In the picture, Ma represents millions of years and Ga represents billions of years.

Earth's Geologic History

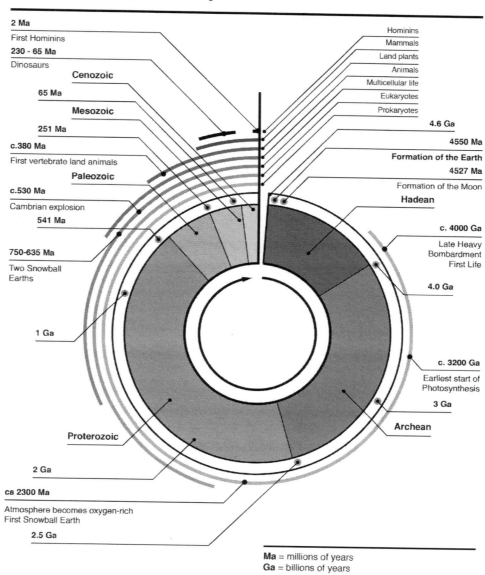

2 Ma
First Hominins
230 - 65 Ma
Dinosaurs
Cenozoic
65 Ma
Mesozoic
251 Ma
c.380 Ma
First vertebrate land animals
Paleozoic
c.530 Ma
Cambrian explosion
541 Ma
750-635 Ma
Two Snowball Earths
1 Ga
Proterozoic
2 Ga
ca 2300 Ma
Atmosphere becomes oxygen-rich
First Snowball Earth
2.5 Ga

Hominins
Mammals
Land plants
Animals
Multicellular life
Eukaryotes
Prokaryotes
4.6 Ga
4550 Ma
Formation of the Earth
4527 Ma
Formation of the Moon
Hadean
c. 4000 Ga
Late Heavy Bombardment
First Life
4.0 Ga
c. 3200 Ga
Earliest start of Photosynthesis
3 Ga
Archean

Ma = millions of years
Ga = billions of years

<u>Fossil Record as Evidence of the Origin and Development of Life</u>
The *fossil record* is the location of fossils throughout the Earth's surface layers. Deeper fossils are older than the fossils above. Scientists use the fossil record to determine when certain organisms existed and how they evolved. There are several ways a fossil can form:

- *Perimineralization:* when an organism is buried and its empty spaces fill with mineral-rich groundwater

- <u>Casts</u>: when the original remains are completely destroyed and an organism-shaped hole is left in the existing rock

- *Replacement or recrystallization:* when shell or bone is replaced with another mineral

The fossil record provides evidence of *mass extinctions*, which occurred when there was a faster rate of extinction than speciation. It also provides evidence of five ice ages in the Earth's history. *Ice ages* are lengthy periods when the temperature of the Earth's surface and atmosphere are greatly reduced. During these periods, animals that require warmer temperatures for survival can become extinct. *Meteors* are fragments of rock that come from outside of the Earth's atmosphere. A meteor impact can induce a massive change in the atmosphere, also causing mass extinction.

The Earth's Atmosphere

Basic Structure and Composition of the Earth's Atmosphere

<u>Layers</u>
The Earth's atmospheric layers are determined by their temperatures but are reported by their distance above sea level. Listed from closest to sea level on upward, the levels are:

- Troposphere: sea level to 11 miles above sea level
- Stratosphere: 11 miles to 31 miles above sea level
- Mesosphere: 31 miles to 50 miles above sea level
- Ionosphere: 50 miles to 400 miles above sea level
- Exosphere: 400 miles to 800 miles above sea level

The ionosphere and exosphere are together considered the thermosphere. The ozone layer is in the stratosphere and weather experienced on Earth's surface is a product of factors in the troposphere.

<u>Composition of the Atmosphere</u>
The Earth's atmosphere is composed of gas particles: 78% nitrogen, 21% oxygen, 1% other gases such as argon, and 0.039% carbon dioxide. The atmospheric layers are created by the number of particles in the air and gravity's pull upon them.

<u>Atmospheric Pressure and Temperature</u>
The lower atmospheric levels have higher atmospheric pressures due to the mass of the gas particles located above. The air is less dense (it contains fewer particles per given volume) at higher altitudes. The temperature changes from the bottom to top of each atmospheric layer. The tops of the troposphere and mesosphere are colder than their bottoms, but the reverse is true for the stratosphere and thermosphere. Some of the warmest temperatures are actually found in the thermosphere because of a type of radiation that enters that layer.

Basic Concepts of Meteorology

Relative Humidity

Relative humidity is the ratio of the partial pressure of water vapor to water's equilibrium vapor pressure at a given temperature. At low temperatures, less water vapor is required to reach a high relative humidity. More water vapor is needed to reach a high relative humidity in warm air, which has a greater capacity for water vapor. At ground level or other areas of higher pressure, relative humidity increases as temperatures decrease because water vapor condenses as the temperature falls below the dew point. As relative humidity cannot be greater than 100%, the dew point temperature cannot be greater than the air temperature.

Dew Point

The *dewpoint* is the temperature at which the water vapor in air at constant barometric pressure condenses into liquid water due to saturation. At temperatures below the dew point, the rate of condensation will be greater than the rate of evaporation, forming more liquid water. When condensed water forms on a surface, it's called *dew*; when it forms in the air, it's called *fog* or *clouds*, depending on the altitude.

Wind

Wind is the movement of gas particles across the Earth's surface. Winds are generated by differences in atmospheric pressure. Air inherently moves from areas of higher pressure to lower pressure, which is what causes wind to occur. Surface friction from geological features, such as mountains or man-made features can decrease wind speed. In meteorology, winds are classified based on their strength, duration, and direction. *Gusts* are short bursts of high-speed wind, *squalls* are strong winds of intermediate duration (around one minute), and winds with a long duration are given names based on their average strength. *Breezes* are the weakest, followed by *gales*, *storms*, and *hurricanes*.

Cloud Types and Formation

Water in the atmosphere can exist as visible masses called *clouds* composed of water droplets, tiny crystals of ice, and various chemicals. Clouds exist primarily in the troposphere. They can be classified based on the altitude at which they occur:

- *High clouds*—between 5,000 and 13,000 meters above sea level
- Cirrus: thin and wispy "mare's tail" appearance
- Cirrocumulus: rows of small puffy pillows
- Cirrostratus: thin sheets that cover the sky
- *Middle clouds*—between 2,000 and 7,000 meters above sea level
- Altocumulus: gray and white and made up of water droplets
- Altostratus: grayish or bluish gray clouds
- *Low clouds*—below 2,000 meters above sea level
- Stratus: gray clouds made of water droplets that can cover the sky

- Stratocumulus: gray and lumpy low-lying clouds
- Nimbostratus: dark gray with uneven bases; typical of rain or snow clouds

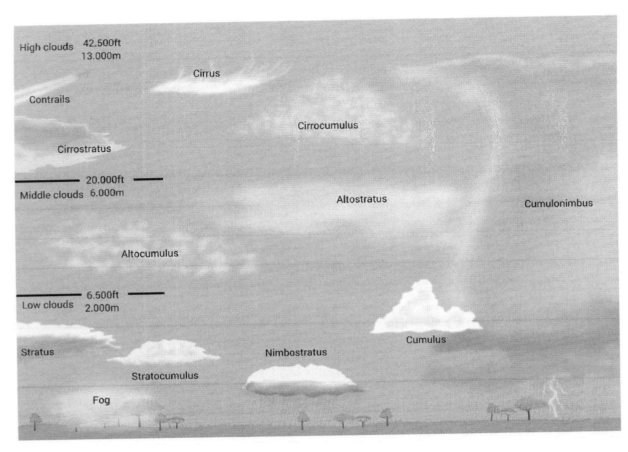

Types of Precipitation

There are three distinct processes by which precipitation occurs. *Convection precipitation* occurs when air rises vertically in a forceful manner, quickly overturning the atmosphere and resulting in heavy precipitation. It's generally more intense and shorter in duration than *stratiform precipitation*, which occurs when large masses of air move over each other. *Orographic precipitation* occurs when moist air is forced upwards over rising terrain, such as a mountain. Most storms are a result of convection precipitation.

Precipitation can fall in liquid or solid phases, as well as any form in between. Liquid precipitation includes rain and drizzle. Frozen precipitation includes snow, sleet, and hail. Intensity is classified by rate of fall or visibility restriction. The forms of precipitation are:

- *Rain*: water vapor that condenses on dust particles in the troposphere until it becomes heavy enough to fall to Earth

- *Sleet*: rain that freezes on its way down; it starts as ice that melts and then freezes again before hitting the ground

- *Hail*: balls of ice thrown up and down several times by turbulent winds, so that more and more water vapor can condense and freeze on the original ice; hail can be as large as golf balls or even baseballs

- *Snow*: loosely packed ice crystals that fall to Earth

Air Masses, Fronts, Storms, and Severe Weather

Airmasses are volumes of air defined by their temperature and the amount of water vapor they contain. A *front* is where two air masses of different temperatures and water vapor content meet. Fronts can be the site of extreme weather, such as thunderstorms, which are caused by water particles rubbing against each other. When they do so, electrons are transferred and energy and electrical currents accumulate. When enough energy accumulates, thunder and lightning occur. *Lightning* is a massive electric spark created by a cloud, and *thunder* is the sound created by an expansion of air caused by the sudden increase in pressure and temperature around lightning.

Extreme weather includes tornadoes and hurricanes. *Tornadoes* are created by changing air pressure and winds that can exceed 300 miles per hour. *Hurricanes* occur when warm ocean water quickly evaporates and rises to a colder, low-pressure portion of the atmosphere. Hurricanes, typhoons, and tropical cyclones are all created by the same phenomena but they occur in different regions. *Blizzards* are similar to hurricanes in that they're created by the clash of warm and cold air, but they only occur when cold Arctic air moves toward warmer air. They usually involve large amounts of snow.

Development and Movement of Weather Patterns

A *weather pattern* is weather that's consistent for a period of time. Weather patterns are created by fronts. A *cold front* is created when two air masses collide in a high-pressure system. A *warm front* is created when a low-pressure system results from the collision of two air masses; they are usually warmer and less dense than high-pressure systems. When a cold front enters an area, the air from the warm front is forced upwards. The temperature of the warm front's air decreases, condenses, and often creates clouds and precipitation. When a warm front moves into an area, the warm air moves slowly upwards at an angle. Clouds and precipitation form, but the precipitation generally lasts longer because of how slowly the air moves.

The Water Cycle

Evaporation and Condensation

The *water cycle* is the cycling of water between its three physical states: solid, liquid, and gas. The Sun's thermal energy heats surface water so it evaporates. As water vapor collects in the atmosphere from evaporation, it eventually reaches a saturation level where it condenses and forms clouds heavy with water droplets.

Precipitation

When the droplets condense as clouds get heavy, they fall as different forms of precipitation, such as rain, snow, hail, fog, and sleet. *Advection* is the process of evaporated water moving from the ocean and falling over land as precipitation.

Runoff and Infiltration

Runoff and *infiltration* are important parts of the water cycle because they provide water on the surface available for evaporation. Runoff can add water to oceans and aid in the advection process. Infiltration provides water to plants and aids in the transpiration process.

Transpiration

Transpiration is an evaporation-like process that occurs in plants and soil. Water from the stomata of plants and from pores in soil evaporates into water vapor and enters the atmosphere.

Major Factors that Affect Climate and Seasons

Effects of Latitude, Geographical Location, and Elevation

The climate and seasons of different geographical areas are primarily dictated by their sunlight exposure. Because the Earth rotates on a tilted axis while travelling around the Sun, different latitudes get different amounts of direct sunlight throughout the year, creating different climates. Polar regions experience the greatest variation, with long periods of limited or no sunlight in the winter and up to 24 hours of daylight in the summer. Equatorial regions experience the least variance in direct sunlight exposure. Coastal areas experience breezes in the summer as cooler ocean air moves ashore, while areas southeast of the Great Lakes can get "lake effect" snow in the winter, as cold air travels over the warmer water and creates snow on land. Mountains are often seen with snow in the spring and fall. Their high elevation causes mountaintops to stay cold. The air around the mountaintop is also cold and holds less water vapor than air at sea level. As the water vapor condenses, it creates snow.

Effects of Atmospheric Circulation

Global winds are patterns of wind circulation and they have a major influence on global weather and climate. They help influence temperature and precipitation by carrying heat and water vapor around the Earth. These winds are driven by the uneven heating between the polar and equatorial regions created by the Sun. Cold air from the polar regions sinks and moves toward the equator, while the warm air from the equator rises and moves toward the poles. The other factor driving global winds is the *Coriolis*

Effect. As air moves from the North Pole to the equator, the Earth's rotation makes it seem as if the wind is also moving to the right, or westbound, and eastbound from South Pole to equator.

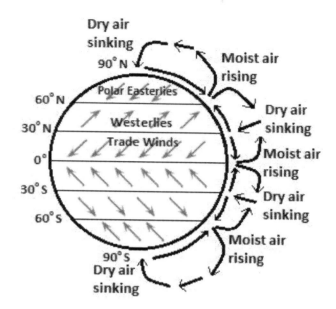

Global wind patterns are given names based on which direction they blow. There are three major wind patterns in each hemisphere. Notice the image above diagramming the movement of warm (dry) air and moist (cold) air.

Tradewinds—easterly surface winds found in the troposphere near the equator—blow predominantly from the northeast in the Northern Hemisphere and from the southeast in the Southern Hemisphere. These winds direct the tropical storms that develop over the Atlantic, Pacific, and Indian Oceans and land in North America, Southeast Asia, and eastern Africa, respectively. *Jet streams* are westerly winds that follow a narrow, meandering path. The two strongest jet streams are the polar jets and the subtropical jets. In the Northern Hemisphere, the polar jet flows over the middle of North America, Europe, and Asia, while in the Southern Hemisphere, it circles Antarctica.

Effects of Ocean Circulation
Ocean currents are similar to global winds because winds influence how the oceans move. Ocean currents are created by warm water moving from the equator towards the poles while cold water travels from the poles to the equator. The warm water can increase precipitation in an area because it evaporates faster than the colder water.

Characteristics and Locations of Climate Zones
Climate zones are created by the Earth's tilt as it travels around the Sun. These zones are delineated by the equator and four other special latitudinal lines: the Tropic of Cancer or Northern Tropic at 23.5° North; the Tropic of Capricorn or Southern Tropic at 23.5° South; the Arctic Circle at 66.5° North; and the Antarctic Circle at 66.5° South. The areas between these lines of latitude represent different climate zones. Tropical climates are hot and wet, like rainforests, and tend to have abundant plant and animal life, while polar climates are cold and usually have little plant and animal life. Temperate zones can vary and experience the four seasons.

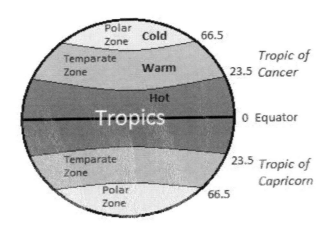

Effect of the Tilt of the Earth's Axis on Seasons

In addition to the equator and the prime meridian, other major lines of latitude and longitude divide the world into regions relative to the direct rays of the Sun. These lines correspond with the Earth's 23.5-degree tilt, and are responsible—along with the Earth's revolution around the Sun—for the seasons. For example, the Northern Hemisphere is tilted directly toward the Sun from June 22 to September 23, which creates the summer. Conversely, the Southern Hemisphere is tilted away from the Sun and experiences winter during those months. The area between the Tropic of Cancer and the Tropic of Capricorn tends to be warmer and experiences fewer variations in seasonal temperatures because it's constantly subject to the direct rays of the Sun, no matter which direction the Earth is tilted.

The area between the Tropic of Cancer and the Arctic Circle, which is at 66.5° North, and the Antarctic Circle, which is at 66.5° South, is where most of Earth's population resides and is called the *middle latitudes*. Here, the seasons are more pronounced, and milder temperatures generally prevail. When the Sun's direct rays are over the equator, it's known as an *equinox*, and day and night are almost equal throughout the world. Equinoxes occur twice a year: the fall, or autumnal equinox, occurs on September 22, while the spring equinox occurs on March 20.

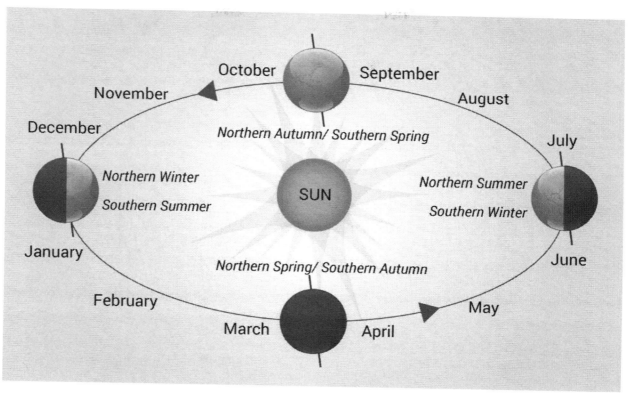

Effects of Natural Phenomena

Natural phenomena can have a sizeable impact on climate and weather. Chemicals released from volcanic eruptions can fall back to Earth in acid rain. In addition, large amounts of carbon dioxide released into the atmosphere can warm the climate. Carbon dioxide creates the *greenhouse effect* by trapping solar energy from sunlight reflected off the Earth's surface within the atmosphere. The amount of solar radiation emitted from the Sun varies and has recently been discovered to be cyclical.

El Niño and La Niña

El Niño and *La Niña* are terms for severe weather anomalies associated with torrential rainfall in the Pacific coastal regions, mainly in North and South America. These events occur irregularly every few years, usually around December, and are caused by a band of warm ocean water that accumulates in the central Pacific Ocean around the equator. The warm water changes the wind patterns over the Pacific and stops cold water from rising toward the American coastlines. The rise in ocean temperature also leads to increased evaporation and rain. These events are split into two phases—a warm, beginning phase called El Niño and a cool end phase called La Niña.

The Earth's Water

Characteristics and Processes of the Earth's Oceans and Other Bodies of Water

Distribution and Location of the Earth's Water

A *body of water* is any accumulation of water on the Earth's surface. It usually refers to oceans, seas, and lakes, but also includes ponds, wetlands, and puddles. Rivers, streams, and canals are bodies of water that involve the movement of water.

Most bodies of water are naturally occurring geographical features, but they can also be artificially created like lakes created by dams. Saltwater oceans make up 96% of the water on the Earth's surface. Freshwater makes up 2.5% of the remaining water.

Seawater Composition

Seawater is water from a sea or ocean. On average, seawater has a salinity of about 3.5%, meaning every kilogram of seawater has approximately 35 grams of dissolved sodium chloride salt. The average density of saltwater at the surface is 1.025 kg/L, making it denser than pure or freshwater, which has a density of 1.00 kg/L. Because of the dissolved salts, the freezing point of saltwater is also lower than that of pure water; salt water freezes at −2 °C (28 °F). As the concentration of salt increases, the freezing point decreases. Thus, it's more difficult to freeze water from the Dead Sea—a saltwater lake known to have water with such high salinity that swimmers cannot sink.

Coastline Topography and the Topography of Ocean Floor

Topography is the study of natural and artificial features comprising the surface of an area. *Coastlines* are an intermediate area between dry land and the ocean floor. The ground progressively slopes from the dry coastal area to the deepest depth of the ocean floor. At the continental shelf, there's a steep descent of the ocean floor. Although it's often believed that the ocean floor is flat and sandy like a beach, its topography includes mountains, plateaus, and valleys.

Tides, Waves, and Currents

Tides are caused by the pull of the Moon and the Sun. When the Moon is closer in its orbit to the Earth, its gravity pulls the oceans away from the shore. When the distance between the Moon and the Earth is greater, the pull is weaker, and the water on Earth can spread across more land. This relationship creates low and high tides. Waves are influenced by changes in tides as well as the wind. The energy transferred from wind to the top of large bodies of water creates *crests* on the water's surface and *waves* below. Circular movements in the ocean are called *currents*. They result from the Coriolis Effect, which is caused by the Earth's rotation. Currents spin in a clockwise direction above the equator and counterclockwise below the equator.

Estuaries and Barrier Islands

An *estuary* is an area of water located on a coast where a river or stream meets the sea. It's a transitional area that's partially enclosed, has a mix of salty and fresh water, and has calmer water than the open sea. *Barrier islands* are coastal landforms created by waves and tidal action parallel to the mainland coast. They usually occur in chains, and they protect the coastlines and create areas of protected waters where wetlands may flourish.

Islands, Reefs, and Atolls

Islands are land that is completely surrounded by water. *Reefs* are bars of rocky, sandy, or coral material that sit below the surface of water. They may form from sand deposits or erosion of underwater rocks.

An *atoll* is a coral reef in the shape of a ring (but not necessarily circular) that encircles a lagoon. In order for an atoll to exist, the rate of its erosion must be slower than the regrowth of the coral that composes the atoll.

Polar Ice, Icebergs, Glaciers

Polar ice is the term for the sheets of ice that cover the poles of a planet. *Icebergs* are large pieces of freshwater ice that break off from glaciers and float in the water. A *glacier* is a persistent body of dense ice that constantly moves because of its own weight. Glaciers form when snow accumulates at a faster rate than it melts over centuries. They form only on land, in contrast to *icecaps*, which can form from sheets of ice in the ocean. When glaciers deform and move due to stresses created by their own weight, they can create crevasses and other large distinguishing land features.

Lakes, Ponds, and Wetlands

Lakes and *ponds* are bodies of water that are surrounded by land. They aren't part of the ocean and don't contain flowing water. Lakes are larger than ponds, but otherwise the two bodies don't have a scientific distinction. *Wetlands* are areas of land saturated by water. They have a unique soil composition and provide a nutrient-dense area for vegetation and aquatic plant growth. They also play a role in water purification and flood control.

Streams, Rivers, and River Deltas

A *river* is a natural flowing waterway usually consisting of freshwater that flows toward an ocean, sea, lake, or another river. Some rivers flow into the ground and become dry instead of reaching another body of water. Small rivers are usually called *streams* or *creeks*. River *deltas* are areas of land formed from the sediment carried by a river and deposited before it enters another body of water. As the river reaches its end, the flow of water slows, and the river loses the power to transport the sediment so it falls out of suspension.

Geysers and Springs

A *spring* is a natural occurrence where water flows from an aquifer to the Earth's surface. A *geyser* is a spring that intermittently and turbulently discharges water. Geysers form only in certain hydrogeological conditions. They require proximity to a volcanic area or magma to provide enough heat to boil or vaporize the water. As hot water and steam accumulate, pressure grows and creates the spraying geyser effect.

Properties of Water that Affect Earth Systems

Water is a chemical compound composed of two hydrogen atoms and one oxygen atom (H_2O) and has many unique properties. In its solid state, water is less dense than its liquid form; therefore, ice floats in water. Water also has a very high heat capacity, allowing it to absorb a high amount of the Sun's energy without getting too hot or evaporating. Its chemical structure makes it a polar compound, meaning one side has a negative charge while the other is positive. This characteristic—along with its ability to form strong intermolecular hydrogen bonds with itself and other molecules—make water an effective solvent for other chemicals.

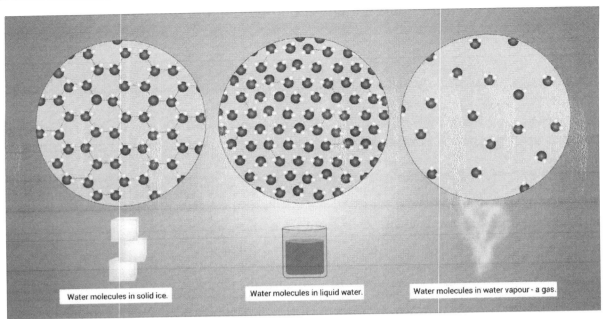

Water molecules in solid ice.

Water molecules in liquid water.

Water molecules in water vapour - a gas.

Number Sense

Numbers, Relationships Among Numbers, and Number Systems

Place Value of a Given Digit

The number system that is used consists of only ten different digits or characters. However, this system is used to represent an infinite number of values. The place value system makes this infinite number of values possible. The position in which a digit is written corresponds to a given value. Starting from the decimal point (which is implied, if not physically present), each subsequent place value to the left represents a value greater than the one before it. Conversely, starting from the decimal point, each subsequent place value to the right represents a value less than the one before it.

The names for the place values to the left of the decimal point are as follows:

...	Billions	Hundred-Millions	Ten-Millions	Millions	Hundred-Thousands	Ten-Thousands	Thousands	Hundreds	Tens	Ones

*Note that this table can be extended infinitely further to the left.

The names for the place values to the right of the decimal point are as follows:

Decimal Point (.)	Tenths	Hundredths	Thousandths	Ten-Thousandths	...

*Note that this table can be extended infinitely further to the right.

When given a multi-digit number, the value of each digit depends on its place value. Consider the number 682,174.953. Referring to the chart above, it can be determined that the digit 8 is in the ten-thousands place. It is in the fifth place to the left of the decimal point. Its value is 8 ten-thousands or 80,000. The digit 5 is two places to the right of the decimal point. Therefore, the digit 5 is in the hundredths place. Its value is 5 hundredths or $\frac{5}{100}$ (equivalent to .05).

Base-10 System

Value of Digits

In accordance with the base-10 system, the value of a digit increases by a factor of ten each place it moves to the left. For example, consider the number 7. Moving the digit one place to the left (70), increases its value by a factor of 10 ($7 \times 10 = 70$). Moving the digit two places to the left (700) increases its value by a factor of 10 twice ($7 \times 10 \times 10 = 700$). Moving the digit three places to the left (7,000) increases its value by a factor of 10 three times ($7 \times 10 \times 10 \times 10 = 7,000$), and so on.

Conversely, the value of a digit decreases by a factor of ten each place it moves to the right. (Note that multiplying by $\frac{1}{10}$ is equivalent to dividing by 10). For example, consider the number 40. Moving the digit one place to the right (4) decreases its value by a factor of 10 ($40 \div 10 = 4$). Moving the digit two places to the right (0.4), decreases its value by a factor of 10 twice ($40 \div 10 \div 10 = 0.4$) or

$(40 \times \frac{1}{10} \times \frac{1}{10} = 0.4)$. Moving the digit three places to the right (0.04) decreases its value by a factor of 10 three times $(40 \div 10 \div 10 \div 10 = 0.04)$ or $(40 \times \frac{1}{10} \times \frac{1}{10} \times \frac{1}{10} = 0.04)$, and so on.

Exponents to Denote Powers of 10

The value of a given digit of a number in the base-10 system can be expressed utilizing powers of 10. A power of 10 refers to 10 raised to a given exponent such as 10^0, 10^1, 10^2, 10^3, etc. For the number 10^3, 10 is the base and 3 is the exponent. A base raised by an exponent represents how many times the base is multiplied by itself. Therefore, $10^1 = 10$, $10^2 = 10 \times 10 = 100$, $10^3 = 10 \times 10 \times 10 = 1,000$, $10^4 = 10 \times 10 \times 10 \times 10 = 10,000$, etc. Any base with a zero exponent equals one.

Powers of 10 are utilized to decompose a multi-digit number without writing all the zeroes. Consider the number 872,349. This number is decomposed to $800,000 + 70,000 + 2,000 + 300 + 40 + 9$. When utilizing powers of 10, the number 872,349 is decomposed to $(8 \times 10^5) + (7 \times 10^4) + (2 \times 10^3) + (3 \times 10^2) + (4 \times 10^1) + (9 \times 10^0)$. The power of 10 by which the digit is multiplied corresponds to the number of zeroes following the digit when expressing its value in standard form. For example, 7×10^4 is equivalent to 70,000 or 7 followed by four zeros.

Comparing, Classifying, and Ordering Rational Numbers

Rational numbers are any number that can be written as a fraction or ratio. Within the set of rational numbers, several subsets exist that are referenced throughout the mathematics topics. Counting numbers are the first numbers learned as a child. Counting numbers consist of 1,2,3,4, and so on. Whole numbers include all counting numbers and zero (0,1,2,3,4,...). Integers include counting numbers, their opposites, and zero (..., -3, -2, -1, 0, 1, 2, 3, ...). Rational numbers are inclusive of integers, fractions, and decimals that terminate, or end (1.7, 0.04213) or repeat ($0.136\overline{5}$).

When comparing or ordering numbers, the numbers should be written in the same format (decimal or fraction), if possible. For example, $\sqrt{49}$, 7.3, and $\frac{15}{2}$ are easier to order if each one is converted to a decimal, such as 7, 7.3, and 7.5 (converting fractions and decimals is covered in the following section). A number line is used to order and compare the numbers. Any number that is to the right of another number is greater than that number. Conversely, a number positioned to the left of a given number is less than that number.

Structure of the Number System

The mathematical number system is made up of two general types of numbers: real and complex. *Real numbers* are those that are used in normal settings, while *complex numbers* are those composed of both a real number and an imaginary one. Imaginary numbers are the result of taking the square root of -1, and $\sqrt{-1} = i$.

The real number system is often explained using a Venn diagram similar to the one below. After a number has been labeled as a real number, further classification occurs when considering the other groups in this diagram. If a number is a never-ending, non-repeating decimal, it falls in the irrational category. Otherwise, it is rational. More information on these types of numbers is provided in the previous section. Furthermore, if a number does not have a fractional part, it is classified as an integer, such as -2, 75, or zero. Whole numbers are an even smaller group that only includes positive integers and zero. The last group of natural numbers is made up of only positive integers, such as 2, 56, or 12.

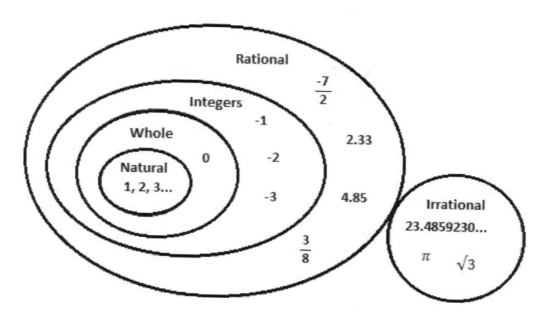

Real numbers can be compared and ordered using the number line. If a number falls to the left on the real number line, it is less than a number on the right. For example, $-2 < 5$ because -2 falls to the left of zero, and 5 falls to the right. Numbers to the left of zero are negative while those to the right are positive.

Complex numbers are made up of the sum of a real number and an imaginary number. Some examples of complex numbers include $6 + 2i$, $5 - 7i$, and $-3 + 12i$. Adding and subtracting complex numbers is similar to collecting like terms. The real numbers are added together, and the imaginary numbers are added together. For example, if the problem asks to simplify the expression $6 + 2i - 3 + 7i$, the 6 and -3 are combined to make 3, and the $2i$ and $7i$ combine to make $9i$. Multiplying and dividing complex numbers is similar to working with exponents. One rule to remember when multiplying is that $i * i = -1$. For example, if a problem asks to simplify the expression $4i(3 + 7i)$, the $4i$ should be distributed throughout the 3 and the $7i$. This leaves the final expression $12i - 28$. The 28 is negative because $i * i$ results in a negative number. The last type of operation to consider with complex numbers is the conjugate. The *conjugate* of a complex number is a technique used to change the complex number into a real number. For example, the conjugate of $4 - 3i$ is $4 + 3i$. Multiplying $(4 - 3i)(4 + 3i)$ results in $16 + 12i - 12i + 9$, which has a final answer of $16 + 9 = 25$.

The order of operations—PEMDAS—simplifies longer expressions with real or imaginary numbers. Each operation is listed in the order of how they should be completed in a problem containing more than one operation. Parenthesis can also mean grouping symbols, such as brackets and absolute value. Then, exponents are calculated. Multiplication and division should be completed from left to right, and addition and subtraction should be completed from left to right.

Simplification of another type of expression occurs when radicals are involved. As explained previously, root is another word for radical. For example, the following expression is a radical that can be simplified: $\sqrt{24x^2}$. First, the number must be factored out to the highest perfect square. Any perfect square can be taken out of a radical. Twenty-four can be factored into 4 and 6, and 4 can be taken out of the radical. $\sqrt{4} = 2$ can be taken out, and 6 stays underneath. If $x > 0$, x can be taken out of the radical because it is a perfect square. The simplified radical is $2x\sqrt{6}$. An approximation can be found using a calculator.

There are also properties of numbers that are true for certain operations. The *commutative* property allows the order of the terms in an expression to change while keeping the same final answer. Both addition and multiplication can be completed in any order and still obtain the same result. However, order does matter in subtraction and division. The *associative* property allows any terms to be "associated" by parenthesis and retain the same final answer. For example, $(4 + 3) + 5 = 4 + (3 + 5)$. Both addition and multiplication are associative; however, subtraction and division do not hold this property. The *distributive* property states that $a(b + c) = ab + ac$. It is a property that involves both addition and multiplication, and the *a* is distributed onto each term inside the parentheses.

Integers can be factored into prime numbers. To *factor* is to express as a product. For example, $6 = 3 \cdot 2$, and $6 = 6 \cdot 1$. Both are factorizations, but the expression involving the factors of 3 and 2 is known as a *prime factorization* because it is factored into a product of two *prime numbers*—integers which do not have any factors other than themselves and 1. A *composite number* is a positive integer that can be divided into at least one other integer other than itself and 1, such as 6. Integers that have a factor of 2 are even, and if they are not divisible by 2, they are odd. Finally, a *multiple* of a number is the product of that number and a counting number—also known as a *natural number*. For example, some multiples of 4 are 4, 8, 12, 16, etc.

Properties of Exponents

Exponents are used in mathematics to express a number or variable multiplied by itself a certain number of times. For example, x^3 means *x* is multiplied by itself three times. In this expression, x is called the *base*, and 3 is the *exponent*. Exponents can be used in more complex problems when they contain fractions and negative numbers.

Fractional exponents can be explained by looking first at the inverse of exponents, which are *roots*. Given the expression x^2, the square root can be taken, $\sqrt{x^2}$, cancelling out the 2 and leaving x by itself, if x is positive. Cancellation occurs because $\sqrt{x}$ can be written with exponents, instead of roots, as $x^{\frac{1}{2}}$. The numerator of 1 is the exponent, and the denominator of 2 is called the root (which is why it's referred to as *square root*). Taking the square root of x^2 is the same as raising it to the $\frac{1}{2}$ power. Written out in mathematical form, it takes the following progression: $\sqrt{x^2} = (x^2)^{\frac{1}{2}} = x$.

From properties of exponents, $2 \cdot \frac{1}{2} = 1$ is the actual exponent of x. Another example can be seen with $x^{\frac{4}{7}}$. The variable *x,* raised to four-sevenths, is equal to the seventh root of x to the fourth power: $\sqrt[7]{x^4}$. In general, $x^{\frac{1}{n}} = \sqrt[n]{x}$ and $x^{\frac{m}{n}} = \sqrt[n]{x^m}$.

Negative exponents also involve fractions. Whereas y^3 can also be rewritten as $\frac{y^3}{1}$, y^{-3} can be rewritten as $\frac{1}{y^3}$. A negative exponent means the exponential expression must be moved to the opposite spot in a fraction to make the exponent positive. If the negative appears in the numerator, it moves to the denominator. If the negative appears in the denominator, it is moved to the numerator. In general, $a^{-n} = \frac{1}{a^n}$, and a^{-n} and a^n are reciprocals.

Take, for example, the following expression: $\frac{a^{-4}b^2}{c^{-5}}$. Since *a* is raised to the negative fourth power, it can be moved to the denominator. Since *c* is raised to the negative fifth power, it can be moved to the numerator. The *b* variable is raised to the positive second power, so it does not move. The simplified expression is as follows: $\frac{b^2 c^5}{a^4}$.

In mathematical expressions containing exponents and other operations, the order of operations must be followed. *PEMDAS* states that exponents are calculated after any parenthesis and grouping symbols, but before any multiplication, division, addition, and subtraction.

Ratios and Proportions

Ratios are used to show the relationship between two quantities. The ratio of oranges to apples in the grocery store may be 3 to 2. That means that for every 3 oranges, there are 2 apples. This comparison can be expanded to represent the actual number of oranges and apples. Another example may be the number of boys to girls in a math class. If the ration of boys to girls is given as 2 to 5, that means there are 2 boys to every 5 girls in the class. Ratios can also be compared if the units in each ratio are the same. The ratio of boys to girls in the math class can be compared to the ratio of boys to girls in a science class by stating which ratio is higher and which is lower.

Rates are used to compare two quantities with different units. *Unit rates* are the simplest form of rate. With unit rates, the denominator in the comparison of two units is one. For example, if someone can type at a rate of 1000 words in 5 minutes, then his or her unit rate for typing is $\frac{1000}{5} = 200$ words in one minute or 200 words per minute. Any rate can be converted into a unit rate by dividing to make the denominator one. 1000 words in 5 minutes has been converted into the unit rate of 200 words per minute.

Ratios and rates can be used together to convert rates into different units. For example, if someone is driving 50 kilometers per hour, that rate can be converted into miles per hour by using a ratio known as the *conversion factor*. Since the given value contains kilometers and the final answer needs to be in miles, the ratio relating miles to kilometers needs to be used. There are 0.62 miles in 1 kilometer. This, written as a ratio and in fraction form, is $\frac{0.62 \; miles}{1 \; km}$. To convert 50km/hour into miles per hour, the following conversion needs to be set up: $\frac{50 \; km}{hour} * \frac{0.62 \; miles}{1 \; km} = 31 \; miles \; per \; hour$.

The ratio between two similar geometric figures is called the *scale factor*. For example, a problem may depict two similar triangles, A and B. The scale factor from the smaller triangle A to the larger triangle B is given as 2 because the length of the corresponding side of the larger triangle, 16, is twice the corresponding side on the smaller triangle, 8.This scale factor can also be used to find the value of a missing side, x, in triangle A. Since the scale factor from the smaller triangle (A) to larger one (B) is 2, the larger corresponding side in triangle B (given as 25), can be divided by 2 to find the missing side in A (x= 12.5). The scale factor can also be represented in the equation $2A = B$ because two times the lengths of A gives the corresponding lengths of B. This is the idea behind similar triangles.

Much like a scale factor can be written using an equation like $2A = B$, a *relationship* is represented by the equation $Y = kX$. X and Y are proportional because as values of X increase, the values of Y also increase. A relationship that is inversely proportional can be represented by the equation $Y = \frac{k}{x}$, where the value of Y decreases as the value of x increases and vice versa.

Proportional reasoning can be used to solve problems involving ratios, percentages, and averages. Ratios can be used in setting up proportions and solving them to find unknowns. For example, if student completes an average of 10 pages of math homework in 3 nights, how long would it take the student to complete 22 pages? Both ratios can be written as fractions. The second ratio would contain the unknown. The following proportion represents this problem, where x is the unknown number of nights:

$$\frac{10\ pages}{3\ nights} = \frac{22\ pages}{x\ nights}$$

Solving this proportion entails cross-multiplying and results in the following equation: $10x = 22 * 3$. Simplifying and solving for x results in the exact solution: $x = 6.6\ nights$. The result would be rounded up to 7 because the homework would be actually be completed on the 7th night.

The following problem uses ratios involving percentages:

If 20% of the class is girls and 30 students are in the class, how many girls are in the class?

To set up this problem, it is helpful to use the common proportion: $\frac{\%}{100} = \frac{is}{of}$. Within the proportion, % is the percentage of girls, 100 is the total percentage of the class, *is* is the number of girls, and *of* is the total number of students in the class. Most percentage problems can be written using this language. To solve this problem, the proportion should be set up as $\frac{20}{100} = \frac{x}{30}$, and then solved for x. Cross-multiplying results in the equation $20 * 30 = 100x$, which results in the solution $x = 6$. There are 6 girls in the class.

Problems involving volume, length, and other units can also be solved using ratios. For example, a problem may ask for the volume of a cone to be found that has a radius, $r = 7m$ and a height, $h = 16m$. Referring to the formulas provided on the test, the volume of a cone is given as: $V = \pi r^2 \frac{h}{3}$, where r is the radius, and h is the height. Plugging $r = 7$ and $h = 16$ into the formula, the following is obtained: $V = \pi(7^2)\frac{16}{3}$. Therefore, volume of the cone is found to be approximately 821m^3. Sometimes, answers in different units are sought. If this problem wanted the answer in liters, 821m^3 would need to be converted. Using the equivalence statement 1m^3 = 1000L, the following ratio would be used to solve for liters: $821m^3 * \frac{1000L}{1m^3}$. Cubic meters in the numerator and denominator cancel each other out, and the answer is converted to 821,000 liters, or $8.21 * 10^5$ L.

Other conversions can also be made between different given and final units. If the temperature in a pool is 30°C, what is the temperature of the pool in degrees Fahrenheit? To convert these units, an equation is used relating Celsius to Fahrenheit. The following equation is used: $T_{\circ F} = 1.8T_{\circ C} + 32$. Plugging in the given temperature and solving the equation for T yields the result: $T_{\circ F} = 1.8(30) + 32 = 86°F$. Both units in the metric system and U.S. customary system are widely used.

Scientific Notation

Scientific Notation is used to represent numbers that are either very small or very large. For example, the distance to the sun is approximately 150,000,000,000 meters. Instead of writing this number with so many zeros, it can be written in scientific notation as $1.5 * 10^{11}$ meters. The same is true for very small numbers, but the exponent becomes negative. If the mass of a human cell is 0.000000000001 kilograms, that measurement can be easily represented by $1.0 * 10^{-12}$ kilograms. In both situations, scientific notation makes the measurement easier to read and understand. Each number is translated to an expression with one digit in the tens place times an expression corresponding to the zeros.

When two measurements are given and both involve scientific notation, it is important to know how these interact with each other:

- In addition and subtraction, the exponent on the ten must be the same before any operations are performed on the numbers. For example, $(1.3 * 10^4) + (3.0 * 10^3)$ cannot be added until one of the exponents on the ten is changed. The $3.0 * 10^3$ can be changed to $0.3 * 10^4$, then the 1.3 and 0.3 can be added. The answer comes out to be $1.6 * 10^4$.

- For multiplication, the first numbers can be multiplied and then the exponents on the tens can be added. Once an answer is formed, it may have to be converted into scientific notation again depending on the change that occurred.

  ○ The following is an example of multiplication with scientific notation: $(4.5 * 10^3) * (3.0 * 10^{-5}) = 13.5 * 10^{-2}$. Since this answer is not in scientific notation, the decimal is moved over to the left one unit, and 1 is added to the ten's exponent. This results in the final answer: $1.35 * 10^{-1}$.

- For division, the first numbers are divided, and the exponents on the tens are subtracted. Again, the answer may need to be converted into scientific notation form, depending on the type of changes that occurred during the problem.

- *Order of magnitude* relates to scientific notation and is the total count of powers of 10 in a number. For example, there are 6 orders of magnitude in 1,000,000. If a number is raised by an order of magnitude, it is multiplied times 10. Order of magnitude can be helpful in estimating results using very large or small numbers. An answer should make sense in terms of its order of magnitude.

  ○ For example, if area is calculated using two dimensions with 6 orders of magnitude, because area involves multiplication, the answer should have around 12 orders of magnitude. Also, answers can be estimated by rounding to the largest place value in each number. For example, 5,493,302 * 2,523,100 can be estimated by 5 * 3 = 15 with 6 orders of magnitude.

Computational Tools, Procedures, and Strategies

Basic Concepts of Number Theory

Prime and Composite Numbers

Whole numbers are classified as either prime or composite. A prime number can only be divided evenly by itself and one. For example, the number 11 can only be divided evenly by 11 and one; therefore, 11 is a prime number. A helpful way to visualize a prime number is to use concrete objects and try to divide them into equal piles. If dividing 11 coins, the only way to divide them into equal piles is to create 1 pile of 11 coins or to create 11 piles of 1 coin each. Other examples of prime numbers include 2, 3, 5, 7, 13, 17, and 19.

A composite number is any whole number that is not a prime number. A composite number is a number that can be divided evenly by one or more numbers other than itself and one. For example, the number 6 can be divided evenly by 2 and 3. Therefore, 6 is a composite number. If dividing 6 coins into equal piles, the possibilities are 1 pile of 6 coins, 2 piles of 3 coins, 3 piles of 2 coins, or 6 piles of 1 coin. Other examples of composite numbers include 4, 8, 9, 10, 12, 14, 15, 16, 18, and 20.

To determine if a number is a prime or composite number, the number is divided by every whole number greater than one and less than its own value. If it divides evenly by any of these numbers, then the number is composite. If it does not divide evenly by any of these numbers, then the number is prime. For example, when attempting to divide the number 5 by 2, 3, and 4, none of these numbers divide evenly. Therefore, 5 must be a prime number.

Factors and Multiples of Numbers
The factors of a number are all integers that can be multiplied by another integer to produce the given number. For example, 2 is multiplied by 3 to produce 6. Therefore, 2 and 3 are both factors of 6. Similarly, $1 \times 6 = 6$ and $2 \times 3 = 6$, so one, 2, 3, and 6 are all factors of 6. Another way to explain a factor is to say that a given number divides evenly by each of its factors to produce an integer. For example, 6 does not divide evenly by 5. Therefore, 5 is not a factor of 6.

Multiples of a given number are found by taking that number and multiplying it by any other whole number. For example, 3 is a factor of 6, 9, and 12. Therefore, 6, 9, and 12 are multiples of 3. The multiples of any number are an infinite list. For example, the multiples of 5 are 5, 10, 15, 20, and so on. This list continues without end. A list of multiples is used in finding the least common multiple, or LCM, for fractions when a common denominator is needed. The denominators are written down and their multiples listed until a common number is found in both lists. This common number is the LCM.

Prime factorization breaks down each factor of a whole number until only prime numbers remain. All composite numbers can be factored into prime numbers. For example, the prime factors of 12 are 2, 2, and 3 ($2 \times 2 \times 3 = 12$). To produce the prime factors of a number, the number is factored and any composite numbers are continuously factored until the result is the product of prime factors only. A factor tree, such as the one below, is helpful when exploring this concept.

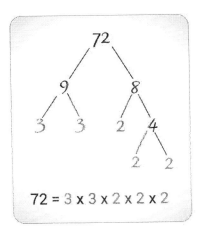

Number Relationships
The set of natural numbers can be separated into a variety of different types such as odds, evens, perfect squares, cubes, primes, composite, Fibonacci, etc. Number theory concepts can be used to prove relationships between these subsets of natural numbers. One of the main goals of number theory is to discover relationships between different subsets and prove that they are true. For example, some number theory proofs involve showing that the sum of two odd numbers is odd and the sum of two even numbers is even.

Order of Operations

When solving equations with multiple operations, special rules apply. These rules are known as the Order of Operations. The order is as follows: Parentheses, Exponents, Multiplication and Division from left to right, and Addition and Subtraction from left to right. A popular pneumonic device to help remember the order is Please Excuse My Dear Aunt Sally (PEMDAS). Evaluate the following two problems to understand the Order of Operations:

1) $4 + (3 \times 2)^2 \div 4$

First, solve the operation within the parentheses: $4 + 6^2 \div 4$.
Second, solve the exponent: $4 + 36 \div 4$.
Third, solve the division operation: $4 + 9$.
Fourth, finish the operation with addition for the answer, 13.

2) $2 \times (6 + 3) \div (2 + 1)^2$

$2 \times 9 \div (3)^2$
$2 \times 9 \div 9$
$18 \div 9$
2

Positive and Negative Numbers

Signs
Aside from 0, numbers can be either positive or negative. The sign for a positive number is the plus sign or the + symbol, while the sign for a negative number is minus sign or the − symbol. If a number has no designation, then it's assumed to be positive.

Absolute Values
Both positive and negative numbers are valued according to their distance from 0. Look at this number line for +3 and -3:

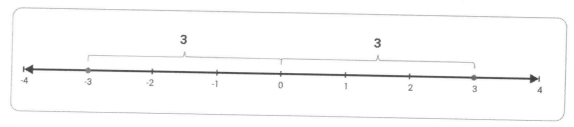

Both 3 and -3 are three spaces from 0. The distance from 0 is called its absolute value. Thus, both -3 and 3 have an absolute value of 3 since they're both three spaces away from 0.

An absolute number is written by placing | | around the number. So, |3| and |−3| both equal 3, as that's their common absolute value.

Implications for Addition and Subtraction

For addition, if all numbers are either positive or negative, simply add them together. For example, 4 + 4 = 8 and -4 + -4 = -8. However, things get tricky when some of the numbers are negative and some are positive.

Take 6 + (-4) as an example. First, take the absolute values of the numbers, which are 6 and 4. Second, subtract the smaller value from the larger. The equation becomes 6– 4 = 2. Third, place the sign of the original larger number on the sum. Here, 6 is the larger number, and it's positive, so the sum is 2.

Here's an example where the negative number has a larger absolute value: (-6) + 4. The first two steps are the same as the example above. However, on the third step, the negative sign must be placed on the sum, as the absolute value of (-6) is greater than 4. Thus, -6 + 4 = -2.

The absolute value of numbers implies that subtraction can be thought of as flip the sign of the number following the subtraction sign and simply adding the two numbers. This means that subtracting a negative number will in fact be adding the positive absolute value of the negative number. Here are some examples:

$$-6 - 4 = -6 + -4 = -10$$

$$3 - -6 = 3 + 9 = 12$$

$$-3 - 2 = -3 + -2 = -5$$

Implications for Multiplication and Division

For multiplication and division, if both numbers are positive, then the product or quotient is always positive. If both numbers are negative, then the product or quotient is also positive. However, if the numbers have opposite signs, the product or quotient is always negative.

Simply put, the product in multiplication and quotient in division is always positive, unless the numbers have opposing signs, in which case it's negative. Here are some examples:

$$(-6) \times (-5) = 30$$

$$(-50) \div 10 = -5$$

$$8 \times |-7| = 56$$

$$(-48) \div (-6) = 8$$

If there are more than two numbers in a multiplication or division problem, then whether the product or quotient is positive or negative depends on the number of negative numbers in the problem. If there is an odd number of negatives, then the product or quotient is negative. If there is an even number of negative numbers, then the result is positive.

Here are some examples:

$$(-6) \times 5 \times (-2) \times (-4) = -240$$

$$(-6) \times 5 \times 2 \times (-4) = 240$$

Strategies and Algorithms to Perform Operations on Rational Numbers

A rational number is any number that can be written in the form of a ratio or fraction. Integers can be written as fractions with a denominator of 1 ($5 = \frac{5}{1}$; $-342 = \frac{-342}{1}$; etc.). Decimals that terminate and/or repeat can also be written as fractions ($47 = \frac{47}{100}$; $.\overline{33} = \frac{1}{3}$). For more on converting decimals to fractions, see the section *Converting Between Fractions, Decimals,* and *Percent.*

When adding or subtracting fractions, the numbers must have the same denominators. In these cases, numerators are added or subtracted and denominators are kept the same. For example, $\frac{2}{7} + \frac{3}{7} = \frac{5}{7}$ and $\frac{4}{5} - \frac{3}{5} = \frac{1}{5}$. If the fractions to be added or subtracted do not have the same denominator, a common denominator must be found. This is accomplished by changing one or both fractions to a different but equivalent fraction. Consider the example $\frac{1}{6} + \frac{4}{9}$. First, a common denominator must be found. One method is to find the least common multiple (LCM) of the denominators 6 and 9. This is the lowest number that both 6 and 9 will divide into evenly. In this case the LCM is 18. Both fractions should be changed to equivalent fractions with a denominator of 18. To obtain the numerator of the new fraction, the old numerator is multiplied by the same number by which the old denominator is multiplied. For the fraction $\frac{1}{6}$, 6 multiplied by 3 will produce a denominator of 18. Therefore, the numerator is multiplied by 3 to produce the new numerator $\left(\frac{1\times3}{6\times3} = \frac{3}{18}\right)$. For the fraction $\frac{4}{9}$, multiplying both the numerator and denominator by 2 produces $\frac{8}{18}$. Since the two new fractions have common denominators, they can be added $\left(\frac{3}{18} + \frac{8}{18} = \frac{11}{18}\right)$.

When multiplying or dividing rational numbers, these numbers may be converted to fractions and multiplied or divided accordingly. When multiplying fractions, all numerators are multiplied by each other and all denominators are multiplied by each other. For example, $\frac{1}{3} \times \frac{6}{5} = \frac{1\times6}{3\times5} = \frac{6}{15}$ and $\frac{-1}{2} \times \frac{3}{1} \times \frac{11}{100} = \frac{-1\times3\times11}{2\times1\times100} = \frac{-33}{200}$. When dividing fractions, the problem is converted by multiplying by the reciprocal of the divisor. This is done by changing division to multiplication and "flipping" the second fraction, or divisor. For example, $\frac{1}{2} \div \frac{3}{5} \rightarrow \frac{1}{2} \times \frac{5}{3}$ and $\frac{5}{1} \div \frac{1}{3} \rightarrow \frac{5}{1} \times \frac{3}{1}$. To complete the problem, the rules for multiplying fractions should be followed.

Note that when adding, subtracting, multiplying, and dividing mixed numbers (ex. $4\frac{1}{2}$), it is easiest to convert these to improper fractions (larger numerator than denominator). To do so, the denominator is kept the same. To obtain the numerator, the whole number is multiplied by the denominator and added to the numerator. For example, $4\frac{1}{2} = \frac{9}{2}$ and $7\frac{2}{3} = \frac{23}{3}$. Also, note that answers involving fractions should be converted to the simplest form.

Converting Between Fractions, Decimals, and Percent

To convert a fraction to a decimal, the numerator is divided by the denominator. For example, $\frac{3}{8}$ can be converted to a decimal by dividing 3 by 8 ($\frac{3}{8} = 0.375$). To convert a decimal to a fraction, the decimal point is dropped and the value is written as the numerator. The denominator is the place value farthest to the right with a digit other than zero. For example, to convert .48 to a fraction, the numerator is 48 and the denominator is 100 (the digit 8 is in the hundredths place). Therefore, $.48 = \frac{48}{100}$. Fractions should be written in the simplest form, or reduced. To reduce a fraction, the numerator and denominator are divided by the largest common factor. In the previous example, 48 and 100 are both divisible by 4. Dividing the numerator and denominator by 4 results in a reduced fraction of $\frac{12}{25}$.

To convert a decimal to a percent, the number is multiplied by 100. To convert .13 to a percent, .13 is multiplied by 100 to get 13 percent. To convert a fraction to a percent, the fraction is converted to a decimal and then multiplied by 100. For example, $\frac{1}{5}$ = .20 and .20 multiplied by 100 produces 20 percent.

To convert a percent to a decimal, the value is divided by 100. For example, 125 percent is equal to 1.25 ($\frac{125}{100}$). To convert a percent to a fraction, the percent sign is dropped and the value is written as the numerator with a denominator of 100. For example, 80% = $\frac{80}{100}$. This fraction can be reduced ($\frac{80}{100} = \frac{4}{5}$).

Representing Rational Numbers and Their Operations

Concrete Models
Concrete objects are used to develop a tangible understanding of operations of rational numbers. Tools such as tiles, blocks, beads, and hundred charts are used to model problems. For example, a hundred chart (10 × 10) and beads can be used to model multiplication. If multiplying 5 by 4, beads are placed across 5 rows and down 4 columns producing a product of 20. Similarly, tiles can be used to model division by splitting the total into equal groups. If dividing 12 by 4, 12 tiles are placed one at a time into 4 groups. The result is 4 groups of 3. This is also an effective method for visualizing the concept of remainders.

Representations of objects can be used to expand on the concrete models of operations. Pictures, dots, and tallies can help model these concepts. Utilizing concrete models and representations creates a foundation upon which to build an abstract understanding of the operations.

Rational Numbers on a Number Line
A number line typically consists of integers (...3, 2, 1, 0, -1, -2, -3...), and is used to visually represent the value of a rational number. Each rational number has a distinct position on the line determined by comparing its value with the displayed values on the line. For example, if plotting -1.5 on the number line below, it is necessary to recognize that the value of -1.5 is .5 less than -1 and .5 greater than -2. Therefore, -1.5 is plotted halfway between -1 and -2.

Number lines can also be useful for visualizing sums and differences of rational numbers. Adding a value indicates moving to the right (values increase to the right), and subtracting a value indicates moving to the left (numbers decrease to the left). For example, 5 − 7 is displayed by starting at 5 and moving to the left 7 spaces, if the number line is in increments of 1. This will result in an answer of -2.

Multiplication and Division Problems

Multiplication and division are inverse operations that can be represented by using rectangular arrays, area models, and equations. Rectangular arrays include an arrangement of rows and columns that correspond to the factors and display product totals.

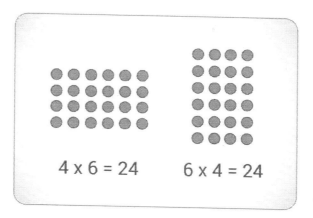

Another method of multiplication can be done with the use of an *area model*. An area model is a rectangle that is divided into rows and columns that match up to the number of place values within each number. For example, $29 \times 65 = 25 + 4$ and $66 = 60 + 5$. The products of those 4 numbers are found within the rectangle and then summed up to get the answer. The entire process is: $(60 \times 25) + (5 \times 25) + (60 \times 4) + (5 \times 4) = 1,500 + 240 + 125 + 20 = 1,885$.

Here is the actual area model:

	25	**4**
60	60x25 1,500	60x4 240
5	5x25 125	5x4 20

$$
\begin{array}{r}
1,500 \\
240 \\
125 \\
+\quad 20 \\
\hline
1,885
\end{array}
$$

Dividing a number by a single digit or two digits can be turned into repeated subtraction problems. An area model can be used throughout the problem that represents multiples of the divisor. For example, the answer to $8580 \div 55$ can be found by subtracting 55 from 8580 one at a time and counting the total number of subtractions necessary.

However, a simpler process involves using larger multiples of 55. First, $100 \times 55 = 5,500$ is subtracted from 8,580, and 3,080 is leftover. Next, $50 \times 55 = 2,750$ is subtracted from 3,080 to obtain380. $5 \times 55 = 275$ is subtracted from 330 to obtain 55, and finally, $1 \times 55 = 55$ is subtracted from 55 to obtain zero. Therefore, there is no remainder, and the answer is $100 + 50 + 5 + 1 = 156$.

Here is a picture of the area model and the repeated subtraction process:

Counting Techniques

There are many counting techniques that can help solve problems involving counting possibilities. For example, the *Addition Principle* states that if there are m choices from Group 1 and n choices from Group 2, then $n + m$ is the total number of choices possible from Groups 1 and 2. For this to be true, the groups can't have any choices in common. The *Multiplication Principle* states that if Process 1 can be completed n ways and Process 2 can be completed m ways, the total number of ways to complete both Process 1 and Process 2 is $n \times m$. For this rule to be used, both processes must be independent of each other. Counting techniques also involve permutations. A *permutation* is an arrangement of elements in a set for which order must be considered. For example, if three letters from the alphabet are chosen, ABC and BAC are two different permutations. The multiplication rule can be used to determine the total number of possibilities. If each letter can't be selected twice, the total number of possibilities is $26 \times 25 \times 24 = 15,600$. A formula can also be used to calculate this total. In general, the notation $P(n, r)$ represents the number of ways to arrange r objects from a set of n and, the formula is $P(n, r) = \frac{n!}{(n-r)!}$. In the previous example, $P(26, 3) = \frac{26!}{23!} = 15,600$. Contrasting permutations, a *combination* is an arrangement of elements in which order doesn't matter. In this case, ABC and BAC are the same combination. In the previous scenario, there are six permutations that represent each single combination. Therefore, the total number of possible combinations is $15,600 \div 6 = 2,600$. In general, $C(n, r)$ represents the total number of combinations of n items selected r at a time where order doesn't matter, and the formula is $C(n, r) = \frac{n!}{(n-r)!\, r!}$. Therefore, the following relationship exists between permutations and combinations: $C(n, r) = \frac{P(n,r)}{n!} = \frac{P(n,r)}{P(r,r)}$.

Determining the Reasonableness of Results

When solving math word problems, the solution obtained should make sense within the given scenario. The step of checking the solution will reduce the possibility of a calculation error or a solution that may be *mathematically* correct but not applicable in the real world. Consider the following scenarios:

A problem states that Lisa got 24 out of 32 questions correct on a test and asks to find the percentage of correct answers. To solve the problem, a student divided 32 by 24 to get 1.33, and then multiplied by 100 to get 133 percent. By examining the solution within the context of the problem, the student should recognize that getting all 32 questions correct will produce a perfect score of 100 percent. Therefore, a score of 133 percent with 8 incorrect answers does not make sense and the calculations should be checked.

A problem states that the maximum weight on a bridge cannot exceed 22,000 pounds. The problem asks to find the maximum number of cars that can be on the bridge at one time if each car weighs 4,000 pounds. To solve this problem, a student divided 22,000 by 4,000 to get an answer of 5.5. By examining the solution within the context of the problem, the student should recognize that although the calculations are mathematically correct, the solution does not make sense. Half of a car on a bridge is not possible, so the student should determine that a maximum of 5 cars can be on the bridge at the same time.

Mental Math Estimation

Once a result is determined to be logical within the context of a given problem, the result should be evaluated by its nearness to the expected answer. This is performed by approximating given values to perform mental math. Numbers should be rounded to the nearest value possible to check the initial results.

Consider the following example: A problem states that a customer is buying a new sound system for their home. The customer purchases a stereo for $435, 2 speakers for $67 each, and the necessary cables for $12. The customer chooses an option that allows him to spread the costs over equal payments for 4 months. How much will the monthly payments be?

After making calculations for the problem, a student determines that the monthly payment will be $145.25. To check the accuracy of the results, the student rounds each cost to the nearest ten (440 + 70 + 70 + 10) and determines that the total is approximately $590. Dividing by 4 months gives an approximate monthly payment of $147.50. Therefore, the student can conclude that the solution of $145.25 is very close to what should be expected.

When rounding, the place-value that is used in rounding can make a difference. Suppose the student had rounded to the nearest hundred for the estimation. The result ($400 + 100 + 100 + 0 = 600$; $600 \div 4 = 150$) will show that the answer is reasonable, but not as close to the actual value as rounding to the nearest ten.

Precision and Accuracy

Precision and accuracy are used to describe groups of measurements. *Precision* describes a group of measures that are very close together, regardless of whether the measures are close to the true value. *Accuracy* describes how close the measures are to the true value.

Since accuracy refers to the closeness of a value to the true measurement, the level of accuracy depends on the object measured and the instrument used to measure it. This will vary depending on the situation. If measuring the mass of a set of dictionaries, kilograms may be used as the units. In this case, it is not vitally important to have a high level of accuracy. If the measurement is a few grams away from the true value, the discrepancy might not make a big difference in the problem.

In a different situation, the level of accuracy may be more significant. Pharmacists need to be sure they are very accurate in their measurements of medicines that they give to patients. In this case, the level of accuracy is vitally important and not something to be estimated. In the dictionary situation, the measurements were given as whole numbers in kilograms. In the pharmacist's situation, the measurements for medicine must be taken to the milligram and sometimes further, depending on the type of medicine.

When considering the accuracy of measurements, the error in each measurement can be shown as absolute and relative. *Absolute error* tells the actual difference between the measured value and the true value. The *relative error* tells how large the error is in relation to the true value. There may be two problems where the absolute error of the measurements is 10 grams. For one problem, this may mean the relative error is very small because the measured value is 14,990 grams, and the true value is 15,000 grams. Ten grams in relation to the true value of 15,000 is small: 0.06%. For the other problem, the measured value is 290 grams, and the true value is 300 grams. In this case, the 10-gram absolute error means a high relative error because the true value is smaller. The relative error is 10/300=0.03, or 3%.

Algebra and Functions

Patterns and Functional Relationships

Number Patterns

Given a sequence of numbers, a mathematical rule can be defined that represents the numbers if a pattern exists within the set. For example, consider the sequence of numbers 1, 4, 9, 16, 25, etc. This set of numbers represents the positive integers squared, and an explicitly defined sequence that represents this set is $f_n = n^2$. An important mathematical concept is recognizing patterns in sequences and translating the patterns into an explicit formula. Once the pattern is recognized and the formula is defined, the sequence can be extended easily. For example, the next three numbers in the sequence are 36, 49, and 64.

Predicting Values

In a similar sense, patterns can be used to make conjectures, predictions, and generalizations. If a pattern is recognized in a set of numbers, values can be predicted that aren't originally provided. For example, if an experiment results in the sequence of numbers 1, 4, 9, 16, and 25, where 1 represents the first trial, 2 represents the second trial, etc., one expects the tenth trial to result in a value of 100 because that value is equal to the square of the trial number.

Recursively Defined Functions

Similar to recursively defined sequences, recursively defined functions are not explicitly defined in terms of a variable. A recursive function builds on itself and consists of a smaller argument, such as $f(0)$ or $f(1)$ and the actual definition of the function. For example, a recursively defined function is the following:

$$f(0) = 3$$

$$f(n) = f(n-1) + 2n$$

Contrasting an explicitly defined function, a recursively defined function must be evaluated in order. The first five terms of this function are $f(0) = 3, f(1) = 5, f(2) = 9, f(3) = 15,$ and $f(4) = 23$. Some recursively defined functions have an explicit counterpart and, like sequences, they can be used to model real-life applications. The Fibonacci numbers can also be thought of as a recursively defined function if $f(n) = f_n$.

Closed-Form Functions

A *closed-form function* can be evaluated using a finite number of operations such as addition, subtraction, multiplication, and division. An example of a function that's not a closed-form function is one involving an infinite sum. For example, $y = \sum_{n=1}^{\infty} x$ isn't a closed-form function because it consists of a sum of infinitely many terms. Many recursively defined functions can be expressed as a closed-form expression. To convert to a closed-form expression, a formula must be found for the nth term. This means that the recursively defined sequence must be converted to its explicit formula.

Translating Between Verbal and Symbolic Forms

Being able to translate verbal scenarios into symbolic forms is a critical skill in mathematics. This idea is seen mostly when solving word problems. First, the problem needs to be read carefully several times until one can state clearly what is being sought. Then, variables that represent the unknown quantities need to be defined. Equations can be defined using those variables that model the verbal conditions of the given problem. The equations then need to be solved to answer the problem's questions. The problem-solving skills learned in these types of problems is an invaluable skill, and is ultimately more important than finding the answer to each individual problem.

Solving Problems by Quantitative Reasoning

Dimensional analysis is the process of converting between different units using equivalent measurement statements. For instance, running 5 kilometers is approximately the same as running 3.1 miles. This conversion can be found by knowing that 1 kilometer is equal to approximately 0.62 miles.

When setting up the dimensional analysis calculations, the original units need to be opposite one another in each of the two fractions: one in the original amount (essentially in the numerator) and one in the denominator of the conversion factor. This enables them to cancel after multiplying, leaving the converted result.

Calculations involving formulas, such as determining volume and area, are a common situation in which units need to be interpreted and used. However, graphs can also carry meaning through units. The graph below is an example. It represents a graph of the position of an object over time. The y-axis represents the position or the number of meters the object is from the starting point at time s, in seconds. Interpreting this graph, the origin shows that at time zero seconds, the object is zero meters away from the starting point. As the time increases to one second, the position increases to five meters away. This trend continues until 6 seconds, where the object is 30 meters away from the starting position. After this point in time—since the graph remains horizontal from 6 to 10 seconds—the object must have stopped moving.

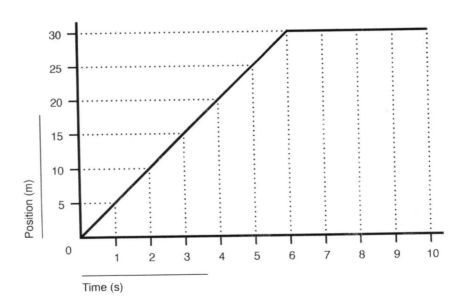

In each of the previous problem examples, the units were important to the answer. When solving problems with units, it's important to consider the reasonableness of the answer. If conversions are used, it's helpful to have an estimated value to compare the final answer to. This way, if the final answer is too distant from the estimate, it will be obvious that a mistake was made.

Functions

A *function* is defined as a relationship between inputs and outputs where there is only one output value for a given input. As an example, the following function is in function notation: $f(x) = 3x - 4$. The $f(x)$ represents the output value for an input of x. If $x = 2$, the equation becomes $f(2) = 3(2) - 4 = 6 - 4 = 2$. The input of 2 yields an output of 2, forming the ordered pair $(2, 2)$. The following set of ordered pairs corresponds to the given function: $(2, 2), (0, -4), (-2, -10)$. The set of all possible inputs of a function is its *domain*, and all possible outputs is called the *range*. By definition, each member of the domain is paired with only one member of the range.

Functions can also be defined recursively. In this form, they are not defined explicitly in terms of variables. Instead, they are defined using previously-evaluated function outputs, starting with either $f(0)$ or $f(1)$. An example of a recursively-defined function is $f(1) = 2, f(n) = 2f(n - 1) + 2n, n > 1$. The domain of this function is the set of all integers.

Domain and Range

The domain and range of a function can be found visually by its plot on the coordinate plane. In the function $f(x) = x^2 - 3$, for example, the domain is all real numbers because the parabola stretches as far left and as far right as it can go, with no restrictions. This means that any input value from the real number system will yield an answer in the real number system. For the range, the inequality $y \geq -3$ would be used to describe the possible output values because the parabola has a minimum at $y = -3$. This means there will not be any real output values less than -3 because -3 is the lowest value it reaches on the y-axis.

These same answers for domain and range can be found by observing a table. The table below shows that from input values $x = -1$ to $x = 1$, the output results in a minimum of -3. On each side of $x = 0$, the numbers increase, showing that the range is all real numbers greater than or equal to -3.

x (domain/input)	y (range/output)
-2	1
-1	-2
0	-3
-1	-2
2	1

Finding the Zeros of a Function

The zeros of a function are the points where its graph crosses the x-axis. At these points, $y = 0$. One way to find the zeros is to analyze the graph. If given the graph, the x-coordinates can be found where the line crosses the x-axis. Another way to find the zeros is to set $y = 0$ in the equation and solve for x. Depending on the type of equation, this could be done by using opposite operations, by factoring the equation, by completing the square, or by using the quadratic formula. If a graph does not cross the x-axis, then the function may have complex roots.

Translating Functions

A function can be translated in many ways. Typical translations involve shifting, reflecting, and scaling graphs. A shift is a translation that does not change the original shape of the function. A vertical shift adds or subtracts a constant from every y-coordinate, and is represented as $y = f(x) + c$. A horizontal shift adds or subtracts a constant from every x-coordinate, and is represented as $y = f(x) - c$. A reflection involves flipping a function over an axis. To reflect about the y-axis, every x-coordinate needs to be multiplied times -1. This reflection is represented as $y = f(-x)$. To reflect about the x-axis, every y-coordinate needs to be multiplied times -1. This reflection is represented as $y = -f(x)$. Finally, a scale involves changing the shape of the graph through either a shrink or stretch. A scale either multiplies or divides each coordinate by a constant. A vertical scale involves multiplying or dividing every y-coordinate by a constant. This scaling is represented by $y = kf(x)$ and is a vertical stretch if $k > 1$ and vertical shrink if $0 < k < 1$. A horizontal scale involves multiplying or dividing every x-coordinate by a constant. This scaling is represented by $y = f(kx)$ and is a horizontal stretch if $0 < k < 1$ and horizontal shrink if $k > 1$.

Graphing Functions

Typically, a function can be graphed using a graphing calculator. However, some characteristics can be found that allow for enough information to be compounded to graph a very good sketch without technology. Such information includes significant points such as zeros, local extrema, and points where a function is not continuous and not differentiable. Zeros are points in which a function crosses the y-axis. These points are found by plugging 0 into the independent variable x and solving for the dependent variable y. Local extrema are points in which a function is either a local maxima or minima. These points occur where the derivative of the function is either equal to zero or undefined, and those points are known as critical values. The first derivative test can be used to decide whether a critical value is a maximum or minimum. If a function increases to a point, showing that the first derivative is positive over that interval, and if a function decreases after that same point, showing that the derivative is negative over that interval, then the point is a local maximum. The opposite occurs at a local minimum. Finally, points in which a function is not continuous or not differentiable are also important points. A function is continuous over its domain. A function is not differentiable at a point if there exists a vertical tangent at that point, if there is a corner or a cusp at that point, or if the function is not defined at that point.

Asymptotes

An *asymptote* is a line that approaches the graph of a given function, but never meets it. Vertical asymptotes correspond to denominators of zero for a rational function. They also exist in logarithmic functions and trigonometric functions, such as tangent and cotangent. In rational functions and trigonometric functions, the asymptotes exist at x-values that cause a denominator equal to zero. For example, vertical asymptotes exist at $x = \pm 2$ for the function $f(x) = \frac{x+1}{(x-2)(x+2)}$. Horizontal and oblique asymptotes correspond to the behavior of a curve as the x-values approach either positive or negative infinity. For example, the graph of $f(x) = e^x$ has a horizontal asymptote of $y = 0$ as x approaches negative infinity. In regards to rational functions, there is a rule to follow. Consider the following rational function: $f(x) = \frac{ax^n + \cdots}{bx^m + \cdots}$. The numerator is an nth degree polynomial and the denominator is an mth degree polynomial. If $m < n$, the line $y = 0$ is a horizontal asymptote. If $n = m$, the line $y = \frac{a}{b}$ is a horizontal asymptote. If $m > n$, then there is an oblique asymptote. In order to find the equation of the oblique asymptote, the denominator is divided into the numerator using long division. The result, minus the remainder, gives the equation of the oblique asymptote.

Here is a graph that shows an example of both a slant and a vertical asymptote:

Graphed Asymptotes

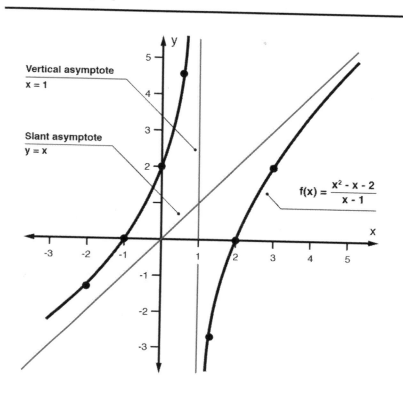

Inverse Variation and Rational Functions

The variable y varies inversely with respect to x if $y = \frac{k}{x}$, where k is the constant of variation. This means that as x decreases, y increases, and y is said to be inversely proportional to x. Also, this can be written as $k = xy$, and this specific example is known as inverse linear variation. The function $f(x) = \frac{k}{x}$ is a rational function because it is a rational fraction in which both the numerator and denominator are polynomials. Other types of inverse variation exist with nonlinear factors. The variable y can vary inversely with respect to x^2, and in this case: $y = \frac{k}{x^2}$. The exponent on the variable x can be any positive real number. In any case, the function will always be a rational function.

Rate of Change

Rate of change for any line calculates the steepness of the line over a given interval. Rate of change is also known as the slope or rise/run. The rates of change for nonlinear functions vary depending on the interval being used for the function. The rate of change over one interval may be zero, while the next interval may have a positive rate of change. The equation plotted on the graph below, $y = x^2$, is a quadratic function and non-linear.

The average rate of change from points $(0, 0)$ to $(1, 1)$ is 1 because the vertical change is 1 over the horizontal change of 1. For the next interval, $(1, 1)$ to $(2, 4)$, the average rate of change is 3 because the slope is $\frac{3}{1}$.

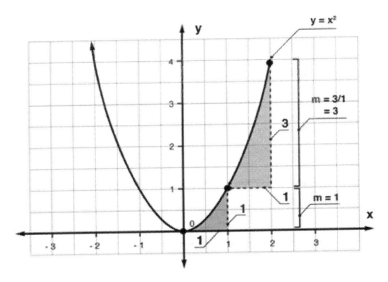

The rate of change for a linear function is constant and can be determined based on a few representations. One method is to place the equation in slope-intercept form: $y = mx + b$. Thus, m is the slope, and b is the y-intercept. In the graph below, the equation is $y = x + 1$, where the slope is 1 and the y-intercept is 1. For every vertical change of 1 unit, there is a horizontal change of 1 unit. The x-intercept is -1, which is the point where the line crosses the x-axis.

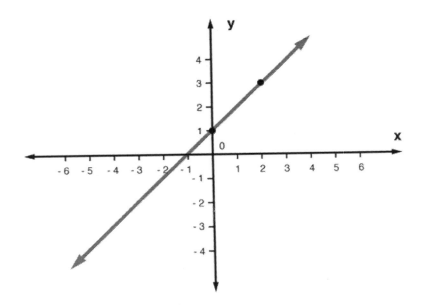

Solving Line Problems

As mentioned, two lines are parallel if they have the same slope. Two lines are perpendicular if the product of their slope equals -1. Parallel lines never intersect unless they are the same line, and perpendicular lines intersect at a right angle. If two lines aren't parallel, they must intersect at one point. Determining equations of lines based on properties of parallel and perpendicular lines appears in word problems. To find an equation of a line, both the slope and a point the line goes through are necessary. Therefore, if an equation of a line is needed that's parallel to a given line and runs through a specified point, the slope of the given line and the point are plugged into the point-slope form of an equation of a line. Secondly, if an equation of a line is needed that's perpendicular to a given line running through a specified point, the negative reciprocal of the slope of the given line and the point are plugged into the point-slope form. Also, if the point of intersection of two lines is known, that point will be used to solve the set of equations. Therefore, to solve a system of equations, the point of intersection must be found. If a set of two equations with two unknown variables has no solution, the lines are parallel.

Modeling Functions

Mathematical functions such as polynomials, rational functions, radical functions, absolute value functions, and piecewise-defined functions can be utilized to approximate, or model, real-life phenomena. For example, a function can be built that approximates the average amount of snowfall on a given day of the year in Chicago. This example could be as simple as a polynomial. Modeling situations using such functions has limitations; the most significant issue is the error that exists between the exact amount and the approximate amount. Typically, the model will not give exact values as outputs. However, the choosing the type of function that provides the best fit of the data will reduce this error. Technology can be used to model situations. For example, given a set of data, the data can be inputted into tools such as graphing calculators or spreadsheet software that output a function with a good fit. Some examples of polynomial modeling are linear, quadratic, and cubic regression.

Representing Exponential and Logarithmic Functions

The logarithmic function with base b is denoted $y = \log_b x$. Its base must be greater than 0 and not equal to 1, and the domain is all $x > 0$. The exponential function with base b is denoted $y = b^x$. Exponential and logarithmic functions with base b are inverses. By definition, if $y = \log_b x$, $x = b^y$. Because exponential and logarithmic functions are inverses, the graph of one is obtained by reflecting the other over the line $y = x$. A common base used is e, and in this case $y = e^x$ and its inverse $y = \log_e x$ is commonly written as the natural logarithmic function $y = \ln x$.

Here is the graph of both functions:

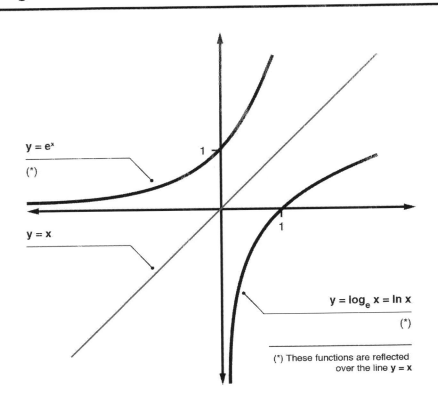

The Graphs of Exponential and Logarithmic Functions are Inverses

$y = e^x$

(*)

$y = x$

1

1

$y = \log_e x = \ln x$

(*)

(*) These functions are reflected over the line y = x

Graphing Functions

The x-intercept of the logarithmic function $y = \log_b x$ with any base is always the ordered pair $(1, 0)$. Bythe definition of inverse, the point $(0, 1)$ always lies on the exponential function $y = b^x$. This is true because any real number raised to the power of 0 equals 1. Therefore, the exponential function only has a y-intercept. The exponential function also has a horizontal asymptote of the x-axis as x approaches negative infinity. Because the graph is reflected over the line $y = x$, to obtain the graph of the logarithmic function, the asymptote is also reflected. Therefore, the logarithmic function has a one-sided vertical asymptote at $y = 0$. These asymptotes can be seen in the above graphs of $y = e^x$ and $y = \ln x$.

Solving Logarithmic and Exponential Functions

To solve an equation involving exponential expressions, the goal is to isolate the exponential expression. Once this process is completed, the logarithm—with the base equaling the base of the exponent of both sides—needs to be taken to get an expression for the variable. If the base is e, the natural log of both sides needs to be taken.

To solve an equation with logarithms, the given equation needs to be written in exponential form, using the fact that $\log_b a = x$ means $b^x = y$, and then solved for the given variable. Lastly, properties of logarithms can be used to simplify more than one logarithmic expression into one.

Some equations involving exponential and logarithmic functions can be solved algebraically, or analytically. To solve an equation involving exponential functions, the goal is to isolate the exponential expression. Then, the logarithm of both sides is found in order to yield an expression for the variable. Laws of Logarithms will be helpful at this point.

To solve an equation with logarithms, the equation needs to be rewritten in exponential form. The definition that $\log_b x = y$ means $b^y = x$ needs to be used. Then, one needs to solve for the given variable. Properties of logarithms can be used to simplify multiple logarithmic expressions into one.

Other methods can be used to solve equations containing logarithmic and exponential functions. Graphs and graphing calculators can be used to see points of intersection. In a similar manner, tables can be used to find points of intersection. Also, numerical methods can be utilized to find approximate solutions.

Exponential Growth and Decay
Exponential growth and decay are important concepts in modeling real-world phenomena. The growth and decay formula is $A(t) = Pe^{rt}$, where the independent variable t represents temperature, P represents an initial quantity, r represents the rate of increase or decrease, and $A(t)$ represents the amount of the quantity at time t. If $r > 0$, the equation models exponential growth and a common application is population growth. If $r < 0$, the equation models exponential decay and a common application is radioactive decay. Exponential and logarithmic solving techniques are necessary to work with the growth and decay formula.

Logarithmic Scales
A logarithmic scale is a scale of measurement that uses the logarithm of the given units instead of the actual given units. Each tick mark on such a scale is the product of the previous tick mark multiplied by a number. The advantage of using such a scale is that if one is working with large measurements, this technique reduces the scale into manageable quantities that are easier to read. The Richter magnitude scale is the famous logarithmic scale used to measure the intensity of earthquakes and the decibel scale is commonly used to measure sound level in electronics.

Using Exponential and Logarithmic Functions in Finance Problems
Modeling within finance also involves exponential and logarithmic functions. Compound interest results when the bank pays interest on the original amount of money – the principal – and the interest that has accrued. The compound interest equation is $A(t) = P\left(1 + \frac{r}{n}\right)^{nt}$, where P is the principal, r is the interest rate, n is the number of times per year the interest is compounded, and t is the time in years. The result, $A(t)$, is the final amount after t years. Mathematical problems of this type that are frequently encountered involve receiving all but one of these quantities and solving for the missing quantity. The solving process then involves employing properties of logarithmic and exponential functions. Interest can also be compounded continuously. This formula is given as $A(t) = Pe^{rt}$. If $1,000 was compounded continuously at a rate of 2% for 4 years, the result would be $A(4) = 1000e^{0.02 \cdot 4} = \$1,083$.

Rate of Change Proportional to the Current Quantity
Many quantities grow or decay as fast as exponential functions. Specifically, if such a quantity grows or decays at a rate proportional to the quantity itself, it shows exponential behavior. If a data set is given

with such specific characteristics, the initial amount and an amount at a specific time, t, can be plugged into the exponential function $A(t) = Pe^{rt}$ for A and P. Using properties of exponents and logarithms, one can then solve for the rate, r. This solution yields enough information to have the entire model, which can allow for an estimation of the quantity at any time, t, and the ability to solve various problems using that model.

Mathematical Models to Represent Real-World Situations

A mathematical model is a representation in mathematical terms of a real-world situation, and is widely used in science and engineering. Formulas are derived that model phenomena such as population growth and decay. In any model, simplifications must be made to create such formulas, and parameters within the model usually do not represent the physical world exactly. Once the model is formulated, its output can be compared to real-world scenarios to judge how valid the model is. If a model is deemed to be inaccurate, original assumptions and restrictions can be lifted that initially simplified the model.

Using Multiple Representations of a Mathematical Concept

There are many different areas of mathematics, and a single mathematical concept can have meaning in more than one area. Some of the main divisions of math include arithmetic, algebra, calculus, geometry, and statistics. A concept that spans across those divisions is *area*. Many different formulas in geometry involve calculating the area of different shapes. For example, area of a circle $A = \pi r^2$ is a quadratic function in r, the radius of the circle. In calculus, an area problem can involve calculating the area under a curve from two points on the x-axis, which is known as the definite integral. Also, the area between two curves is discussed. Finally, in statistics, the area under a density curve is defined to be probability.

Communicating Mathematical Ideas

Many different types of representations are useful in mathematics, and the most widely-used are written symbols, pictures or diagrams, models, spoken words, and real-world experiences. Real-world experiences and spoken words are both representations that can be expressed by written symbols that impart mathematical meaning to the situation being discussed. Pictures or diagrams, including graphs and geometric figures, allow for visual representations of mathematical concepts. These external representations are widely used and have been developed for centuries. Similarly, written representations, such as symbolic methods like equations and functions, are also widely used and are used the most in math classes.

Using Visual Media

Students benefit from the use of visual media that represents mathematical information, and teachers should be able to go back and forth between each type. They should know which type of representation is useful in given a scenario. For example, a function can be represented by a diagram, a table, a graph, and a set of numbers simultaneously. Here is such an example:

Multiple Representations of a Function

Mapping

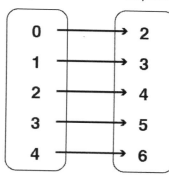

Domain
inputs

Range
outputs

Table

x	y
0	2
1	3
2	4
3	5
4	6

Graph

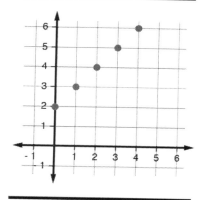

Ordered Pairs

{(0,2),(1,3),(2,4),(3,5),(4,6)}

Using Math Terminology

Using appropriate vocabulary that represents mathematical ideas is a critical skill in both being able to teach mathematics and use mathematical techniques to solve real-world situations. Each area in mathematics has its own set of definitions, and the translation of ideas onto paper requires a deep understanding of all the terminology. An important application of this idea is being able to translate word problems into equations that can be solved.

Linear and Quadratic Equations and Inequalities

Rewriting Expressions

Algebraic expressions are made up of numbers, variables, and combinations of the two, using mathematical operations. Expressions can be rewritten based on their factors. For example, the expression $6x + 4$ can be rewritten as $2(3x + 2)$ because 2 is a factor of both $6x$ and 4. More complex expressions can also be rewritten based on their factors. The expression $x^4 - 16$ can be rewritten as $(x^2 - 4)(x^2 + 4)$. This is a different type of factoring, where a difference of squares is factored into a sum and difference of the same two terms. With some expressions, the factoring process is simple and only leads to a different way to represent the expression. With others, factoring and rewriting the expression leads to more information about the given problem.

In the following quadratic equation, factoring the binomial leads to finding the zeros of the function: $x^2 - 5x + 6 = y$. This equations factors into $(x - 3)(x - 2) = y$, where 2 and 3 are found to be the zeros of the function when y is set equal to zero. The zeros of any function are the x-values where the graph of the function on the coordinate plane crosses the x-axis.

Factoring an equation is a simple way to rewrite the equation and find the zeros, but factoring is not possible for every quadratic. Completing the square is one way to find zeros when factoring is not an option. The following equation cannot be factored: $x^2 + 10x - 9 = 0$. The first step in this method is to move the constant to the right side of the equation, making it $x^2 + 10x = 9$. Then, the coefficient of x is divided by 2 and squared. This number is then added to both sides of the equation, to make the equation still true. For this example, $\left(\frac{10}{2}\right)^2 = 25$ is added to both sides of the equation to obtain: $x^2 + 10x + 25 = 9 + 25$. This expression simplifies to $x^2 + 10x + 25 = 34$, which can then be factored into $(x + 5)^2 = 34$. Solving for x then involves taking the square root of both sides and subtracting 5. This leads to two zeros of the function: $x = \pm\sqrt{34} - 5$. Depending on the type of answer the question seeks, a calculator may be used to find exact numbers.

Given a quadratic equation in standard form—$ax^2 + bx + c = 0$—the sign of a tells whether the function has a minimum value or a maximum value. If $a > 0$, the graph opens up and has a minimum value. If $a < 0$, the graph opens down and has a maximum value. Depending on the way the quadratic equation is written, multiplication may need to occur before a max/min value is determined.

Exponential expressions can also be rewritten, just as quadratic equations. Properties of exponents must be understood. Multiplying two exponential expressions with the same base involves adding the exponents: $a^m a^n = a^{m+n}$. Dividing two exponential expressions with the same base involves subtracting the exponents: $\frac{a^m}{a^n} = a^{m-n}$. Raising an exponential expression to another exponent includes multiplying the exponents: $(a^m)^n = a^{mn}$. The zero power always gives a value of 1: $a^0 = 1$. Raising either a product or a fraction to a power involves distributing that power:$(ab)^m = a^m b^m$ and $\left(\frac{a}{b}\right)^m = \frac{a^m}{b^m}$. Finally, raising a number to a negative exponent is equivalent to the reciprocal including the positive exponent: $a^{-m} = \frac{1}{a^m}$.

Polynomial Identities

Difference of squares refers to a binomial composed of the difference of two squares. For example, $a^2 - b^2$ is a difference of squares. It can be written $(a)^2 - (b)^2$, and it can be factored into $(a - b)(a + b)$. Recognizing the difference of squares allows the expression to be rewritten easily because of the form it takes. For some expressions, factoring consists of more than one step. When factoring, it's important to always check to make sure that the result cannot be factored further. If it can, then the expression should be split further. If it cannot be, the factoring step is complete, and the expression is completely factored.

A sum and difference of cubes is another way to factor a polynomial expression. When the polynomial takes the form of addition or subtraction of two terms that can be written as a cube, a formula is given. The following graphic shows the factorization of a difference of cubes:

$$a^3 - b^3 = (a - b)(a^2 + ab + b^2)$$

same sign

opposite sign

always +

This form of factoring can be useful in finding the zeros of a function of degree 3. For example, when solving $x^3 - 27 = 0$, this rule needs to be used. $x^3 - 27$ is first written as the difference two cubes, $(x)^3 - (3)^3$ and then factored into $(x - 3)(x^2 + 3x + 9)$. This expression may not be factored any further. Each factor is then set equal to zero. Therefore, one solution is found to be $x = 3$, and the other two solutions must be found using the quadratic formula. A sum of squares would have a similar process. The formula for factoring a sum of squares is $a^3 + b^3 = (a + b)(a^2 - ab + b^2)$.

The opposite of factoring is multiplying. Multiplying a square of a binomial involves the following rules: $(a + b)^2 = a^2 + 2ab + b^2$ and $(a - b)^2 = a^2 - 2ab + b^2$. The binomial theorem for expansion can be used when the exponent on a binomial is larger than 2, and the multiplication would take a long time. The binomial theorem is given as:

$$(a + b)^n = \sum_{k=0}^{n} \binom{n}{k} a^{n-k} b^k \qquad \binom{n}{k} = \frac{n!}{k!(n-k)!}$$

where

The *Remainder Theorem* can be helpful when evaluating polynomial functions $P(x)$ for a given value of x. A polynomial can be divided by $(x - a)$, if there is a remainder of 0. This also means that $P(a) = 0$ and $(x - a)$ is a factor of $P(x)$. In a similar sense, if P is evaluated at any other number b, $P(b)$ is equal to the remainder of dividing $P(x)$ by $(x - b)$.

Zeros of Polynomials

Finding the zeros of polynomial functions is the same process as finding the solutions of polynomial equations. These are the points at which the graph of the function crosses the x-axis. As stated previously, factors can be used to find the zeros of a polynomial function. The degree of the function shows the number of possible zeros. If the highest exponent on the independent variable is 4, then the degree is 4, and the number of possible zeros is 4. If there are complex solutions, the number of roots is less than the degree.

Given the function $y = x^2 + 7x + 6$, y can be set equal to zero, and the polynomial can be factored. The equation turns into $0 = (x + 1)(x + 6)$, where $x = -1$ and $x = -6$ are the zeros. Since this is a quadratic equation, the shape of the graph will be a parabola. Knowing that zeros represent the points where the parabola crosses the x-axis, the maximum or minimum point is the only other piece needed to sketch a rough graph of the function. By looking at the function in standard form, the coefficient of x is positive; therefore, the parabola opens *up*. Using the zeros and the minimum, the following rough sketch of the graph can be constructed:

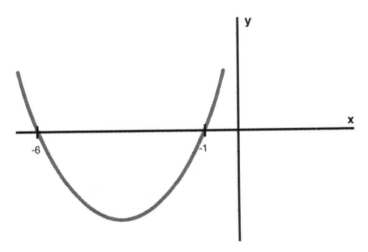

Operations with Polynomials

Addition and subtraction operations can be performed on polynomials with like terms. *Like terms refers to terms* that have the same variable and exponent. The two following polynomials can be added together by collecting like terms: $(x^2 + 3x - 4) + (4x^2 - 7x + 8)$. The x^2 terms can be added as $x^2 + 4x^2 = 5x^2$. The x terms can be added as $3x + -7x = -4x$, and the constants can be added as $-4 + 8 = 4$. The following expression is the result of the addition: $5x^2 - 4x + 4$. When subtracting polynomials, the same steps are followed, only subtracting like terms together.

Multiplication of polynomials can also be performed. Given the two polynomials, $(y^3 - 4)$ and $(x^2 + 8x - 7)$, each term in the first polynomial must be multiplied by each term in the second polynomial. The steps to multiply each term in the given example are as follows:

$$(y^3 * x^2) + (y^3 * 8x) + (y^3 * -7) + (-4 * x^2) + (-4 * 8x) + (-4 * -7)$$

Simplifying each multiplied part, yields $x^2y^3 + 8xy^3 - 7y^3 - 4x^2 - 32x + 28$. None of the terms can be combined because there are no like terms in the final expression. Any polynomials can be multiplied by each other by following the same set of steps, then collecting like terms at the end.

Equations and Inequalities

The sum of a number and 5 is equal to 10 times the number. To find this unknown number, a simple equation can be written to represent the problem. Key words such as *sum*, *equal*, and *times* are used to form the following equation with one variable: $n + 5 = 10n$. When solving for n, opposite operations are used. First, n is subtracted from $10n$ across the equals sign, resulting in $5 = 9n$. Then, 9 is divided on both sides, leaving $n = \frac{5}{9}$. This solution can be graphed on the number line with a dot as shown below:

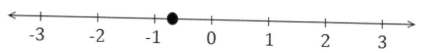

If the problem were changed to say, "The sum of a number and 5 is greater than 10 times the number," then an inequality would be used instead of an equation. Using key words again, *greater than* is represented by the symbol >. The inequality $n + 5 > 10n$ can be solved using the same techniques, resulting in $n < \frac{5}{9}$. The only time solving an inequality differs from solving an equation is when a negative number is either multiplied times or divided by each side of the inequality. The sign must be switched in this case. For this example, the graph of the solution changes to the following graph because the solution represents all real numbers less than $\frac{5}{9}$. Not included in this solution is $\frac{5}{9}$ because it is a *less than* symbol, not *equal to*.

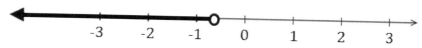

Equations and inequalities in two variables represent a relationship. Jim owns a car wash and charges $40 per car. The rent for the facility is $350 per month. An equation can be written to relate the number of cars Jim cleans to the money he makes per month. Let x represent the number of cars and y represent the profit Jim makes each month from the car wash. The equation $y = 40x - 350$ can be used to show Jim's profit or loss. Since this equation has two variables, the coordinate plane can be used to show the relationship and predict profit or loss for Jim. The following graph shows that Jim must wash at least nine cars to pay the rent, where $x = 9$. Anything nine cars and above yield a profit shown in the value on the y-axis.

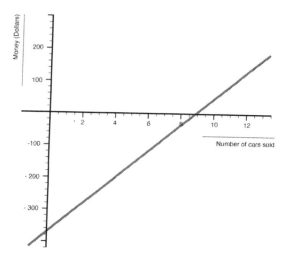

With a single equation in two variables, the solutions are limited only by the situation the equation represents. When two equations or inequalities are used, more constraints are added. For example, in a system of linear equations, there is often—although not always—only one answer. The point of intersection of two lines is the solution. For a system of inequalities, there are infinitely many answers.

The intersection of two solution sets gives the solution set of the system of inequalities. In the following graph, the darker shaded region is where two inequalities overlap. Any set of x and y found in that region satisfies both inequalities. The line with the positive slope is solid, meaning the values on that line are included in the solution. The with the negative line is dotted, so the coordinates on that line are not included.

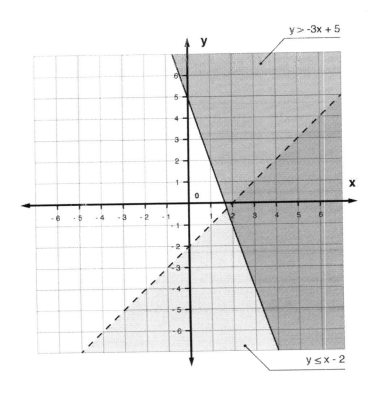

Formulas with two variables are equations used to represent a specific relationship. For example, the formula $d = rt$ represents the relationship between distance, rate, and time. If Bob travels at a rate of 35 miles per hour on his road trip from Westminster to Seneca, the formula $d = 35t$ can be used to represent his distance traveled in a specific length of time. Formulas can also be used to show different roles of the variables, transformed without any given numbers. Solving for r, the formula becomes $\frac{d}{t} = r$. The t is moved over by division so that *rate* is a function of distance and time.

Solving Equations

Solving equations in one variable is the process of For example, in $3x - 7 = 20$, the variable x needs to be isolated. Using opposite operations, the -7 is moved to the right side of the equation by adding seven to both sides: $3x - 7 + 7 = 20 + 7$, resulting in $3x = 27$. Dividing by three on each side, $\frac{3x}{3} = \frac{27}{3}$, results in isolation of the variable. It is important to note that if an operation is performed on one side of the equals sign, it has to be performed on the other side to maintain equality. The solution is found to be $x = 9$. This solution can be checked for accuracy by plugging $x=7$ in the original equation. After simplifying the equation, $20 = 20$ is found, which is a true statement.

When solving radical and rational equations, extraneous solutions must be accounted for when finding the answers. For example, the equation $\frac{x}{x-5} = \frac{3x}{x+3}$ has two values that create a 0 denominator: $x \neq 5, -3$. When solving for x, these values must be considered because they cannot be solutions. In the given equation, solving for x can be done using cross-multiplication, yielding the equation $x(x + 3) = 3x(x - 5)$. Distributing results in the quadratic equation yields $x^2 + 3x = 3x^2 - 15x$; therefore, all terms must be moved to one side of the equals sign. This results in $2x^2 - 18x = 0$, which in factored form is $2x(x - 9) = 0$. Setting each factor equal to zero, the apparent solutions are $x = 0$ and $x = 9$. These two solutions are neither 5 nor -3, so they are viable solutions. Neither 0 nor 9 create a 0 denominator in the original equation.

A similar process exists when solving radical equations. One must check to make sure the solutions are defined in the original equations. Solving an equation containing a square root involves isolating the root and then squaring both sides of the equals sign. Solving a cube root equation involves isolating the radical and then cubing both sides. In either case, the variable can then be solved for because there are no longer radicals in the equation.

Methods for Solving Equations

Equations with one variable can be solved using the addition principle and multiplication principle. If $a = b$, then $a + c = b + c$, and $ac = bc$. Given the equation $2x - 3 = 5x + 7$, the first step is to combine the variable terms and the constant terms. Using the principles, expressions can be added and subtracted onto and off both sides of the equals sign, so the equation turns into $-10 = 3x$. Dividing by 3 on both sides through the multiplication principle with $c = \frac{1}{3}$ results in the final answer of $x = \frac{-10}{3}$.

Some equations have a higher degree and are not solved by simply using opposite operations. When an equation has a degree of 2, completing the square is an option. For example, the quadratic equation $x^2 - 6x + 2 = 0$ can be rewritten by completing the square. The goal of completing the square is to get the equation into the form $(x - p)^2 = q$. Using the example, the constant term 2 first needs to be moved over to the opposite side by subtracting. Then, the square can be completed by adding 9 to both sides, which is the square of half of the coefficient of the middle term $-6x$. The current equation is $x^2 - 6x + 9 = 7$. The left side can be factored into a square of a binomial, resulting in $(x - 3)^2 = 7$. To solve for x, the square root of both sides should be taken, resulting in $(x - 3) = \pm\sqrt{7}$, and $x = 3 \pm \sqrt{7}$.

Other ways of solving quadratic equations include graphing, factoring, and using the quadratic formula. The equation $y = x^2 - 4x + 3$ can be graphed on the coordinate plane, and the solutions can be observed where it crosses the x-axis. The graph will be a parabola that opens up with two solutions at 1 and 3.

The equation can also be factored to find the solutions. The original equation, $y = x^2 - 4x + 3$ can be factored into $y = (x - 1)(x - 3)$. Setting this equal to zero, the x-values are found to be 1 and 3, just as on the graph. Solving by factoring and graphing are not always possible. The quadratic formula is a method of solving quadratic equations that always results in exact solutions. The formula is $x = \frac{-b \pm \sqrt{b^2 - 4ac}}{2a}$, where a, b, and c are the coefficients in the original equation in standard form $y = ax^2 + bx + c$. For this example, $x = \frac{4 \pm \sqrt{(-4)^2 - 4(1)(3)}}{2(1)} = \frac{4 \pm \sqrt{16 - 12}}{2} = \frac{4 \pm 2}{2} = 1, 3$.

285

The expression underneath the radical is called the *discriminant*. Without working out the entire formula, the value of the discriminant can reveal the nature of the solutions. If the value of the discriminant $b^2 - 4ac$ is positive, then there will be two real solutions. If the value is zero, there will be one real solution. If the value is negative, the two solutions will be imaginary or complex. If the solutions are complex, it means that the parabola never touches the x-axis. An example of a complex solution can be found by solving the following quadratic: $y = x^2 - 4x + 8$. By using the quadratic formula, the solutions are found to be: $x = \frac{4 \pm \sqrt{(-4)^2 - 4(1)(8)}}{2(1)} = \frac{4 \pm \sqrt{16 - 32}}{2} = \frac{4 \pm \sqrt{-16}}{2} = 2 \pm 2i$. The solutions both have a real part, 2, and an imaginary part, $2i$.

Systems of Equations

A *system of equations* is a group of equations that have the same variables or unknowns. These equations can be linear, but they are not always so. Finding a solution to a system of equations means finding the values of the variables that satisfy each equation. For a linear system of two equations and two variables, there could be a single solution, no solution, or infinitely many solutions.

A single solution occurs when there is one value for x and y that satisfies the system. This would be shown on the graph where the lines cross at exactly one point. When there is no solution, the lines are parallel and do not ever cross. With infinitely many solutions, the equations may look different, but they are the same line. One equation will be a multiple of the other, and on the graph, they lie on top of each other.

The process of elimination can be used to solve a system of equations. The word "elmination" should be un-bolded, and one variable cancels out. For example, the following equations make up a system: $x + 3y = 10$ and $2x - 5y = 9$. Immediately adding these equations does not eliminate a variable, but it is possible to change the first equation by multiplying the whole equation by -2. This changes the first equation to $-2x - 6y = -20$. The equations can be then added to obtain $-11y = -11$. Solving for y yields $y = 1$. To find the rest of the solution, 1 can be substituted in for y in either original equation to find the value of $x = 7$. The solution to the system is (7, 1) because it makes both equations true, and it is the point in which the lines intersect. If the system is *dependent*—having infinitely many solutions— then both variables will cancel out when the elimination method is used, resulting in an equation that is true for many values of x and y. Since the system is dependent, both equations can be simplified to the same equation or line.

A system can also be solved using *substitution*. This involves solving one equation for a variable and then plugging that solved equation into the other equation in the system. This equation can be solved for one variable, which can then be plugged in to either original equation and solved for the other variable. For example, $x - y = -2$ and $3x + 2y = 9$ can be solved using substitution. The first equation can be solved for x, where $x = -2 + y$. Then it can be plugged into the other equation: $3(-2 + y) + 2y = 9$. Solving for y yields $-6 + 3y + 2y = 9$, where $y = 3$. If $y = 3$, then $x = 1$. This solution can be checked by plugging in these values for the variables in each equation to see if it makes a true statement.

Finally, a solution to a system of equations can be found graphically. The solution to a linear system is the point or points where the lines cross. The values of x and y represent the coordinates (x, y) where the lines intersect. Using the same system of equation as above, they can be solved for y to put them in slope-intercept form, $y = mx + b$. These equations become $y = x + 4$ and $y = -\frac{3}{2}x + 4.5$. The slope is the coefficient of x, and the y-intercept is the constant value. This system with the solution is shown below:

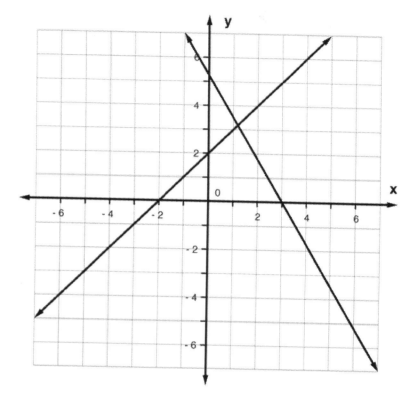

A system of equations may also be made up of a linear and a quadratic equation. These systems may have one solution, two solutions, or no solutions. The graph of these systems involves one straight line and one parabola. Algebraically, these systems can be solved by solving the linear equation for one variable and plugging that answer in to the quadratic equation. If possible, the equation can then be solved to find part of the answer. The graphing method is commonly used for these types of systems. On a graph, these two lines can be found to intersect at one point, at two points across the parabola, or at no points.

Matrices can also be used to solve systems of linear equations. Specifically, for systems, the coefficients of the linear equations in standard form are the entries in the matrix. Using the same system of linear equations as above, $x - y = -2$ and $3x + 2y = 9$, the matrix to represent the system is $\begin{bmatrix} 1 & -1 \\ 3 & 2 \end{bmatrix}\begin{bmatrix} x \\ y \end{bmatrix} = \begin{bmatrix} -2 \\ 9 \end{bmatrix}$. To solve this system using matrices, the inverse matrix must be found. For a general 2x2 matrix, $\begin{bmatrix} a & b \\ c & d \end{bmatrix}$, the inverse matrix is found by the expression $\frac{1}{ad-bc}\begin{bmatrix} d & -b \\ -c & a \end{bmatrix}$. The inverse matrix for the system given above is $\frac{1}{2--3}\begin{bmatrix} 2 & 1 \\ -3 & 1 \end{bmatrix} = \frac{1}{5}\begin{bmatrix} 2 & 1 \\ -3 & 1 \end{bmatrix}$. The next step in solving is to multiply this identity matrix by the system matrix above.

This is given by the following equation:

$$\frac{1}{5}\begin{bmatrix} 2 & 1 \\ -3 & 1 \end{bmatrix}\begin{bmatrix} 1 & -1 \\ 3 & 2 \end{bmatrix}\begin{bmatrix} x \\ y \end{bmatrix} = \begin{bmatrix} -2 \\ 9 \end{bmatrix}\begin{bmatrix} 2 & 1 \\ -3 & 1 \end{bmatrix}\frac{1}{5}$$

287

This simplifies to $\frac{1}{5}\begin{bmatrix} 5 & 0 \\ 0 & 5 \end{bmatrix}\begin{bmatrix} x \\ y \end{bmatrix} = \frac{1}{5}\begin{bmatrix} 5 \\ 15 \end{bmatrix}$. Solving for the solution matrix, the answer is $\begin{bmatrix} 1 & 0 \\ 0 & 1 \end{bmatrix}\begin{bmatrix} x \\ y \end{bmatrix} = \begin{bmatrix} 1 \\ 3 \end{bmatrix}$. Since the first matrix is the identity matrix, the solution is $x = 1$ and $y = 3$.

Finding solutions to systems of equations is essentially finding what values of the variables make both equations true. It is finding the input value that yields the same output value in both equations. For functions $g(x)$ and $f(x)$, the equation $g(x) = f(x)$ means the output values are being set equal to each other. Solving for the value of x means finding the x-coordinate that gives the same output in both functions. For example, $f(x) = x + 2$ and $g(x) = -3x + 10$ is a system of equations. Setting $f(x) = g(x)$ yields the equation $x + 2 = -3x + 10$. Solving for x, gives the x-coordinate $x = -2$ where the two lines cross. This value can also be found by using a table or a graph. On a table, both equations can be given the same inputs, and the outputs can be recorded to find the point(s) where the lines cross. Any method of solving finds the same solution, but some methods are more appropriate for some systems of equations than others.

Systems of Linear Inequalities

Systems of *linear inequalities* are like systems of equations, but the solutions are different. Since inequalities have infinitely many solutions, their systems also have infinitely many solutions. Finding the solutions of inequalities involves graphs. A system of two equations and two inequalities is linear; thus, the lines can be graphed using slope-intercept form. If the inequality has an equals sign, the line is solid. If the inequality only has a greater than or less than symbol, the line on the graph is dotted. Dashed lines indicate that points lying on the line are not included in the solution. After the lines are graphed, a region is shaded on one side of the line. This side is found by determining if a point—known as a *test point*—lying on one side of the line produces a true inequality. If it does, that side of the graph is shaded. If the point produces a false inequality, the line is shaded on the opposite side from the point. The graph of a system of inequalities involves shading the intersection of the two shaded regions.

Measurement and Geometry

Two- and Three-Dimensional Geometric Objects

Points, Lines, Planes, and Angles

A point is a place, not a thing, and therefore has no dimensions or size. A set of points that lies on the same line is called collinear. A set of points that lies on the same plane is called coplanar.

The image above displays point *A*, point *B*, and point *C*.

A line is as series of points that extends in both directions without ending. It consists of an infinite number of points and is drawn with arrows on both ends to indicate it extends infinitely. Lines can be named by two points on the line or with a single, cursive, lower case letter. The lines below are named: line *AB* or line *BA* or $\overleftrightarrow{AB}$ or $\overleftrightarrow{BA}$; and line *m*.

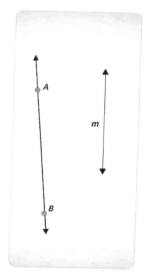

Two lines are considered parallel to each other if, while extending infinitely, they will never intersect (or meet). Parallel lines point in the same direction and are always the same distance apart. Two lines are

289

considered perpendicular if they intersect to form right angles. Right angles are 90°. Typically, a small box is drawn at the intersection point to indicate the right angle.

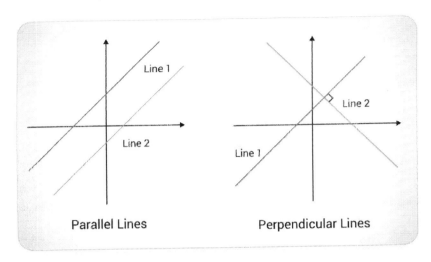

| Parallel Lines | Perpendicular Lines |

Line 1 is parallel to line 2 in the left image and is written as line 1 || line 2. Line 1 is perpendicular to line 2 in the right image and is written as line 1 ⊥ line 2.

A ray has a specific starting point and extends in one direction without ending. The endpoint of a ray is its starting point. Rays are named using the endpoint first, and any other point on the ray. The following ray can be named ray *AB* and written $\overrightarrow{AB}$.

A line segment has specific starting and ending points. A line segment consists of two endpoints and all the points in between. Line segments are named by the two endpoints. The example below is named segment *GH* or segment *HG*, written $\overline{GH}$ or $\overline{HG}$.

Two- and Three-Dimensional Shapes

A polygon is a closed geometric figure in a plane (flat surface) consisting of at least 3 sides formed by line segments. These are often defined as two-dimensional shapes. Common two-dimensional shapes include circles, triangles, squares, rectangles, pentagons, and hexagons. Note that a circle is a two-dimensional shape without sides.

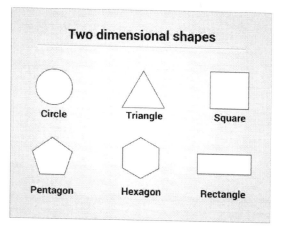

A solid figure, or simply solid, is a figure that encloses a part of space. Some solids consist of flat surfaces only while others include curved surfaces. Solid figures are often defined as three-dimensional shapes. Common three-dimensional shapes include spheres, prisms, cubes, pyramids, cylinders, and cones.

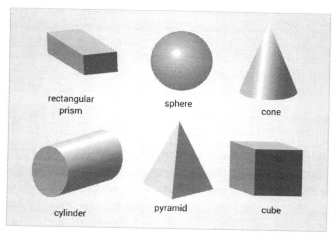

Composing two- or three-dimensional shapes involves putting together two or more shapes to create a new larger figure. For example, a semi-circle (half circle), rectangle, and two triangles can be used to compose the figure of the sailboat shown below.

Similarly, solid figures can be placed together to compose an endless number of three-dimensional objects.

Decomposing two- and three-dimensional figures involves breaking the shapes apart into smaller, simpler shapes. Consider the following two-dimensional representations of a house:

This complex figure can be decomposed into the following basic two-dimensional shapes: large rectangle (body of house); large triangle (roof); small rectangle and small triangle (chimney). Decomposing figures is often done more than one way. To illustrate, the figure of the house could also be decomposed into: two large triangles (body); two medium triangles (roof); two smaller triangles of unequal size (chimney).

Polygons and Solids

A polygon is a closed two-dimensional figure consisting of three or more sides. Polygons can be either convex or concave. A polygon that has interior angles all measuring less than 180° is convex. A concave polygon has one or more interior angles measuring greater than 180°. Examples are shown below.

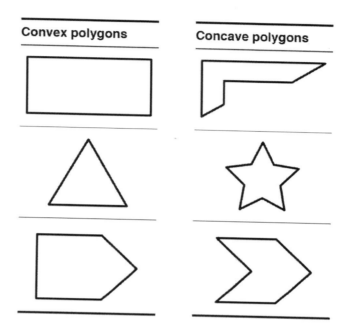

Polygons can be classified by the number of sides (also equal to the number of angles) they have. The following are the names of polygons with a given number of sides or angles:

# of sides	3	4	5	6	7	8	9	10
Name of polygon	Triangle	Quadrilateral	Pentagon	Hexagon	Septagon (or heptagon)	Octagon	Nonagon	Decagon

Equiangular polygons are polygons in which the measure of every interior angle is the same. The sides of equilateral polygons are always the same length. If a polygon is both equiangular and equilateral, the polygon is defined as a regular polygon. Examples are shown below.

Triangles can be further classified by their sides and angles. A triangle with its largest angle measuring 90° is a right triangle. A triangle with the largest angle less than 90° is an acute triangle. A triangle with the largest angle greater than 90° is an obtuse triangle.

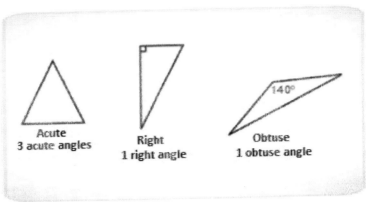

A triangle consisting of two equal sides and two equal angles is an isosceles triangle. A triangle with three equal sides and three equal angles is an equilateral triangle. A triangle with no equal sides or angles is a scalene triangle.

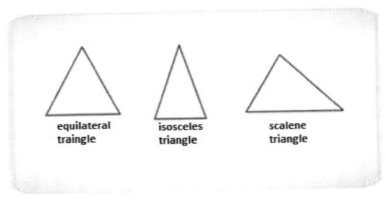

Quadrilaterals can be further classified according to their sides and angles. A quadrilateral with exactly one pair of parallel sides is called a trapezoid. A quadrilateral that shows both pairs of opposite sides parallel is a parallelogram. Parallelograms include rhombuses, rectangles, and squares. A rhombus has four equal sides. A rectangle has four equal angles (90° each). A square has four 90° angles and four equal sides. Therefore, a square is both a rhombus and a rectangle.

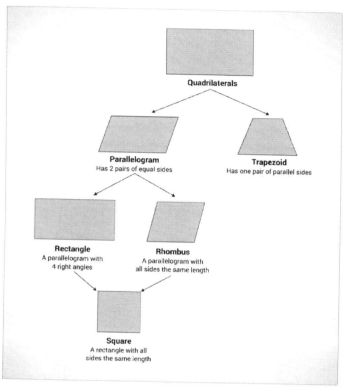

A solid is a three-dimensional figure that encloses a part of space. Solids consisting of all flat surfaces that are polygons are called polyhedrons. The two-dimensional surfaces that make up a polyhedron are called faces. Types of polyhedrons include prisms and pyramids. A prism consists of two parallel faces that are congruent (or the same shape and same size), and lateral faces going around (which are parallelograms). A prism is further classified by the shape of its base, as shown below:

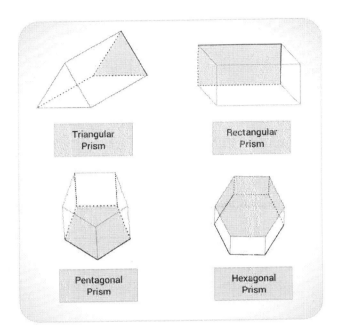

A pyramid consists of lateral faces (triangles) that meet at a common point called the vertex and one other face that is a polygon, called the base. A pyramid can be further classified by the shape of its base, as shown below.

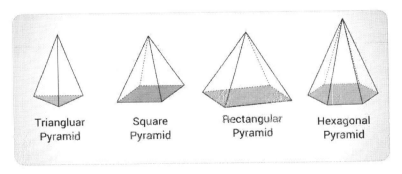

A tetrahedron is another name for a triangular pyramid. All the faces of a tetrahedron are triangles.

Solids that are not polyhedrons include spheres, cylinders, and cones. A sphere is the set of all points a given distance from a given center point. A sphere is commonly thought of as a three-dimensional circle. A cylinder consists of two parallel, congruent (same size) circles and a lateral curved surface. A cone consists of a circle as its base and a lateral curved surface that narrows to a point called the vertex.

Similar polygons are the same shape but different sizes. More specifically, their corresponding angle measures are congruent (or equal) and the length of their sides is proportional. For example, all sides of one polygon may be double the length of the sides of another. Likewise, similar solids are the same shape but different sizes. Any corresponding faces or bases of similar solids are the same polygons that are proportional by a consistent value.

Properties of certain polygons allow that the perimeter may be obtained by using formulas. A rectangle consists of two sides called the length (*l*), which have equal measures, and two sides called the width (*w*), which have equal measures. Therefore, the perimeter (*P*) of a rectangle can be expressed as $P = l + l + w + w$. This can be simplified to produce the following formula to find the perimeter of a rectangle: $P = 2l + 2w$ or $P = 2(l + w)$.

A regular polygon is one in which all sides have equal length and all interior angles have equal measures, such as a square and an equilateral triangle. To find the perimeter of a regular polygon, the length of one side is multiplied by the number of sides. For example, to find the perimeter of an equilateral triangle with a side of length of 4 feet, 4 feet is multiplied by 3 (number of sides of a triangle). The perimeter of a regular octagon (8 sides) with a side of length of $\frac{1}{2}$cm is $\frac{1}{2} cm \times 8 = 4cm$.

Classification of Angles

An angle consists of two rays that have a common endpoint. This common endpoint is called the vertex of the angle. The two rays can be called sides of the angle. The angle below has a vertex at point *B* and the sides consist of ray *BA* and ray *BC*. An angle can be named in three ways:

1. Using the vertex and a point from each side, with the vertex letter in the middle.
2. Using only the vertex. This can only be used if it is the only angle with that vertex.
3. Using a number that is written inside the angle.

The angle below can be written ∠*ABC* (read angle *ABC*), ∠*CBA*, ∠*B*, or ∠1.

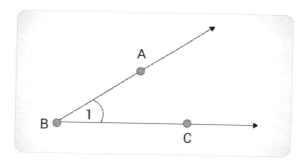

An angle divides a plane, or flat surface, into three parts: the angle itself, the interior (inside) of the angle, and the exterior (outside) of the angle. The figure below shows point *M* on the interior of the angle and point *N* on the exterior of the angle.

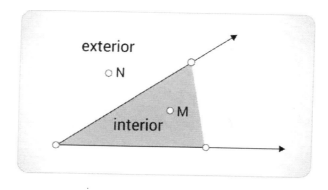

Angles can be measured in units called degrees, with the symbol °. The degree measure of an angle is between 0° and 180° and can be obtained by using a protractor.

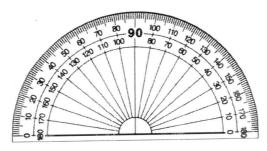

A straight angle (or simply a line) measures exactly 180°. A right angle's sides meet at the vertex to create a square corner. A right-angle measures exactly 90° and is typically indicated by a box drawn in the interior of the angle. An acute angle has an interior that is narrower than a right angle. The measure of an acute angle is any value less than 90° and greater than 0°. For example, 89.9°, 47°, 12°, and 1°. An obtuse angle has an interior that is wider than a right angle. The measure of an obtuse angle is any value greater than 90° but less than 180°. For example, 90.1°, 110°, 150°, and 179.9°.

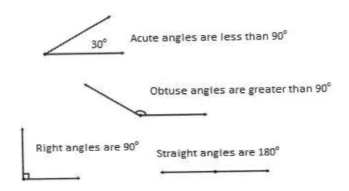

Solving Line Problems

As mentioned, two lines are parallel if they have the same slope. Two lines are perpendicular if the product of their slope equals -1. Parallel lines never intersect unless they are the same line, and perpendicular lines intersect at a right angle. If two lines aren't parallel, they must intersect at one point. Determining equations of lines based on properties of parallel and perpendicular lines appears in word problems. To find an equation of a line, both the slope and a point the line goes through are necessary. Therefore, if an equation of a line is needed that's parallel to a given line and runs through a specified point, the slope of the given line and the point are plugged into the point-slope form of an equation of a line. Secondly, if an equation of a line is needed that's perpendicular to a given line running through a specified point, the negative reciprocal of the slope of the given line and the point are plugged into the point-slope form. Also, if the point of intersection of two lines is known, that point will be used to solve the set of equations. Therefore, to solve a system of equations, the point of intersection must be found. If a set of two equations with two unknown variables has no solution, the lines are parallel.

Solving Problems with Parallel and Perpendicular Lines

Two lines can be parallel, perpendicular, or neither. If two lines are parallel, they have the same slope. This is proven using the idea of similar triangles. Consider the following diagram with two parallel lines, L1 and L2:

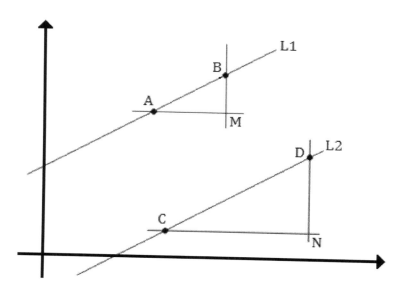

A and B are points on L1, and C and D are points on L2. Right triangles are formed with vertex M and N where lines BM and DN are parallel to the y-axis and AM and CN are parallel to the x-axis. Because all three sets of lines are parallel, the triangles are similar. Therefore, $\frac{BM}{DN} = \frac{MA}{NC}$. This shows that the rise/run is equal for lines L1 and L2. Hence, their slopes are equal.

Secondly, if two lines are perpendicular, the product of their slopes equals -1. This means that their slopes are negative reciprocals of each other. Consider two perpendicular lines, *l* and *n*:

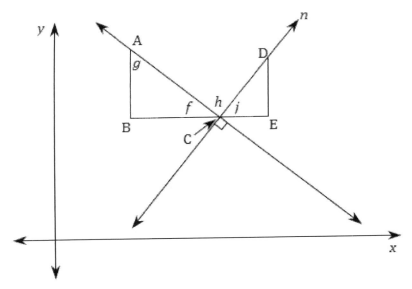

Right triangles ABC and CDE are formed so that lines BC and CE are parallel to the *x*-axis, and AB and DE are parallel to the *y*-axis. Because line BE is a straight line, angles $f + h + i = 180 \ degrees$. However, angle *h* is a right angle, so $f + j = 90 \ degrees$. By construction, $f + g = 90$, which means that $g = j$. Therefore, because angles $B = E$ and $g = j$, the triangles are similar and $\frac{AB}{BC} = \frac{CE}{DE}$. Because slope is equal to rise/run, the slope of line *l* is $-\frac{AB}{BC}$ and the slope of line *n* is $\frac{DE}{CE}$. Multiplying the slopes together gives $-\frac{AB}{BC} \cdot \frac{DE}{CE} = -\frac{CE}{DE} \cdot \frac{DE}{CE} = -1$. This proves that the product of the slopes of two perpendicular lines equals -1. Both parallel and perpendicular lines can be integral in many geometric proofs, so knowing and understanding their properties is crucial for problem-solving.

Effects of Changes to Dimensions on Area and Volume

Similar polygons are figures that are the same shape but different sizes. Likewise, similar solids are different sizes but are the same shape. In both cases, corresponding angles in the same positions for both figures are congruent (equal), and corresponding sides are proportional in length. For example, the triangles below are similar. The following pairs of corresponding angles are congruent: ∠A and ∠D; ∠B and $\angle E$; $\angle C$ and $\angle F$. The corresponding sides are proportional: $\frac{AB}{DE} = \frac{6}{3} = 2, \frac{BC}{EF} = \frac{9}{4.5} = 2, \frac{CA}{FD} = \frac{10}{5} = 2$. In other words, triangle *ABC* is the same shape but twice as large as triangle *DEF*.

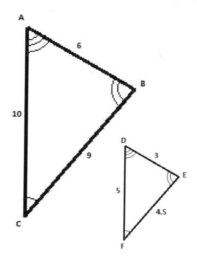

An example of similar triangular pyramids is shown below.

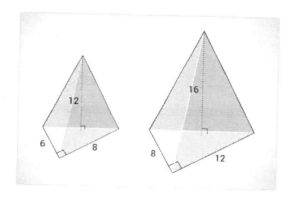

Given the nature of two- and three-dimensional measurements, changing dimensions by a given scale (multiplier) does not change the area of volume by the same scale. Consider a rectangle with a length of 5 centimeters and a width of 4 centimeters. The area of the rectangle is $20cm^2$. Doubling the dimensions of the rectangle (multiplying by a scale factor of 2) to 10 centimeters and 8 centimeters *does not* double the area to $40cm^2$. Area is a two-dimensional measurement (measured in square units). Therefore, the dimensions are multiplied by a scale that is squared (raised to the second power) to determine the scale of the corresponding areas. For the previous example, the length and width are multiplied by 2. Therefore, the area is multiplied by 2^2, or 4. The area of a 5cm × 4cm rectangle is $20cm^2$. The area of a 10cm × 8cm rectangle is $80cm^2$.

Volume is a three-dimensional measurement, which is measured in cubic units. Therefore, the scale between dimensions of similar solids is cubed (raised to the third power) to determine the scale between their volumes. Consider similar right rectangular prisms: one with a length of 8 inches, a width of 24 inches, and a height of 16 inches; the second with a length of 4 inches, a width of 12 inches, and a height of 8 inches. The first prism, multiplied by a scalar of $\frac{1}{2}$, produces the measurement of the second prism. The volume of the first prism, multiplied by $(\frac{1}{2})^3$, which equals $\frac{1}{8}$, produces the volume of the second prism. The volume of the first prism is 8in × 24in × 16in which equals $3,072in^3$. The volume of the second prism is 4in × 12in × 8in which equals $384in^3$ ($3,072in^3 \times \frac{1}{8} = 384in^3$).

The rules for squaring the scalar for area and cubing the scalar for volume only hold true for similar figures. In other words, if only one dimension is changed (changing the width of a rectangle but not the length) or dimensions are changed at different rates (the length of a prism is doubled and its height is tripled) the figures are not similar (same shape). Therefore, the rules above do not apply.

Trigonometric Ratios in Right Triangles

Trigonometric Functions
Within similar triangles, corresponding sides are proportional and angles are congruent. In addition, within similar triangles, the ratio of the side lengths is the same. This property is true even if side lengths are different. Within right triangles, trigonometric ratios can be defined for the acute angle within the triangle. The functions are defined through ratios in a right triangle. Sine of acute angle, A, is opposite over hypotenuse, cosine is adjacent over hypotenuse, and tangent is opposite over adjacent. Note that expanding or shrinking the triangle won't change the ratios. However, changing the angle measurements will alter the calculations.

Complementary Angles
Angles that add up to 90 degrees are *complementary*. Within a right triangle, two complementary angles exist because the third angle is always 90 degrees. In this scenario, the *sine* of one of the complementary angles is equal to the *cosine* of the other angle. The opposite is also true. This relationship exists because sine and cosine will be calculated as the ratios of the same side lengths.

The Pythagorean Theorem
The *Pythagorean theorem* is an important relationship between the three sides of a right triangle. It states that the square of the side opposite the right triangle, known as the *hypotenuse* (denoted as c^2), is equal to the sum of the squares of the other two sides ($a^2 + b^2$). Thus, $a^2 + b^2 = c^2$.

Both the trigonometric functions and the Pythagorean theorem can be used in problems that involve finding either a missing side or a missing angle of a right triangle. To do so, one must look to see what sides and angles are given and select the correct relationship that will help find the missing value. These relationships can also be used to solve application problems involving right triangles. Often, it's helpful to draw a figure to represent the problem to see what's missing.

Congruence and Similarity in Terms of Transformations

Rigid Motion
A *rigid motion* is a transformation that preserves distance and length. Every line segment in the resulting image is congruent to the corresponding line segment in the pre-image. Congruence between two figures means a series of transformations (or a rigid motion) can be defined that maps one of the figures onto the other. Basically, two figures are congruent if they have the same shape and size.

Dilation

A shape is dilated, or a *dilation* occurs, when each side of the original image is multiplied by a given scale factor. If the scale factor is less than 1 and greater than 0, the dilation contracts the shape and the resulting shape is smaller. If the scale factor equals 1, the resulting shape is the same size and the dilation is a rigid motion. Finally, if the scale factor is greater than 1, the resulting shape is larger and the dilation expands the shape. The *center of dilation* is the point where the distance from it to any point on the new shape equals the scale factor times the distance from the center to the corresponding point in the pre-image. Dilation isn't an isometric transformation because distance isn't preserved. However, angle measure, parallel lines, and points on a line all remain unchanged. This following figure is an example of translation, rotation, dilation, and reflection:

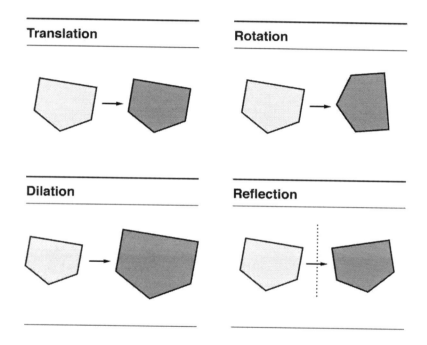

Determining Congruence

Two figures are congruent if there is a rigid motion that can map one figure onto the other. Therefore, all pairs of sides and angles within the image and pre-image must be congruent. For example, in triangles, each pair of the three sides and three angles must be congruent. Similarly, in two four-sided figures, each pair of the four sides and four angles must be congruent.

Similarity

Two figures are *similar* if there is a combination of translations, reflections, rotations, and dilations, which maps one figure onto the other. The difference between congruence and similarity is that dilation can be used in similarity. Therefore, side lengths between each shape can differ. However, angle measure must be preserved within this definition. If two polygons differ in size so that the lengths of corresponding line segments differ by the same factor, but corresponding angles have the same measurement, they are similar.

Triangle Congruence

There are five theorems to show that triangles are congruent when it's unknown whether each pair of angles and sides are congruent. Each theorem is a shortcut that involves different combinations of sides and angles that must be true for the two triangles to be congruent. For example, *side-side-side (SSS)* states that if all sides are equal, the triangles are congruent. *Side-angle-side (SAS)* states that if two pairs of sides are equal and the included angles are congruent, then the triangles are congruent. Similarly, *angle-side-angle (ASA)* states that if two pairs of angles are congruent and the included side lengths are equal, the triangles are similar. *Angle-angle-side (AAS)* states that two triangles are congruent if they have two pairs of congruent angles and a pair of corresponding equal side lengths that aren't included. Finally, *hypotenuse-leg (HL)* states that if two right triangles have equal hypotenuses and an equal pair of shorter sides, then the triangles are congruent. An important item to note is that angle-angle-angle *(AAA)* is not enough information to have congruence. It's important to understand why these rules work by using rigid motions to show congruence between the triangles with the given properties. For example, three reflections are needed to show why *SAS* follows from the definition of congruence.

Similarity for Two Triangles
If two angles of one triangle are congruent with two angles of a second triangle, the triangles are similar. This is because, within any triangle, the sum of the angle measurements is 180 degrees. Therefore, if two are congruent, the third angle must also be congruent because their measurements are equal. Three congruent pairs of angles mean that the triangles are similar.

Proving Congruence and Similarity
The criteria needed to prove triangles are congruent involves both angle and side congruence. Both pairs of related angles and sides need to be of the same measurement to use congruence in a proof. The criteria to prove similarity in triangles involves proportionality of side lengths. Angles must be congruent in similar triangles; however, corresponding side lengths only need to be a constant multiple of each other. Once similarity is established, it can be used in proofs as well. Relationships in geometric figures other than triangles can be proven using triangle congruence and similarity. If a similar or congruent triangle can be found within another type of geometric figure, their criteria can be used to prove a relationship about a given formula. For instance, a rectangle can be broken up into two congruent triangles.

Relationships between Angles
Supplementary angles add up to 180 degrees. *Vertical angles* are two nonadjacent angles formed by two intersecting lines. *Corresponding angles* are two angles in the same position whenever a straight line (known as a *transversal*) crosses two others. If the two lines are parallel, the corresponding angles are equal. *Alternate interior angles* are also a pair of angles formed when two lines are crossed by a transversal. They are opposite angles that exist inside of the two lines. In the corresponding angles diagram above, angles 2 and 7 are alternate interior angles, as well as angles 6 and 3. *Alternate exterior angles* are opposite angles formed by a transversal but, in contrast to interior angles, exterior angles exist outside the two original lines. Therefore, angles 1 and 8 are alternate exterior angles and so are angles 5 and 4. Finally, *consecutive interior angles* are pairs of angles formed by a transversal. These angles are located on the same side of the transversal and inside the two original lines. Therefore, angles 2 and 3 are a pair of consecutive interior angles, and so are angles 6 and 7. These definitions are instrumental in solving many problems that involve determining relationships between angles.

Medians, Midpoints, and Altitudes
A *median* of a triangle is the line drawn from a vertex to the midpoint on the opposite side. A triangle has three medians, and their point of intersection is known as the *centroid*. An *altitude* is a line drawn from a vertex perpendicular to the opposite side. A triangle has three altitudes, and their point of intersection is known as the *orthocenter*. An altitude can actually exist outside, inside, or on the triangle depending on the placement of the vertex. Many problems involve these definitions. For example, given

one endpoint of a line segment and the midpoint, the other endpoint can be determined by using the midpoint formula. In addition, area problems heavily depend on these definitions. For example, it can be proven that the median of a triangle divides it into two regions of equal areas. The actual formula for the area of a triangle depends on its altitude.

Special Triangles

An *isosceles triangle* contains at least two equal sides. Therefore, it must also contain two equal angles and, subsequently, contain two medians of the same length. An isosceles triangle can also be labelled as an *equilateral triangle* (which contains three equal sides and three equal angles) when it meets these conditions. In an equilateral triangle, the measure of each angle is always 60 degrees. Also within an equilateral triangle, the medians are of the same length. A *scalene triangle* can never be an equilateral or an isosceles triangle because it contains no equal sides and no equal angles. Also, medians in a scalene triangle can't have the same length. However, a *right triangle*, which is a triangle containing a 90-degree angle, can be a scalene triangle. There are two types of special right triangles. The *30-60-90 right triangle* has angle measurements of 30 degrees, 60 degrees, and 90 degrees. Because of the nature of this triangle, and through the use of the Pythagorean theorem, the side lengths have a special relationship. If x is the length opposite the 30-degree angle, the length opposite the 60-degree angle is $\sqrt{3}x$, and the hypotenuse has length $2x$. The *45-45-90 right triangle* is also special as it contains two angle measurements of 45 degrees. It can be proven that, if x is the length of the hypotenuse, the other two side lengths are $\sqrt{2}x/2$. The properties of all of these special triangles are extremely useful in determining both side lengths and angle measurements in problems where some of these quantities are given and some are not.

Special Quadrilaterals

A special quadrilateral is one in which both pairs of opposite sides are parallel. This type of quadrilateral is known as a *parallelogram*. A parallelogram has six important properties:

- Opposite sides are congruent.
- Opposite angles are congruent.
- Within a parallelogram, consecutive angles are supplementary, so their measurements total 180 degrees.
- If one angle is a right angle, all of them have to be right angles.
- The diagonals of the angles bisect each other.
- These diagonals form two congruent triangles.

A parallelogram with four congruent sides is a *rhombus*. A quadrilateral containing only one set of parallel sides is known as a *trapezoid*. The parallel sides are known as bases and the other two sides are known as legs. If the legs are congruent, the trapezoid can be labelled an *isosceles trapezoid*. An important property of a trapezoid is that their diagonals are congruent. Also, the median of a trapezoid is parallel to the bases, and its length is equal to half of the sum of the base lengths.

Quadrilateral Relationships

Rectangles, squares, and rhombuses are *polygons* with four sides. By definition, all rectangles are parallelograms, but only some rectangles are squares. However, some parallelograms are rectangles. Also, it's true that all squares are rectangles, and some rhombuses are squares. There are no rectangles, squares, or rhombuses that are trapezoids though, because they have more than one set of parallel sides.

Diagonals and Angles

Diagonals are lines (excluding sides) that connect two vertices within a polygon. *Mutually bisecting diagonals* intersect at their midpoints. Parallelograms, rectangles, squares, and rhombuses have mutually bisecting diagonals. However, trapezoids don't have such lines. *Perpendicular diagonals* occur when they form four right triangles at their point of intersection. Squares and rhombuses have perpendicular diagonals, but trapezoids, rectangles, and parallelograms do not. Finally, *perpendicular bisecting* diagonals (also known as *perpendicular bisectors*) form four right triangles at their point of intersection, but this intersection is also the midpoint of the two lines. Both rhombuses and squares have perpendicular bisecting angles, but trapezoids, rectangles, and parallelograms do not. Knowing these definitions can help tremendously in problems that involve both angles and diagonals.

Polygons with More Than Four Sides

A *pentagon* is a five-sided figure. A six-sided shape is a *hexagon*. A seven-sided figure is classified as a *heptagon*, and an eight-sided figure is called an *octagon*. An important characteristic is whether a polygon is regular or irregular. If it's *regular*, the side lengths and angle measurements are all equal. An *irregular* polygon has unequal side lengths and angle measurements. Mathematical problems involving polygons with more than four sides usually involve side length and angle measurements. The sum of all internal angles in a polygon equals $180(n-2)$ degrees, where n is the number of sides. Therefore, the total of all internal angles in a pentagon is 540 degrees because there are five sides so $180(5-2) = 540$ degrees. Unfortunately, area formulas don't exist for polygons with more than four sides. However, their shapes can be split up into triangles, and the formula for area of a triangle can be applied and totaled to obtain the area for the entire figure.

Congruency

Two figures are congruent if they have the same shape and same size. The two figures could have been rotated, reflected, or translated. Two figures are similar if they have been rotated, reflected, translated, and resized. Angle measure is preserved in similar figures. Both angle and side length are preserved in congruent figures.

Representational Systems

Three-Dimensional Figures with Nets

A net is a construction of two-dimensional figures that can be folded to form a given three-dimensional figure. More than one net may exist to fold and produce the same solid, or three-dimensional figure. The bases and faces of the solid figure are analyzed to determine the polygons (two-dimensional figures) needed to form the net.

Consider the following triangular prism:

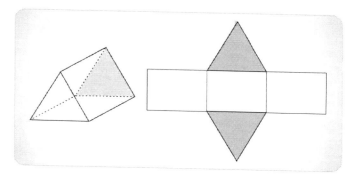

The surface of the prism consists of two triangular bases and three rectangular faces. The net beside it can be used to construct the triangular prism by first folding the triangles up to be parallel to each other, and then folding the two outside rectangles up and to the center with the outer edges touching.

Consider the following cylinder:

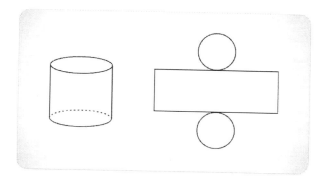

The surface consists of two circular bases and a curved lateral surface that can be opened and flattened into a rectangle. The net beside it can be used to construct the cylinder by first folding the circles up to be parallel to each other, and then curving the sides of the rectangle up to touch each other. The top and bottom of the folded rectangle should be touching the outside of both circles.

Consider the following square pyramid below on the left. The surface consists of one square base and four triangular faces. The net below on the right can be used to construct the square pyramid by folding each triangle towards the center of the square. The top points of the triangle meet at the vertex.

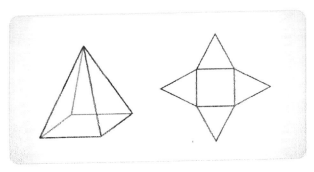

Simplifying Three-Dimensional Objects
Three-dimensional objects can be simplified into related two-dimensional shapes to solve problems. This simplification can make problem-solving a much easier experience. An isometric representation of a three-dimensional object can be completed so that important properties (e.g., shape, relationships of faces and surfaces) are noted. Edges and vertices can be translated into two-dimensional objects as well. For example, below is a three-dimensional object that's been partitioned into two-dimensional representations of its faces:

The net represents the sum of the three different faces. Depending on the problem, using a smaller portion of the given shape may be helpful, by simplifying the steps necessary to solve.

Visualizing Relationships Between Two-Dimensional and Three-Dimensional Objects

Cross-Sections and Nets of Three-Dimensional Shapes
One way to analyze a three-dimensional shape is to view its cross-sections in a two-dimensional plane. A cross-section is an intersection of the shape with a plane. Also, a three-dimensional shape can be represented in a two-dimensional plane by its net, which is an unfolded, flat representation of the all

sides of the shape. For example, a rectangular prism has cross sections that are squares and rectangles and the following figure shows its net:

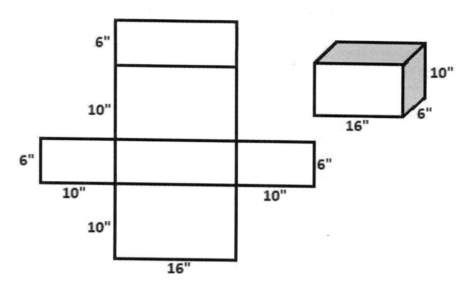

Cross Sections and Rotations

Two-dimensional objects are formed when three-dimensional objects are "sliced" in various ways. For example, any cross section of a sphere is a circle. Some three-dimensional objects have different cross sections depending on how the object is sliced. For example, the cross section of a cylinder can be a circle or a rectangle, and the cross section of a pyramid can be a square or a triangle. In addition, three-dimensional objects can be formed by rotating two-dimensional objects. Certain rotations can relate the two-dimensional cross sections back to the original three-dimensional objects. The objects must be rotated around an imaginary line known as the *rotation axis*. For example, a right triangle can be rotated around one of its legs to form a cone. A sphere can be formed by rotating a semicircle around a line segment formed from its diameter. Finally, rotating a square around one of its sides forms a cylinder.

Solving Problems in the Coordinate Plane

The location of a point on a coordinate grid is identified by writing it as an ordered pair. An ordered pair is a set of numbers indicating the *x*-and *y*-coordinates of the point. Ordered pairs are written in the form (*x*, *y*) where *x* and *y* are values which indicate their respective coordinates. For example, the point (3, -2) has an *x*-coordinate of 3 and a *y*-coordinate of -2.

Plotting a point on the coordinate plane with a given coordinate means starting from the origin (0, 0). To determine the value of the *x*-coordinate, move right (positive number) or left (negative number) along the *x*-axis. Next, move up (positive number) or down (negative number) to the value of the *y*-coordinate. Finally, plot and label the point. For example, plotting the point (1, -2) requires starting from the origin and moving right along the *x*-axis to positive one, then moving down until straight across from negative

2 on the *y*-axis. The point is plotted and labeled. This point, along with three other points, are plotted and labeled on the graph below.

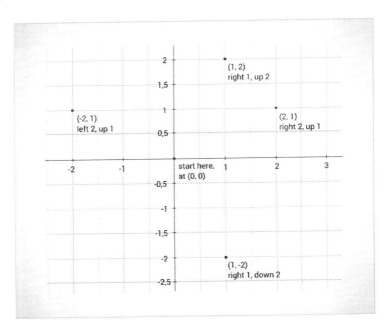

To write the coordinates of a point on the coordinate grid, a line should be traced directly above or below the point until reaching the *x*-axis (noting the value on the *x*-axis). Then, returning to the point, a line should be traced directly to the right or left of the point until reaching the *y*-axis (noting the value on the *y*-axis). The ordered pair (*x*, *y*) should be written with the values determined for the *x*- and *y*-coordinates.

Polygons can be drawn in the coordinate plane given the coordinates of their vertices. These coordinates can be used to determine the perimeter and area of the figure. Suppose triangle *RQP* has vertices located at the points: *R*(-2, 0), *Q*(2, 2), and *P*(2, 0). By plotting the points for the three vertices, the triangle can be constructed as follows:

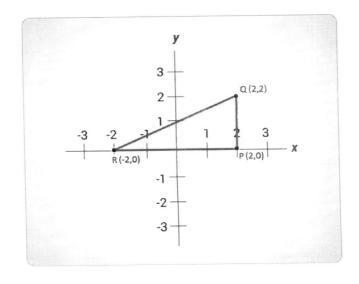

Because points R and P have the same y-coordinates (they are directly across from each other), the distance between them is determined by subtracting their x-coordinates (or simply counting units from one point to the other): 1– (-4) = 5. Therefore, the length of side RP is 5 units. Because points Q and P have the same x-coordinate (they are directly above and below each other), the distance between them is determined by subtracting their y-coordinates (or counting units between them): 6 – 2=4. Therefore, the length of side PQ is 4 units. Knowing the length of side RP, which is the base of the triangle, and the length of side PQ, which is the height of the triangle, the area of the figure can be determined by using the formula $A = \frac{1}{2}bh$.

To determine the perimeter of the triangle, the lengths of all three sides are needed. Points R and Q are neither directly across nor directly above and below each other. Therefore, the distance formula must be used to find the length of side RQ. The distance formula is as follows:

$$d = \sqrt{(x_2 - x_1)^2 + (y_2 - y_1)^2}$$

$$d = \sqrt{(1 - (-4))^2 + (6 - 2)^2}$$

$$d = \sqrt{(5)^2 + (4)^2}$$

$$d = \sqrt{25 + 16}$$

$$d = \sqrt{41}$$

The perimeter is determined by adding the lengths of the three sides of the triangle.

Techniques, Tools, and Formulas for Determining Measurements

Perimeter and Area

Perimeter is the measurement of a distance around something. Think of perimeter as the length of the boundary, like a fence. In contrast, area is the space occupied by a defined enclosure, like a field enclosed by a fence.

The perimeter of a polygon is the distance around the outside of the two-dimensional figure. Perimeter is a one-dimensional measurement and is therefore expressed in linear units such as centimeters (*cm*), feet (*ft.*), and miles (*mi*). The perimeter (*P*) of the figure below is calculated by: P = 9m + 5m + 4m + 6m + 8m → P = 32 m.

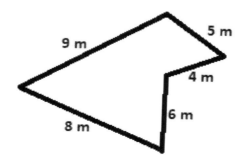

The perimeter of a square is measured by adding together all of the sides. Since a square has four equal sides, its perimeter can be calculated by multiplying the length of one side by 4. Thus, the formula is $P = 4 \times s$, where s equals one side. The area of a square is calculated by squaring the length of one side, which is expressed as the formula $A = s^2$.

Like a square, a rectangle's perimeter is measured by adding together all of the sides. But as the sides are unequal, the formula is different. A rectangle has equal values for its lengths (long sides) and equal values for its widths (short sides), so the perimeter formula for a rectangle is $P = l + l + w + w = 2l + 2w$, where l equals length and w equals width. The area is found by multiplying the length by the width, so the formula is $A = l \times w$.

A triangle's perimeter is measured by adding together the three sides, so the formula is $P = a + b + c$, where a, b, and c are the values of the three sides. The area is calculated by multiplying the length of the base times the height times ½, so the formula is $A = \frac{1}{2} \times b \times h = \frac{bh}{2}$. The base is the bottom of the triangle, and the height is the distance from the base to the peak. If a problem asks to calculate the area of a triangle, it will provide the base and height.

A circle's perimeter—also known as its circumference—is measured by multiplying the diameter (the straight line measured from one end to the direct opposite end of the circle) by π, so the formula is $\pi \times d$. This is sometimes expressed by the formula $C = 2 \times \pi \times r$, where r is the radius of the circle. These formulas are equivalent, as the radius equals half of the diameter. The area of a circle is calculated through the formula $A = \pi \times r^2$. The test will indicate either to leave the answer with π attached or to calculate to the nearest decimal place, which means multiplying by 3.14 for π.

The perimeter of a parallelogram is measured by adding the lengths and widths together. Thus, the formula is the same as for a rectangle, $P = l + l + w + w = 2l + 2w$. However, the area formula differs from the rectangle. For a parallelogram, the area is calculated by multiplying the length by the height: $A = h \times l$

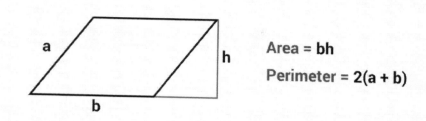

Area = bh

Perimeter = 2(a + b)

The perimeter of a trapezoid is calculated by adding the two unequal bases and two equal sides, so the formula is $P = a + b_1 + c + b_2$. Although unlikely to be a test question, the formula for the area of a trapezoid is $A = \frac{b_1 + b_2}{2} \times h$, where h equals height, and b_1 and b_2 equal the bases.

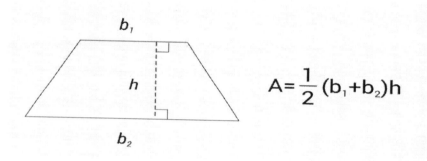

$$A = \frac{1}{2}(b_1 + b_2)h$$

Irregular Shapes

The perimeter of an irregular polygon is found by adding the lengths of all of the sides. In cases where all of the sides are given, this will be very straightforward, as it will simply involve finding the sum of the provided lengths. Other times, a side length may be missing and must be determined before the perimeter can be calculated. Consider the example below:

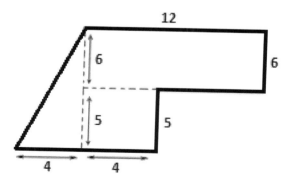

All of the side lengths are provided except for the angled side on the left. Test takers should notice that this is the hypotenuse of a right triangle. The other two sides of the triangle are provided (the base is 4

and the height is 6 + 5 = 11). The Pythagorean Theorem can be used to find the length of the hypotenuse, remembering that $a^2 + b^2 = c^2$.

Substituting the side values provided yields $(4)^2 + (11)^2 = c^2$.

Therefore, $c = \sqrt{16 + 121} = 11.7$

Finally, the perimeter can be found by adding this new side length with the other provided lengths to get the total length around the figure: 4 + 4 + 5 + 6 + 12 + 11.7 = 42.7. Although units are not provided in this figure, remember that reporting units with a measurement is important.

The area of an irregular polygon is found by decomposing, or breaking apart, the figure into smaller shapes. When the area of the smaller shapes is determined, these areas are added together to produce the total area of the area of the original figure. Consider the same example provided before:

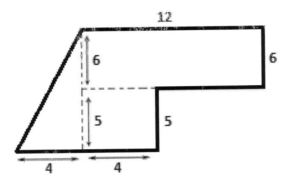

The irregular polygon is decomposed into two rectangles and a triangle. The area of the large rectangles ($A = l \times w \rightarrow A = 12 \times 6$) is 72 square units. The area of the small rectangle is 20 square units ($A = 4 \times 5$). The area of the triangle ($A = \frac{1}{2} \times b \times h \rightarrow A = \frac{1}{2} \times 4 \times 11$) is 22 square units. The sum of the areas of these figures produces the total area of the original polygon: $A = 72 + 20 + 22 \rightarrow A = 114$ square units.

Surface Area of Three-Dimensional Figures

The area of a two-dimensional figure refers to the number of square units needed to cover the interior region of the figure. This concept is similar to wallpaper covering the flat surface of a wall. For example, if a rectangle has an area of 21 square centimeters (written $21cm^2$), it will take 21 squares, each with sides one centimeter in length, to cover the interior region of the rectangle. Note that area is measured in square units such as: square feet or ft^2; square yards or yd^2; square miles or mi^2.

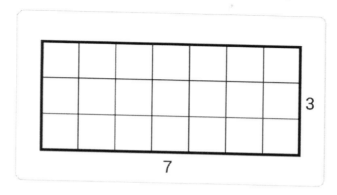

The surface area of a three-dimensional figure refers to the number of square units needed to cover the entire surface of the figure. This concept is similar to using wrapping paper to completely cover the outside of a box. For example, if a triangular pyramid has a surface area of 17 square inches (written $17in^2$), it will take 17 squares, each with sides one inch in length, to cover the entire surface of the pyramid. Surface area is also measured in square units.

Many three-dimensional figures (solid figures) can be represented by nets consisting of rectangles and triangles. The surface area of such solids can be determined by adding the areas of each of its faces and bases. Finding the surface area using this method requires calculating the areas of rectangles and triangles. To find the area (A) of a rectangle, the length (l) is multiplied by the width (w) → $A = l \times w$. The area of a rectangle with a length of 8cm and a width of 4cm is calculated: $A = (8cm) \times (4cm) →$ $A = 32cm^2$.

To calculate the area (A) of a triangle, the product of $\frac{1}{2}$, the base (b), and the height (h) is found → $A = \frac{1}{2} \times b \times h$. Note that the height of a triangle is measured from the base to the vertex opposite of it forming a right angle with the base. The area of a triangle with a base of 11cm and a height of 6cm is calculated: $A = \frac{1}{2} \times (11cm) \times (6cm) → A = 33cm^2$.

Consider the following triangular prism, which is represented by a net consisting of two triangles and three rectangles.

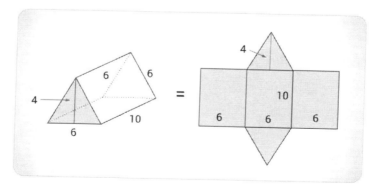

315

The surface area of the prism can be determined by adding the areas of each of its faces and bases. The surface area (*SA*) = area of triangle + area of triangle + area of rectangle + area of rectangle + area of rectangle.

$$SA = \left(\frac{1}{2} \times b \times h\right) + \left(\frac{1}{2} \times b \times h\right) + (l \times w) + (l \times w) + (l \times w)$$

$$SA = \left(\frac{1}{2} \times 6 \times 4\right) + \left(\frac{1}{2} \times 6 \times 4\right) + (6 \times 10) + (6 \times 10) + (6 \times 10)$$

$$SA = (12) + (12) + (60) + (60) + (60)$$

$$SA = 204 \text{square units}$$

Circles

Circle Angles

The *radius* of a circle is the distance from the center of the circle to any point on the circle. A *chord* of a circle is a straight line formed when its endpoints are allowed to be any two points on the circle. Many angles exist within a circle. A *central angle* is formed by using two radii as its rays and the center of the circle as its vertex. An inscribed angle is formed by using two chords as its rays, and its vertex is a point on the circle itself. Finally, a *circumscribed angle* has a vertex that is a point outside the circle and rays that intersect with the circle. Some relationships exist between these types of angles, and, in order to define these relationships, arc measure must be understood. An *arc* of a circle is a portion of the circumference. Finding the *arc measure* is the same as finding the degree measure of the central angle that intersects the circle to form the arc. The measure of an inscribed angle is half the measure of its intercepted arc. It's also true that the measure of a circumscribed angle is equal to 180 degrees minus the measure of the central angle that forms the arc in the angle.

Quadrilateral Angles

If a quadrilateral is inscribed in a circle, the sum of its opposite angles is 180 degrees. Consider the quadrilateral ABCD centered at the point O:

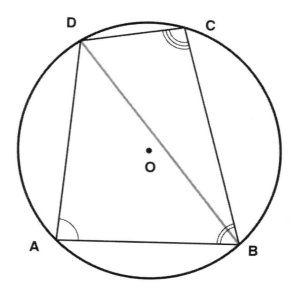

Each of the four line segments within the quadrilateral is a chord of the circle. Consider the diagonal DB. Angle DAB is an inscribed angle leaning on the arc DCB. Therefore, angle DAB is half the measure of the arc DCB. Conversely, angle DCB is an inscribed angle leaning on the arc DAB. Therefore, angle DCB is half the measure of the arc DAB. The sum of arcs DCB and DAB is 360 degrees because they make up the entire circle. Therefore, the sum of angles DAB and DCB equals half of 360 degrees, which is 180 degrees.

Circle Lines

A *tangent line* is a line that touches a curve at a single point without going through it. A *compass* and a *straightedge* are the tools necessary to construct a tangent line from a point *P* outside the circle to the circle. A tangent line is constructed by drawing a line segment from the center of the circle *O* to the point *P*, and then finding its midpoint *M* by bisecting the line segment. By using *M* as the center, a compass is used to draw a circle through points *O* and *P*. *N* is defined as the intersection of the two circles. Finally, a line segment is drawn through *P* and *N*. This is the tangent line. Each point on a circle has only one tangent line, which is perpendicular to the radius at that point. A line similar to a tangent line is a *secant line.* Instead of intersecting the circle at one point, a secant line intersects the circle at two points. A *chord* is a smaller portion of a secant line.

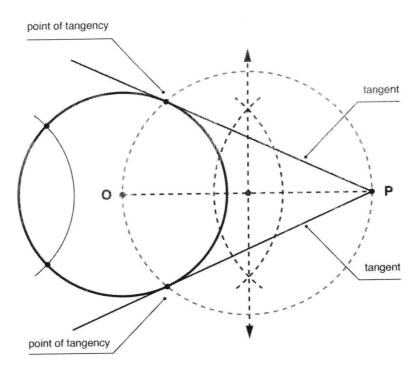

Applying Geometric Concepts to Real-World Situations

Real-World Geometry
Many real-world objects can be compared to geometric shapes. Describing certain objects using the measurements and properties of two- and three-dimensional shapes is an important part of geometry. For example, basic ideas such as angles and line segments can be seen in real-world objects. The corner of any room is an angle, and the intersection of a wall with the floor is like a line segment. Building upon this idea, entire objects can be related to both two- and three-dimensional shapes. An entire room can be thought of as square, rectangle, or a sum of a few three-dimensional shapes. Knowing what properties and measures are needed to make decisions in real life is why geometry is such a useful branch of mathematics. One obvious relationship between a real-life situation and geometry exists in construction. For example, to build an addition onto a house, several geometric measurements will be used.

Density
The *density* of a substance is the ratio of mass to area or volume. It's a relationship between the mass and how much space the object actually takes up. Knowing which units to use in each situation is crucial. Population density is an example of a real-life situation that's modeled by using density concepts. It involves calculating the ratio of the number of people to the number of square miles. The amount of material needed per a specific unit of area or volume is another application. For example, estimating the number of BTUs per cubic foot of a home is a measurement that relates to heating or cooling the house based on the desired temperature and the house's size.

<u>Solving Design Problem</u>

Design problems are an important application of geometry (e.g., building structures that satisfy physical constraints and/or minimize costs). These problems involve optimizing a situation based on what's given and required. For example, determining what size barn to build, given certain dimensions and a specific budget, uses both geometric properties and other mathematical concepts. Equations are formed using geometric definitions and the given constraints. In the end, such problems involve solving a system of equations and rely heavily on a strong background in algebra. *Typographic grid systems* also help with such design problems. A grid made up of intersecting straight or curved lines can be used as a visual representation of the structure being designed. This concept is seen in the blueprints used throughout the graphic design process.

Converting Within and Between Standard and Metric Systems

<u>American Measuring System</u>

The measuring system used today in the United States developed from of the British units of measurement during colonial times. The most typically used units in this customary system are those used to measure weight, liquid volume, and length, whose common units are found below. In the customary system, the basic unit for measuring weight is the ounce (oz); there are 16 ounces (oz) in 1 pound (lb) and 2000 pounds in 1 ton. The basic unit for measuring liquid volume is the ounce (oz); 1 ounce is equal to 2 tablespoons (tbsp) or 6 teaspoons (tsp), and there are 8 ounces in 1 cup, 2 cups in 1 pint (pt), 2 pints in 1 quart (qt), and 4 quarts in 1 gallon (gal). For measurements of length, the inch (in) is the base unit; 12 inches make up 1 foot (ft), 3 feet make up 1 yard (yd), and 5280 feet make up 1 mile (mi). However, as there are only a set amount of units in the customary system, with extremely large or extremely small amounts of material, the numbers can become awkward and difficult to compare.

Common Customary Measurements		
Length	**Weight**	**Capacity**
1 foot = 12 inches	1 pound = 16 ounces	1 cup = 8 fluid ounces
1 yard = 3 feet	1 ton = 2,000 pounds	1 pint = 2 cups
1 yard = 36 inches		1 quart = 2 pints
1 mile = 1,760 yards		1 quart = 4 cups
1 mile = 5,280 feet		1 gallon = 4 quarts
		1 gallon = 16 cups

<u>Metric System</u>

Aside from the United States, most countries in the world have adopted the metric system embodied in the International System of Units (SI). The three main SI base units used in the metric system are the meter (m), the kilogram (kg), and the liter (L); meters measure length, kilograms measure mass, and liters measure volume.

These three units can use different prefixes, which indicate larger or smaller versions of the unit by powers of ten. This can be thought of as making a new unit which is sized by multiplying the original unit in size by a factor.

These prefixes and associated factors are:

Metric Prefixes			
Prefix	Symbol	Multiplier	Exponential
kilo	k	1,000	10^3
hecto	h	100	10^2
deca	da	10	10^1
no prefix		1	10^0
deci	d	0.1	10^{-1}
centi	c	0.01	10^{-2}
milli	m	0.001	10^{-3}

The correct prefix is then attached to the base. Some examples:

1 milliliter equals .001 liters.

1 kilogram equals 1,000 grams.

Choosing the Appropriate Measuring Unit
Some units of measure are represented as square or cubic units depending on the solution. For example, perimeter is measured in units, area is measured in square units, and volume is measured in cubic units.

Also be sure to use the most appropriate unit for the thing being measured. A building's height might be measured in feet or meters while the length of a nail might be measured in inches or centimeters. Additionally, for SI units, the prefix should be chosen to provide the most succinct available value. For example, the mass of a bag of fruit would likely be measured in kilograms rather than grams or milligrams, and the length of a bacteria cell would likely be measured in micrometers rather than centimeters or kilometers.

Conversion
Converting measurements in different units between the two systems can be difficult because they follow different rules. The best method is to look up an English to Metric system conversion factor and then use a series of equivalent fractions to set up an equation to convert the units of one of the

measurements into those of the other. The table below lists some common conversion values that are useful for problems involving measurements with units in both systems:

English System	Metric System
1 inch	2.54 cm
1 foot	0.3048 m
1 yard	0.914 m
1 mile	1.609 km
1 ounce	28.35 g
1 pound	0.454 kg
1 fluid ounce	29.574 mL
1 quart	0.946 L
1 gallon	3.785 L

Consider the example where a scientist wants to convert 6.8 inches to centimeters. The table above is used to find that there are 2.54 centimeters in every inch, so the following equation should be set up and solved: $6.8 \; in \; \times \; \frac{2.54 \; cm}{1 \; in} = 17.272 \; cm$. Notice how the inches in the numerator of the initial figure and the denominator of the conversion factor cancel out. (This equation could have been written simply as $6.8 \; in \; \times \; 2.54 \; cm = 17.272 \; cm$, but it was shown in detail to illustrate the steps). The goal in any conversion equation is to set up the fractions so that the units you are trying to convert from cancel out and the units you desire remain.

For a more complicated example, consider converting 2.15 kilograms into ounces. The first step is to convert kilograms into grams and then grams into ounces:

$$2.15 \; kg \; \times \frac{1000 g}{kg} = 2150 \; g$$

Then, use the conversion factor from the table to convert grams to ounces:

$$2150 g \; \times \; \frac{1 \; oz}{28.35 g} = 75.8 \; oz$$

Statistics, Data Analysis, and Probability

Collection, Organization, and Representation of Data

Interpreting Displays of Data

A set of data can be visually displayed in various forms allowing for quick identification of characteristics of the set. Histograms, such as the one shown below, display the number of data points (vertical axis) that fall into given intervals (horizontal axis) across the range of the set. The histogram below displays the heights of black cherry trees in a certain city park. Each rectangle represents the number of trees with heights between a given five-point span. For example, the furthest bar to the right indicates that two trees are between 85 and 90 feet. Histograms can describe the center, spread, shape, and any unusual characteristics of a data set.

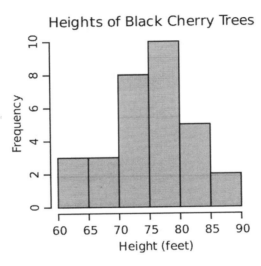

A box plot, also called a box-and-whisker plot, divides the data points into four groups and displays the five-number summary for the set, as well as any outliers. The five-number summary consists of:

- The lower extreme: the lowest value that is not an outlier
- The higher extreme: the highest value that is not an outlier
- The median of the set: also referred to as the second quartile or Q_2
- The first quartile or Q_1: the median of values below Q_2
- The third quartile or Q_3: the median of values above Q_2

To construct a box (or box-and-whisker) plot, the five-number summary for the data set is calculated as follows: the second quartile (Q_2) is the median of the set. The first quartile (Q_1) is the median of the values below Q_2. The third quartile (Q_3) is the median of the values above Q_2. The upper extreme is the highest value in the data set if it is not an outlier (greater than 1.5 times the interquartile range $Q_3 - Q_1$). The lower extreme is the least value in the data set if it is not an outlier (more than 1.5 times lower than the interquartile range). To construct the box-and-whisker plot, each value is plotted on a number line, along with any outliers. The box consists of Q_1 and Q_3 as its top and bottom and Q_2 as the dividing line inside the box. The whiskers extend from the lower extreme to Q_1 and from Q_3 to the upper extreme.

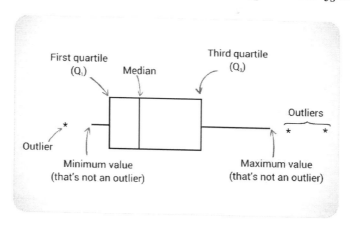

Suppose the box plot displays IQ scores for 12th grade students at a given school. The five-number summary of the data consists of: lower extreme (67); upper extreme (127); Q_2 or median (100); Q_1 (91); Q_3 (108); and outliers (135 and 140). Although all data points are not known from the plot, the points are divided into four quartiles each, including 25% of the data points. Therefore, 25% of students scored between 67 and 91, 25% scored between 91 and 100, 25% scored between 100 and 108, and 25% scored between 108 and 127. These percentages include the normal values for the set and exclude the outliers. This information is useful when comparing a given score with the rest of the scores in the set.

A scatter plot is a mathematical diagram that visually displays the relationship or connection between two variables. The independent variable is placed on the x-axis, or horizontal axis, and the dependent variable is placed on the y-axis, or vertical axis. When visually examining the points on the graph, if the points model a linear relationship, or a line of best-fit can be drawn through the points with the points relatively close on either side, then a correlation exists. If the line of best-fit has a positive slope (rises from left to right), then the variables have a positive correlation. If the line of best-fit has a negative slope (falls from left to right), then the variables have a negative correlation. If a line of best-fit cannot be drawn, then no correlation exists. A positive or negative correlation can be categorized as strong or weak, depending on how closely the points are graphed around the line of best-fit.

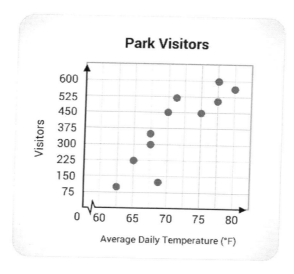

Graphical Representation of Data

Like a scatter plot, a line graph compares variables that change continuously, typically over time. Paired data values (ordered pair) are plotted on a coordinate grid with the *x*- and *y*-axis representing the variables. A line is drawn from each point to the next, going from left to right. The line graph below displays cell phone use for given years (two variables) for men, women, and both sexes (three data sets).

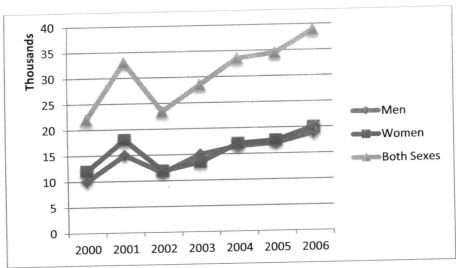

A line plot, also called dot plot, displays the frequency of data (numerical values) on a number line. To construct a line plot, a number line is used that includes all unique data values. It is marked with x's or dots above the value the number of times that the value occurs in the data set.

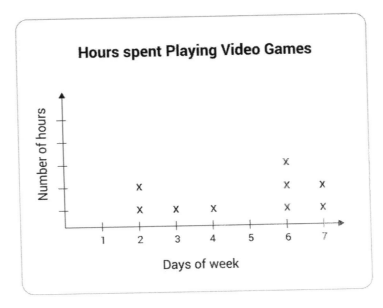

A *bar graph* is a diagram in which the quantity of items within a specific classification is represented by the height of a rectangle. Each type of classification is represented by a rectangle of equal width. Here is an example of a bar graph:

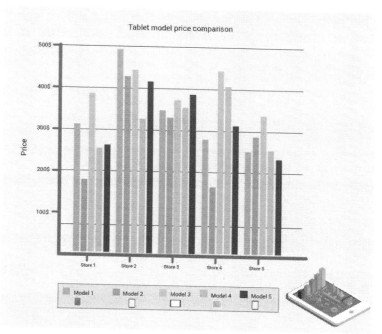

A circle graph, also called a pie chart, shows categorical data with each category representing a percentage of the whole data set. To make a circle graph, the percent of the data set for each category must be determined. To do so, the frequency of the category is divided by the total number of data points and converted to a percent. For example, if 80 people were asked what their favorite sport is and 20 responded basketball, basketball makes up 25% of the data ($\frac{20}{80} = .25 = 25\%$). Each category in a data set is represented by a *slice* of the circle proportionate to its percentage of the whole.

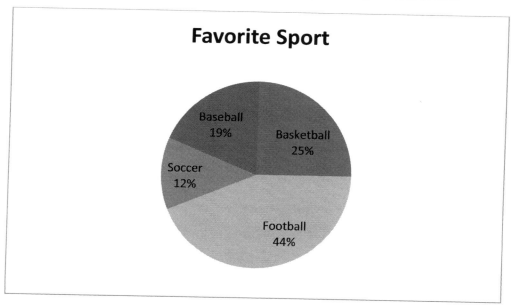

Choice of Graphs to Display Data

Choosing the appropriate graph to display a data set depends on what type of data is included in the set and what information must be displayed. Histograms and box plots can be used for data sets consisting of individual values across a wide range. Examples include test scores and incomes. Histograms and box plots will indicate the center, spread, range, and outliers of a data set. A histogram will show the shape of the data set, while a box plot will divide the set into quartiles (25% increments), allowing for comparison between a given value and the entire set.

Scatter plots and line graphs can be used to display data consisting of two variables. Examples include height and weight, or distance and time. A correlation between the variables is determined by examining the points on the graph. Line graphs are used if each value for one variable pairs with a distinct value for the other variable. Line graphs show relationships between variables.

Line plots, bar graphs, and circle graphs are all used to display categorical data, such as surveys. Line plots and bar graphs both indicate the frequency of each category within the data set. A line plot is used when the categories consist of numerical values. For example, the number of hours of TV watched by individuals is displayed on a line plot. A bar graph is used when the categories consists of words. For example, the favorite ice cream of individuals is displayed with a bar graph. A circle graph can be used to display either type of categorical data. However, unlike line plots and bar graphs, a circle graph does not indicate the frequency of each category. Instead, the circle graph represents each category as its percentage of the whole data set.

Describing a Set of Data

A set of data can be described in terms of its center, spread, shape and any unusual features. The center of a data set can be measured by its mean, median, or mode. The spread of a data set refers to how far the data points are from the center (mean or median). The spread can be measured by the range or the quartiles and interquartile range. A data set with data points clustered around the center will have a small spread. A data set covering a wide range will have a large spread.

When a data set is displayed as a histogram or frequency distribution plot, the shape indicates if a sample is normally distributed, symmetrical, or has measures of skewness or kurtosis. When graphed, a data set with a normal distribution will resemble a bell curve.

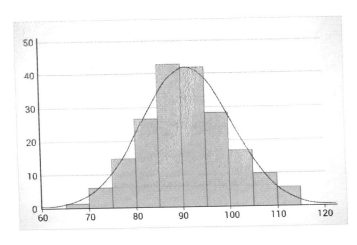

If the data set is symmetrical, each half of the graph when divided at the center is a mirror image of the other. If the graph has fewer data points to the right, the data is skewed right. If it has fewer data points to the left, the data is skewed left.

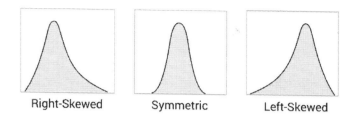

Right-Skewed   Symmetric   Left-Skewed

Kurtosis is a measure of whether the data is heavy-tailed with a high number of outliers, or light-tailed with a low number of outliers.

A description of a data set should include any unusual features such as gaps or outliers. A gap is a span within the range of the data set containing no data points. An outlier is a data point with a value either extremely large or extremely small when compared to the other values in the set.

Normal Distribution

A *normal distribution* of data follows the shape of a bell curve. In a normal distribution, the data set's median, mean, and mode are equal. Therefore, 50 percent of its values are less than the mean and 50 percent are greater than the mean. Data sets that follow this shape can be generalized using normal distributions. Normal distributions are described as *frequency distributions* in which the data set is plotted as percentages rather than true data points. A *relative frequency distribution* is one where the y-axis is between zero and 1, which is the same as 0% to 100%. Within a standard deviation, 68 percent of the values are within 1 standard deviation of the mean, 95 percent of the values are within 2 standard deviations of the mean, and 99.7 percent of the values are within 3 standard deviations of the mean. The number of standard deviations that a data point falls from the mean is called the *z-score*. The formula for the z-score is $Z = \frac{x - \mu}{\sigma}$, where μ is the mean, σ is the standard deviation, and x is the data point. This formula is used to fit any data set that resembles a normal distribution to a standard normal distribution, in a process known as *standardizing*. Here is a normal distribution with labelled z-scores:

Normal Distribution with Labelled Z-Scores

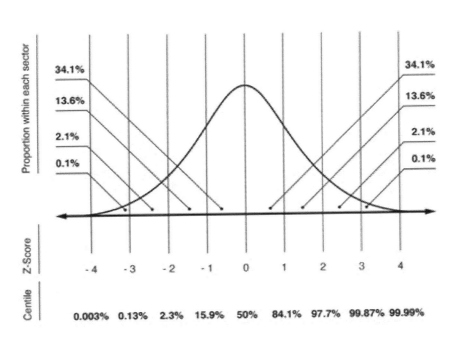

Population percentages can be estimated using normal distributions. For example, the probability that a data point will be less than the mean, or that the z-score will be less than 0, is 50%. Similarly, the probability that a data point will be within 1 standard deviation of the mean, or that the z-score will be between -1 and 1, is about 68.2%. When using a table, the left column states how many standard deviations (to one decimal place) away from the mean the point is, and the row heading states the second decimal place. The entries in the table corresponding to each column and row give the probability, which is equal to the area.

Measures of Center and Range

The center of a set of data (statistical values) can be represented by its mean, median, or mode. These are sometimes referred to as measures of central tendency. The mean is the average of the data set. The mean can be calculated by adding the data values and dividing by the sample size (the number of data points). Suppose a student has test scores of 93, 84, 88, 72, 91, and 77. To find the mean, or average, the scores are added and the sum is divided by 6 because there are 6 test scores:

$\frac{93+84+88+72+91+77}{6} = \frac{505}{6} = 84.17.$

Given the mean of a data set and the sum of the data points, the sample size can be determined by dividing the sum by the mean. Suppose you are told that Kate averaged 12 points per game and scored a total of 156 points for the season. The number of games that she played (the sample size or the number of data points) can be determined by dividing the total points (sum of data points) by her average (mean of data points): $\frac{156}{12} = 13$. Therefore, Kate played in 13 games this season.

If given the mean of a data set and the sample size, the sum of the data points can be determined by multiplying the mean and sample size. Suppose you are told that Tom worked 6 days last week for an average of 5.5 hours per day. The total number of hours worked for the week (sum of data points) can be determined by multiplying his daily average (mean of data points) by the number of days worked (sample size): $5.5 \times 6 = 33$. Therefore, Tom worked a total of 33 hours last week.

The median of a data set is the value of the data point in the middle when the sample is arranged in numerical order. To find the median of a data set, the values are written in order from least to greatest. The lowest and highest values are simultaneously eliminated, repeating until the value in the middle remains. Suppose the salaries of math teachers are: $35,000; $38,500; $41,000; $42,000; $42,000; $44,500; $49,000. The values are listed from least to greatest to find the median. The lowest and highest values are eliminated until only the middle value remains. Repeating this step three times reveals a median salary of $42,000. If the sample set has an even number of data points, two values will remain after all others are eliminated. In this case, the mean of the two middle values is the median. Consider the following data set: 7, 9, 10, 13, 14, 14. Eliminating the lowest and highest values twice leaves two values, 10 and 13, in the middle. The mean of these values $\left(\frac{10+13}{2}\right)$ is the median. Therefore, the set has a median of 11.5.

The mode of a data set is the value that appears most often. A data set may have a single mode, multiple modes, or no mode. If different values repeat equally as often, multiple modes exist. If no value repeats, no mode exists. Consider the following data sets:

- A: 7, 9, 10, 13, 14, 14
- B: 37, 44, 33, 37, 49, 44, 51, 34, 37, 33, 44
- C: 173, 154, 151, 168, 155

Set A has a mode of 14. Set B has modes of 37 and 44. Set C has no mode.

The range of a data set is the difference between the highest and the lowest values in the set. The range can be considered the span of the data set. To determine the range, the smallest value in the set is subtracted from the largest value. The ranges for the data sets A, B, and C above are calculated as follows: A: $14 - 7 = 7$; B: $51 - 33 = 18$; C: $173 - 151 = 22$.

Best Description of a Set of Data

Measures of central tendency, namely mean, median, and mode, describe characteristics of a set of data. Specifically, they are intended to represent a *typical* value in the set by identifying a central position of the set. Depending on the characteristics of a specific set of data, different measures of central tendency are more indicative of a typical value in the set.

When a data set is grouped closely together with a relatively small range and the data is spread out somewhat evenly, the mean is an effective indicator of a typical value in the set. Consider the following data set representing the height of sixth grade boys in inches: 61 inches, 54 inches, 58 inches, 63 inches, 58 inches. The mean of the set is 58.8 inches. The data set is grouped closely (the range is only 9 inches) and the values are spread relatively evenly (three values below the mean and two values above the mean). Therefore, the mean value of 58.8 inches is an effective measure of central tendency in this case.

When a data set contains a small number of values either extremely large or extremely small when compared to the other values, the mean is not an effective measure of central tendency. Consider the following data set representing annual incomes of homeowners on a given street: $71,000; $74,000; $75,000; $77,000; $340,000. The mean of this set is $127,400. This figure does not indicate a typical value in the set, which contains four out of five values between $71,000 and $77,000. The median is a much more effective measure of central tendency for data sets such as these. Finding the middle value diminishes the influence of outliers, or numbers that may appear out of place, like the $340,000 annual income. The median for this set is $75,000 which is much more typical of a value in the set.

The mode of a data set is a useful measure of central tendency for categorical data when each piece of data is an option from a category. Consider a survey of 31 commuters asking how they get to work with results summarized below.

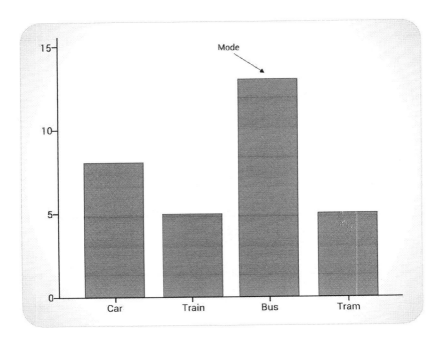

The mode for this set represents the value, or option, of the data that repeats most often. This indicates that the bus is the most popular method of transportation for the commuters.

Effects of Changes in Data
Changing all values of a data set in a consistent way produces predictable changes in the measures of the center and range of the set. A linear transformation changes the original value into the new value by either adding a given number to each value, multiplying each value by a given number, or both. Adding (or subtracting) a given value to each data point will increase (or decrease) the mean, median, and any modes by the same value. However, the range will remain the same due to the way that range is calculated. Multiplying (or dividing) a given value by each data point will increase (or decrease) the mean, median, and any modes, and the range by the same factor.

Consider the following data set, call it set P, representing the price of different cases of soda at a grocery store: $4.25, $4.40, $4.75, $4.95, $4.95, $5.15. The mean of set P is $4.74. The median is $4.85. The mode of the set is $4.95. The range is $0.90. Suppose the state passes a new tax of $0.25 on every case of soda sold. The new data set, set T, is calculated by adding $0.25 to each data point from set P.

330

Therefore, set T consists of the following values: $4.50, $4.65, $5.00, $5.20, $5.20, $5.40. The mean of set T is $4.99. The median is $5.10. The mode of the set is $5.20. The range is $.90. The mean, median and mode of set T is equal to $0.25 added to the mean, median, and mode of set P. The range stays the same.

Now suppose, due to inflation, the store raises the cost of every item by 10 percent. Raising costs by 10 percent is calculated by multiplying each value by 1.1. The new data set, set I, is calculated by multiplying each data point from set T by 1.1. Therefore, set I consists of the following values: $4.95, $5.12, $5.50, $5.72, $5.72, $5.94. The mean of set I is $5.49. The median is $5.61. The mode of the set is $5.72. The range is $0.99. The mean, median, mode, and range of set I is equal to 1.1 multiplied by the mean, median, mode, and range of set T because each increased by a factor of 10 percent.

Comparing Data

Data sets can be compared by looking at the center and spread of each set. Measures of central tendency involve median, mean, midrange, and mode. The *mode* of a data set is the data value or values that appears the most frequently. The *midrange* is equal to the maximum value plus the minimum value divided by two. The *median* is the value that is halfway into each data set; it splits the data into two intervals. The *mean* is the sum of all data values divided by the number of data points. Two completely different sets of data can have the same mean. For example, a data set having values ranging from 0 to 100 and a data set having values ranging from 44 to 46 could both have means equal to 50. The first data set would have a much wider range, which is known as the *spread* of the data. It measures how varied the data is within each set. Spread can be defined further as either interquartile range or standard deviation. The *interquartile range (IQR)* is the range of the middle fifty percent of the data set. The *standard deviation, s,* quantifies the amount of variation with respect to the mean. A lower standard deviation shows that the data set does not differ much from the mean. A larger standard deviation shows that the data set is spread out farther away from the mean. The formula for standard deviation is $s = \sqrt{\frac{\sum(x-\bar{x})^2}{n-1}}$, where x is each value in the data set, $\bar{x}$ is the mean, and n is the total number of data points in the sample set. The square of the standard deviation is known as the *variance* of the data set. A data set can have outliers, and measures of central tendency that are not affected by outliers are the mode and median. Those measures are labeled as resistant measures of center.

Inferences, Predictions, and Arguments Based on Data

Making Inferences and Justifying Conclusions from Samples, Experiments, and Observational Studies

Data Gathering Techniques

Statistics involves making decisions and predictions about larger sets of data based on smaller data sets. The information from a small subset can help predict what happens in the entire set. The smaller data set is called a *sample* and the larger data set for which the decision is being made is called a *population*. The three most common types of data gathering techniques are sample surveys, experiments, and observational studies. *Sample surveys* involve collecting data from a random sample of people from a desired population. The measurement of the variable is only performed on this set of people. To have accurate data, the sampling must be unbiased and random. For example, surveying students in an advanced calculus class on how much they enjoy math classes is not a useful sample if the population should be all college students based on the research question. There are many methods to form a random sample, and all adhere to the fact that every sample that could be chosen has a predetermined probability of being chosen. Once the sample is chosen, statistical experiments can then be carried out to investigate real-world problems.

An *experiment* is the method in which a hypothesis is tested using a trial-and-error process. A cause and the effect of that cause are measured, and the hypothesis is accepted or rejected. Experiments are usually completed in a controlled environment where the results of a control population are compared to the results of a test population. The groups are selected using a randomization process in which each group has a representative mix of the population being tested. Finally, an *observational study* is similar to an experiment. However, this design is used when there cannot be a designed control and test population because of circumstances (e.g., lack of funding or unrealistic expectations). Instead, existing control and test populations must be used, so this method has a lack of randomization.

Interpreting Statistical Information

To make decisions concerning populations, data must be collected from a sample. The sample must be large enough to be able to make conclusions. A common way to collect data is via surveys and polls. Every survey and poll must be designed so that there is no bias. An example of a biased survey is one with loaded questions, which are either intentionally worded or ordered to obtain a desired response. Once the data is obtained, conclusions should not be made that are not justified by statistical analysis. One must make sure the difference between correlation and causation is understood. Correlation implies there is an association between two variables, and correlation does not imply causation.

Population Mean and Proportion

Both the population mean and proportion can be calculated using data from a sample. The *population mean (μ)* is the average value of the parameter for the entire population. Due to size constraints, finding the exact value of μ is impossible, so the mean of the sample population is used as an estimate instead. The larger the sample size, the closer the sample mean gets to the population mean. An alternative to finding μ is to find the *proportion* of the population, which is the part of the population with the given characteristic. The proportion can be expressed as a decimal, a fraction, or a percentage, and can be given as a single value or a range of values. Because the population mean and proportion are both estimates, there's a *margin of error*, which is the difference between the actual value and the expected value.

T-Tests

A *randomized experiment* is used to compare two treatments by using statistics involving a *t-test,* which tests whether two data sets are significantly different from one another. To use a t-test, the test statistic must follow a normal distribution. The first step of the test involves calculating the *t* value, which is given as $t = \frac{\bar{x}_1 - \bar{x}_2}{s_{\bar{x}_1 - \bar{x}_2}}$, where $\bar{x}_1$ and $\bar{x}_2$ are the averages of the two samples. Also, $s_{\bar{x}_1 - \bar{x}_2} = \sqrt{\frac{s_1^2}{n_1} + \frac{s_2^2}{n_2}}$, where s_1 and s_2 are the standard deviations of each sample and n_1 and n_2 are their respective sample sizes. The *degrees of freedom* for two samples are calculated as $df = \frac{(n_1 - 1) + (n_2 - 1)}{2}$ rounded to the lowest whole number. Also, a significance level α must be chosen, where a typical value is $\alpha = 0.05$. Once everything is compiled, the decision is made to use either a *one-tailed test* or a *two-tailed test*. If there's an assumed difference between the two treatments, a one-tailed test is used. If no difference is assumed, a two-tailed test is used.

Analyzing Test Results

Once the type of test is determined, the t-value, significance level, and degrees of freedom are applied to the published table showing the *t* distribution. The row is associated with degrees of freedom and each column corresponds to the probability. The t-value can be exactly equal to one entry or lie between two entries in a row. For example, consider a t-value of 1.7 with degrees of freedom equal to 30. This *test statistic* falls between the p values of 0.05 and 0.025. For a one-tailed test, the corresponding p value lies between 0.05 and 0.025. For a two-tailed test, the p values need to be doubled so the corresponding p value falls between 0.1 and 0.05. Once the probability is known, this range is compared to α. If $p < \alpha$, the hypothesis is rejected. If $p > \alpha$, the hypothesis isn't rejected. In a two-tailed test, this scenario means the hypothesis is accepted that there's no difference in the two treatments. In a one-tailed test, the hypothesis is accepted, indicating that there's a difference in the two treatments.

Evaluating Completed Tests

In addition to applying statistical techniques to actual testing, evaluating completed tests is another important aspect of statistics. Reports can be read that already have conclusions, and the process can be evaluated using learned concepts. For example, deciding if a sample being used is appropriate. Other things that can be evaluated include determining if the samples are randomized or the results are significant. Once statistical concepts are understood, the knowledge can be applied to many applications.

Sample Statistics

A *point estimate* is a single value used to approximate a population parameter. The sample proportion is the best point estimate of the population proportion. It is used because it is an *unbiased estimator*, meaning that it is a statistic that targets the value of the population parameter by assuming the mean of the sampling distribution is equal to the mean of the population distribution. Other unbiased estimators include the mean and variance. *Biased estimators* do not target the value of the population parameter, and such values include median, range, and standard deviation. A *confidence interval* consists of a range of values that is utilized to approximate the true value of a population parameter. The *confidence level* is the probability that the confidence interval does contain the population parameter, assuming the estimation process is repeated many times.

Population Inferences Using Distributions

Samples are used to make inferences about a population. The sampling distribution of a sample mean is a distribution of all sample means for a fixed sample size, *n*, which is part of a population. Depending on different criteria, either a binomial, normal, or geometric distribution can be used to determine probabilities. A normal distribution uses a continuous random variable, and is bell-shaped and symmetric. A binomial distribution uses a discrete random variable, has a finite number of trials, and only has two possible outcomes: a success and a failure. A geometric distribution is very similar to a binomial distribution; however, the number of trials does not have to be finite.

Creating and Interpreting Linear Regression Models

Linear Regression

Regression lines are a way to calculate a relationship between the independent variable and the dependent variable. A straight line means that there's a linear trend in the data. The average daily temperature example above is one in which a straight line represents the data because the shape of the scatterplot resembles a straight line. Technology can be used to find the equation of this line (e.g., a graphing calculator or Microsoft Excel®). In either case, all of the data points are entered and a line is "fit" that best represents the shape of the data. Other functions used to model data sets include quadratic and exponential models.

Estimating Data Points

Regression lines can be used to estimate data points not already given. For example, if an equation of a line is found that fit the temperature and beach visitor data set, its input is the average daily temperature and its output is the projected number of visitors. Thus, the number of beach visitors on a 100-degree day can be estimated. The output is a data point on the regression line, and the number of daily visitors is expected to be greater than on a 96-degree day because the regression line has a positive slope.

Plotting and Analyzing Residuals

Once the function is found that fits the data, its accuracy can be calculated. Therefore, how well the line fits the data can be determined. The difference between the actual dependent variable from the data set and the estimated value located on the regression line is known as a *residual.* Therefore, the residual is known as the predicted value $\hat{y}$ minus the actual value y. A residual is calculated for each data point and can be plotted on the scatterplot. If all the residuals appear to be approximately the same distance from the regression line, the line is a good fit. If the residuals seem to differ greatly across the board, the line isn't a good fit.

Interpreting the Regression Line

The formula for a regression line is $y = mx + b$, where m is the slope and b is the y-intercept. Both the slope and y-intercept are found in the *Method of Least Squares*, which is the process of finding the equation of the line through minimizing residuals. The slope represents the rate of change in y as x gets larger. Therefore, because y is the dependent variable, the slope actually provides the predicted values given the independent variable. The y-intercept is the predicted value for when the independent variable equals zero. In the temperature example, the y-intercept is the expected number of beach visitors for a very cold average daily temperature of zero degrees.

Correlation Coefficient

The *correlation coefficient (r)* measures the association between two variables. Its value is between -1 and 1, where -1 represents a perfect negative linear relationship, 0 represents no relationship, and 1 represents a perfect positive linear relationship. A *negative linear relationship* means that as x values increase, y values decrease. A *positive linear relationship* means that as x values increase, y values increase. The formula for computing the correlation coefficient is $r = \dfrac{n\sum xy - (\sum x)(\sum y)}{\sqrt{n(\sum x^2) - (\sum x)^2}\sqrt{n(\sum y^2) - (y)^2}}$, where n is the number of data points. Both Microsoft Excel® and a graphing calculator can evaluate this easily once the data points are entered. A correlation greater than 0.8 or less than -0.8 is classified as "strong" while a correlation between -0.5 and 0.5 is classified as "weak."

Correlation Versus Causation

Correlation and causation have two different meanings. As stated previously, if two values are *correlated*, there is an association between them. However, correlation doesn't necessarily mean that one variable causes the other. *Causation*(or "cause and effect") occurs when one variable causes the other. Average daily temperature and number of beachgoers are correlated and have causation. If the temperature increases, the change in weather causes more people to go to the beach. However, alcoholism and smoking are correlated but don't have causation. The more someone drinks the more likely they are to smoke, but drinking alcohol doesn't cause someone to smoke.

Regression Models

Regression lines are straight lines that calculate a relationship between nonlinear data involving an independent variable and a dependent variable. A regression line is of the form $y = mx + b$, where m is the slope and b is the y-intercept. Both the slope and y-intercept are found using the *Method of Least Squares*, which involves minimizing residuals – the difference between the dependent variable from the data set and the estimated value located on the regression line. The slope represents the rate of change in y as x increases. The y-intercept is the predicted value when the independent variable is equal to 0. Technology, such as a graphing calculator or Microsoft Excel®, can also be utilized to find the equation of this line. In either case, the data points are entered and a line is "fit" that best represents the shape of the data.

Here is an example of a data set and its regression line:

The Regression Line is the Line of Best Fit

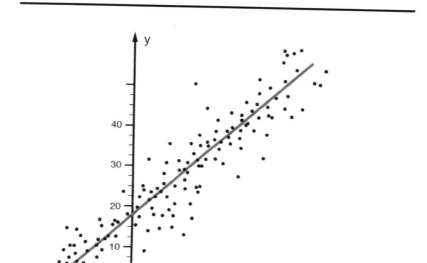

Regression models are highly used for forecasting, and linear regression techniques are the simplest models. If the nonlinear data follows the shape of exponential, logarithmic, or power functions, those types of functions can be used to more accurately model the data rather than lines.

Here is an example of both an exponential regression and logarithmic regression model:

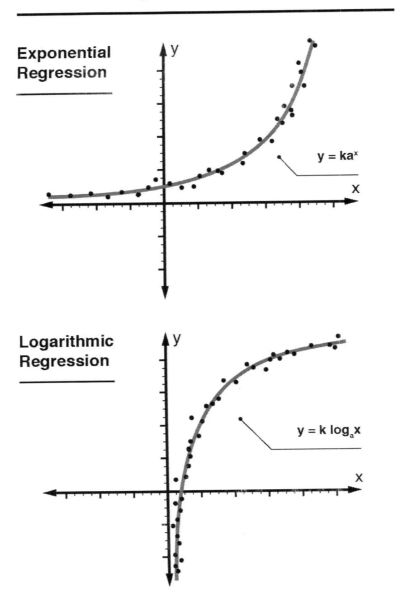

Nonlinear Regression

Exponential Regression

$y = ka^x$

Logarithmic Regression

$y = k \log_a x$

<u>The Law of Large Numbers and the Central Limit Theorem</u>
The *Law of Large Numbers* states that as the number of experiments increase, the actual ratio of outcomes will approach the theoretical probability. The *Central Limit Theorem* states that through using a sufficiently large sample size N, meaning over 30, the sampling distribution of the mean approaches a normal distribution with a mean of μ and variance of σ^2/N. The variance of the actual population is σ^2 and its mean is μ. In other words, as the sample size increases, the distribution will behave normally.

Estimating Parameters

A point estimate of a population parameter is a single statistic. For example, the sample mean is a point estimate of the population mean. Once all calculations are made, a confidence interval is used to express the accuracy of the sampling method used. The confidence interval consists of a confidence level, the statistic, and a margin of error. A 95% confidence level indicates that 95% of all confidence intervals will contain the population parameter. Also, the margin of error gives a range of values above and below the sample statistic, which helps to form a confidence interval.

The Principles of Hypotheses Testing

The P-value approach to hypothesis testing involves assuming a null hypothesis is true and then determining the probability of a test statistic in the direction of the alternative hypothesis. The test statistic is defined as the t-statistic $t^* = \frac{\bar{x} - \mu}{s/\sqrt{n}}$, which follows a t-distribution with n-1 degrees of freedom. The P-value is then calculated as the probability that if the null hypothesis is true, a more extreme test statistic in the direction of the alternative hypothesis would be observed. A significance level, α, is set (usually at 0.05 or 0.001) and the P-value is compared to α. If $P \leq \alpha$, one rejects the null hypothesis and accepts the alternative hypothesis. If $P > \alpha$, one accepts the null hypothesis.

Measuring Probabilities with Two-Way Frequency Tables

When measuring event probabilities, two-way frequency tables can be used to report the raw data and then used to calculate probabilities. If the frequency tables are translated into relative frequency tables, the probabilities presented in the table can be plugged directly into the formulas for conditional probabilities. By plugging in the correct frequencies, the data from the table can be used to determine if events are independent or dependent.

Differing Probabilities

The probability that event A occurs differs from the probability that event A occurs given B. When working within a given model, it's important to note the difference. $P(A|B)$ is determined using the formula $P(A|B) = \frac{P(A \text{ and } B)}{P(B)}$ and represents the total number of A's outcomes left that could occur after B occurs. $P(A)$ can be calculated without any regard for B. For example, the probability of a student finding a parking spot on a busy campus is different once class is in session.

Uniform and Non-Uniform Probability Models

A *uniform probability model* is one where each outcome has an equal chance of occurring, such as the probabilities of rolling each side of a die. A *non-uniform probability model* is one where each outcome has an unequal chance of occurring. In a uniform probability model, the conditional probability formulas for $P(B|A)$ and $P(A|B)$ can be multiplied by their respective denominators to obtain two formulas for $P(A \text{ and } B)$. Therefore, the multiplication rule is derived as $P(A \text{ and } B) = P(A)P(B|A) = P(B)P(A|B)$. In a model, if the probability of either individual event is known and the corresponding conditional probability is known, the multiplication rule allows the probability of the joint occurrence of A and B to be calculated.

Binomial Experiments

In statistics, a *binomial experiment* is an experiment that has the following properties. The experiment consists of n repeated trial that can each have only one of two outcomes. It can be either a success or a failure. The probability of success, p, is the same in every trial. Each trial is also independent of all other trials. An example of a binomial experiment is rolling a die 10 times with the goal of rolling a 5. Rolling a 5 is a success while any other value is a failure. In this experiment, the probability of rolling a 5 is $\frac{1}{6}$. In any binomial experiment, x is the number of resulting successes, n is the number of trials, p is the probability of success in each trial, and $q = 1 - p$ is the probability of failure within each trial. The probability of obtaining x successes within n trials is:

$$P(X = x) = \frac{n!}{x!\,(n-x)!} p^x (1-p)^{n-x}$$

With the following being the *binomial coefficient*:

$$\binom{n}{x} = \frac{n!}{x!\,(n-x)!}$$

Within this calculation, $n!$ is n factorial that's defined as:

$$n \cdot (n-1) \cdot (n-2) \ldots 1$$

Let's look at the probability of obtaining 2 rolls of a 5 out of the 10 rolls.

Start with $P(X = 2)$, where 2 is the number of successes. Then fill in the rest of the formula with what is known, n=10, x=2, p=1/6, q=5/6:

$$P(X = 2) = \left(\frac{10!}{2!\,(10-2)!} \right) \left(\frac{1}{6} \right)^2 \left(1 - \frac{1}{6} \right)^{10-2}$$

Which simplifies to:

$$P(X = 2) = \left(\frac{10!}{2!\,8!} \right) \left(\frac{1}{6} \right)^2 \left(\frac{5}{6} \right)^8$$

Then solve to get:

$$P(X = 2) = \left(\frac{3628800}{80640} \right) (.0277)(.2325) = .2898$$

Statistical Questions

A statistical question is answered by collecting data with variability. Data consists of facts and/or statistics (numbers), and variability refers to a tendency to shift or change. Data is a broad term, inclusive of things like height, favorite color, name, salary, temperature, gas mileage, and language. Questions requiring data as an answer are not necessarily statistical questions. If there is no variability in the data, then the question is not statistical in nature. Consider the following examples: what is Mary's favorite color? How much money does your mother make? What was the highest temperature last week? How many miles did your car get on its last tank of gas? How much taller than Bob is Ed?

None of the above are statistical questions because each case lacks variability in the data needed to answer the question. The questions on favorite color, salary, and gas mileage each require a single piece of data, whether a fact or statistic. Therefore, variability is absent. Although the temperature question requires multiple pieces of data (the high temperature for each day), a single, distinct number is the answer. The height question requires two pieces of data, Bob's height and Ed's height, but no difference in variability exists between those two values. Therefore, this is not a statistical question. Statistical questions typically require calculations with data.

Consider the following statistical questions:

How many miles per gallon of gas does the 2016 Honda Civic get? To answer this question, data must be collected. This data should include miles driven and gallons used. Different cars, different drivers, and different driving conditions will produce different results. Therefore, variability exists in the data. To answer the question, the mean (average) value could be determined.

Are American men taller than Chinese men? To answer this question, data must be collected. This data should include the heights of American men and the heights of Chinese men. All American men are not the same height and all Chinese men are not the same height. Some American men are taller than some Chinese men and some Chinese men are taller than some American men. Therefore, variability exists in the data. To answer the question, the median values for each group could be determined and compared.

The following are more examples of statistical questions: What proportion of 4th graders have a favorite color of blue? How much money do teachers make? Is it colder in Boston or Chicago?

Statistical Processes

<u>Samples and Populations</u>
Statistics involves making decisions and predictions about larger data sets based on smaller data sets. Basically, the information from one part or subset can help predict what happens in the entire data set or population at large. The entire process involves guessing, and the predictions and decisions may not be 100 percent correct all of the time; however, there is some truth to these predictions, and the decisions do have mathematical support. The smaller data set is called a *sample* and the larger data set (in which the decision is being made) is called a *population*. A *random sample* is used as the sample, which is an unbiased collection of data points that represents the population as well as it can. There are many methods of forming a random sample, and all adhere to the fact that every potential data point has a predetermined probability of being chosen.

<u>Goodness of Fit</u>
Goodness of fit tests show how well a statistical model fits a given data set. They allow the differences between the observed and expected quantities to be summarized to determine if the model is consistent with the results. The *Chi-Squared Goodness of Fit Test* (or *Chi-Squared Test* for short) is used with one categorical variable from one population, and it concludes whether or not the sample data is consistent with a hypothesized distribution. Chi-Squared is evaluated using the following formula: $\chi^2 = \sum \frac{(O-E)^2}{E}$, where O is the observed frequency value and E is the expected frequency value. Also, the *degree of freedom* must be calculated, which is the number of categories in the data set minus one. Then a Chi-Squared table is used to test the data. The *degree of freedom value* and a *significance value*, such as 0.05, are located on the table. The corresponding entry represents a critical value.

If the calculated χ^2 is greater than the critical value, the data set does not work with the statistical model. If the calculated χ^2 is less than the critical value, the statistical model can be used.

Basic Notions of Chance and Probability

Counting Techniques

There are many counting techniques that can help solve problems involving counting possibilities. For example, the *Addition Principle* states that if there are m choices from Group 1 and n choices from Group 2, then $n + m$ is the total number of choices possible from Groups 1 and 2. For this to be true, the groups can't have any choices in common. The *Multiplication Principle* states that if Process 1 can be completed n ways and Process 2 can be completed m ways, the total number of ways to complete both Process 1 and Process 2 is $n \times m$ .For this rule to be used, both processes must be independent of each other. Counting techniques also involve permutations. A *permutation* is an arrangement of elements in a set for which order must be considered. For example, if three letters from the alphabet are chosen, ABC and BAC are two different permutations. The multiplication rule can be used to determine the total number of possibilities. If each letter can't be selected twice, the total number of possibilities is $26 \times 25 \times 24 = 15,600$.A formula can also be used to calculate this total. In general, the notation $P(n,r)$ represents the number of ways to arrange r objects from a set of n and, the formula is $P(n,r) = \frac{n!}{(n-r)!}$.In the previous example, $P(26,3) = \frac{26!}{23!} = 15,600$. Contrasting permutations, a *combination* is an arrangement of elements in which order doesn't matter. In this case, ABC and BAC are the same combination. In the previous scenario, there are six permutations that represent each single combination. Therefore, the total number of possible combinations is $15,600 \div 6 = 2,600$. In general, $C(n,r)$ represents the total number of combinations of n items selected r at a time where order doesn't matter, and the formula is $C(n,r) = \frac{n!}{(n-r)!\,r!}$. Therefore, the following relationship exists between permutations and combinations: $C(n,r) = \frac{P(n,r)}{n!} = \frac{P(n,r)}{P(r,r)}$.

Probabilities Involving Finite Sample Spaces and Independent Trials

Fundamental Counting Principle
The *fundamental counting principle* states that if there are m possible ways for an event to occur, and n possible ways for a second event to occur, there are $m \cdot n$ possible ways for both events to occur. For example, there are two events that can occur after flipping a coin and six events that can occur after rolling a die, so there are $2 \cdot 6 = 12$ total possible event scenarios if both are done simultaneously. This principle can be used to find probabilities involving finite sample spaces and independent trials because it calculates the total number of possible outcomes. For this principle to work, the events must be independent of each other.

Computing Probabilities of Simple Events, Probabilities of Compound Events, and Conditional Probabilities

Simple and Compound Events
A *simple event* consists of only one outcome. The most popular simple event is flipping a coin, which results in either heads or tails. A *compound event* results in more than one outcome and consists of more than one simple event. An example of a compound event is flipping a coin while tossing a die. The result is either heads or tails on the coin and a number from one to six on the die. The probability of a simple event is calculated by dividing the number of possible outcomes by the total number of outcomes. Therefore, the probability of obtaining heads on a coin is $1/2$, and the probability of rolling a 6 on a die is $1/6$.The probability of compound events is calculated using the basic idea of the probability of simple events. If the two events are independent, the probability of one outcome is equal to the product of the probabilities of each simple event. For example, the probability of obtaining heads on a coin and rolling a 6 is equal to $1/2 \times 1/6 = 1/12$. The probability of either A or B occurring is equal to the sum of the probabilities minus the probability that both A and B will occur. Therefore, the probability of obtaining either heads on a coin or rolling a 6 on a die is $1/2 + 1/6 - 1/12 = 7/12$.The two events aren't mutually exclusive because they can happen at the same time. If two events are mutually exclusive, and the probability of both events occurring at the same time is zero, the probability

of event A or B occurring equals the sum of both probabilities. An example of calculating the probability of two mutually exclusive events is determining the probability of pulling a king or a queen from a deck of cards. The two events cannot occur at the same time.

Sample Spaces
Probabilities are based on observations of events. The probability of an event occurring is equal to the ratio of the number of favorable outcomes over the total number of possible outcomes. The total number of possible outcomes is found by constructing the sample space. The sum of probabilities of all possible distinct outcomes is equal to 1. A simple example of a sample space involves a deck of cards. They contain 52 distinct cards, and therefore the sample space contains each individual card. To find the probability of selecting a queen on one draw from the deck, the ratio would be equal to $\frac{4}{52} = \frac{1}{13}$, which equals 4 possible queens over the total number of possibilities in the sample space.

Probability with Combinations and Permutations
Probability problems require that the total number of simple events is known, which means the entire sample space must be recognized. Different methods can be used to count the number of possible outcomes, depending on whether different arrangements of the same items are counted only once or separately. *Permutations* are arrangements in which different sequences are counted separately. Therefore, order matters in permutations. *Combinations* are arrangements in which different sequences are not counted separately. Therefore, order does not matter in combinations. If the sample space contains n different permutations of n different items and all of them must be selected, there are $n!$ different possibilities. For example, 5 different books can be rearranged $5!=120$ times. The probability of two people ordering the books in the same way is $1/120$. A different calculation is necessary if a number less than n is to be selected or if order does not matter. In general, the notation $P(n,r)$ represents the number of ways to arrange r objects from a set of n if order does not matter, and $P(n,r) = \frac{n!}{(n-r)!}$. Secondly, $C(n,r)$ represents the total number of r combinations selected out of n items when order does not matter and $C(n,r) = \frac{n!}{(n-r)!\,r!}$. Therefore, the following relationship exists between permutations and combinations: $C(n,r) = \frac{P(n,r)}{n!}$.

Solving Probability Problems Using Geometric Ratios
The ratio between two similar geometric figures is called the *scale factor*. In the following example, there are two similar triangles. The scale factor from figure A to figure B is 2 because the length of the corresponding side of the larger triangle, 14, is twice the corresponding side on the smaller triangle, 7.

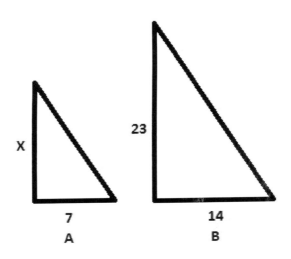

This scale factor can also be used to find the value of X. Since the scale factor from small to large is 2, the larger number, 23, can be divided by 2 to find the missing side: X = 11.5. The scale factor can also be represented in the equation $2A = B$ because two times the lengths of A gives the corresponding lengths of B. This is the idea behind similar triangles.

Problems involving volume, length, and other units can also be solved using ratios. If the following graphic of a cone is given, the problem may ask for the volume to be found.

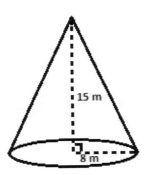

Referring to the formulas provided on the test, the volume of a cone is given as: $V = \pi r^2 \frac{h}{3}$, where r is the radius, and h is the height. Plugging $r = 7$ and $h = 16$ from the graphic in to the formula, the following is obtained: $V = \pi(7^2)\frac{16}{3}$. Therefore, volume of the cone is found to be approximately $821m^3$. Sometimes, answers in different units are sought. If this problem wanted the answer in liters, $821m^3$ would need to be converted. Using the equivalence statement $1m^3 = 1000L$, the following ratio would be used to solve for liters: $821m^3 * \frac{1000L}{1m^3}$. Cubic meters in the numerator and denominator cancel each other out, and the answer is converted to 821,000 liters, or $8.21 * 10^5$ L.

Other conversions can also be made between different given and final units. If the temperature in a pool is 30°C, what is the temperature of the pool in degrees Fahrenheit? To convert these units, an equation is used relating Celsius to Fahrenheit. The following equation is used: $T_{°F} = 1.8T_{°C} + 32$. Plugging in the given temperature and solving the equation for T yields the result: $T_{°F} = 1.8(30) + 32 = 86°F$. Both units in the metric system and U.S. customary system are widely used.

Probability Axioms

The *addition rule* is necessary to find the probability of event A or event B occurring, or both occurring at the same time. If events A and B are mutually exclusive, which means they cannot occur at the same time, $P(A \text{ or } B) = P(A) + P(B)$. If events A and B are not mutually exclusive, $P(A \text{ or } B) = P(A) + P(B) - P(A \text{ and } B)$, where $P(A \text{ and } B)$ represents the probability of event A and B both occurring at the same time. The *multiplication rule* is necessary to find the probability that both A and B occur in two separate trials. This rule differs if the events are independent or dependent. Two events, A and B, are labeled as *independent* if the occurrence of one event does not affect the probability that the other event will occur. If A and be are not independent, they are *dependent.* If events A and B are independent, $P(A \text{ and } B) = P(A)P(B)$, and if events A and B are dependent, $P(A \text{ and } B) = P(A)P(B|A)$ where $P(B|A)$ represents the probability event B occurs given that event A has already occurred. $P(B|A)$ represents *conditional probability.* $P(B|A)$ can be found using the formula $P(B|A) = \frac{P(A \text{ and } B)}{P(A)}$, and represents the total number of outcomes remaining for B to occur after A occurs.

Probability Distributions

Probability is a measure of the likelihood of something happening or being the case. The probability of an event A is written P(A) and is assigned a value between zero (can't happen) and one (is certain to happen): $0 \leq P(A) \leq 1$.

Probabilities can be objectively assigned by sampling or reviewing historical data to determine how frequently the outcome has occurred in the past.

If the probability of a parameter's value is calculated and plotted along its entire possible range, a probability distribution function (PDF) can be determined. The normal probability distribution is a continuous PDF.

The binomial probability distribution is an important discrete PDF giving the probability of getting exactly k successes in n trials of a "yes-no," or *binomial*, test: $P(k) = \binom{n}{k} p^k (1 - p)^{n-k}$, where p is the probability of success for each trial. The binomial coefficient $\binom{n}{k}$ is the number of possible ways k values can be selected from a group of n items and is calculated as $n!/(k!(n-k)!$, where $k! = k \times (k-1) \times (k-2) \times \ldots \times 2 \times 1$. The value of 0! is defined as 1 to allow calculation of the probability of zero occurrences of the event in a time interval.

For example, to determine the probability of getting exactly 4 heads in 10 tosses of a fair coin: p(H) = p(T) = 0.5 and $P(4) = \binom{10}{4} 0.5^4 (1 - 0.5)^6 = 0.2051$.

The Poisson discrete PDF is used for modeling the number of times a discrete event occurs in an interval of time. It is valid for events occurring with a known average rate, λ, and probability independent of the time since the last event: $P(k \text{ events}) = \frac{\lambda^k e^{-\lambda}}{k!}$, where λ is the average number of events per interval, e is the base of natural logarithms (2.7182...), and k! is calculated as discussed above.

Discrete and Continuous Random Variables

A *discrete random variable* consists of a collection of values that is either finite or countable. If there are infinitely many values, being countable means that each individual value can be counted. For example, the number of coin tosses before getting heads could potentially be infinite, but the total number of tosses is countable. A *continuous random variable* has infinitely many values, and is not countable. The individual items cannot be counted and an example is a measurement. Because of the use of decimals, there are infinitely many heights of human beings. Each type of variable has its own *probability distribution*, which is a description that shows the probability for each potential value of the random variable. They are usually seen in tables, formulas, or graphs. The *expected value* of a random variable represents what the mean value should be in either a large sample size or after many trials. According to the Law of Large Numbers, after many trials, the actual mean and that of the probability distribution should be approximately equal to the expected value. The expected value is a weighted average that is calculated as $E(X) = \sum x_i p_i$, where x_i represent the value of each outcome and p_i represent the probability of each outcome. The expected value if all probabilities are equal is $E(X) = \frac{x_1 + x_2 + \cdots + x_n}{n}$. Expected value is often called the *mean of the random variable*, and is also a measure of central tendency. A *binomial probability distribution* is a probability distribution that has a fixed number of trials, all trials are independent, each trial has an outcome classified as either success or failure, and the probability of a success is the same in each trial. Within any binomial experiment, x is the number of resulting successes, n is the number of trials, P is the probability of success within each trial, and $Q = 1 - P$ is the probability of failure within each trial. The probability of obtaining x successes within n trials is $\binom{n}{x} P^x (1 - P)^{n-x}$, where $\binom{n}{x} = \frac{n!}{x!(n-x)!}$ is called the *binomial coefficient*. A *geometric probability distribution* is a binomial probability distribution where the number of trials is not fixed. A *uniform probability distribution* exists when there is constant probability. Each random variable has equal probability and its graph is a rectangle. Finally, a *uniform probability distribution* has a graph that is symmetric and bell-shaped.

Population percentages can be estimated using normal distributions. For example, the probability that a data point will be less than the mean is 50%. Similarly, the probability that a data point will be within one standard deviation of the mean, or that the z-score will be between -1 and 1, is about 68.2%. When using a table, the left column states how many standard deviations (to one decimal place) away from the mean the point lies, and the row heading states the second decimal place. The entries in the table corresponding to each column and each row gives the probability, which is equal to the area under the curve. The area under the entire curve of a standard normal distribution is equal to 1.

Independence and Conditional Probability

Sample Subsets
A sample can be broken up into subsets that are smaller parts of the whole. For example, consider a sample population of females. The sample can be divided into smaller subsets based on the characteristics of each female. There can be a group of females with brown hair and a group of females that wear glasses. There also can be a group of females that have brown hair *and* wear glasses. This "and" relates to the *intersection* of the two separate groups of brunettes and those with glasses. Every female in that intersection group has both characteristics. Similarly, there also can be a group of females that either have brown hair *or* wear glasses. The "or" relates to the union of the two separate groups of brunettes and glasses. Every female in this group has at least one of the characteristics. Finally, the group of females who do *not* wearing glasses can be discussed. This "not" relates to the *complement* of the glass-wearing group. No one in the complement has glasses. *Venn diagrams* are useful in highlighting these ideas. When discussing statistical experiments, this idea can also relate to events instead of characteristics.

Verifying Independent Events
Two events aren't always independent. For examples, females with glasses and brown hair aren't independent characteristics. There definitely can be overlap because females with brown hair can wear glasses. Also, two events that exist at the same time don't have to have a relationship. For example,

even if all females in a given sample are wearing glasses, the characteristics aren't related. In this case, the probability of a brunette wearing glasses is equal to the probability of a female being a brunette multiplied by the probability of a female wearing glasses. This mathematical test of $P(A \cap B) = P(A)P(B)$ verifies that two events are independent.

Conditional Probability

Conditional probability is the probability that event A will happen given that event B has already occurred. An example of this is calculating the probability that a person will eat dessert once they have eaten dinner. This is different than calculating the probability of a person just eating dessert. The formula for the conditional probability of event A occurring given B is $P(A|B) = \frac{P(A \text{ and } B)}{P(B)}$, and it's defined to be the probability of both A and B occurring divided by the probability of event B occurring. If A and B are independent, then the probability of both A and B occurring is equal to $P(A)P(B)$, so $P(A|B)$ reduces to just $P(A)$. This means that A and B have no relationship, and the probability of A occurring is the same as the conditional probability of A occurring given B. Similarly, $P(B|A) = \frac{P(B \text{ and } A)}{P(A)} = P(B)$ if A and B are independent.

Independent Versus Related Events

To summarize, conditional probability is the probability that an event occurs given that another event has happened. If the two events are related, the probability that the second event will occur changes if the other event has happened. However, if the two events aren't related and are therefore independent, the first event to occur won't impact the probability of the second event occurring.

Practice Questions

1. How many daughter cells are formed from one parent cell during meiosis?
    a. One
    b. Two
    c. Three
    d. Four

2. What is the total mechanical energy of a system?
    a. The total potential energy
    b. The total kinetic energy
    c. Kinetic energy plus potential energy
    d. Kinetic energy minus potential energy

3. What does the Lewis Dot structure of an element represent?
    a. The outer electron valence shell population
    b. The inner electron valence shell population
    c. The positioning of the element's protons
    d. The positioning of the element's neutrons

4. What is the name of this compound: CO?
    a. Carbonite oxide
    b. Carbonic dioxide
    c. Carbonic oxide
    d. Carbon monoxide

5. What is the molarity of a solution made by dissolving 4.0 grams of $NaCl$ into enough water to make 120 mL of solution? The atomic mass of Na is 23.0 g/mol and Cl is 35.5 g/mol.
    a. 0.34 M
    b. 0.57 M
    c. 0.034 M
    d. 0.057 M

6. Considering a gas in a closed system, at a constant volume, what will happen to the temperature if the pressure is increased?
    a. The temperature will stay the same
    b. The temperature will decrease
    c. The temperature will increase
    d. It cannot be determined with the information given

7. What is the current when a 3.0 V battery is wired across a lightbulb that has a resistance of 6.0 ohms?
    a. 0.5 A
    b. 18.0 A
    c. 0.5 J
    d. 18.0 J

8. According to Newton's Three Laws of Motion, which of the following is true?
   a. Two objects cannot exert a force on each other without touching.
   b. An object at rest has no inertia.
   c. The weight of an object is the same as the mass of the object.
   d. The weight of an object is equal to the mass of an object multiplied by gravity.

9. What is the chemical reaction when a compound is broken down into its elemental components called?
   a. A synthesis reaction
   b. A decomposition reaction
   c. An organic reaction
   d. An oxidation reaction

10. Which of the following is a balanced chemical equation?
   a. $Na + Cl_2 \rightarrow NaCl$
   b. $2Na + Cl_2 \rightarrow NaCl$
   c. $2Na + Cl_2 \rightarrow 2NaCl$
   d. $2Na + 2Cl_2 \rightarrow 2NaCl$

11. What effect changes the oscillations of a wave and can alter the appearance of light waves?
   a. Reflection
   b. Refraction
   c. Dispersion
   d. Polarization

12. The Sun transferring heat to the Earth through space is an example of which of the following?
   a. Convection
   b. Conduction
   c. Induction
   d. Radiation

13. What is the acceleration of a vehicle starting from rest and reaching a velocity of 15 m/s in 5.0 s?
   a. 3.0 m/s
   b. 75 m/s
   c. 3.0 m/s^2
   d. 75 m/s^2

14. What is 45 °C converted to °F?
   a. 113 °F
   b. 135 °F
   c. 57 °F
   d. 88 °F

15. What is the force that opposes motion?
   a. Reactive force
   b. Responsive force
   c. Friction
   d. Momentum

16. What type of chemical reaction produces a salt?
    a. An oxidation reaction
    b. A neutralization reaction
    c. A synthesis reaction
    d. A decomposition reaction

17. If a reading is above the curve on a solubility curve, the solvent is considered to be which of the following?
    a. Unsaturated
    b. Supersaturated
    c. Stable
    d. Saturated

18. Which factor is NOT a consideration in population dynamics?
    a. Size and age of population
    b. Immigration
    c. Hair color
    d. Number of births

19. Which rock is formed from cooling magma underneath the Earth's surface?
    a. Extrusive sedimentary rocks
    b. Sedimentary rocks
    c. Igneous rocks
    d. Metamorphic rocks

20. Water that has seeped into rock cracks and freezes will most likely result in what process?
    a. Chemical weathering
    b. Mechanical weathering
    c. Erosion
    d. Deposition

21. Which soil is the least permeable to water?
    a. Pure sand
    b. Pure silt
    c. Pure clay
    d. Loam

22. Which of the Earth's layers is thickest?
    a. The crust
    b. The shell
    c. The mantle
    d. The inner core

23. Which level of protein structure is defined by the folds and coils of the protein's polypeptide backbone?
    a. Primary
    b. Secondary
    c. Tertiary
    d. Quaternary

24. What is the process called in which a tectonic plate moves over another plate?
    a. Fault
    b. Diversion
    c. Subduction
    d. Drift

25. What is transpiration?
    a. Evaporation from moving water
    b. Evaporation from plant life
    c. Movement of water through the ground
    d. Precipitation that falls on trees

26. Absolute dating involves which of the following?
    a. Measuring radioactive decay
    b. Comparing rock stratification
    c. Fossil location
    d. Fossil record

27. Which of the following will freeze last?
    a. Freshwater from a pond
    b. Pure water
    c. Seawater from the Pacific Ocean
    d. Seawater from the Dead Sea

28. Which of the following is true of glaciers?
    a. They form in water.
    b. They float.
    c. They form on land.
    d. They are formed from icebergs.

29. What is the broadest, or LEAST specialized, classification of the Linnean taxonomic system?
    a. Species
    b. Family
    c. Domain
    d. Phylum

30. Which of the following is most abundant in the Earth's atmosphere?
    a. Carbon dioxide
    b. Oxygen
    c. Nitrogen
    d. Water

31. Dew point is a measure of which of the following?
       I. Pressure
       II. Temperature at which water vapor condenses
       III. Temperature at which water evaporates
    a. I and III
    b. I and II
    c. II and III
    d. All the above

32. The Coriolis Effect is created by which of the following?
   a. Wind
   b. Earth's rotation
   c. Earth's axis
   d. Mountains

33. Dark storm clouds are usually located where?
   a. Between 5,000 and 13,000 meters above sea level
   b. Between 2,000 and 7,000 meters above sea level
   c. Below 2,000 meters above sea level
   d. Outer space

34. What is the solution to the following system of equations?
$$x^2 - 2x + y = 8$$
$$x - y = -2$$

   a. $(-2, 3)$
   b. There is no solution.
   c. $(-2, 0)\ (1, 3)$
   d. $(-2, 0)\ (3, 5)$

35. How could the following equation be factored to find the zeros?
$$y = x^3 - 3x^2 - 4x$$

   a. $0 = x^2(x - 4), x = 0, 4$
   b. $0 = 3x(x + 1)(x + 4), x = 0, -1, -4$
   c. $0 = x(x + 1)(x + 6), x = 0, -1, -6$
   d. $0 = x(x + 1)(x - 4), x = 0, -1, 4$

36. What is the simplified quotient of $\frac{5x^3}{3x^2y} \div \frac{25}{3y^9}$?
   a. $\frac{125x}{9y^{10}}$
   b. $\frac{x}{5y^8}$
   c. $\frac{5}{xy^8}$
   d. $\frac{xy^8}{5}$

37. Mom's car drove 72 miles in 90 minutes. How fast did she drive in feet per second?
   a. 0.8 feet per second
   b. 48.9 feet per second
   c. 0.009 feet per second
   d. 70. 4 feet per second

38. For the following similar triangles, what are the values of x and y (rounded to one decimal place)?

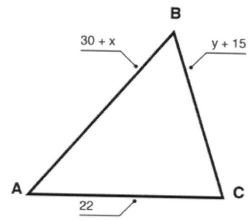
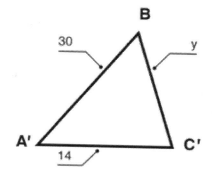

a. $x = 16.5, y = 25.1$
b. $x = 19.5, y = 24.1$
c. $x = 17.1, y = 26.3$
d. $x = 26.3, y = 17.1$

39. What are the center and radius of a circle with equation $4x^2 + 4y^2 - 16x - 24y + 51 = 0$?
   a. Center $(3, 2)$ and radius ½
   b. Center $(2, 3)$ and radius ½
   c. Center $(3, 2)$ and radius ¼
   d. Center $(2, 3)$ and radius ¼

40. If the ordered pair $(-3, -4)$ is reflected over the x-axis, what's the new ordered pair?
   a. $(-3, -4)$
   b. $(3, -4)$
   c. $(3, 4)$
   d. $(-3, 4)$

41. If the volume of a sphere is 288π cubic meters, what are the radius and surface area of the same sphere?
   a. Radius 6 meters and surface area 144π square meters
   b. Radius 36 meters and surface area 144π square meters
   c. Radius 6 meters and surface area 12π square meters
   d. Radius 36 meters and surface area 12π square meters

42. Which of the following is the result of simplifying the expression: $\frac{4a^{-1}b^3}{a^4b^{-2}} * \frac{3a}{b}$?
   a. $12a^3b^5$
   b. $12\frac{b^4}{a^4}$
   c. $\frac{12}{a^4}$
   d. $7\frac{b^4}{a}$

43. The area of a given rectangle is 24 centimeters. If the measure of each side is multiplied by 3, what is the area of the new figure?

    a. 48cm

    b. 72cm

    c. 216cm

    d. 13,824cm

44. The perimeter of a 6-sided polygon is 56 cm. The length of three sides is 9 cm each. The length of two other sides is 8 cm each. What is the length of the missing side?

    a. 11 cm

    b. 12 cm

    c. 13 cm

    d. 10 cm

45. Two cards are drawn from a shuffled deck of 52 cards. What's the probability that both cards are Kings if the first card isn't replaced after it's drawn?

    a. $1/169$

    b. $1/221$

    c. $1/13$

    d. $4/13$

46. For a group of 20 men, the median weight is 180 pounds and the range is 30 pounds. If each man gains 10 pounds, which of the following would be true?

    a. The median weight will increase, and the range will remain the same.

    b. The median weight and range will both remain the same.

    c. The median weight will stay the same, and the range will increase.

    d. The median weight and range will both increase.

47. A pair of dice is thrown and the sum of the two scores is calculated. What's the expected value of the roll?

    a. 5

    b. 6

    c. 7

    d. 8

48. Which measure for the center of a small sample set is most affected by outliers?

    a. Mean

    b. Median

    c. Mode

    d. None of the above

49. Given the value of a given stock at monthly intervals, which graph should be used to best represent the trend of the stock?

    a. Box plot

    b. Line plot

    c. Line graph

    d. Circle graph

50. What is the probability of randomly picking the winner and runner-up from a race of 4 horses and distinguishing which is the winner?

    a. $\dfrac{1}{4}$

    b. $\dfrac{1}{2}$

    c. $\dfrac{1}{16}$

    d. $\dfrac{1}{12}$

51. In Jim's school, there are 3 girls for every 2 boys. There are 650 students in total. Using this information, how many students are girls?

    a. 260

    b. 130

    c. 65

    d. 390

52. Five of six numbers have a sum of 25. The average of all six numbers is 6. What is the sixth number?

    a. 8

    b. 10

    c. 11

    d. 12

Answer Explanations

1. D: Meiosis has the same phases as mitosis, except that they occur twice—once in meiosis I and once in meiosis II. During meiosis I, the cell splits into two. Each cell contains two sets of chromosomes. Next, during meiosis II, the two intermediate daughter cells divide again, producing four total haploid cells that each contain one set of chromosomes.

2. C: In any system, the total mechanical energy is the sum of the potential energy and the kinetic energy. Either value could be zero but it still must be included in the total. Choices *A* and *B* only give the total potential or kinetic energy, respectively. Choice *D* gives the difference in the kinetic and potential energy.

3. A: A Lewis Dot diagram shows the alignment of the valence (outer) shell electrons and how readily they can pair or bond with the valence shell electrons of other atoms to form a compound. Choice *B* is incorrect because the Lewis Dot structure aids in understanding how likely an atom is to bond or not bond with another atom, so the inner shell would add no relevance to understanding this likelihood. The positioning of protons and neutrons concerns the nucleus of the atom, which again would not lend information to the likelihood of bonding.

4. D: The naming of compounds focuses on the second element in a chemical compound. Elements from the non-metal category are written with an "ide" at the end. The compound CO has one carbon and one oxygen, so it is called carbon monoxide. Choice *B* represents that there are two oxygen atoms, and Choices *A* and *B* incorrectly alter the name of the first element, which should remain as carbon.

5. B: To solve this, the number of moles of NaCl needs to be calculated:

First, to find the mass of NaCl, the mass of each of the molecule's atoms is added together as follows:

$$23.0g \text{ (Na)} + 35.5g \text{ (Cl)} = 58.8g \text{ NaCl}$$

Next, the given mass of the substance is multiplied by one mole per total mass of the substance:

$$4.0g \text{ NaCl} \times (1 \text{ mol NaCl}/58.5g \text{ NaCl}) = 0.068 \text{ mol NaCl}$$

Finally, the moles are divided by the number of liters of the solution to find the molarity:

$$(0.068 \text{ mol NaCl})/(0.120L) = 0.57 \text{ M NaCl}$$

Choice *A* incorporates a miscalculation for the molar mass of NaCl, and Choices *C* and *D* both incorporate a miscalculation by not converting mL into liters (L), so they are incorrect by a factor of 10.

6. C: According to the *ideal gas law* ($PV = nRT$), if volume is constant, the temperature is directly related to the pressure in a system. Therefore, if the pressure increases, the temperature will increase in direct proportion. Choice *A* would not be possible, since the system is closed and a change is occurring, so the temperature will change. Choice *B* incorrectly exhibits an inverse relationship between pressure and temperature, or $P = 1/T$. Choice *D* is incorrect because even without actual values for the variables, the relationship and proportions can be determined.

7. A: According to Ohm's Law: $V = IR$, so using the given variables: $3.0 \text{ V} = I \times 6.0 \text{ }\Omega$

Solving for I: $I = 3.0 \text{ V}/6.0 \text{ }\Omega = 0.5 \text{ A}$

Choice B incorporates a miscalculation in the equation by multiplying 3.0 V by 6.0 Ω, rather than dividing these values. Choices C and D are labeled with the wrong units; Joules measure energy, not current.

8. D: The weight of an object is equal to the mass of the object multiplied by gravity. According to Newton's Second Law of Motion, $F = m \times a$. Weight is the force resulting from a given situation, so the mass of the object needs to be multiplied by the acceleration of gravity on Earth: $W = m \times g$. Choice A is incorrect because, according to Newton's first law, all objects exert some force on each other, based on their distance from each other and their masses. This is seen in planets, which affect each other's paths and those of their moons. Choice B is incorrect because an object in motion or at rest can have inertia; inertia is the resistance of a physical object to change its state of motion. Choice C is incorrect because the mass of an object is a measurement of how much substance of there is to the object, while the weight is gravity's effect of the mass.

9. B: A decomposition reaction breaks down a compound into its constituent elemental components. Choice A is incorrect because a synthesis reaction joins two or more elements into a single compound. Choice C, an organic reaction, is not possible, since it needs carbon and hydrogen for a reaction. Choice D, oxidation/reduction (redox or half) reaction, is incorrect because it involves the loss of electrons from one species (oxidation) and the gain of electrons to the other species (reduction). There is no notation of this occurring within the given reaction, so it is not correct.

10. C:

$$2Na + Cl_2 \longrightarrow 2NaCl$$

The number of each element must be equal on both sides of the equation:

Choice C is the only correct option: $2Na + Cl_2 \rightarrow 2NaCl$

2 Na + 2 Cl does equal 2 Na + 2 Cl (the number of sodium atoms and chlorine atoms match)

Choice A: $Na + Cl_2 \rightarrow NaCl$

1 Na + 2 Cl does not equal 1 Na + 1 Cl (the number of chlorine atoms do not match)

Choice B: $2Na + Cl_2 \rightarrow NaCl$

2 Na + 2 Cl does not equal 1 Na + 1 Cl (neither the number of sodium atoms nor chlorine atoms match)

Choice D: $2Na + 2Cl_2 \rightarrow 2NaCl$

2 Na + 4 Cl does not equal 2 Na + 2 Cl (the number of chlorine atoms do not match)

11. D: Polarization changes the oscillations of a wave and can alter the appearance in light waves. For example, polarized sunglasses remove the "glare" from sunlight by altering the oscillation pattern observed by the wearer. Choice A, reflection, is the bouncing back of a wave, such as in a mirror; Choice B is the bending of a wave as it travels from one medium to another, such as going from air to water; and Choice C, dispersion, is the spreading of a wave through a barrier or a prism.

12. D: Radiation can be transmitted through electromagnetic waves and needs no medium to travel; it can travel in a vacuum. This is how the Sun warms the Earth and it typically applies to large objects with great amounts of heat, or objects that have a large difference in their heat measurements. Choice A, convection, involves atoms or molecules traveling from areas of high concentration to those of low concentration and transferring energy or heat with them. Choice B, conduction, involves the touching or bumping of atoms or molecules to transfer energy or heat. Choice C, induction, deals with charges and does not apply to the transfer of energy or heat. Choices A, B, and C need a medium in which to travel, while radiation requires no medium.

13. C: Review the following:

$$a = \frac{\Delta v}{\Delta t}$$

$$a = \frac{15 - 0}{5 - 0}$$

$$a = \frac{15}{5}$$

$$= 3.0 \text{ m/s}^2$$

Choices A and B have the wrong units for acceleration; they are labeled with the units for velocity. Choices B and D integrate a miscalculation with the formula—multiplying, rather than dividing, 15 and 5.

14. A: Review the following conversion:

$$^\circ F = \frac{9}{5}(^\circ C) + 32$$

$$^\circ F = \frac{9}{5}(45) + 32$$

$$^\circ F = 113 \text{ }^\circ F$$

Choices B, C, and D all incorporate a mistake in the order of operations necessary for this calculation: divide, multiply, and then add.

15. C: The force that opposes motion is called *friction*. It also provides the resistance necessary for walking, running, braking, etc. In order for something to slide down a ramp, it must be acted upon by a force stronger than that of friction. Choices A and B are not actual terms, and Choice C is the measure of mass multiplied by velocity ($p = mv$).

16. B: A solid produced during a reaction is called a precipitate. In a neutralization reaction, the products (an acid and a base) react to form a salt and water. Choice A, an oxidation reaction, involves the transfer of an electron. Choice C, a synthesis reaction, involves the joining of two molecules to form a single molecule. Choice D, a decomposition reaction, involves the separation of a molecule into two other molecules.

17. B: When a solution is on the verge of—or in the process of—crystallization, it is called a *supersaturated* solution. This can also occur in a solution that seems stable, but if it is disturbed, the change can begin the crystallization process. To display the relationship between the mass of a solute that a solvent holds and a given temperature, a *solubility curve* is used. If a reading is on the solubility curve, the solvent is *saturated*; it is full and cannot hold more solute. If a reading is above the curve, the solvent is *supersaturated* and unstable from holding more solute than it should. If a reading is below the curve, the solvent is *unsaturated* and could hold more solute. Choices A, C, and D are all stable, whereas Choice B is unstable.

18. C: Population dynamics looks at the composition of populations, including size and age, and the biological and environmental processes that cause changes. These can include immigration, emigration, births, and deaths.

19. C: Igneous rocks are formed from the cooling of magma, both on and below the Earth's surface, which are classified as extrusive and intrusive, respectively. Sedimentary rocks are formed from deposition and cementation on the surface, and metamorphic rocks are formed from the transformation of sedimentary or igneous rocks through heat and pressure.

20. B: Freezing water expands because ice is less dense than liquid water. This expansion can break up solid rocks, which describes a form of mechanical weathering. Chemical weathering occurs when water dissolves rocks. Erosion is the movement of broken rock, and deposition is the process of laying down rocks from erosion.

21. C: Pure clay has small particles that pack together tightly and are impermeable to water. Sand is the least permeable type of soil because it has the largest grains. Loam is a combination of all three types of soil in relatively equal proportions.

22. C: The mantle is the Earth's thickest layer; it holds most of the Earth's material. The crust is thin, and the inner core is also small compared to the mantle. There is no such thing as Earth's shell.

23. B: The secondary structure of a protein refers to the folds and coils that are formed by hydrogen bonding between the slightly charged atoms of the polypeptide backbone. The primary structure is the sequence of amino acids, similar to the letters in a long word. The tertiary structure is the overall shape of the molecule that results from the interactions between the side chains that are linked to the polypeptide backbone. The quaternary structure is the complete protein structure that occurs when a protein is made up of two or more polypeptide chains.

24. C: Subduction occurs when one plate is pushed down by another. A fault is where two plates meet. Diversion occurs when two plates move apart. Drift isn't a term used with tectonic plates.

25. B: Transpiration is water that evaporates from pores in plants called stomata. Evaporation of moving water is still called evaporation. Infiltration is the process of water moving into the ground, and precipitation that falls on trees is called canopy interception.

26. A: Absolute dating involves measuring radioactive decay of elements such as carbon-14 trapped in rocks or minerals and using the known rate of decay to determine how much time has passed. Another element used is uranium-lead, which allows dating for some of the oldest rocks on the Earth.

27. D: Water with a higher salinity has more dissolved salt and a lower freezing point. Water from the Dead Sea has the highest salinity of the answer choices.

28. C: Glaciers are formed only on land and constantly move because of their own weight. Icebergs are formed from glaciers and float.

29. C: In the Linnean system, organisms are classified as follows, moving from comprehensive and specific similarities to fewer and more general similarities: species, genus, family, order, class, phylum, kingdom, and domain. A popular mnemonic device to remember the Linnean system is "Dear King Philip came over for good soup."

30. C: Nitrogen is the most abundant element in the atmosphere at 78%. Carbon dioxide and water don't make up a large percentage. Oxygen makes up only 21% of the atmosphere.

31. C: The dew point is the temperature at which the water vapor in a sample of air at constant barometric pressure condenses into water at the same rate at which it evaporates. It isn't a measure of pressure.

32. B: The Coriolis Effect is created by Earth's rotation. As wind moves toward the equator, the Earth's rotation also makes the wind move to the west. The Earth's axis and mountains don't play a part in the Coriolis Effect.

33. C: Dark storm clouds are considered nimbostratus clouds, which are located below 2,000 meters above sea level. There are no atmospheric clouds in outer space.

34. D: This system of equations involves one quadratic function and one linear function, as seen from the degree of each equation. One way to solve this is through substitution. Solving for y in the second equation yields $y = x + 2$. Plugging this equation in for the y of the quadratic equation yields $x^2 - 2x + x + 2 = 8$. Simplifying the equation, it becomes $x^2 - x + 2 = 8$. Setting this equal to zero and factoring, it becomes $x^2 - x - 6 = 0 = (x - 3)(x + 2)$. Solving these two factors for x gives the zeros $x = 3, -2$. To find the y-value for the point, each number can be plugged in to either original equation. Solving each one for y yields the points $(3, 5)$ and $(-2, 0)$.

35. D: Finding the zeros for a function by factoring is done by setting the equation equal to zero, then completely factoring. Since there was a common x for each term in the provided equation, that is factored out first. Then the quadratic that is left can be factored into two binomials: $(x + 1)(x - 4)$. Setting each factor equation equal to zero and solving for x yields three zeros.

36. D: Dividing rational expressions follows the same rule as dividing fractions. The division is changed to multiplication, and the reciprocal is found in the second fraction. This turns the expression into $\frac{5x^3}{3x^2} * \frac{3y^9}{25}$. Multiplying across and simplifying, the final expression is $\frac{xy^8}{5}$.

37. D: This problem can be solved by using unit conversions. The initial units are miles per minute. The final units need to be feet per second. Converting miles to feet uses the equivalence statement 1 mile=5,280 feet. Converting minutes to seconds uses the equivalence statement 1 minute=60 seconds. Setting up the ratios to convert the units is shown in the following equation: $\frac{72\ miles}{90\ minutes} * \frac{1\ minute}{60\ seconds} * \frac{5280\ feet}{1\ mile} = 70.4$ feet per second. The initial units cancel out, and the new, desired units are left.

38. C: Because the triangles are similar, the lengths of the corresponding sides are proportional. Therefore, $\frac{30+x}{30} = \frac{22}{14} = \frac{y+5}{y}$. This results in the equation $14(30 + x) = 22 \cdot 30$ which, when solved, gives $x = 17.1$. The proportion also results in the equation $14(y + 5) = 22y$ which, when solved, gives $y = 26.3$.

39. B: The technique of completing the square must be used to change $4x^2 + 4y^2 - 16x - 24y + 51 = 0$ into the standard equation of a circle. First, the constant must be moved to the right-hand side of the equals sign, and each term must be divided by the coefficient of the x^2 term (which is 4). The x

andy terms must be grouped together to obtain $x^2 - 4x + y^2 - 6y = -\frac{51}{4}$. Then, the process of completing the square must be completed for each variable. This gives $(x^2 - 4x + 4) + (y^2 - 6y + 9) = -\frac{51}{4} + 4 + 9$. The equation can be written as $(x - 2)^2 + (y - 3)^2 = \frac{1}{4}$. Therefore, the center of the circle is (2, 3) and the radius is $\sqrt{1/4} = 1/2$.

40. D: When an ordered pair is reflected over an axis, the sign of one of the coordinates must change. When it's reflected over the x-axis, the sign of the x coordinate must change. The y value remains the same. Therefore, the new ordered pair is $(-3, 4)$.

41. A: Because the volume of the given sphere is 288π cubic meters, this gives $\frac{4}{3}\pi r^3 = 288\pi$. This equation is solved for r to obtain a radius of 6 meters. When you find this phrase, the comma should go before "so" not after "so" is $4\pi r^2$ so, if $r = 6$ in this formula, the surface area is 144π square meters.

42. B: To simplify the given equation, the first step is to make all exponents positive by moving them to the opposite place in the fraction. This expression becomes $\frac{4b^3 b^2}{a^1 a^4} * \frac{3a}{b}$. Then the rules for exponents can be used to simplify. Multiplying the same bases means the exponents can be added. Dividing the same bases means the exponents are subtracted.

43. C: 216cm. Because area is a two-dimensional measurement, the dimensions are multiplied by a scale that is squared to determine the scale of the corresponding areas. The dimensions of the rectangle are multiplied by a scale of 3. Therefore, the area is multiplied by a scale of 3^2 (which is equal to 9):

$24cm \times 9 = 216cm$.

44. C: The perimeter is found by calculating the sum of all sides of the polygon. $9 + 9 + 9 + 8 + 8 + s = 56$, where s is the missing side length. Therefore, 43 plus the missing side length is equal to 56. The missing side length is 13 cm.

45. B: For the first card drawn, the probability of a King being pulled is $\frac{4}{52}$. Since this card isn't replaced, if a King is drawn first, the probability of a King being drawn second is $\frac{3}{51}$. The probability of a King being drawn in both the first and second draw is the product of the two probabilities: $\frac{4}{52}$ x $\frac{3}{51} = \frac{12}{2652}$ which, divided by 12, equals $\frac{1}{221}$.

46. A: If each man gains 10 pounds, every original data point will increase by 10 pounds. Therefore, the man with the original median will still have the median value, but that value will increase by 10. The smallest value and largest value will also increase by 10 and, therefore, the difference between the two won't change. The range does not change in value and, thus, remains the same.

47. C: The expected value is equal to the total sum of each product of individual score and probability. There are 36 possible rolls. The probability of rolling a 2 is $\frac{1}{36}$. The probability of rolling a 3 is $\frac{2}{36}$. The probability of rolling a 4 is $\frac{3}{36}$. The probability of rolling a 5 is $\frac{4}{36}$. The probability of rolling a 6 is $\frac{5}{36}$. The probability of rolling a 7 is $\frac{6}{36}$. The probability of rolling an 8 is $\frac{5}{36}$. The probability of rolling a 9 is $\frac{4}{36}$. The probability of rolling a 10 is $\frac{3}{36}$. The probability of rolling an 11 is $\frac{2}{36}$. Finally, the probability of rolling a 12 is $\frac{1}{36}$.

Each possible outcome is multiplied by the probability of it occurring. Like this:

$$2 \times \frac{1}{36} = a$$

$$3 \times \frac{2}{36} = b$$

$$4 \times \frac{3}{36} = c$$

And so forth.

Then all of those results are added together:

$$a + b + c \dots = expected\ value$$

In this case, it equals 7.

48. A: An outlier is a data value that is either far above or far below the majority of values in a sample set. The mean is the average of all the values in the set. In a small sample set, a very high or very low number could drastically change the average (or mean) of the data points. Outliers will have no more of an effect on the median (the middle value when arranged from lowest to highest) than any other value above or below the median. If the same outlier does not repeat, outliers will have no effect on the mode (value that repeats most often).

49. C: The scenario involves data consisting of two variables: month and stock value. Box plots display data consisting of values for one variable. Therefore, a box plot is not an appropriate choice. Both line plots and circle graphs are used to display frequencies within categorical data. Neither can be used for the given scenario. Line graphs display two numerical variables on a coordinate grid and show trends among the variables, so this is the correct choice.

50. D: The probability of picking the winner of the race is $\frac{1}{4} \left(\frac{number\ of\ favorable\ outcomes}{number\ of\ total\ outcomes} \right)$. Assuming the winner was picked on the first selection, three horses remain from which to choose the runner-up (these are dependent events). Therefore, the probability of picking the runner-up is $\frac{1}{3}$. To determine the probability of multiple events, the probability of each event is multiplied: $\frac{1}{4} \times \frac{1}{3} = \frac{1}{12}$.

51. D: Three girls for every two boys can be expressed as a ratio: 3:2. This can be visualized as splitting the school into 5 groups: 3 girl groups and 2 boy groups. The number of students in each group can be found by dividing the total number of students by 5:

650 divided by 5 equals 1 part, or 130 students per group

To find the total number of girls, the number of students per group (130) is multiplied by the number of girl groups in the school (3). This equals 390, answer *D*.

52. C: If the average of all six numbers is 6, that means $\frac{a+b+c+d+e+x}{6} = 6$. The sum of the first five numbers is 25, so this equation can be simplified to $\frac{25+x}{6} = 6$. Multiplying both sides by 6 gives $25 + x = 36$, and x, or the sixth number, is found to equal 11.

Movement Skills and Knowledge

Basic Movement Skills

Motor Skills and Movement Patterns in Children

Educators should be familiar with physical and neurological development, especially in terms of motor skills and development, to provide developmentally appropriate motor movement tasks. As young children grow and mature, they develop the ability to handle increasingly complex motor skills. Children learn to move and move to learn and, for this reason, physical activity is especially important in the classroom for young children and it should be incorporated into lessons. As children grow, their physical abilities gradually increase, and educators can begin to modify lessons and activities to continue to challenge and improve new movement patterns and abilities. What looks like "play" actually consists of meaningful movement patterns that help the child move his or her body and use large muscle groups to develop physical competency. This is known as movement education. Children should learn basic movement patterns and skills for daily life so that they can maneuver safely and appropriately in their environment in relation to other people and objects. After basic skills are mastered, more specific sport-related skills can be achieved. Movement competency is the successful ability of the child to manage his or her body in both basic and specialized physical tasks despite obstacles in the environment, while perceptual motor competency includes capabilities involving balance, coordination, lateral and backward movements, kinesthetic sense, and knowledge of one's own body and strength.

Educators should be able to assess the level at which students can control specific movements and identify patterns of physical activity that have been mastered. This information can be used to plan developmentally-appropriate movement tasks and activities. In addition, early childhood educators can be helpful in identifying students who seem to be lagging behind in age-appropriate motor abilities. In such cases, early intervention programming and resources may be beneficial.

There are three general categories of basic skills: locomotor, non-locomotor, and manipulative skills; more complex movement patterns combine skills from multiple categories. Locomotor skills – such as walking, running, jumping, and skipping – are the movement skills that children need to travel within a given space or get from one space to another. Non-locomotor skills are typically completed in a stationary position – such as kneeling, pushing, twisting, bouncing, or standing – and help control the body in relation to gravity. Manipulative skills usually involve using the hands and feet, although other body parts may be used. These skills help the child handle, move, or play with an object. Manipulating objects helps advance hand-eye and foot-eye coordination so that the child can more successfully participate in sports activities like throwing, batting, catching, and kicking.

Young children can begin to learn these skills with balls and beanbags at a less challenging level and progress to more difficult levels and activities with practice and development. Early stages usually involve individual practice first and then progress to involve partners and groups. Throwing and catching are actually quite complex skills that can be as challenging to teach as they are to learn. Early childhood educators should emphasize skill performance and principles such as opposition, following objects with the eyes, weight transfer, follow through, and, eventually, striking targets. Motor planning is the ability of the child to figure out how to complete a new motor task or action and depends on both the sensory motor development of the child as well as his or her thinking and reasoning skills.

361

Motor Development

Typical motor development milestones for various age groups are as follows:

Ages three to four: have mastered walking and standing and are now developing gross motor skills such as single foot hopping and balancing, unsupported ascent and descent of stairs, kicking a ball, overhand throwing, catching a ball off of a bounce, moving forward and backward with coordination, and riding a tricycle. Fine motor skills begin to progress including using scissors with one hand, copying capital letters and more complex shapes, and drawing basic shapes from memory.

Ages four to five: tackling increasingly complex gross motor skills that require some coordination and multiple movement patterns combined together such as doing somersaults, swinging, climbing, and skipping. They also can use utensils to eat independently, dress themselves with clothing containing zippers and buttons, and begin to tie shoelaces. Mastery of fine motor skills begins to progress more rapidly, including cutting and pasting, and drawing shapes, letters, and people with heads, bodies, and arms. They tend to engage in long periods of physical activity followed by a need for a significant amount of rest. Physically, bones are still developing. Girls tend to be more coordinated while boys are stronger, but both sexes lack precise fine motor skills and the ability to focus on small objects for a long time.

Children Enjoy Exercise with Games Like Tag

Age six to eight: skating, biking, skipping with both feet, dribbling a ball. By the end of grade two, children should be able to make smoother transitions between different locomotor skills sequenced together. They can also accomplish more complicated manipulative skills such as dribbling a soccer ball with their feet and can better control their bodies during locomotion, weight-bearing, and balance. Students can begin to use feedback to hone motor skills from a cognitive perspective.

Ages nine to eleven: Children begin to get stronger, leaner, and taller as they enter the pre-adolescent stage and growth accelerates with the beginnings of secondary sex characteristics. Attention span and gross and fine motor skills improve. By the end of grade five, most children can achieve more performance-based outcomes such as hitting targets and can complete specialized sports skills such as fielding baseballs and serving tennis balls. They are also able to combine movements in a more dynamic environment such as moving rhythmically to music. From a cognitive perspective, they can begin to take concepts and feedback learned in other skills or sports and apply them to a new game. An example of this is increasing body stability by bending the knees to lower the center of gravity in basketball during a pick drill; this skill can also be reapplied on the ski slope. Additionally, children begin to observe peers more and can provide feedback to others.

Muscles Involved in Gross Motor Movements

Gross motor skill movement involves using the whole body, especially core stabilizing muscles that involve general functionality, such as those necessary for standing, walking, running, and basic hand-eye coordination. A variety of activities can help improve children's gross motor skills.

Some suggestions to develop balance:

- Using a balance beam
- Participating in an obstacle course
- Jumping around on dots on a marked floor

To develop body control:

- Kicking balls and balloons
- Jumping over objects like lines, boxes, and beanbags

To prepare children for sports:

- Dancing to music
- Running, turning, twisting, and bending in unique ways

Muscles Involved in Fine Motor Movements

Fine motor skill movements involve using smaller muscles in the body like those that control the toes, fingers, wrists, and the eyes. Well-developed fine motor skills help a child complete tasks more efficiently and with more autonomy.

A variety of activities can help improve a child's fine motor skills. Opening and closing jars, manipulating beads and small handicrafts, mini golf, ping-pong, and other hand motor skills can augment these skills.

Physical activity helps children develop and refine their motor skills. Physical activity for children can take on many forms, including exercise, martial arts, walking and running, climbing trees, biking, playing tag, and sporting activities.

Additionally, exercise provides a host of benefits to the brain (creating and strengthening neural-pathways), lungs, muscles, the heart, vascular structures, tendons and ligaments, and bones. To maximize the benefits of exercise, children are encouraged to exercise for at least an hour a day.

Basic Structures of Bones, Skeletal Muscle, and Connective Tissue Bone

The skeleton is divided into the axial (skull, vertebrae, ribs, and sternum) and appendicular (shoulder girdles, arms, hips, legs) skeletons. There are two types of bone or osseous tissue. Compact (cortical) bone comprises 80 percent of bone mass and is made of dense, organized Haversian systems, which are arrangements of minerals, living bone cells, nerves, blood, and lymph vessels. Cancellous (spongy) bone, the other 20 percent of bone mass, lacks Haversian systems, is porous with trabeculae (lattice, branching arrangement), and has marrow and fat storage.

Skeletal Muscle

This muscle is voluntarily controlled by the nervous system and is elastic, extensible, and able to contract. It is striated, and cells have multiple nuclei.

Connective Tissue

The three major structures are tendons (attaching muscle to bone), ligaments (connecting bone to bone), and fascia (attaches, stabilizes, encloses, and separates muscles and other internal organs).

Basic Anatomy of Cardiovascular and Respiratory Systems

The heart has the smaller right and left atria on top of the larger right and left ventricles. A series of valves keeps blood flowing in the correct direction and prevents backflow to optimize cardiac efficiency: the bicuspid, tricuspid, pulmonary semilunar, and aortic semilunar valves.

The aorta is the main blood vessel branching off the top of the heart and sends blood to circulate through the body. The blood vessels, in order of decreasing size away from the heart, are arteries, arterioles, and capillaries. Towards the heart, from smallest to largest, are capillaries, venules, and veins.

Blood enters the (1) right atrium. When it contracts, blood passes through the (2) tricuspid valve into the (3) right ventricle. After filling, the right ventricle contracts, and the tricuspid valve closes, pushing blood through the (4) pulmonary semilunar valve into the (5) pulmonary arteries. These arteries, unlike all other arteries in the body, carry deoxygenated blood to the lungs, where blood travels through the (6) alveolar capillaries. Here, oxygen is absorbed and carbon dioxide is removed.

The newly-oxygenated blood is carried by the (7) pulmonary veins back to the (8) left atrium. Contraction of the left atrium moves blood through the (9) bicuspid valve into the (10) left ventricle (the largest heart chamber). When the bicuspid valve closes and the left ventricle contracts, blood is forced into the (11) aortic valve through the aorta and on to systemic circulation.

Heart Rate and Blood Pressure During Exercise

Both heart rate and systolic blood pressure increase linearly with exercise intensity.

Diastolic pressure may remain constant or decrease slightly over a bout of exercise, due to the reduced peripheral resistance that occurs during activity to facilitate oxygen delivery to muscles.

Age, fitness level, medications, temperature, hydration status, and body position can also affect heart rate. Younger children have faster heart rates and should be provided with more frequent rest breaks to allow the elevated heart rate to return to baseline.

Directions of Body Movements

- Inferior: toward the feet
- Superior: toward the head
- Medial: toward the body's midline
- Lateral: away from the body's midline
- Supination: typically used to describe forearm or ankle motion, rotating up and inward
- Pronation: typically used to describe forearm or ankle motion, rotating down and outward
- Flexion: a reduction in joint angle by two body segments around a joint coming closer together

- Extension: an increase in joint angle by two segments of the body around one joint moving apart
- Adduction: movement toward the body's midline
- Abduction: movement away from the body's midline (typically out to the side)
- Hyperextension: movement beyond the normal extension range of a joint
- Rotation: turning to the right or left, often of the head or neck or ankles
- Circumduction: moving in a circular motion, a compound motion involving flexion, extension, abduction, and adduction into one movement
- Agonist: the primary muscle involved in a motion
- Antagonist: the muscle that opposes a given motion
- Stabilizers: provide stability by contracting to hold joints or segments of the body in place while others around it are free to move

Planes of Body Movement

Physical education instructors should understand planes of body movement in order to diversify workouts and focus on all muscles, even smaller, weaker, or assistive muscles. While the body does not necessarily operate in an isolated plane of motion, exercises should focus on combining movements and planes of motion so that the child can more seamlessly flow from movement to movement with more flexibility and to prevent muscle imbalances. Understanding the proper form in which movement should occur in the planes also helps educators notice improper movements and correct them. The planes of movement of the body include the following:

- Frontal/Coronal: splits the body into front and back sections

- Sagittal: splits the body into right and left sections

- Midsagittal: the specific instance of a sagittal plane that divides the body into equal right and left halves

- Transverse: splits the body into top and bottom sections

Interrelationships Among Center of Gravity, Base of Support, Balance, and Stability

The center of gravity is the location of a theoretical point that represents the total weight of an object. In most humans, the center of gravity is anterior to the second sacral vertebrae.

The base of support refers to the part of an object that serves as the supporting surface, often thought of as feet in contact with the ground. The base of support extends to mean the area between the feet as well, not just the physical structures of the body in contact with the supporting surface. Increasing the base of support makes it easier to be more stable and have an easier time balancing.

Balance is the ability to control the center of mass within the base of support without falling. The wider the base of support and the lower the center of gravity, the easier it is to maintain balance. This concept can be applied to squatting. Teachers can instruct children to widen their base of support, squat back, and bring their hips back (as if they are sitting in a chair) in order to lower their center of mass without disturbing balance. Because younger children have a lower center of mass, they tend to have better balance than older adults.

Stability is the ability to lean or deviate the body in one direction or another without changing base of support (taking a step or replanting the feet). Stability, like balance, is improved with a wider base of support. It can also be improved with core training.

Proper spinal alignment refers to the composition of the spine, which is composed of thirty-three (seven cervical, twelve thoracic, five lumbar, five sacral, and four coccygeal) vertebrae and the discs between them. There are normal curvatures of the spine in the sagittal plane: cervical and lumbar lordosis (convex anteriorly and concave posteriorly) and thoracic and sacral kyphosis (concave anteriorly and convex posteriorly). It is important to utilize good posture during resistance exercises to protect the spine from injury.

Exercise Physiology: Health and Physical Fitness

Aerobic and Anaerobic Energy Systems

ATP is the energy molecule of the body and can be generated from the ATP-PC and glycolysis anaerobic (without oxygen) and aerobic (with oxygen) metabolic pathways.

- ATP-PC system: anaerobic, uses ATP stored in muscles, sufficient only for about ten-second high-intensity bouts of activity

- Glycolysis: anaerobic, creates ATP from carbohydrates (glucose) metabolism, used for two-three minutes of high intensity activity, but produces lactic acid as a byproduct

- Aerobic (Krebs cycle): aerobic, ATP generated through breakdown of carbohydrates, fats and, to a lesser degree, proteins, supplies energy during long duration endurance activities and used when the other energy systems are depleted or insufficient

Normal Acute Response to Cardiovascular and Resistance Training

At the onset of cardiovascular exercise, heart rate, blood pressure, and ventilation all increase immediately in healthy individuals in order to increase oxygen intake and transport, transitioning the body from anaerobic to aerobic energy systems. This same response is seen with resistance training, although these physiological variables do not typically remain elevated as the exercise session progresses because of the greater reliance on anaerobic metabolism for energy.

Normal Chronic Adaptations to Cardiovascular and Resistance Training

Heart and skeletal muscle hypertrophy is one of the chronic adaptations with regular cardiovascular and resistance training, respectively. With cardiovascular training, as the heart enlarges, the chamber sizes increase, allowing for a greater stroke volume and cardiac output. This also enables the heart to be more efficient, which lowers the resting heart rate and blood pressure as well as the submaximal exercise heart rate and blood pressure. It also increases exercise time and intensity tolerance. Total blood volume increases, reflecting both an increase in plasma volume and hemoglobin concentration. These circulatory adaptations increase the blood's oxygen-carrying capacity as well as the rate of removal of metabolic byproducts, such as carbon dioxide and lactate. The liver also becomes better able to metabolize the lactate from glycolysis, so that it can be used more effectively for energy. Endurance performance is often enhanced due to metabolic adaptations such as increased muscle glycogen storage and a greater reliance on fat (rather than carbohydrates) as an energy substrate at higher workloads. The ability to metabolize fat at greater intensities further spares glycogen, which can delay "hitting the wall"—a rapid onset of fatigue when the finite stores are consumed in the later stages of an endurance bout. Vasculature also increases, so blood perfusion of muscles improves. Other positive adaptations include increased bone mineral density, improvements in body composition, and neural adaptations.

Chronic resistance training also affords strength, power, and coordination improvements as well as greater efficiency of the anaerobic systems. Note that organized strength training with external weight is typically contraindicated for young children who are still growing and developing. Strength training can be safely incorporated into a young child's exercise habits, but exercises should entail the use of body weight only or resistance bands.

With strength training, nervous system adaptations occur quickly, as motor units (an alpha motor neuron from the spine and all of the skeletal muscle fibers it innervates) become conditioned to activate more quickly and more often, increasing the efficiency of stimulating muscle fibers to contract. As more motor units activate together and coordinate, a higher percentage of fibers in a muscle contract simultaneously, improving strength. In fact, many of the earliest strength improvements noticed in resistance training programs are due to these neural adaptations rather than muscle hypertrophy (which takes four to eight weeks to occur). A person can experience increased strength and power very quickly as a result of training. Over time, muscle fibers increase in size and bone mineral density increases in load-bearing bones, helping mitigate age-related bone and muscle loss.

Physiologic Response to Warm-Up and Cool-Down

Warm-ups and cool-downs are important components of the workout and help reduce injury risk by gradually transitioning the cardiovascular and musculoskeletal systems of the body between levels of rest and activity. They also improve joint range of motion by increasing the extensibility of connective tissue.

Effective warm-ups should begin by stoking the cardiovascular system with gentle, total body movements to start increasing heart rate and blood pressure, which better circulates oxygen, nutrients, and blood to the muscles. Specific muscles can be targeted (those that the training session will be focusing on) as the warm-up progresses.

The transition from exercise back to resting conditions is equally important and is the function of a cool-down. Without a proper cool-down to slow the heart rate gradually, cardiac dysrhythmias and feelings of dizziness can occur due to the decrease in venous return.

Blood Pressure Responses

It is important to be aware of blood pressure (BP) changes during exercise, especially with the increasing number of people with hypertension. The following are the blood pressure responses:

- Acute exercise: As exercise intensity increases, there is a linear increase in systolic BP, while diastolic may decrease slightly or remain unchanged due to the decreased peripheral resistance.

- Chronic exercise: Resting BP may decrease, and BP is lower at a given level of submaximal work.

- Postural changes: Exercise may produce hypotensive response because of the reduced aortic pressure and improved pliability of blood vessels. If BP gets very low, children may experience orthotic hypotension (dizziness when standing). Teachers should encourage fluid intake and have children change positions more gradually.

Muscle Actions

Physical education instructors need to be familiar with muscle actions and be cognizant that they should incorporate all types of contractions into workouts for optimal functional strength.

- Isotonic: a muscle contraction that exerts a constant tension
- Isometric: a muscle contraction in which there is no change in muscle length
- Isokinetic: a muscle contraction that moves through the range of motion at a constant speed
- Concentric: a muscle contraction with shortening, such as the biceps in the lifting portion of the biceps curl
- Eccentric: a lengthening muscle contraction, such as the biceps in the lowering the weight portion of the movement, frequently the cause of DOMS

Major Muscles

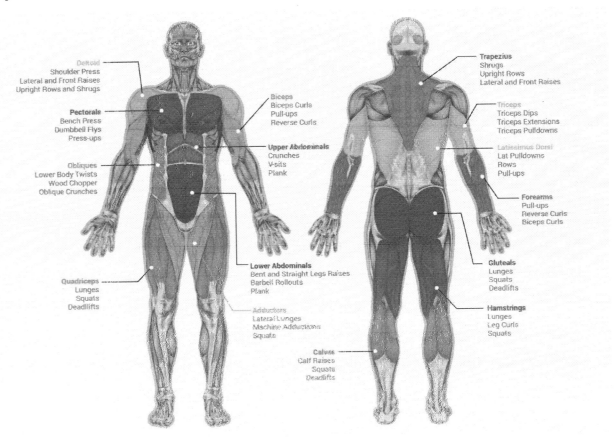

Teachers should not only be aware of muscle names, but also their origins, insertions, primary action, and nerve innervation. An understanding of these criteria can help in identifying injuries. It can also help ensure that exercises are targeting all muscles to maximize strength, strengthen stabilizing muscles, and provide proximal stability for functional distal mobility.

- Upper body muscles: trapezius, pectoralis major, deltoids, serratus anterior, latissimus dorsi, biceps, triceps, rectus abdominis, internal and external obliques, erector spinae, rhomboids, flexor carpi radialis

- Lower body muscles: iliopsoas, gluteus maximus, quadriceps, piriformis, hamstrings, adductors, abductors, soleus, gastrocnemius

Major Bones

Knowledge of bone anatomy enables the physical education instructor to understand the bones involved in joint motions and the bones that may be implicated in certain orthopedic injuries, which is important when communicating with physicians. There are different types of bones. Flat bones, like the cranial bones of the skull and the sternum, protect internal organs. Long bones, like the femur and tibia, support weight and facilitate movement. Short bones, like the carpal bones in the wrist, provide stability and some movement. Irregular bones also protect structures like the vertebrae over the spinal cord. Lastly, sesamoid bones, like the patella, protect tendons from stress.

- Upper body bones: clavicle, scapula, sternum, humerus, carpals, ulna, radius, metacarpals, vertebrae, ribs

- Lower body bones: ilium, ischium, pubis, femur, fibula, tibia, metatarsals, tarsals

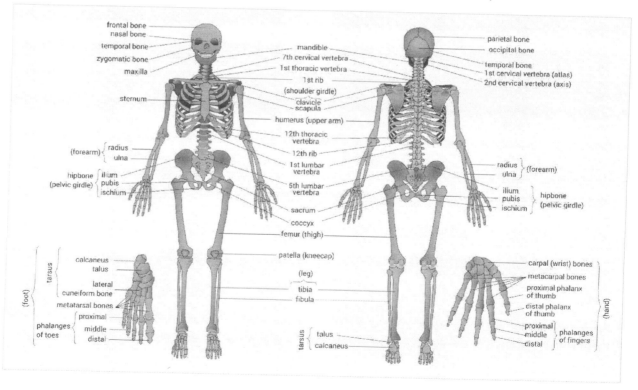

Joint Classifications

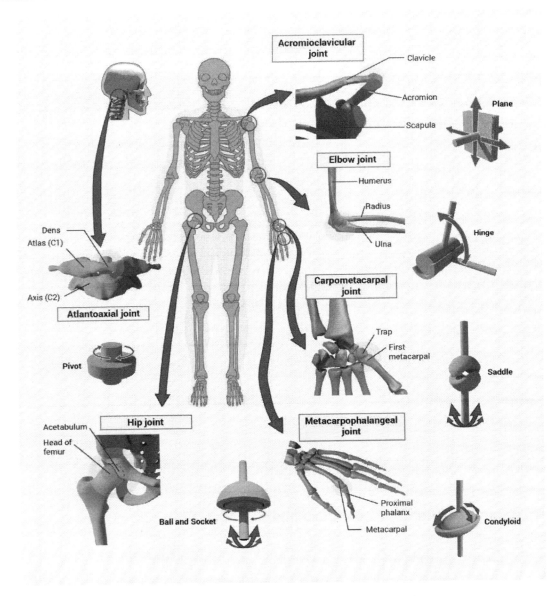

Joints can be classified based on structure of how the bones are connected:

- Fibrous joints: bones joined by fibrous tissue and that lack a joint cavity, e.g., sutures of the skull

- Cartilaginous joints: bones joined by cartilage and lack a joint cavity, e.g., the pubic symphysis

- Synovial joints: bones separated by a fluid-containing joint cavity with articular cartilage covering the ends of the bone and forming a capsule

- Plane joints: flat surfaces that allow gliding and transitional movements, e.g., intercarpal joints

- Hinge joints: cylindrical projection that nests in a trough-shaped structure, single plane of movement (e.g. the elbow)

- Pivot joints: rounded structure that sits into a ring-like shape, allowing uniaxial rotation of the bone around the long axis (e.g. radius head on ulna)

- Condyloid joints: oval articular surface that nests in a complementary depression, allowing all angular movements (e.g. the wrist)

- Saddle joints: articular surfaces that both have complementary concave and convex areas, allowing more movement than condyloid joints (e.g. the thumb)

- Ball-and-socket joints: spherical structure that fits in a cuplike structure, allowing multiaxial movements (e.g. the shoulder)

Primary Action and Joint Range of Motion

Each type of joint permits different movements, controlled by the shape of the joint and the muscles surrounding it. Educators should be aware of these movements and the normal ROM to ensure that students are performing exercises safely, are within a healthy range, and are utilizing a variety of motions to optimize health and muscular balance. Ball-and-socket joints, like the shoulder and hip, are the most mobile and allow flexion, extension, abduction, adduction, internal and external rotation, and circumduction. The elbow is a hinge joint and allows flexion and extension. Intervertebral joints are cartilaginous and allow flexion, extension, lateral flexion, and rotation. The ankle has a hinge joint (dorsiflexion, plantarflexion) and a gliding joint (inversion, eversion).

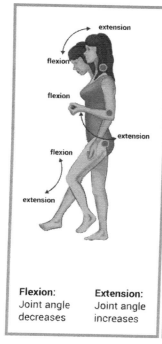
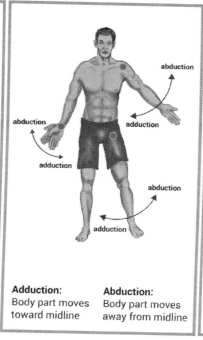
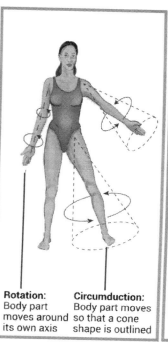
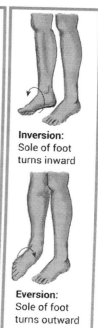

Flexion: Joint angle decreases

Extension: Joint angle increases

Adduction: Body part moves toward midline

Abduction: Body part moves away from midline

Rotation: Body part moves around its own axis

Circumduction: Body part moves so that a cone shape is outlined

Inversion: Sole of foot turns inward

Eversion: Sole of foot turns outward

Muscle Terms

- Hypertrophy: increase in muscle fiber cross-sectional area, often an adaptation from strength training, an increase in fiber size, not fiber number, muscle strength gained from resistance training mostly due to hypertrophy

- Atrophy: reduction in muscle size due to a decrease in fiber cross-sectional area (opposite of hypertrophy) often due to physical inactivity, disease, nutritional inadequacies, or a disease of the muscle or nerve supplying the muscle

- Hyperplasia: an increase in muscle size due to an increase in the number of muscle fibers

Components of Physical Fitness

A well-rounded program addresses all five components of health-related physical fitness:

- Cardiovascular fitness: capacity of circulatory and respiratory systems to supply oxygen during continued activity
- Muscular strength: force capability of a muscle
- Muscular endurance: ability to maintain level of muscular work without fatigue
- Body composition: relative amounts of body fat, muscle, bone, and other tissues
- Flexibility: permitted joint range of motion

Normal Chronic Physiological Adaptations Associated with Cardiovascular, Resistance, and Flexibility Training

Cardiovascular training increases the number of mitochondria and oxidative enzymes on a cellular level, as well as facilitates an increase in capillaries and muscle blood flow, all leading to improved aerobic metabolism. Muscle glycogen storage increases, as well as the enhanced ability to metabolize fat for energy to spare glycogen stores. There are increases in cardiac output and stroke volume (due to increased plasma volume and left ventricle size) during exercise, as well as a lower resting and submaximal heart rate and blood pressure. VO_2 max and lactate threshold can increase as can the maximal pulmonary ventilation rate.

Resistance training increases skeletal muscle force due to hypertrophy (increase in cross-sectional area of muscle fibers) and greater, more coordinated fiber recruitment due to neural adaptations. There is also increased strength and size of tendons and ligaments, ATP-PC and glycogen stores, and improvements in lactate utilization.

Flexibility training increases the elasticity and resting length of muscle and connective tissues and joint ROM before the stretch reflex is initiated (muscle spindle adaptation), reducing injury risk.

Prevention of Common Injuries and Health Problems

One critically important component of health and safety education is the prevention of common injuries and illnesses. By practicing safety and exercising caution, many common injuries and illnesses can be avoided. For example, wearing helmets and seat belts can reduce the risk of injury during automobile or bicycle accidents. Washing hands thoroughly and frequently with antibacterial soap can help prevent the spread of germs, and thus safeguard against viral and bacterial infections. Even very young children should be encouraged to wash hands thoroughly before and after eating, after using the bathroom, after coming in from outdoor play, and when transitioning to a new activity. It is sometimes helpful to demonstrate how to wash in between each finger, under the fingernails, and up to the wrists, modeling not only how to wash hands but for how long. The common song "Row, Row, Row Your Boat" repeated three times is sometimes used to measure the appropriate length of time for hand washing.

By instilling an attitude of mindfulness and awareness, educators can help children to develop practices of safety, which will ultimately keep them healthy. Other longer-term behavioral and lifestyle principles – such as keeping a healthy weight through caloric balance and a healthy diet – will help prevent disease risk factors such as obesity, high triglycerides, hypercholesterolemia, and high blood sugar. Children should be informed about the dangers of smoking and the detrimental health consequences of tobacco products, including ingestion of secondhand smoke. Other simple safety practices include wearing proper footwear, practicing good hygiene, remaining alert when out in traffic, using sidewalks and pedestrian walkways, and wearing sunscreen.

Wearing Seat Belts and Helmets

Children should be informed that they should always wear a seat belt in the car. Children under eighty pounds should be in an appropriate car seat as well to maximize safety in moving vehicles. Many unfortunate traffic injuries and fatalities could have been prevented had the victim appropriately worn a seat belt. Riding bicycles, skateboarding, using scooters, and rollerblading are examples of excellent exercise and recreational pursuits; however, helmets and appropriate padding and protection on elbows and knees should always be worn. Children or their supervisors often neglect to fasten on a helmet when the child is simply trying out a skateboard or scooter around the driveway or park. This is quite dangerous because falls are inevitable in the learning process and even minor head bumps can be damaging. Helmets should fit snugly with the band clipped securely under the chin and the dome of the helmet should cover the entire forehead. Helmets should not move freely on the head and should be snug enough to stay in place. They should be sized appropriately to the child's head with use of additional padding if necessary. Kneepads and shoulder pads are great adjuncts to safety gear for rollerblading, skateboarding, and scooters. Children riding in bicycle trailers should also wear helmets, and children should never ride on the handlebars of a bicycle. Although more stable, tricycles and bicycles with training wheels still require helmets with their use.

Drugs, Alcohol, and Tobacco

Drugs, alcohol, and tobacco are unhealthy substances that early childhood educators should begin informing young children about. Exposure to drugs, cigarettes, and alcohol happens at increasingly younger ages, particularly when children have older siblings. By educating children about the risks and consequences of such substances at young ages, teachers can begin to thwart the risks of unhealthy behaviors. The Drug Abuse Resistance Education (D.A.R.E.) program is often helpful at introducing such substances, their health consequences, and how to navigate social situations involving peer pressure. The difference between alcohol abuse and alcohol in moderation should also be discussed.

Routine Preventative Medical and Dental Care

By practicing routine medical and dental care and adhering to recommended guidelines regarding the frequency of preventative healthcare, certain risks for various diseases and dental issues (such as cavities and gingivitis) can be reduced. It is typically recommended the children see their pediatrician and get dental cleanings at least once every six months. In between these appointments, healthy habits continue to safeguard against health issues. Examples include thoroughly brushing teeth at least twice a day and flossing daily, getting at least sixty minutes of moderate to vigorous exercise a day, meeting healthy sleep requirements (the National Sleep Foundation recommends ten to thirteen hours for preschoolers and nine to eleven hours for elementary school children), consuming an adequate amount of water, and following nutritional guidelines. By keeping children on a routine schedule of preventive care with consistency in providers of that care, the health and wellbeing of each child can be tracked during their growth to ensure health issues do not slip through the cracks.

Food Preparation Choices

Early childhood educators should devote instructional attention to the methods of food preparation and how various choices in preparation affect the nutritive value of the food. For example, baking and steaming are healthier than pan frying, deep frying, and sautéing. Eating whole foods is healthier than eating their processed counterparts because the whole foods retain a greater percentage of the inherent nutrients. For example, apples are healthier than applesauce because applesauce strips away much of the fiber and the vitamins in the apple skin. Similarly, whole grain bread is healthier than refined white breads, which remove the bran from the grain, thereby reducing the fiber, protein, and B vitamin content. Foods that are organic do not have the pesticides and chemicals used with certain conventional foods. This is an important consideration for thin-skinned fruits and vegetables such as spinach, tomatoes, and berries, which can absorb harmful chemicals.

Self-Image and Personal Development

Physical Growth and Development

The Relation Between Healthy Behaviors and a Healthy Person

Early childhood educators can introduce young children to a wide variety of healthy behaviors that will help improve overall health. An important concept to begin teaching students is that optimal health is brought about through routine practice of daily healthy behaviors and an overall commitment to a healthy lifestyle. For example, educators can discuss the importance of establishing regular physical activity and daily healthy eating habits and that, through these habits, students can control their body weight and help avoid obesity. Obesity is a modifiable risk factor for many diseases including insulin-resistant Type 2 diabetes mellitus and cardiovascular disease. It is important and empowering for children to start to understand their roles and responsibilities in healthy habits and disease prevention. By giving them the necessary knowledge and tools to put the information into practice in their lives, educators can increase the self-efficacy and behaviors of even young children. In this way, early childhood educators can be instrumental in bringing about a healthier generation of young children who have an awareness of their health and an understanding of their own influence on risk factors for certain diseases. The following are healthy behaviors that can lead to a healthy body and mind:

Nutrition

Children should be taught how to identify foods and the importance of consuming a daily variety of food within each healthy food group. The benefits of trying new foods, especially those from other cultures, can help students understand diversity and challenge their preconceived notions about different cultures and flavors. Older children can learn how to prepare simple foods, recognize the USDA recommended daily allowances of each food group in order to keep the body healthy, and classify foods based on their group and health benefits. Older students can also learn about the role of various nutrients in the body such as fat, fiber, and protein, and how to select nutrient-dense foods from a given list. Children benefit from understanding what makes a food healthy and knowing options for healthy meals and snacks. By the third grade, students can start learning how to read nutrition labels, how to compare foods based on nutrition labels, and how to modify food choices to improve healthfulness, such as replacing low-fiber foods with higher fiber choices, like opting for apples instead of applesauce. When students are in the fourth grade, educators can start talking about portion sizes and the relationship between food consumption and physical activity on energy balance and weight control. In the context of introducing the basics about calories, prevention of obesity and the ramifications of an unhealthy diet can also be discussed. Children in the fifth and sixth grades can learn about the differences in types of fats, examples of common vitamins and minerals and food sources of these nutrients, the disadvantages of "empty-calories," and how to recognize misleading nutrition information.

Physical Activity

In childhood, regular physical activity improves strength and endurance, helps build healthy bones and muscles, controls weight, reduces anxiety and stress, increases self-esteem, and may improve blood pressure and cholesterol. Children should get at least sixty minutes of physical activity daily. Typically, young children are less concerned about their physical fitness and more concerned about having fun; therefore, physical education should center on fun and play as a means to engage the body in activity. Play-centered physical education programs are an effective means to promote children's movement development and meet their requisite activity needs for health. Early childhood educators should develop physical education programs that focuses on the enjoyment of movement rather than sport-specific skill mastery for two reasons. Firstly, play-centered activity will help the child be more engaged and likely to adopt a positive attitude towards exercise; and secondly, in early childhood, basic general fitness and movement skills are more important than mastery of highly specialized skills unique to certain sports. Young children also tend to lack the gross and fine motor skills and perceptual abilities needed for such highly specialized skills, which can lead to frustration or simply an inability to perform the activity.

For optimal results, it is best for early childhood educators to establish an environment of student-centered learning in regards to physical education. Because young children at any given age can have vastly different motor and physical abilities from each other, it is imperative that the educator simply set standards of enjoyment, movement, and physical discovery rather than specific mastery of skills. This prevents boredom in more physically advanced children and bewilderment and demotivation in less skilled children. It is prudent for educators to provide a variety of options within every activity and game so that children can figure out what appeals and works for them at their own developmental level. This also starts children on the path to understanding themselves and evaluating choices at a young age within a fun, playful environment and begins to get their minds processing not just what to do but how to do it as well.

Educators should use simple instructions that are age-appropriate in terms of the steps and level of complexity, visual demonstrations of movements, and drills that help reinforce the skill. During practice and exploration of the new skill, educators should focus on positive feedback and evaluation to guide the children in learning. When teaching new skills, especially to toddlers and young children, instructions lasting longer than twenty seconds or that contain more than just a couple of steps will cause students to lose interest or get overwhelmed. It is typically advantageous to have very short instructional periods interspersed between longer breaks to play and try out the skills. To help manage a large group of small, active children, simple rules and expectations should be laid out with consequences for improper behavior.

Children should learn about the methods and benefits of a proper warm-up and cool-down, how to set goals to make exercise part of their daily routine, and the benefits of physical activity. Older children can learn about the effects of exercise on the heart and how to locate their pulse during and after exercise, how to stay physically active through more than just sports, and how to create a personal fitness plan.

Sleep
Early childhood educators should talk about the importance of sleep and why parents set a "bedtime," as well as healthy sleep hygiene and establishing a sleep schedule. Children can learn about how much sleep they need and ways to improve the quality of sleep, such as physical activity and avoiding screen time before bed. Young children who may experience nightmares can benefit from learning relaxation techniques as well as talking about their fears and feelings to trusted adults.

Stress Management
Students should be educated about stress management and exposed to techniques such as mental imagery, relaxation, deep breathing, aerobic exercise, and meditation. Children can be guided through progressive muscle relaxation and should be taught signs of excessive nervousness and stress, how to manage test and performance anxiety, and when and how to get help with excessive stress.

Healthy Relationships

Healthy family and social relationships are important to overall health and happiness. Studies have pointed to a negative impact of parental fighting on a child's wellbeing, including sleep and exercise habits, nutrition choices, stress, and social adjustment. Early childhood educators should talk about aspects of healthy relationships such as communication, emotional support, sharing, and respect. Younger children should learn skills that are helpful in making friends, cultivating relationships, and resolving conflict, especially as they relate to peers and siblings. Cooperation, taking turns, using words rather than physical means to communicate feelings, and exploring feelings are helpful concepts to instill. Older children should begin to be exposed to dating etiquette and forming healthy romantic relationships. Educators should work to create a classroom environment of inclusion where students have an awareness of peers who may feel left out and work to include everyone. Within discussions of healthy relationships, educators should talk about accepting and appreciating diversity, including differences in cultures, religions, families, physical appearance and abilities, interests, intellect, emotions, lifestyle, and, in older children, sexual orientations. Life skills – such as having self-esteem, making decisions, calming oneself when angry or upset, and using listening skills – should be addressed.

Hydration

Early childhood educators should teach students about the importance of hydration and signs of dehydration as well as healthy choices for fluids, with a special emphasis on water. Children and their parents should be encouraged to send kids to school with a water bottle, and classrooms or hallways should be equipped with water fountains that children can access and use with limited supervision or assistance.

Safety Behaviors

Children should learn basic safety behaviors and the importance of following rules to prevent common injuries. Basic safety behaviors include wearing sunscreen and sunglasses when going outdoors; wearing protective gear in sports such as bicycle helmets, reflective vests, appropriate pads and cups, etc.; and using a car seat and/or always wearing a seat belt. Young children should learn about household safety such as not touching burners and not putting their fingers in electrical sockets nor opening the door to strangers. Educators should have children practice the "no, go, and tell" procedure for unsafe situations. For example, if a stranger offers the child an unknown substance, the child should know how to firmly refuse, carefully leave the situation, and tell a trusted adult. In this lesson, educators should also help children to identify trusted adults in their families and communities.

Educators can also discuss community safety measures such as using sidewalks, contacting city services (police, fire, and ambulance) in emergencies, and crossing the street safely by using crosswalks, holding hands, and looking both ways before crossing. Children should also learn about the health consequences of smoking, how to avoid secondhand smoke, and how to identify and avoid poisonous household substances. Fire safety such as "stop, drop, and roll" and emergency evacuation procedures should be rehearsed. Older children can learn about safety rules for various types of weather and how weather affects their personal safety, what different traffic signs mean, water/swim safety rules, and the importance of weighing consequences before taking risks.

Hygiene

Young children should learn about germs and the spread of infections. Older children can learn about bacteria and viruses. The importance of washing hands (including appropriate demonstration) cannot be overstated in elementary and preschool classrooms.

Other aspects of hygiene such as covering the mouth while coughing and covering the nose while sneezing, not sharing cups, practicing clean bathroom habits, showering and bathing, and, in older children, using deodorants, antiperspirants, and facial cleansers should be included in the curriculum.

Hygiene Stickers Remind Students to Use Healthy Practices

Promoting Physical Fitness, Responsible Behavior, and Respect in Physical Activity Settings

The youngest students enjoy being physically active for the fun of movement itself, and they particularly enjoy non-structured activities in moderate and high intensities followed by sufficient rest. By the end of second grade, students will likely voluntarily incorporate activities from physical education class to leisure time activity and, although they are not typically concerned with structured exercise or activity recommendations for health, they do recognize the physical and mental benefits of activity and they self-select game-like play they enjoy. They are able to recognize the physiologic indicators of exercise such as elevated heart rate, sweating, and heavy breathing; they have a general understanding that physical fitness improves health; and they know that there are five components of health-related fitness: cardiovascular endurance, muscular strength, muscular endurance, flexibility, and body composition.

By the end of fifth grade, students should be aware that participation in regular physical activity is a conscious decision, and they should choose activities based on both enjoyment and health benefits. At this age, they begin to develop an awareness of resources and opportunities in the school and community to support activity and may become more interested in healthy food choices, realizing that personal responsibility and their own choices can affect their health. They also become more aware of their body and voice in a complex dynamic environment with others, and have greater focus towards controlling parts of their body and their movements within an environment with others. Students should also begin to take an interest in improving aspects of fitness for better sports' performance or health indicators, and should apply the results of fitness assessments to gain a deeper understanding of their own personal fitness and health compared with peers and standards. Older students also understand that success comes with practice and effort, and they also enjoy broadening their skills and activities by learning new sports and skills based on prior mastery. They can engage in mutual physical activity with students of differing ability levels.

Influence of Family, Peers, Culture, and Media on Health Behaviors

Health behaviors are heavily influenced by a child's environment, including family, friends, peers, media, and technology. These factors can shape the child's ideas of health, nutrition, and fitness, as well as influence subsequent health behaviors. It is important for educators to help children identify and cultivate positive influences while avoiding or modifying negative ones.

Educators should work with students to develop self-efficacy for healthy behaviors to help safeguard against any negative environmental influences. Children should learn about peer pressure, substance use, wearing seat belts, and how to make independent decisions and stick to them despite peer pressure or group dynamics. Discussed below are a few examples of potential environmental and situational influences.

Family
Family factors include health insurance status, safety and injury prevention education and care, nutritional meal planning and diet composition, family dynamics and stress, family culture during leisure time such as activity vs. inactivity, child care situation, and parental and sibling modeled behavior.

Peers
The peer group that surrounds a child can affect his or her health behaviors depending on those of the group. Example behaviors and influences include the use of helmets and seat belts, interests and activities, inclusion on sports teams or during recess and physical education, aggression and bullying or teasing.

School and Community
Factors in this domain include things such as the availability and choices of food in vending machines, school breakfast and lunch programs, health education and screenings, first aid and AED (automated external defibrillator) access, bike paths and walking trails, parks and community fitness and sports programs, crosswalks, and non-smoking zones.

Public Policy and Government
Tobacco and alcohol sales and policies, seat belt and helmet enforcement, child care laws, and other such regulations fall under the domain of public policy and governmental influences.

Media
Media use and exposure can have a significant impact on young minds. Children have not necessarily developed the critical thinking skills needed to evaluate the truthfulness of media claims. Television programming and commercials, PSAs, advertising, exposure to celebrities, knowledge of current events, and consumer skills all fall under this domain.

Technology
Technological factors including Internet access, handicap accessibility such as audio signals at crosswalks and wheelchair ramps and lifts, health technology apps, and pedometer availability can affect health behaviors.

Health Promotion and Disease Prevention

Early childhood educators should be able to incorporate health and physical education concepts into the classroom for the overall health, wellness, and growth of their students. Physical activity is especially important at young ages, and children need at least sixty minutes of moderate to vigorous physical activity daily according to the U.S. Surgeon General's Recommendations. There are five components of health-related physical fitness: cardiovascular fitness, muscular strength, muscular endurance, flexibility, and body composition. All five areas should be addressed in physical education classes. With cardiovascular training, as the heart enlarges, the volume of the chambers increase, allowing for a greater stroke volume and cardiac output. This also enables the heart to be more efficient, with a resultant lowering of the resting and submaximal exercise heart rate and blood pressure, which increases the body's exercise duration and intensity tolerance. Blood volume—both in terms of plasma and hemoglobin—increases oxygen-carrying capacity and lactic acid metabolism improves, which allows the aerobic system to more effectively metabolize substrates for usable energy. Muscle glycogen storage, another important form of energy storage in the body, also increases. Vasculature increases as well, improving the blood perfusion of muscles.

Other positive results of physical fitness include increased bone mineral density, improvements in body composition, and neural adaptations. Resistance training, even with body weight alone (such as squats and push-ups), affords strength, power, and coordination improvements and leads to greater efficiency of the anaerobic metabolic systems. Nervous system adaptations occur quickly with training as motor units (connections between the spine and other muscles throughout the body) become conditioned to activate more quickly and more often. As a greater number of motor units activate together and coordinate with each other, a higher percentage of fibers in a muscle contract simultaneously, increasing strength. Over time, muscle fibers increase in size and bone mineral density increases in load-bearing bones. Flexibility training increases elasticity and resting length of muscle and connective tissues and joint range of motion (ROM) before the stretch reflex is initiated (muscle spindle adaptation), reducing injury risk.

Health education – even beginning at preschool ages – has been shown to have a significant positive impact on an individual for maintaining healthy behaviors as an adolescent and adult. Preschool children who receive high-quality physical and health education may have improved nutrition and exercise habits and are more likely to receive routine medical and dental care as adults. Early childhood educators can start laying the groundwork for a lifetime of healthier behaviors and attitudes by fostering an environment of enjoyment of physical activity, an understanding of nutrition and hydration, and methods of disease and injury prevention.

Educators can talk with older children about the types, causes, and characteristics of chronic, degenerative, communicable, and non-communicable diseases, as well as ways to detect and prevent them. Students can learn about modifiable risk factors for various diseases and conditions such as diabetes, coronary artery disease, cardiovascular disease, and obesity.

Health Advocacy

Students have a lot to gain by cultivating advocacy skills, especially as they relate to promoting healthy behaviors. Students can learn how to advocate for personal, family, and community health resources and opportunities and establish health-enhancing messages that encourage others to also adopt and maintain a healthy lifestyle. Young children can work on how to advocate for healthy policies in their own schools and communities, such as ensuring easy access to drinking water and banning smoking on school grounds. They can also work on ways to encourage peers to make positive health choices, focusing on supporting one another and getting everyone to join the "team" of good health advocates. Older students can research and learn about various health issues and then make presentations to other students and family members to share accurate health information. The following are a few specific advocacy skills that educators should work to enhance in their students:

Locate Valid Health Resources in the Home, School, Community, and Media
One of the greatest challenges for children and adults alike is vetting various health resources in the home, school, community, and especially media for their validity and accuracy. Unfortunately, fad diets are popularized in the media daily. The weight loss industry is a multi-billion-dollar industry for a reason: people are desperate to lose weight and are often looking for the "quick fix" that many of these diets and exercise gadgets promise. However, many of these fad diets are dangerous, have not been developed by health professionals, or do not have sufficient scientific research to validate their safety or efficacy. For instance, fad diets often eliminate entire food groups or claim that the diet is some sort of health panacea. Other unhealthy methods promising rapid weight loss in popular culture include exercise in saunas or steam rooms to "sweat off pounds," starvation or liquid diets, cleanses, and mega doses of dietary supplements. These can cause dangerous dehydration, overdoses on certain micronutrients, and electrolyte imbalances leading to arrhythmias, and a reduced resting metabolic rate as the body senses starvation, which makes subsequent weight loss harder.

Educators should teach students how to critically evaluate information, particularly from the media, and judge its accuracy. School resources may include things such as the physical education department and health education resources, the Great Body Shop health curriculum, the infirmary or nurse's office, the D.A.R.E program, and other health-informing programs. In the community, additional resources include S.A.D.D. (Students Against Destructive Decisions), the Red Cross, local medical and health offices, and WIC (Women, Infants, and Children) offices.

In the media, students should look for reliable sources of information such as myplate.gov and other government-sponsored health resources, peer-reviewed research journals, PBS or NOVA documentaries, TED Talks, course content from colleges and universities, etc. Students should not only be informed about correct and accurate information, but should also develop the skills to independently determine the validity of resources when they are faced with new information.

Develop Sound Opinions about Health Issues

A critical skill for children to develop is the ability to form informed opinions and back up their opinions with sound evidence. This need extends beyond the realms of health and fitness and can apply to all facets of life, but health information and behaviors are some of the more approachable and applicable topics for young children. Behaviors such as the choice not to smoke or consume drugs and alcohol, the practice of engaging in an active lifestyle over a sedentary one, the consumption of home-cooked or lower fat food choices over fried or fast foods, the intake of water over sodas and juices, and even safety behaviors such as wearing a helmet are all choices and issues that children can begin to consider and establish their own personal standards for.

Early childhood educators can help guide children to the healthful choices by presenting the information and facts about each choice and its consequences as well as engage children in brainstorming sessions to come up with ideas and tactics to support their choices for healthy behaviors. For example, if a family typically stops at the local fast food drive-through after soccer practice, children can talk to their parents about packing healthy snacks for the car ride home instead and even work with parents in the kitchen to make snacks such as vegetable sticks and hummus and cheese and apple slices. Children can even make posters or perform skits to defend their healthy opinions and share such information with younger grades.

The ability to not only form an opinion but also explain and support the reasoning behind it will serve students well throughout their education and lives in general. At the same time, educators should encourage students to keep an open mind and practice critical listening and analytical skills so that they remain open to other people's opinions and can modify their own with changes in research or situations. Particularly in the fields of health and nutrition, where research and science are constantly evolving, the "healthy option" does tend to change. Considering dietary recommendations alone, macronutrient (nutrients required in large amounts, like protein and carbohydrates) intake is constantly changing and the thinking about the healthfulness of saturated fats and carbohydrates shifts. The educated consumer is one who stays abreast of the research and also has the ability to alter his or her own opinions based on changes in the information.

Help Assist Others in Making Healthy Choices

One component of advocacy is supporting and assisting others in making healthy choices. Once students have formulated educated opinions about health-related topics like diet, exercise, safety habits, and substance use, they can become educators and advocates themselves. Students can then share their knowledge and reasoning with peers, family, friends, neighbors, and the community. For example, students can create and posters with health information they have learned and hang them in their schools, homes, or other community areas. Students with younger siblings can help them develop good hygiene and safety habits.

Use Effective Communication Skills

Early childhood educators are instrumental in developing effective communication skills in their students. Verbal and nonverbal communication skills are important in setting a positive, educational, supportive environment to optimize learning. They are equally important for students to master for use in their own daily lives. When communicating with others, students should be mindful to be fully attentive, make eye contact, and use encouraging facial expressions and body language to augment positive verbal feedback. Postures including hands on hips or crossed over the chest may appear standoffish, while smiling and nodding enhance the comfort and satisfaction of the other party. Active listening is the process of trying to understand the underlying meaning in someone else's words, which builds empathy and trust. Asking open-ended questions and repeating or rephrasing in a reflective or clarifying manner is a form of active listening that builds a positive, trusting relationship.

In tandem with different communication styles, educators and students alike should be aware of different learning styles. Auditory learners learn through hearing, so the educator can use verbal descriptions and instructions. Visual learners learn through observation, so the educator can use demonstrations, provide written and pictorial instructional content, and show videos. Kinesthetic learners learn through movement, involvement, and experience, so the educator can prepare lessons with hands-on learning, labs, or games with a physical component.

An important skill for children is the ability to communicate effectively with adults, and developing this comfort from a young age will be helpful throughout life. Educators can facilitate this through providing experiences where children need to talk to adults in the community. For example, educators may take the class on a field trip to the local community library, where students must ask the librarian for help locating certain health resources. Students might also prepare a health fair and invite parents, community members, and those from senior centers to come learn from posters, demonstrations, and presentations. Children can also work on developing communication skills using an array of technologies such as telephone, written word, email, and face-to-face communication.

The Role of Self-esteem, Self-efficacy, and Locus of Control in Self-concept and Self-identity
Self-esteem is the feeling of personal value or worth, and self-efficacy is an individual's feeling of competence in accomplishing a task. Someone who has strong self-esteem and self-efficacy will be proactive and confident, both socially and vocationally. Having an internal locus of control vs. external locus of control also plays a role in one's identity. An internal locus of control is when someone has the perception that he or she have control over his or her environment. An external locus of control is when someone believes that his or her future and life are controlled by factors outside of himself or herself. Those with an internal locus of control have a stronger self-concept and self-identity, leading to superior achievement, greater emotional stability, and more individual responsibility for behaviors.

Engaging in regular physical activity can improve one's self-esteem and self-efficacy. Exercise promotes a sense of physical and psychological wellbeing. Educators should encourage students to adopt a regular practice of physical activity, which enhances positive body image, goal-setting behaviors, and the confidence to achieve such goals.

Learning to Seek Health Care

Early childhood educators can play an instrumental role in the lifelong practice of seeking routine medical and dental care as well as medical support during illness and injury by setting positive attitudes towards such care and explaining the benefits to young children. Not all children will necessarily have health insurance, so information regarding local free and affordable options should be made available to parents. It is important that children learn to identify signs of illness and injury such as sore throats, headaches, stomachaches that do not go away, swelling, etc.

Consistent Feelings of Sadness, Anxiety, Loneliness, and Stress
Just as it is important to get professional help for medical issues, it equally important to seek help with mental and emotional issues. Educators should talk about feelings and emotions and how it is normal to feel sad or anxious at various times, but that if such feelings persist, help may be necessary. Teachers can lead the class through stress management techniques to combat anxiety and talk about the role of physical activity, sound nutrition, and good sleep for mood stabilization. Young children should learn about identifying and communicating their emotions.

<u>Lingering Pains or Aches</u>
Children should be instructed to tell a trusted adult when they have pains, aches, or symptoms that persist for several days so that the adult can help determine if medical attention is needed. Children can also learn basic first-aid such as how to wash a cut and put on a Band-Aid or when and how to use RICES (Rest, Ice, Compression, Elevation, and Stabilization) after an injury.

Social Development

Social Aspects of Physical Activity

Physical education classes provide useful opportunities to encourage students' social development. Life skills such as cooperation, competition, goal setting, respecting and understanding differences, and taking risks can all be discussed while participating in sports and physical activity.

It is important that educators continually address the issues of personal and social behavior, especially as it relates to accepting and respecting differences in abilities, ideas, lifestyles, cultures, and choices. By the end of second grade, students should know how to follow the rules and safety procedures in physical education classes and during activities with little to no need for reinforcement. They also understand the social benefits of playing with others and how activities are more fun while interacting with other people. They should be able to effectively communicate during group activities in a respectful way, and enjoy working collaboratively with others to complete motor tasks or goals by combining movements and skills from many people together. By the end of fifth grade, students should be able to work independently or in small or large groups during physical activities in a cohesive and agreeable manner, while understanding that the group can often achieve more than the individual alone. However, individually, the student should understand that he or she is also responsible for personal health behaviors and movements.

Cultural and Historical Aspects of Movement Forms

Although perhaps less obvious than the arts, some physical activities also have social, cultural, and historical ties. For example, the development of many forms of dance can be traced to particular regions of the world or time periods. For example, ballet began in the Royal Court in Paris, the waltz originated in Venetian ballrooms, tango has its roots in 19th century Buenos Aires, and salsa began in Cuba.

Certain team sports and fitness activities also have cultural significance. For example, soccer, known as football in many countries, is the dominant sport in Brazil and many European nations. Several martial arts disciplines like karate, Judi, and taekwondo have their genesis in Asian nations and remain especially important in the foundations of physical education as well as social sports culture today. Certain East African nations, such as Ethiopia and Kenya produce many of the world's finest distance runners, due to the cultural attitude of prioritizing running as an esteemed pursuit and the natural encouragement of running as a means of transportation and livelihood in the infrastructure of such countries. Many countries have a designated national sport and the popularity of a sport in a country is also often governed by the climate or environment as well as the social reverence of the activity. For example, curling, which originated in Scotland, is common in Canada along with ice hockey, where the cold climate is conducive to ice sports. Not surprisingly, these sports are far less common in tropical nations where access to indoor ice arenas may be limited. Sports that require water access (like sailing, rowing, kayaking, and swimming) are often less popular in landlocked or otherwise dry environments (with the exception of swimming in areas with designated swimming pools).

Educators can tie physical education activities to their historical or cultural significance to help students develop a more well-rounded understanding and appreciation for the activity. Students of different backgrounds may identify socially or culturally with a particular activity once learning about their

385

personal connection to the activity; such education may thus help motivate them to enjoy a lifelong pursuit of the sport.

The historical importance of physical activity throughout several prominent time periods and societies is presented below:

- Primitive Times (up to 10,000 BCE): Nomadic lifestyles were necessary for survival so physical activity was inherent in daily life. Dancing, cultural games, and celebratory walks of up to twenty miles were enjoyed in celebration.

- The Neolithic Agricultural Revolution (10,000-8,000 BCE): Advancements in plant and animal domestication and farming tools and practices transformed the previously physically-demanding hunting and gathering society to a more sedentary one.

- Ancient China (2500-250 BCE): Confucius' ideals encouraged the practice of daily exercise, as it began to be understood that regular physical activity decreased the risk of disease. Cong Fu gymnastics, consisting of different foot positions and animal-inspired movements, was developed. Other forms of exercise, such as badminton, fencing, and dancing, were also practiced.

- Ancient India (2500-250 BCE): In India, exercise outside of various types of Yoga was typically discouraged as the Buddhist and Hindi religions emphasized the spiritual, rather than physical, body.

- The Near East (4000-250 BCE): Rigid fitness training programs starting as early as age six were common in civilizations such as the Persian Empire, Babylonia, and Egypt. Boys were subjected to organized training including marching, javelin throwing, and riding. At the height of the Persian Empire, the goal of such regimented fitness training was to improve strength and stamina to create optimized soldiers, rather than for health benefits.

- Ancient Greece (2500-200 BCE): Ancient Greeks revered the perfection of the human form and encouraged routine exercise for boys and men, especially gymnastics, which took place in supervised arenas. Running, wrestling, throwing, and jumping were also encouraged. Of note, the Spartans also highly valued physical fitness, but mostly for military purposes. Boys, upon reaching the age of six, engaged in military training programs. Females were also encouraged to exercise, with the goal of birthing strong future soldiers.

- The Dark and Middle Ages (476-1400 A.D.): After the fall of the lavish, sedentary Roman Empire, the lifestyle became more physically demanding again (hunting, gathering, farming), so the general fitness of the population improved.

- The Renaissance (1400-1600): The human body was again glorified during this time and organized physical education was implemented in schools to convey the importance of fitness for a healthy body and mind.

- National Period in Europe (1700-1850): Organized gymnastics was particularly popular during this time, especially in countries such as Sweden, Germany, Denmark, and Great Britain. In England, physical educators began recognizing the importance of progressive overload and variation in exercise programs. They also defined elements of purposeful training programs such as the necessary frequency, intensity, and duration of exercise to improve fitness and health.

- United States

  - Colonial Period (1700-1776): The agrarian, herding, and hunting lifestyle provided plentiful opportunities for physical activity but no formal exercise programs existed.

  - National Period (1776 to 1860): European immigrants often brought fitness practices from their nation of origin with them; gymnastics was popular. The importance of regular exercise was also recognized by early American leaders such as Thomas Jefferson and Benjamin Franklin. Jefferson encouraged a minimum of two hours of daily exercise for a healthy body and mind and Franklin expressed the importance of daily activities like running, swimming, and strength training for health.

  - Post-Civil War (1865-1900): Lifestyle physical activity decreased after labor-related advancements developed in the Industrial Revolution. Formal physical education wasn't routinely incorporated into school curriculums until the end of the nineteenth century, also the emphasis was more on sports and game skills rather than fitness for health improvement.

  - Early 20th Century Through the Great Depression: President Theodore Roosevelt strongly encouraged Americans to exercise regularly. Statistics from military training programs during and after World War I reveled that one-third of drafted individuals were physically unfit for services. Consequently, legislation was passed mandating improvements in school physical education programs, although this interest was short-lived, and fitness levels declined during the Depression.

  - World War II: In addition to the importance placed on fitness for the war, the 1940s also saw formal research applied to fitness, particularly through the work of Dr. Thomas Cureton who investigated how to measure physical fitness and the effectiveness of different modalities. He not only identified exercise intensity guidelines for improving health but he developed fitness tests to evaluate muscular strength, cardiovascular endurance, and flexibility.

  - 1950s-1960s: By the 1950s and 1960s, diseases with inactivity as a risk factor (such as cardiovascular disease, Type 2 Diabetes, and certain cancers) emerged. This was due, in large part, to the sedentary lifestyles brought on by advancements in technology, reducing the activity requirements of more jobs and activities for survival. Jack LaLanne encouraged healthy lifestyle habits to prevent disease, and through his television show, he designed aerobics, jumping jacks, water aerobics, and strength programs and developed exercise equipment including several strength training machines. During the Cold War, "Minimum Muscular Fitness Tests in Children" were conducted by Kraus-Hirschland to assess muscular strength and flexibility in the trunk and leg muscles. Results indicated that American children were significantly less fit than European children so President Eisenhower responded by forming the President's Council on Youth Fitness. Several organizations began to promote fitness in the general public such as the American Health Association (AHA) and The American College of Sports Medicine (ACSM). President John F. Kennedy strongly urged Americans to exercise and piloted youth fitness programs. Dr. Ken H. Cooper encouraged aerobics and the necessity if daily exercise to prevent disease.

Cognitive Development from Birth Through Adolescence

Cognitive Development

Typical and Atypical Cognitive Growth and Development

Cognitive development refers to development of a child's capacity for perception, thought, learning, information processing, and other mental processes. The *nature vs. nurture* debate questions whether cognitive development is primarily influenced by genetics or upbringing. Evidence indicates that the interaction between nature and nurture determines the path of development.

Some commonly recognized milestones in early cognitive development:

- One to three months: focuses on faces and moving objects, differentiates between different types of tastes, sees all colors in the spectrum

- Three to six months: recognizes familiar faces and sounds, imitates expressions

- Six to twelve months: begins to determine how far away something is, understands that things still exist when they are not seen (object permanence)

- One to two years: recognizes similar objects, understands and responds to some words

- Two to three years: sorts objects into appropriate categories, responds to directions, names objects

- Three to four years: Demonstrates increased attention span of five to fifteen minutes, shows curiosity and seeks answers to questions, organizes objects by characteristics

- Four to five years: Draws human shapes, counts to five or higher, uses rhyming words

The *Zone of proximal development* is the range of tasks that a child can carry out with assistance, but not independently. Parents and educators can advance a child's learning by providing opportunities within the zone of proximal development, allowing the child to develop the ability to accomplish those actions gradually without assistance.

Piaget's Theory of Cognitive Development

Piaget was the first to study cognitive development systematically. He believed children have a basic cognitive structure and continually restructure cognitive frameworks over time through maturation and experiences.

Key terms:

- Schema: introduced by Piaget, a concept or a mental framework that allows a person to understand and organize new information

- Assimilation: the way in which an individual understands and incorporates new information into their pre-existing cognitive framework (schema)

- Accommodation: in contrast to assimilation, involves altering one's pre-existing cognitive framework in order to adjust to new information

- Equilibrium: occurs when a child can successfully assimilate new information

- Disequilibrium: occurs when a child cannot successfully assimilate new information

- Equilibration: the mechanism that ensures equilibrium takes place

Stages of Cognitive Development

The stages of cognitive development are sensorimotor, pre-operational, concrete operational, and formal operational. *Sensorimotor* occurs from birth to around approximately age two. The key accomplishment here is developing object permanence—the understanding that objects still exist even when the child cannot see them. *Pre-operational* is from two to seven years. Children become capable of symbolic play and using logic. *Concrete operational* is from seven to eleven years of age. Children are able to make generalizations by drawing conclusions from what they observe (inductive reasoning), yet they are generally unable to come to a conclusion or predict an outcome by using logic pertaining to an abstract idea (deductive reasoning). *Formal operational* occurs from adolescence through early adulthood. People develop abstract thought, metacognition (thinking about thinking), and problem-solving ability.

SENSORIMOTOR STAGE

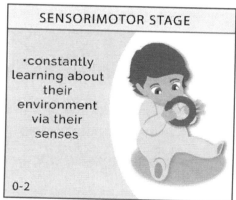

- constantly learning about their environment via their senses

0-2

PREOPERATIONAL STAGE

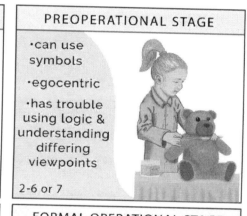

- can use symbols
- egocentric
- has trouble using logic & understanding differing viewpoints

2-6 or 7

CONCRETE OPERATIONAL STAGE

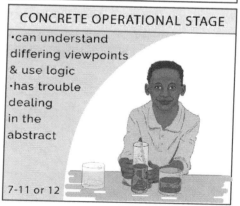

- can understand differing viewpoints & use logic
- has trouble dealing in the abstract

7-11 or 12

FORMAL OPERATIONAL STAGE

- can think in the abstract
- can solve problems systematically

12 - Adulthood

Social and Physical Development from Birth Through Adolescence

Social Development

Typical and Atypical Social Growth, Development, and the Socialization Process

Social development refers to the development of the skills that allow individuals to have effective interpersonal relationships and to contribute in a positive manner to the world around them.

Social learning is taught directly by caregivers and educators, but it is also learned indirectly by the experience of various social relationships.

Social development is commonly influenced by extended family, communities, religious institutions, schools, and sports teams or social groups. Positive social development is supported when caregivers engage in these behaviors:

- Attune to a child's needs and feelings
- Demonstrate respect for others
- Teach children how to handle conflict and solve problems encountered during social experiences
- Help children learn to take the perspective of another person and develop empathy
- Encourage discussion of morals and values and listen to the child's opinions on those topics
- Explain rules and encourage fair treatment of others
- Encourage cooperation, rather than competition

Social development begins from birth as a child learns to attach to their mother and other caregivers. During adolescence, social development focuses on peer relationships and self-identity. In adulthood, social relationships are also important, but the goal is to establish secure and long-term relationships with family and friends.

Another important contributor to social development are social institutions, such as family, church, and school, which assist people in realizing their full potential. Lev Vygotsky was a pioneer in this field with his concept of cultural mediation. This theory emphasizes that one's feelings, thoughts, and behaviors are significantly influenced by others in their environment.

Typical and Atypical Emotional Growth and Development

Emotional development encompasses the development of the following abilities:

- Identifying and understanding the feelings that one experiences
- Identifying and understanding the feelings of others
- Emotional and behavioral regulation
- Empathy
- Establishing relationships with others

Caregivers who are nurturing and responsive enable children to learn to regulate emotions and feel safe in the environment around them.

- By age two to three months, infants express delight and distress, begin smiling, and may be able to be soothed by rocking.

- By three to four months, infants communicate via crying and begin to express interest and surprise.

- Between four to nine months, infants respond differently to strangers in comparison to known individuals, solicit attention, show a particular attachment for a primary caregiver, and have an expanded range of expressed emotions that include anger, fear, and shyness.

- At ten to twelve months, babies show an increase in exploration and curiosity, demonstrate affection, and display a sense of humor.

- Children at age twelve to twenty-four months often demonstrate anger via aggression, laugh in social situations, recognize themselves in a mirror, engage in symbolic play, and have a complete range of emotional expression.

- Around age two, children begin using different facial expressions to show their emotions, begin to play cooperatively, and may transition from being calm and affectionate to temperamental and easily frustrated.

- At age three, children engage in more social and imaginative play, show interest in the feelings of others, begin to learn to manage frustration, and are often inconsistent and stubborn.

- Children at age four show improved cooperation, express sympathy, and may exhibit lying and/or guilty behavior.

- At age five, children can play rule-based games, often want to do what is expected of them, express emotion easily, and choose friends for themselves.

- Children at age six typically describe themselves in terms of their external attributes, have a difficult time coping with challenges and criticism, prefer routines, and show inconsistent self-control.

- Around age seven, children can typically describe causes and outcomes of emotions and show better regulation of emotions in most situations.

- From ages eight to ten, children have an increased need for independence, want to be viewed as intelligent, experience and better understand emotional subtleties, and may be defiant.

- During adolescence, children begin to master emotional skills to manage stress, increase self-awareness, develop identity, show increased ability for empathy, and learn to manage conflict.

Normal versus abnormal behavior is difficult to distinguish because each person is unique, so creating a standard of normal can be challenging. This standard also changes constantly as the culture evolves.

Normal behaviors are those that are common to the majority of the population, as related to emotional functioning, social interactions, and mental capacity. *Abnormal behavior* is generally considered that which is maladaptive, dysfunctional, and disruptive to life. These behaviors may be an exaggeration of a normal behavior or even an absence of a typical response. They do not conform to the accepted patterns or common behaviors of society. Sadness over the death of a loved one is considered normal, but disabling depression that interferes with school and work responsibilities is not.

Social Behavior

Attraction

Attraction occurs when someone is drawn toward others for friendship or romantic love. Familiarity, which often comes through close proximity, contributes to attraction, since people tend to like the things with which they are familiar. Similarity is another determiner of attraction; those who are more alike tend to be drawn to each other and have a liking that lasts. Finally, physical attractiveness, often influenced by social or cultural norms, plays a role in the attraction people feel toward each other.

Aggression

Aggression can be verbal or physical and is intended to harm or destroy someone or something. Many factors contribute to aggressive behavior. Biologically, high levels of testosterone are associated with aggressive behaviors, and aggression is more common in men. Environmental contributors include modeling and observational learning, as illustrated in the Bobo Doll experiment. Another contributor is the frustration-aggression principle that posits that people will act out in anger and aggression if they are thwarted in achieving a goal.

Attachment

Attachment is an emotional bond that a child develops with a primary caregiver and is crucially important during the early months or years of life. If a child establishes an avoidant, disorganized, or anxious attachment rather than a secure attachment with the caregiver, it will impact the child's emotional stability and function, as well as future relationships.

Altruism

Altruism refers to the social phenomenon of people showing an unselfish care or concern for the needs of others. There is conflict about whether pure altruism actually exists among humans, as there is nearly always some type of subtle or intrinsic reward that comes from seemingly selfless behaviors. Either way, acting on behalf of others at the risk or inconvenience to oneself has a positive impact on a person emotionally and physically.

Social Support

Having social support is important for people of all ages and contributes to greater overall health and happiness. Social support can consist of family or friends, and includes the financial, physical, emotional, and psychological care they provide.

Attachment and Bonding

Understanding attachment and bonding has become more important than ever, especially in relation to changes within the U.S. culture's attitudes about child welfare over the last fifty years. Child Protective Service Teams have become more active in every city. The medical profession, the educational system, and the mental health profession are more informed about children at risk. As a result, more children are being taken from parents, sometimes as early as the day of birth. An older child victim may travel from relative to relative, back to the mother, then into foster or group homes. These children do not have an opportunity to form attachments with their caregivers, nor do caregivers have the opportunity to bond with the children.

Bonding refers to a mother's initial connection to her baby. This generally occurs within the first hours or days of the birth. Mothers who are able and willing to hold their child close to them shortly after birth generally have more positive relationships with the child. When a mother fails to bond, the child is at greater risk for having behavioral problems.

Attachment, on the other hand, refers to a more gradual development of the baby's relationship with their caretaker. A secure attachment naturally grows out of a positive, loving relationship in which there is soothing physical contact, emotional and physical safety, and responsiveness to the child's needs. The baby who has a secure attachment will venture out from their safe base, but immediately seek their mother when fearful or anxious, having learned that mommy will be there to protect them. This type of secure relationship becomes impossible if the child is moved from home to home or has experienced abuse or neglect.

A child whose needs have not been met or who has learned through mistreatment that the world is unfriendly and hostile may develop an avoidant attachment or ambivalent attachment. An *avoidant attachment* is characterized by a detached relationship in which the child does not seek out the caregiver when distressed, but acts independently. A child with *ambivalent attachment* shows inconsistency toward the caregiver; sometimes the child clings to them, and at other times, resists their comfort. Establishing a secure, positive attachment with a caregiver is crucial to a child's life-long emotional and social success. The development of attachment disorder is often present in foster children or those adopted later in life and can create much frustration and heartache as the more stable parents step in and attempt to bond with them.

Physical Development

Indicators of Normal Physical Growth and Development

It is important to understand normal developmental milestones. While not all children progress at the same rate, one must know some benchmarks to determine if the child has any developmental delays that prevent him or her from reaching goals by a certain age.

Infancy Through Age 5: During the first year of life, abundant changes occur. The child learns basic, but important, skills. The child is learning to manipulate objects, hold his or her head without support, crawl, and pull up into a standing position. The toddler should be able walk without assistance by 18 months. By age two, the child should be running and able to climb steps one stair at a time. By age three, the child should be curious and full of questions about how the world works or why people behave in certain ways. The child should have the balance and coordination to climb stairs using only one foot per stair. By age four, the child is increasingly independent, demonstrating skills like attending to toilet needs and dressing with some adult assistance.

School Age to Adolescence: By age five, speech is becoming more fluent, and the ability to draw simple figures improves. Dressing without help is achieved. By age six, speech should be fluent, and motor skills are strengthened. The youth is now able to navigate playground equipment and kick and throw a ball. Social skills, such as teamwork or friendship development, are evolving. The child must learn to deal with failure or frustration and find ways to be accepted by peers. They become more proficient in reading, math, and writing skills. Towards the end of this phase, around age 12, secondary sexual characteristics, such as darker body hair or breast development may occur.

Adolescence: This is a period of extraordinary change. The process of *individuation* is occurring. The teen views himself or herself as someone who will someday live independently. More time is spent with peers and less with family. Identity formation arises now, and the teen often experiments with different kinds of clothing, music, and hairstyles to see what feels comfortable and what supports his or her view of the world. Sexuality is explored, and determinations are being made about sexual preferences and orientation. Sexual experimentation is common, and some teens actually form long-term intimate relationships, although others are satisfied to make shorter-term intimate connections. There is sometimes a period of experimentation with drugs or alcohol. As the thinking process matures, there may be a questioning of rules and expectations of those in authority. Moodiness is common, and troubled teens are likely to "act out" their emotions, sometimes in harmful ways.

Influences on Development from Birth Through Adolescence

Influences on Development

The Impact of Physical, Mental, and Cognitive Impairment on Human Development

Approximately 7 percent of U.S. children have some type of disability. The most common physical disabilities that impact development are cerebral palsy, hearing issues, and visual issues. Learning disabilities are also common—these could be Down's syndrome or other developmental delays. Common psychiatric disabilities are ADHD and autism spectrum disorders. Others include mood disorders, oppositional disorders, anxiety disorders, and, in rare cases, schizophrenia. The impact upon the child and family corresponds to the family's ability to adapt to the condition, and their ability to connect to community resources.

How the individual develops and copes with the disability depends greatly upon the social context and the child's own personal attributes. Raising a disabled child puts tremendous stress on parents and siblings. There are issues of stigma, financial burden, missed days of work for parents, and the time and energy needed to seek useful resources. Siblings may be called upon to take roles of parenting to help out. These siblings may be bullied by peers who make fun of their disabled family member. They may feel neglected by parents. Additionally, there may be a need for special housing and special schools. Low-income families may face barriers to accessing services such as transportation, medical specialists, or assistance with childcare.

The Interplay of Biological, Psychological, Social, and Spiritual Factors

The *biopsychosocial model* (developed by George Engle) posits that health and illness result from the interplay between biological, psychological, and social factors. This model incorporates more factors than the traditional biomedical model of illness, which attributed causation only to biological factors, disregarding any other influences.

Biological Factors: Genetics and other biological factors play a substantial role in human development. Examples of these factors are physical features, such as height, weight, or degree of attractiveness. Is the person healthy or disabled? Can he or she walk, talk, see, and hear? While most believe that others should not be judged by physical appearance, studies show that healthy, attractive, fit persons have certain advantages in life. More people will be attracted to these individuals, which creates an expanded circle of friends and eligible partners. In general, being disabled restricts social, educational, and vocational opportunities.

Psychological Factors: Psychological factors encompass a wide range of symptoms and conditions. These can range from a diagnosis of schizophrenia to mild social anxiety. Many psychological factors can directly impact biological ones and vice versa. Depression may cause insomnia. Anxiety can cause gastrointestinal distress. Anorexia causes restricted food intake to the point of starvation. Chronic pain can cause irritability, anger, depression, and social withdrawal.

Social Factors: Social factors are intimately intertwined with both biological and psychological factors. These are developed in response to the social institutions and influences that one is exposed to. These can include family, school, religious organizations, government, and neighborhoods. The media contributes to people's social context, telling them what is desirable, what is undesirable, and what they need in their lives to be happy. Media influences attitudes about sexuality, violence, consumption of goods, the government, and the way people treat one another. Experiences are based on interpretation, and interpretation is influenced by social context.

In Western culture, it is commonly accepted that the interaction of the aforementioned factors determines health outcomes. An individual's health status, their perceptions of and beliefs about health, and their barriers to accessing healthcare exert a combined influence on the likelihood of that individual engaging in healthy behaviors, such as exercising, getting physical exams, or eating well-balanced meals.

The biopsychosocial model is helpful in understanding why some individuals are more likely to develop mental health problems. This perspective is also helpful in fighting the stigmatization of mental illness because it promotes the understanding that anyone can develop mental health problems, if there is a disruption to the balance of biological, psychological, or social influences. In social work, this perspective is often expanded and referred to as the *biopsychosocial-spiritual perspective*—the idea that one must also consider the ways in which individuals find meaning in their lives.

Identity Development
Identity includes *self-concept* and *self-esteem*. Self-concept is the beliefs one holds about one's self. Self-esteem is how one feels about one's self-concept.

The physical changes of adolescence can have a strong influence on an adolescent's self-esteem. Adolescents also incorporate comments from others, particularly parents and friends, into their identity. Adolescents also undergo important emotional development and begin to hone the skills that are necessary for stress management and effective relationships with others. Some of the skills necessary for stress management are recognizing and managing one's own emotions, developing empathy for others, learning appropriate and constructive methods of managing conflict, and learning to work cooperatively rather than competitively.

A normal part of adolescence is a yearning for independence. Teachers can educate both parents and adolescents about the importance of positive peer relationships during this time. Peer groups help adolescents learn about the world outside of their families and identify how they differ from their parents. Adolescents who are accepted by their peers and who have positive peer relationships may have better psychosocial outcomes in both adolescence and adulthood.

An increase in conflict with parents is normal during adolescence and seems to be most prevalent between girls and mothers. Parents may need reassurance that this conflict does not represent rejection, but rather a normal striving for independence.

Some theories seek to explain the prevalence of risk-taking behaviors among adolescents. One theory of risk-taking behavior explains that the need for excitement and sensation seeking outweighs any potential dangers that may come from sensation seeking. Another theory says that risk-taking often occurs within groups as a way to gain status and acceptance among peers. Additionally, adolescents who engage in risk-taking behavior may be modeling adult behavior that has been romanticized.

There are many ways in which teachers and parents can provide guidance to young people with regard to their risk-taking behavior. They should become comfortable discussing uncomfortable topics, so that adolescents can safely talk about their decision-making and peer pressure. Additionally, it is wise to steer adolescents toward healthy outlets that channel their talents or get them involved in positive activities.

Adolescent resilience and positive outcomes are associated with these factors:

- Having a stable and positive relationship with at least one involved and caring adult (e.g., parent, coach, teacher, family member, community member)
- Developing a sense of self-meaning, often through a church or spiritual outlet
- Attending a school that has high, but realistic, expectations and supports its students
- Living in a warm and nurturing home
- Having adequate ability to manage stress

Basic Human Needs

Abraham Maslow is the most notable researcher in the area of basic human needs. Maslow theorized that human needs could be described in the form of a pyramid, with the base of the pyramid representing the most basic needs and the higher layers representing loftier goals and needs. Unless the basic needs are met, a person cannot move on to higher needs. For example, a homeless woman living under a bridge will need food, shelter and safety before she can consider dealing with her alcoholism. The foundational layer in Maslow's hierarchy is physiological needs, and the final layer at the pinnacle of the pyramid is self-transcendence.

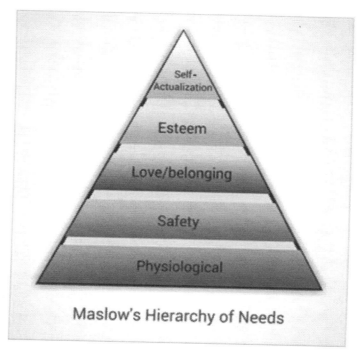

Maslow's Hierarchy of Needs

<u>Maslow's Hierarchy of Needs</u>
Physiological Needs: These needs must be met first and pertain to what humans need to survive. This includes basics, such as food, water, clothing, and housing.

Safety Needs: Once primary needs are met, the person may now focus on safety issues. This would include safety from abuse and neglect, natural disaster, or war.

Love and Belonging: Once the first levels of need have been satisfied, people are next driven to find a sense of acceptance and belonging within social groups, such as family, community, or religious organizations. Maslow suggests that humans have a basic need for love, affection, and sexual intimacy. Failure to achieve this level can lead to difficulty in forming and maintaining close relationships with others.

Esteem: The need for esteem is driven by a desire for recognition, respect, and acceptance within a social context.

Self-Actualization: The U.S. Army slogan, "Be All You Can Be," expresses this layer of need. Reaching one's highest potential is the focus. According to Maslow, this cannot be achieved until all the others are mastered.

Self-Transcendence: Devised by Maslow in his later years, he felt self-actualization did not completely satisfy his image of a person reaching their highest potential. To achieve self-transcendence, one must commit to a goal that is outside of one's self, such as practicing altruism or finding deeper level of spirituality.

Visual and Performing Arts

Foundations of Art Education

The four general categories of arts are visual arts, dance, music, and theater arts. As children progress through elementary school, they should be exposed to the basic foundations, creative expression and production of each type of art, and the ability to critically analyze a work of art and make connections within a cultural and historical context. Art education should build progressively during childhood so that older children are able to eventually take on these more sophisticated and advanced applications.

There are a wide variety of visual and performing arts that can enhance a child's creativity and learning experience. It is optimal to expose young children to many different types of art – both as a creator and observer – for well-rounded cultural, creative, and comprehensive learning. Depending on the child's age, early childhood educators can tailor art assignments and activities to meet the child's interests, motor skills, attention, and needs.

Each of the four forms of art have a vast list of terminology unique to that art form. Educators should be familiar with such terms to help effectively communicate with and educate students and, more importantly, to empower students to have intelligent and meaningful conversations about artwork with peers, artists, and community members.

Fundamental Concepts Related to the Arts

Artists, regardless of medium, typically rely on the following six main principles in art: emphasis, rhythm, balance, contrast, harmony, and movement.

Emphasis
Artists often want to make one part of their work stand out from the rest and guide viewers to pay attention to specific components of their piece. For example, lines and textures in paintings and sculptures may direct viewers to specific details or target features, and altering the texture of one area may make it stand out in contrast to the rest of the work.

Rhythm
Rhythm involves repeating elements within a work such as colors, shapes, lines, notes, or steps to create a pattern of visual or auditory motion.

Balance

Balance is positioning objects or using size, color, shape and lighting in the artwork so that all of the elements are equally present with no particular component overpowering the rest. Symmetrical balance is when two halves of an image create a mirror image, so that if the work is folded in half, each half is the same. Balance can also be asymmetrical, wherein the composition is balanced but the two halves are not the same. For example, a large central object is balanced by a smaller figure on one edge.

Contrast

Contrast exemplifies differences between two unlike things such as loud and soft music, major and minor tones, fast and slow dancing movements, and light and dark colors.

Harmony

Somewhat opposite of contrast, harmony highlights the similarities in separate but related parts of a composition. Rather than emphasizing their dissimilarities, harmony shows that different things can actually be related to each other and blend together.

Movement

Artwork that contains a sense of motion or action has movement. Even stationary art, like painting and sculpture, can imply movement based on the positioning of objects or the artist's use of lines, which draw the viewer's eye to different areas of the artwork.

Self-Expression and Communication through Art

One of the fundamental benefits of the arts is their ability to be used as forms of self-expression, creativity, and self-identity, and a means to communicate emotions, culture, and personal and societal narratives. While the youngest students may not fully grasp the ability to express themselves through art, even fairly young children can use art to communicate ideas, stories, and feelings. Early childhood educators can encourage students to use all forms of art for self-expression and should engage children in active critical thinking and analysis to uncover the meanings and emotions behind artwork generated by others. For example, educators can play a variety of music clips with different tempos, moods, tones, and keys and ask students to explain how the music makes them feel and what they think the composer was trying to express. Compositions in minor keys, at slower largo and adagio tempos, and music with harmonic dissonance may evoke feelings of sadness, trepidation, anxiety, or fear, whereas lively, spirited songs in major keys at faster allegro tempos are likely expressing happier feelings. Students can begin to contrast different moods and types of music and talk about how the moods are conveyed by differences in the music.

Similarly, the students can look at visual artwork and analyze the artist's use of different colors, textures, brushstrokes, etc. to express the feelings behind the artwork. Students can also try to discern the narrative within art, particularly in theater, music, and dance. They can try to understand how stories can be told abstractly and recognize that not every story is told through concrete narrative writing. For example, operatic works and ballets often tell elaborate stories with few or no words. Yet, even when they are presented in foreign languages, operas and ballets can be universally understood by varying audiences due to the emotions and movements present on stage. While these abstract concepts are likely too complex for young children, as students mature and develop, they will gradually become more aware of the nuances and arts' function as a vehicle of expression. Young children are able to understand how their pictorial drawings or paintings convey a narrative in their mind; from there, they can begin to understand how artwork generated by another person conveys his or her storyline. Educators can also encourage students to use art as a cathartic release when they are feeling sad, angry, frustrated, or nervous. Dance, visual arts, and music are constructive, safe, and appropriate ways to temper difficult emotions. Children can use dance choreography and improvisation to express feelings and ideas as well.

Strategies to Promote Critical Analysis and Understanding of the Arts

Early childhood educators should use techniques that foster their students' ability to critically analyze a variety of art forms. Students should develop a toolbox with the appropriate language and terminology to be able to intelligently discuss artwork from a critical standpoint with others. Each form of art has its own unique terms that are important for students to understand, both for their own appreciation and fluency in the arts and for their ability to communicate with others about arts. As students mature and develop their own interests, they will become increasingly able to effectively talk about why they may or may not enjoy a piece of artwork and how it makes them feel. Educators should emphasize that the artistic process is creative and subjective and that each person will have his or her own opinions about various art forms, but that in every case, the universal principles of respect, diversity, and acceptance apply.

Although generally there is no "right or wrong" in art, the ability to critique creative works is a skill that takes time, maturity, exposure, and intellectual understanding and appreciation of art. Early childhood educators can best help students improve these skills through a broad exposure to many arts, detailed explanations about the intricacies of various types of artwork, and discussions about self-expression through art. For example, a young student may inherently not enjoy a classical piece of music arranged in a quartet, but he or she can learn to critique it from an unbiased position based on that type of music. By understanding the details taking place in the piece (such as how the composer changes the key from major to minor halfway through to invoke sadness or mystery, or how the cello and violin feed off each other as if conversing), students can become more impartial and able to understand art for art's sake.

Educators should instruct students to evaluate questions such as: what was the artist's purpose in creating the work, and is the purpose achieved? Is the style the artist chose appropriate for the expressed purpose of the work? Does the artist have a unique idea in their work? The dialogue underlying these lessons should always focus on showing respect for artwork and creative ideas that are different from the student's own and celebrating diversity of preferences and art forms.

Arts in Various Cultures and Throughout History

It is imperative that early childhood educators focus on the fact that artwork has been used throughout history and in every culture as a means of expression and storytelling. Even seemingly new forms of art were not created out of nowhere, but rather, they have evolved from other previously existing forms of art. One of the best ways to discuss art is actually through embedding it in discussions of history and culture. The evolution of music can easily be discussed through various time periods. For example, the assassination of President John F. Kennedy, the Hippie movement, the Vietnam War, and the Beatles coexisted in the same time period, so students can find similarities and differences among these social and artistic ideals within their historical context.

Students can also study different time periods of art and architecture. In the Classical period, Greek artists focused on physical beauty and the human form, paying particular attention to Olympian gods and their idealized proportions in their works. The Medieval period that occurred in Europe from 500-1400 CE saw a flourish of Romanesque style art that shifted the emphasis from portraying realism to conveying a message, particularly symbolic Christian ideals. Students should also learn about the history of art in other countries such as China, with its jade, pottery, bronze, porcelain, and calligraphy.

Educators should focus on how various influences over time affected the predominant artwork each period. For example, Buddhism in the early first century BCE increased calligraphy on silks, the Song dynasty created landscape paintings that were popular, and the Ming and Qing dynasties developed color painting and printing with an evolution towards individualism. As China became increasingly influenced by Western society in the nineteenth and early twentieth century's, social realism predominated. In addition to covering other Asian nations, educators should expose students to traditional African art, which generally demonstrates moral values, focuses on human subjects, and seeks to please the viewer. Educators can also introduce art from the American Indians such as woodcarving, weaving, stitchery, and beading. Art in American Indian populations varies widely from tribe to tribe but tends to beautify everyday objects and create items of spiritual significance. Students should be exposed to music and theater from other cultures and observe the costumes, movements, instruments, and themes in performing arts from places like the Caribbean islands, Japan, Mexico, Australia, Africa, Italy, and Russia.

Dance

Dance

Dance incorporates not only music, creativity, and arts, but also physical activity, which is very important to young children. Dance can help improve kinesthetic sense or awareness of one's body in space, rhythm and mathematical thinking, fluidity of motion, and coordination and balance. There are many varieties of dance, and educators should pick age-appropriate music and dances. The youngest children tend to do best with free movement to music or simple choreographed dances such as the hokey pokey, which are accompanied by easy sing-along songs.

Dance Terminology

In dance, a *step* is one isolated movement, and *choreography* refers to the arrangement of a series of steps. Even young students can learn simple choreography that they rehearse with an instructor and perform with classmates as a group. Older students can learn about different styles of dance such as the waltz, tap, jazz, and ballet, as well as more contemporary styles like *lyrical dance* (combining ballet and jazz) or *fusion dance* (a highly rhythmical dance form). Students of ballet should be familiar with terms like *pirouette* (spinning on one foot or on the points of the toes), *arabesque* (standing on one leg while extending one arm in front and the other arm and leg behind), *plié* (bending at the knees while holding the back straight), *elevé* (rising up from flat foot to pointed feet), and *pivot* (turning the body without traveling to a new location; a pirouette is a type of pivot). Students can also learn about folk dances, partner dances, and line dances.

Tools and Techniques in Dance

Dance simultaneously incorporates a variety of elements, including the following:

Body: refers to *who* – the dancer – and may describe the whole body or its parts, the shape of the body (such as angular, twisted, symmetrical), the systems of the body and its anatomy, or inner aspects of the body such as emotions, intention, and identity.

Action: refers to *what* – the movement created in the dance such as the steps, facial changes, or actions with the body – and can occur in short bouts or long, continuous actions.

Time: refers to *when*, and may be metered or free. Time may also refer to clock time or relationships of time such as before, after, in unison with, or faster than something else.

Space: refers to *where* through space, and how the dancer fills the space and interacts with it. For example, it can refer to whether the dancer's body is low to the ground or up high; moving or in place; going forward, backwards, or sideways; in a curved or random pattern; in front or behind others; or in a group or alone.

Energy: refers to *how*. It is with energy that a force or action causes movement. Dancers may play with flow, tension, and weight. Their energy may be powerful or it may be gentle and light.

Music

Music

Studies show that learning an instrument, especially at a young age, improves thinking mathematical skills, attention, and brain activity. Children benefit from being exposed to a variety of instruments and musical genres including woodwinds, strings, brass, piano, vocals, jazz, blues, classical, folk, etc. Older children can learn basic music theory and how to read music, and may be able to take on more advanced instrument lessons and play or sing collaboratively in groups. As children mature, their attention spans, fine motor skills, ability to understand and maintain rhythm and pitch, and musical fluency improve. Activities and expectations should be age-appropriate. Smaller versions of some instruments are also manufactured and available to very young children to fit their small bodies and fingers.

For young children, learning to identify and maintain rhythm and beat is an important early skill and can be practiced by listening to music accompanied by physical movements such as clapping, stomping, dancing, or following the beat with percussive instruments like tambourines or small drums. They can learn to recognize musical notes and the position of the notes on a staff as well as the various characteristics of basic note types such as eighth notes, quarter notes, half notes, and whole notes. Singing and learning basic traditional and folk songs are simple ways to expose children to music as an easy, low-cost group activity. As children get older and more experienced, the group can be divided into sections to create harmonies and maintain separate singing roles within a varied group, which is a more advanced skill requiring concentration, attention, and group coordination.

Music Terminology

Students should be familiar with terms related to *meter*, which is the repeating pattern of stressed and unstressed sounds in a piece of music. While meter is a somewhat complex concept, students can easily understand the idea of a musical beat, which is the audible result of meter. In written music, meter is noted by a time signature, which looks like a fraction with one number on the top and one number on the bottom, like ¾. The bottom number expresses the beat as a division of a whole note (for example, the number four means that it is a quarter note), while the top number shows how many beats make up a bar (so ¾ means that three quarter note beats make up one bar).

In addition to patterns of stress, music also contains an arrangement of sounds, known as its *melody*. *Melody* refers to the development of a single tone; when many tones are combined simultaneously in a way that sounds pleasing to the listener, it is referred to as *harmony*. Other sound elements related to tone include *chords* (the combination of musical tones), *keys* (the principal tone in a piece of music), and *scales* (a series of tones at fixed intervals, either ascending or descending, usually beginning at a certain note). These elements can be described as either major or minor.

Words to describe the *tempo*, or the speed of a piece of music, include, from slowest to fastest: *largo, adagio, andante, allegro, vivace,* and *presto*. In terms of the intensity of the sound, *piano* refers to music that is played softly whereas *forte* means played with force. Students should also be familiar with vocabulary terms that describe different instruments, different genres of music, and different musical periods.

Tools and Techniques in Music

Instruments used in the early education classroom typically fall into one of the following categories: melodic instruments (melody bells, xylophones, flutes, and recorders), rhythmic instruments (drums, triangles, tambourines, and blocks), or harmonic instruments (chording instruments such as the autoharp). The key elements of music include rhythm, melody, harmony, form (the structure or design of the music, usually referring to the music's different sections and their repetition, such as binary (AB), ternary (ABA), theme and variation and rondo (ABACA), and the musical phrases), and expression [dynamics (volumes) and timbre].

Theater

Theater

Educators can expose young children to theater, both as participants and audience members. Young children may enjoy puppets, and older children can begin to take on roles and learn and memorize short lines. Memorization and recitation skills are transferable to educational activities in other subjects such as spelling words, learning history dates, and memorizing state capitals. Theater activities provide opportunities for imaginative play for children who enjoy dressing up, pretending to be various characters, imagining and acting out scenes, improvising lines, and mimicking jobs, characters, and roles in society. This is healthy and developmentally-appropriate.

Theater Arts Terminology

Students can become familiar with a host of terms related to theater productions. In terms of people working in theater, there is the *director* leading the production and *actors* performing it. The *cast* is comprised of a group of actors, and an organization of actors and other theater workers is known as a *company*. During the casting process, actors usually need to *audition* for parts in a play, and they may get a *callback* if their audition goes well! In addition to a main performer, leading roles in a production might also have an *understudy*, an actor who can step into the role when the main performer is unable to appear in the show.

On the technical side, students can learn about *props, sets, costumes* and *wardrobe, effects,* and *staging*. Theater arts education also presents an opportunity to teach students about the literary aspects of a play, such as the *narrator, act* and *scene* divisions, and stage directions contained in the script. Students can also become familiar with different dramatic modes like *comedy* and *tragedy*. They can learn about the structure of classic drama as well as more open ended structures like *ad lib* and *improvisation*.

Tools and Techniques in Theater Arts

The main skills of the theatrical arts are literary, technical, and performance elements. For theater, teachers can use a variety of techniques to incorporate dramatic arts into the classroom, including the following:

Theater-in-Education (TIE)
This is performed by teachers and students using curriculum material or social issues. Participants take on roles that enable them to explore and problem-solve in a flexible structure that is also educational. TIE productions are conducted with clear educational objectives, such as teaching facts or communicating a lesson to the audience.

Puppetry
Puppetry can be used for creative drama with either simple puppets and stages made of bags, cardboard, socks, or more elaborate, artistic materials. Using puppets in theater allows students to tell stories about a wide variety of characters and settings without requiring large and complex costumes, props, or sets. Telling stories with puppets also allows children to develop their motor skills.

More formal theater works for children are typically product-oriented and audience-centered, and children can be either participants or audience members. Such forms may include the following:

Traditional Theater

Actors use characters and storylines to communicate and the audience laughs, applauds, or provides other feedback. The performers and audience are separate entities and the acting takes place on a stage, supported by technical workers.

Participation Theater

Students can engage their voices or bodies in the work by contributing ideas, joining the actors, or contributing in other ways. This is more interactive than traditional theater.

Story Theater

Often told with simple sets, story theater can take place easily in the classroom with minimal scenery and costumes. Due to the sparse use of sets, props, and costumes, story theater often incorporates improvisational strategies to communicate character and setting to the audience. The actors function as characters and narrators and play multiple parts, often commenting on their own actions in their roles.

Readers' Theater

Readers perform a dramatic presentation while reading lines (typically from children's literature), enabling performance opportunities in the absence of elaborate staging or script memorization. This allows students to focus on emotional expression and speaking skills while reading their lines. The students can sit or stand but no movement is needed.

Readers' Theater

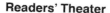

Visual Arts

Visual Arts

Visual arts include things like drawing, painting, sketching, collage, sculpture, etc. Before the age of three, most artwork is produced less in an artistic way and more in a scientific and sensory way. Children at these youngest ages are more interested in the textures, colors, and shapes of what they create rather than expressing any sort of emotion or symbol. There are a variety of crafting activities that young children enjoy and can benefit from including finger painting, pasting, modeling with Play-Doh and clay, folding paper for origami, tracing and making models, and using a variety of craft supplies in creative ways including pom-poms, googly eyes, glitter, pipe cleaners, felt, and yarn. Craft activities help small children develop fine motor skills as they use instruments such as scissors and try to make precise movements like stringing beads and coloring within boundaries. As children develop, they can focus for longer periods of time and can handle more precise movements with smaller materials and areas. For example, a three- to four-year-old child may make simple Play-Doh snakes or snowmen, while a six- to eight-year-old child can add spots, a tongue, and facial features to the snowman with smaller bits of material laid in more exact locations. Through arts and crafts, young children can learn about colors and observe colors in the world around them, recognizing things such as green grass and blue sky. Working on arts and crafts projects helps children develop skills in planning, attention and focusing, problem-solving, and originality. It also helps them learn how to observe the world around them, be appreciative of other people's interpretations and ideas, deal with frustrations when things do not go as planned, and develop hand-eye coordination.

Early childhood educators should strive to expose children to a vast array of arts and craft materials and different types of arts. Activities should be age-appropriate. For example, four- to five-year-old children are likely unable to use small beads and fine pencils and markers, and do better with wider drawing utensils and larger beads that are easier to grasp and manipulate. Children who are ten to twelve are able to work with more intricate objects and may be bored with crayons and coloring books. There are a variety of other art forms that students may view or try to create such as jewelry, pottery, stained glass, wire art, sewing, quilting, knitting, and decoupage.

Terminology in the Visual Arts

Early learners can focus on the basic vocabulary of visual art like identifying colors and shapes. Older students can be exposed to more nuanced terms in the world of visual art. Some visual art is *representational* and depicts objects as they appear in the real world. One visual tool that heightens the realistic accuracy of visual art is *perspective*, an artistic technique that creates the illusion of depth through the use of line (for example, lines in the foreground converge in the background), size and placement of objects (objects that are supposed to be closer to the viewer appear larger than objects that are further away), or color (for example, a hill that is close to the viewer is depicted in a vibrant green, while a distant mountain appears with a more muted, hazy color).

In contrast to representational art, other visual art is *abstract*. When artists use abstraction, they use line, color, and other elements to communicate the presence of objects and emotions rather than realistically portraying the objects. For example, a swirl of warm colors like red and orange might represent anger or anxiety; cool colors like blue and gray could communicate sadness or passivity. In this way, the artist's *palette*, or range of colors used in their work, can communicate a mood or emotion to the viewer. Some works are *monochromatic*, meaning that they only use one color (although the artist might use different shades of the same color—for example, dark blue and light blue). Different shades of color can also create the illusion of shape or represent different lighting.

Other tools of both abstract and representational visual art include *contrast* (the pairing of dissimilar elements to make each other stand out), *positive* and *negative space* (positive space refers to the areas of the artwork occupied by its subject, whereas negative space includes all the areas that do not contain any subject), *balance*, and *symmetry*. Some artistic techniques to introduce to students might include caricature, collage, painting, sculpture, portraiture, landscape, and still life. If educators are able to take students one museum field trips, students should know museum-related vocabulary terms like *gallery, exhibit,* and *curator.*

Basic Techniques, Tools, and Materials for Producing Art

Art has personal (self-expression, gratification, narrative functions), social (collective meaning for a group of people, such as symbolic art honoring a god or political art), and physical (such as a pottery mug for tea) functions that often overlap within a single piece of work. As children go through elementary school, they become familiar with an increasing variety and complexity of visual art forms beginning with things like drawing, painting, and sculpting, then adding printmaking, sponge painting, film animation, and graphics in third and fourth grades, and dabbling in environmental design and art based on personal experience and observation by the fifth grade. They may also try computer-generated art, photography, metalworking, textile arts, and ceramics. Materials include scissors, brushes, papers, glue, beads, clay, film, and computers.

Practice Questions

1. Which of the following would NOT be included on a list of nutrition recommendations for children?
    a. Replace higher fat foods with lower-fat alternatives
    b. Replace higher fiber foods with lower-fiber options
    c. Reduce intake of sugary beverages
    d. Replace refined foods with foods in their more natural form

2. The optimal physical education curriculum for five- to six-year-old children should focus on which of the following?
    a. Movement for enjoyment
    b. Sport-specific skills
    c. Hand-eye coordination
    d. Low intensity, endurance activities

3. Which of the following is true regarding classroom instruction of new movement skills for young children?
    a. It should occur in one long session at the beginning of the class, followed by time for children to play and attempt the skill.
    b. It should contain many small steps for the children to keep track of during play.
    c. It should be limited to short twenty-second stretches of instruction interspersed with long periods of play.
    d. It should be given in written form so children can read it at their leisure.

4. Which of the following is a healthy lifestyle habit for children?
    a. Getting eight hours of sleep every night
    b. Keeping their emotions to themselves
    c. Following safety procedures like wearing a seat belt
    d. Brushing their teeth once a day before bed

5. Educators should teach students about the importance of visiting a doctor for all EXCEPT which of the following reasons?
    a. Routine medical care and check-ups
    b. Consistent feelings of sadness, anxiety, loneliness, and stress
    c. Pains or aches that do not go away
    d. When insurance coverage changes

6. Health insurance status, safety and injury prevention education and care, nutritional meal planning and diet composition, social dynamics and stress, and culture around leisure time are all potential health behavior influences related to which factor?
    a. Family
    b. Peers
    c. School
    d. Media

7. Which of the following is true regarding motor skill development in children?
   a. Motor skill development shouldn't begin until after kindergarten.
   b. Sports skills are learned more readily than generalized body movements such as skipping.
   c. Gross motor skills are mastered before fine motor skills.
   d. Students benefit from formal movement training rather than free play.

8. Which of the following is NOT a general category of basic movement skills?
   a. Locomotor skills
   b. Sports-specific skills
   c. Non-locomotor skills
   d. Manipulative skills

9. In a kindergarten classroom, physical education should include a focus on all EXCEPT which of the following?
   a. Hitting targets
   b. Weight transfer
   c. Following objects with the eyes
   d. Running and stopping

10. Which of the following age groups is likely to be most interested in the health-based benefits of physical activity?
   a. Two- to four-year-old children
   b. Five- to seven-year-old children
   c. Seven- to nine-year-old children
   d. Nine- to twelve-year-old children

11. Which of the following are the major categories of the arts that educators should focus curricular activities on?
   a. Music, dance, theater, visual arts
   b. Music, performing arts, visual arts, sculpture
   c. Painting, drawing, woodworking, visual arts
   d. Language arts, music, theater, visual arts

12. The youngest children just beginning in art tend to create art with a focus on which of the following?
   a. Self-expression
   b. Narrative storytelling
   c. Scientific and sensory observations
   d. Creative and artistic ideas

13. Which of the following is true of art education for children?
   a. Children should focus on learning about art from their own culture and time-period.
   b. It is important for children to see professional art before creating their own works.
   c. It is important for children to study art theory before beginning their own projects.
   d. Children should experiment with a variety of methods and materials to create art.

14. Which of the following is a way for young students to easily learn rhythm in music class?
   a. Have students memorize each song on multiple instruments.
   b. Have students sit still and focus intently on the music.
   c. Have students read the lyrics before they listen to the music.
   d. Have students accompany music with simple instruments like tambourines.

15. Which of the following is performed by teachers and students using curriculum material or social issues?
    a. Puppetry
    b. Participation Theater
    c. Reader's Theater
    d. Theater-in-Education (TIE)

16. The main skills in theatrical arts for children include all EXCEPT which of the following?
    a. Staging
    b. Literary
    c. Technical
    d. Performance

17. A three- to four-year-old child would likely create a drawing emphasizing which of the following?
    a. The emotions expressed in their work.
    b. The figural accuracy of the drawing.
    c. The symbolic meaning of their work.
    d. The colors they use and how they look.

18. Which of the following is a technique used to make flat objects look as though they have depth?
    a. Balance
    b. Perspective
    c. Optical illusion
    d. Abstraction

19. Art serves all EXCEPT which of the following main functional categories?
    a. Religious functions
    b. Personal functions
    c. Social functions
    d. Physical functions

20. Which of the following is a principle in art that highlights the similarities in separate but related parts of a composition?
    a. Contrast
    b. Harmony
    c. Movement
    d. Balance

21. What term best describes a feeling of personal worth or value?
    a. Self-identity
    b. Self-concept
    c. Self-efficacy
    d. Self-esteem

22. Which of the following is not considered one of the five main components of health-related physical fitness?
    a. Muscular power
    b. Flexibility
    c. Muscular endurance
    d. Body composition

23. Ligaments connect what?
    a. Muscle to muscle
    b. Bone to bone
    c. Bone to muscle
    d. Muscle to tendon

24. Which of the following reflects the correct blood flow pathway (heart-valve-vessel)?
    a. Right atrium, left atrium, right ventricle, mitral valve, left ventricle, aorta
    b. Right atrium, tricuspid valve, right ventricle, left atrium, left ventricle, aorta
    c. Right atrium, right ventricle, left atrium, tricuspid valve, left ventricle, aorta
    d. Right atrium, right ventricle, pulmonary circulation, left atrium, mitral valve, left ventricle, aorta

25. Which of the following terms means "movement away from the body's midline"?
    a. Abduction
    b. Adduction
    c. Pronation
    d. Supination

26. What muscle is the primary antagonist in knee flexion?
    a. Hamstrings
    b. Quadriceps
    c. Gastrocnemius
    d. Tibialis anterior

27. In what plane does shoulder flexion occur?
    a. Sagittal
    b. Frontal
    c. Transverse
    d. Coronal

28. What is the primary energy pathway for ATP production for an intense two-minute bout of activity?
    a. Aerobic metabolism
    b. Krebs cycle
    c. Glycolysis
    d. ATP-PC system

29. Which of the following is NOT an adaptation to chronic cardiovascular exercise?
    a. Increased heart chambers' sizes
    b. Increased stroke volume
    c. Increased cardiac output
    d. Increased submaximal heart rate

30. Pectoralis major is doing what type of contraction during a pushup?
    a. Isokinetic
    b. Isometric
    c. Isotonic
    d. Eccentric

31. Which of the following types of joints are correctly matched with the anatomic joint example given?
   - I. Cartilaginous: pubic symphysis
   - II. Saddle: thumb carpal metacarpal
   - III. Plane: sutures in skull
   - IV. Pivot: radial head on ulna
   - a. Choices I, II, III
   - b. Choices I, II, IV
   - c. Choices I, III, IV
   - d. All are correct

32. Balance is facilitated by _____ the base of support and _____ the center of mass.
   - a. Widening, lowering
   - b. Widening, raising
   - c. Lowering, widening
   - d. Raising, raising

33. Where did the waltz originate?
   - a. Paris
   - b. Copenhagen
   - c. Venice
   - d. Vienna

34. Which of the following is true regarding the origin of the tango?
   - a. It has its roots in 19th century Buenos Aires
   - b. It began in Cuba in the 19th century
   - c. It is a recently developed dance from Argentina
   - d. It is a modern popular ballroom dance from Cuba

35. In which country did curling originate?
   - a. Scotland
   - b. Finland
   - c. United States
   - d. Canada

36. Which of the following correctly lists the order of stages of cognitive development?
   - a. Pre-operational, formal operational, concrete operational, sensorimotor
   - b. Pre-operational, concrete operational, formal operational, sensorimotor
   - c. Sensorimotor, pre-operational, formal operational, concrete operational
   - d. Sensorimotor, pre-operational, concrete operational, formal operational

37. In considering the importance of fitness in different regions and time periods throughout history, which of the following statements is most accurate?
   - a. After the prevalence of hypokinetic (lack of movement) diseases increased, organized fitness programs were finally implemented.
   - b. Times of war often saw increases in organized fitness training programs, particularly for boys and men.
   - c. Gymnastics is a relatively new sport but it is enjoyed in many areas around the world.
   - d. The practice of yoga began in Ancient China in response to the philosophies and teachings of Confucius.

38. Which of the following is often experienced by foster children?
    a. Bonding disorder
    b. Attachment disorder
    c. Maslow's Hierarchy of Needs
    d. Altruism

39. Engaging in physical movements such as clapping, stomping, or dancing while listening to music is one way that educators can help students do which of the following?
    a. Learn about melody and harmony
    b. Figure out the key in which the song is played
    c. Learn about rhythm and tempo
    d. Learn about instruments and chords

Answer Explanations

1. B: Nutrition recommendations for children include replacing higher fat foods with lower-fat alternatives, reducing the intake of sugary beverages, and replacing more refined foods like applesauce with foods in their natural form, such as a fresh, whole apple. Answer choice *B* is incorrect because fiber is beneficial in the diet because it increases the feeling of satiety, which can lower caloric intake, and fiber can also reduce LDL cholesterol by binding to it and helping the body excrete it. Lower fiber refined grains have the bran stripped away and should be replaced by higher fiber options.

2. A: The optimal physical education curriculum for five- to six-year-old children should focus on movement for enjoyment. Children at this age are motivated by fun and playing and will be active if it is fun. They are not necessarily ready to focus on sports-specific skills requiring significant hand-eye coordination. They do best with moderate- and high-intensity activities with adequate rest.

3. C: When teaching new skills, especially to toddlers and young children, instructions lasting longer than twenty seconds or containing more than just a couple of steps or cues will lead students to losing interest or getting overwhelmed. It is typically advantageous to have very short instructional periods interspersed between longer breaks to play and try out the introduced skills. Reading material is likely not appropriate for this age group, many of whom do not yet know how to read.

4. C: Following safety procedures like wearing a seatbelt is the best choice. Experts recommend that children get over nine hours of sleep per night. Also, children should brush their teeth after every meal, not just before bed. Finally, it is important for children to learn how to express their emotions in a healthy way and let a trusted adult know if they are struggling with persistent feelings of sadness or anxiety.

5. D: Teachers should educate students on the importance of visiting doctors for routine medical care and check-ups (every six months or so); consistent feelings of sadness, anxiety, loneliness, and stress; and pains or aches that do not go away. Research has found that even at the preschool level, talking about the importance of visiting the doctor can positively impact health behaviors in adulthood.

6. A: Family influences on health behaviors include health insurance status, safety and injury prevention education and care, nutritional meal planning and diet composition, social dynamics and stress, and the family's culture around leisure time.

7. C: Gross motor skills are mastered before fine motor skills. Students begin developing basic motor skills like walking, balancing, and manipulating objects from a very early age. They master gross motor skills before they move on to fine motor skills. Sports skills are not learned more readily than generalized body movements, because sports skills require more fine motor skills, complex motions, and cognitive abilities (e.g. locating and aiming for targets). Also, what looks like play actually helps children develop movement patterns and abilities.

8. B: The general categories of basic movement skills include locomotor skills like walking, running, and skipping; non-locomotor skills such as squatting and twisting; and manipulative skills such as throwing and catching.

9. A: In a kindergarten classroom, hitting targets is not an appropriate focus for physical education because children at this age have not mastered the fine motor abilities and complex skills to aim and hit targets. Hitting targets is more appropriate for fifth grade students. In kindergarten, activities should focus on foundational skills such as weight transfer, balance, following objects with the eyes, and basic skills like jumping and skipping.

10. D: Of the listed age groups, nine- to twelve-year-old students are likely to be more interested in health-based benefits of physical activity than younger children, who are primarily interested in movement for fun and enjoyment. As children mature, they gain a deeper understanding of physiology and healthy lifestyle choices and they become more interested in the health benefits of exercise.

11. A: Educators should focus curricular activities on the major categories of arts: music, dance, theater, and visual arts (painting, drawing, sculpture, pottery, etc.).

12. C: The youngest children tend to create art with a focus on the scientific and sensory aspects of the project rather than artistic creativity, self-expression, or conveying a narrative or story. They enjoy art more as a means to which explore the textures they make (for example, making texture rubbings with crayon on paper), the contrast of colors they use, and the various shapes they make as they move the drawing utensil around (although they are not making shapes for symbolic reasons, they are simply enjoying and exploring what they make when they use the supplies).

13. D: Children should experiment with a variety of methods and materials to create art. Educators should provide children with a wide range of materials like finger paint, glitter, and felt so that children experiment with different textures. *A* is not the best answer because art education should expose students to the historical and cultural context of art beyond that of their everyday experiences. Students can learn about famous artists and art history, but those lessons can be incorporated into creative coursework; they are not a prerequisite for student experimentation.

14. D: Have students accompany the music with simple instruments like tambourines. Students can easily beat along to simple songs using rhythmic instruments like tambourines, maracas, or small drums. Young children enjoy moving around more than sitting and focusing on one thing for an extended time, so learning rhythm through actions like shaking rhythmic instruments or stomping and clapping is more effective for students at this age. Also, *C* is not the best answer because many young children are not yet strong readers.

15. D: Theater-in-education (TIE) is performed by teachers and students using curriculum material or social issues. Participants take on roles, which enable them to explore and problem-solve in a flexible structure, yet in an educational theatrical way. In Readers' Theater, readers perform a dramatic presentation sitting on stools reading the lines typically from children's literature, enabling performance opportunities in the absence of elaborate staging or script memorization. Puppetry can be used for creative drama with either simple puppets and stages made of bags, cardboard, socks, or more elaborate, artistic materials.

16. A: The main skills in theatrical arts for children include literary (reading and writing the script and memorizing lines), technical (includes the staging, lighting, sound effects, etc.), and performance elements (such as the set design and the musical score). Staging is part of the technical elements.

17. D: A three- to four-year-old child's drawing usually emphasizes his or her color choices. At this young age, children typically do not use art for self-expression, symbolism, or realistic figural accuracy. These are all artistic skills that students develop when they are older. Young students tend to focus on sensory exploration involving color, shape, and texture.

18. B: Perspective is a technique used to make flat objects look as though they have depth. Balance is using size, position, color, shape and lighting in the artwork so that all of the elements are equally present with no particular component overpowering. Abstraction is unrealistic artwork that typically has geometric lines or patterns.

19. A: Art has personal (self-expression, gratification, narrative functions), social (collective meaning for a group of people such as symbolic art honoring a god or political art), and physical functions (such as a pottery mug for tea) that often overlap in a project. Religious functions fall under the realm of social functions.

20. B: Harmony is a principle in art that highlights the similarities in separate but related parts of a composition to show how different things can actually be similar and blend together. Balance is positioning objects or using size, color, shape and lighting in a way that makes all of the elements equally present. Contrast is exemplifying differences between two unlike things such as loud and soft music, major and minor tones, fast and slow dancing movements, and light and dark colors.

21. D: Self-esteem is the term that best describes a feeling of personal worth or value. Self-efficacy refers to a person's feelings of competency to perform or achieve a particular task. Self-identity and self-concept have to do with one's overall view of self.

22. A: The five main components of health-related physical fitness are cardiovascular fitness, muscular strength/endurance, flexibility, body composition, and flexibility. Muscular power is related to exercise and performance and is a measure of strength to speed. It isn't one of the five components of fitness that directly relates to health.

23. B: Ligaments connect bone to bone. Tendons connect muscle to bone. Both are made of dense, fibrous connective tissue (primary Type 1 collagen) to give strength. However, tendons are more organized, especially in the long axis direction like muscle fibers themselves, and they have more collagen. This arrangement makes more sense because muscles have specific orientations of their fibers, so they contract in somewhat predictable directions. Ligaments are less organized and more of a woven pattern because bone connections are not as organized as bundles or muscle fibers, so ligaments must have strength in multiple directions to protect against injury.

24. D: Blood returning to the heart from the body enters the right atrium and then moves through the tricuspid valve into the right ventricle. After filling, the right ventricle contracts, and the tricuspid valve closes, pushing blood through the pulmonary semilunar valve into the pulmonary arteries for pulmonary circulation, after which it enters the left atrium. Contraction of the left atrium moves blood through the bicuspid valve into the left ventricle (the largest heart chamber). When the bicuspid valve closes and the left ventricle contracts, blood is forced into the aortic valve through the aorta and on to systemic circulation.

25. A: Abduction is movement away from the body's midline (out to the side). Side-lying leg raises is a common exercise used to strengthen the gluteus medius and is an example of abduction. Adduction is the opposite—movement towards the body's centerline. Pronation is rotating up or inward, while supination is rotating down or outward. These latter two terms often describe movement of the forearm or ankle.

26. B: Antagonists are muscles that oppose the action of the agonist (the primary muscle causing a motion). Hamstrings are the primary knee flexors (the agonists), and the quadriceps fire in opposition. The gastrocnemius does cross the knee joint, so it is a knee flexor, although secondary to the hamstrings. Tibialis anterior is on the shin and is involved in dorsiflexion.

27. A: Shoulder flexion occurs in the sagittal plane (as does most flexion from anatomical position). Shoulder flexion is bringing the arm forward up towards overhead. The sagittal plane is viewing the body from the side, dividing the body into right and left sections. Abduction and adduction occur in the frontal plane and in rotation, such as trunk twists, and typically occur in the transverse plane.

28. C: Glycolysis is one of the anaerobic (without oxygen) metabolic pathways for producing ATP. It generates ATP from carbohydrate (glucose) metabolism that is used for two to three minutes of high intensity activity. The ATP-PC system is the other anaerobic pathway. It uses ATP stored in muscles; however, there is very little, so it is sufficient only for about ten-second high intensity bouts of activity at a time. The aerobic pathway involves the Krebs cycle. ATP is generated through the breakdown of carbohydrates and fats and, to a lesser degree, proteins. It supplies energy during long-duration endurance activities and is used when the other energy systems are depleted or insufficient, but this takes a relatively long time and would be inefficient for short bursts of energy.

29. D: Increased submaximal heart rate is not a chronic adaptation to cardiovascular exercise; in fact, heart rate decreases at a given submaximal workload due to improvements in cardiorespiratory economy. Heart chamber size increases as does preload (the amount of blood that fills a chamber before it contracts to eject it), resulting in a higher stroke volume per heartbeat. This means that more blood, oxygen, and nutrients get moved per pump of the heart. Blood volume and hemoglobin content of the blood also increases.

30. C: In isotonic contractions, the muscle exerts constant tension such as in a pushup or squat. Isometric contractions, like planks, are ones in which there is no change in muscle length. The body is static, and muscles are contracting to stabilize and hold the body stable against gravity. Isokinetic contractions are ones that move through the range of motion at a constant speed, but they are rarely used in practice due to the limited manufactured isokinetic equipment (some Cybex machines are isokinetic as are dynamometers). Eccentric are lengthening contractions, such as the lowering phase of a biceps curl.

31. B: Choices I, II, and IV are correct. Here are the correct matches:

- Fibrous: sutures in skull
- Plane: intercarpal
- Saddle: thumb
- Hinge: elbow
- Condyloid: wrist
- Pivot: radial head on ulna
- Cartilaginous: pubic symphysis

32. A: Balance is the ability to control the center of mass within the base of support without falling. The wider the base of support and the lower the center of gravity, the easier it is to maintain balance. Center of Gravity is the location of a theoretical point that represents the total weight of an object. Base of support is the part of an object that serves as the supporting surface, often thought of as feet in contact with the ground. The base of support also refers to the area between the feet as well, not just the physical structures of the body in contact with the supporting surface. Choice C is incorrect because a person cannot easily widen the center of gravity of the body. The center is a fixed point, so it can be moved, but not expanded. Choices B and D would make it harder to balance if the center of mass is raised.

33. C: Waltzes first appeared in Venetian ballrooms in the 13th century.

34. A: The tango is an energetic ballroom dance originating in the suburbs of Buenos Aires in the late ninetieth century. It quickly gained popularity in other cultures.

35. A: Curling began in Scotland in the 1500s. It is now particularly popular in Canada, although it has also gained popularity in other European nations, Japan, Korea, and Australia, among other countries.

36. D: The stages of cognitive development in the order in which they occur are sensorimotor, pre-operational, concrete operational, and formal operational. The first stage, sensorimotor occurs from birth to around approximately age two and the child develops object permanence. In the pre-operational stage, from two to seven years of age, children engage in symbolic play and can use logic. The concrete operational stage is from around age seven to eleven years. Children use inductive reasoning to make generalizations by drawing conclusions from what they observe, yet they are generally unable to use deductive reasoning or come to a conclusion. The formal operational stage occurs from adolescence through early adulthood. People develop abstract thought, metacognition, and problem-solving ability.

37. B: Times of war or conflict often spurred nations to organize regimented fitness training programs for young boys and men to prepare them to be strong soldiers. This can be seen as early as 4000 BCE in the Persian Empire as well as later in Ancient Greece and Sparta and all the way into the twentieth century in the United States in preparation for the World Wars. Choice A is incorrect because although the attention given to fitness increased with the awareness of the danger of a sedentary lifestyle in the 1950s and 1960s, people recognized the importance of fitness around the world well before that time. Choice C is incorrect because gymnastics dates back all the way to Ancient China with Cong Fu gymnastics and Choice D is incorrect because yoga originated in India.

38. B: Establishing a secure, positive attachment with a caregiver is crucial to a child's life-long emotional and social success and foster children of those adopted later in life can develop an attachment disorder as a result of an inconsistent or lacking caregiver. While bonding is the initial relationship between a mother and a baby just after giving birth, attachment grows more slowly over time as the relationship with the caregiver develops into a trusting and loving, dependable bond. Children who lack this stability or care can develop an attachment disorder. Maslow's Hierarchy of Needs is thought to apply equally to all people and altruism is a someone controversial construct in which people show an unselfish care or concern for the needs of others.

39. C: Teachers can help students learn about the rhythm or tempo of a piece of music by accompanying the listening experience with physical movements such as clapping, stomping, dancing, or following the beat with percussive instruments like tambourines or small drums. The other answer choices pertain to the melodic arrangement of the particular pitches or sounds so stomping or clapping (a rhythmic activity) would not facilitate learning these concepts.

Photo Credits

The following photo is licensed under CC BY 2.5 (creativecommons.org/licenses/by/2.5/)

"Black cherry tree histogram" by Mwtoews
(https://commons.wikimedia.org/wiki/Histogram#/media/File:Black_cherry_tree_histogram.svg)

FREE Test Taking Tips DVD Offer

To help us better serve you, we have developed a Test Taking Tips DVD that we would like to give you for FREE. **This DVD covers world-class test taking tips that you can use to be even more successful when you are taking your test.**

All that we ask is that you email us your feedback about your study guide. Please let us know what you thought about it – whether that is good, bad or indifferent.

To get your **FREE Test Taking Tips DVD**, email freedvd@studyguideteam.com with "FREE DVD" in the subject line and the following information in the body of the email:

    a. The title of your study guide.

    b. Your product rating on a scale of 1-5, with 5 being the highest rating.

    c. Your feedback about the study guide. What did you think of it?

    d. Your full name and shipping address to send your free DVD.

If you have any questions or concerns, please don't hesitate to contact us at freedvd@studyguideteam.com.

Thanks again!

Made in the USA
San Bernardino, CA
20 November 2017